BUSINESS, THE INTERNET AND THE LAW

SUSAN SINGLETON

SIMON HALBERSTAM

Tolley's

 A member of the Reed Elsevier plc group

Whilst every care has been taken to ensure the accuracy of the contents of this work, no responsibility for any loss occasioned to any person acting or refraining from action as a result of any statement or examples in it can be accepted by any of the authors or the publisher.

Published by
Tolley
2 Addiscombe Road
Croydon CR9 5AF
0181-686 9141

Typeset in Great Britain
by
Letterpart Ltd, Reigate, Surrey

Printed in Great Britain
by
Redwood Books,
Trowbridge, Wiltshire

To my husband, Martin and our children Rachel, Rebecca and Benjamin and our new twins, Joseph and Samuel

Preface

Most people underestimate the impact of electronic commerce. The equivalent of the population of the UK joins the internet every six months. E-mail accounts for ten times as many messages as written letters. However, by the time of publication of this book even these statistics will be out-dated. Electronic commerce is here to stay and the law is catching up. English and US common law are well placed to regulate internet transactions. Flexible and largely based on the parties wishes expressed in a contract, they are the ideal tool to apply to E-commerce transactions.

This book examines the principal legal areas which apply to what are loosely described as 'internet transactions'. From engaging a web designer to contracting with an internet service provider, preparing a web page and introducing an E-mail policy for employees, this book aims above all to be practical in its application of the law. Although largely describing English and where relevant EU law, it also seeks to provide useful advice which could be applied in other jurisdictions too.

This is the writer's twentieth book and never has there been so much change in the course of writing. The EU Electronic Commerce Directive and other relevant directives and the UK Electronic Commerce Bill are all in a state of flux and case law on trade marks, the internet, jurisdiction, defamation and internet service provider (ISP) liability continue to change the law remorselessly. Indeed, the only way to stay entirely ahead is to surf the net in the relevant areas.

After much thought it has been decided to include as many web site addresses as possible in this book so that access to the wealth of information on legal issues concerning the internet can be made available to the reader easily, quickly and cheaply. However, bear in mind that such addresses do change. The author apologises in advance for the time any reader will waste. Having the resources of the world available on virtually all topics gives an author a remarkable library accessible from the computer screen but it certainly increases the burden of sifting the information to ascertain that which is relevant, helpful and practical to include and explain in this book.

The appendices are as important as the text. There are few books with internet contracts in publication. It is hoped a start can be made in filling that gap. For lawyers and those involved in running internet businesses the greatest resource is time. This book aims to save time – time spent searching the internet and time spent reinventing the wheel in relation to contracts and words to use on web sites. However, it cannot be a substitute for careful thought applied to contracts and legal advice should always be sought. Where draft legislation is given, the website addresses are given too where possible, so that the reader can always check the latest position.

'Everything you ever thought possible through internet-working technologies will pale into insignificance compared with what is to come in the next few years. Our report predicts a period of unprecedented change in terms of the way we work, live, play and learn as we see the rise of "no-collar" workers who move from job to job rather than align themselves to one employer.'

(June 1999 report of Cisco Systems, The Impact of the Internet Economy in Europe).

The words above echo the author's views. Nothing in the world of E-commerce will be the same again and the change will largely be for the better. The test of the legislators will be whether they can resist the temptation to devise laws and regulations for the internet which are unwanted by business. The EU, UK and US all appear to have reached the consensus that laws should be technology neutral.

Thanks are due to those companies and individuals listed who have given permission for their work to be included in the book. Where this is so their authorship is acknowledged. Otherwise the book and any errors or omissions are the author's.

The clients of Singletons have also played their part. Their many computer and internet queries have ensured there is always the chance to consider the practical side of E-commerce.

The book is up-to-date to 1 October 1999.

Susan Singleton
Pinner Hill

The author welcomes comments or queries on the book.

Singletons
The Ridge
South View Road
Pinner
Middlesex
HA5 3YD
UK

Tel +44 (0)20 8866 1934
Fax +44 (0)20 8429 9212
Email essingleton@link.org
[www.singletons.co.uk]

About Singletons

Singletons is a virtual law firm run by Susan Singleton. A solicitor admitted in 1985, in 1994 she founded her own technology based legal firm, Singletons, working from home, after serving with major London law firms Nabarro Nathanson, Slaughter and May and Bristows.

Singletons advises over 200 clients from around the world on UK and EU computer/IT, intellectual property, competition and commercial law.

Singletons is a member of the technology law practice, a network of similar firms on whose resources calls can be made when necessary.

Singletons
The Ridge
South View Road
Pinner
Middlesex
HA5 3YD
UK

Tel +44 (0)20 8866 1934
Fax +44 (0)20 8429 9212
Email essingleton@link.org
[www.singletons.co.uk]

Contents

Appendix 1: Web Contracts

Appendix 2: Web Page Design Guidelines

Appendix 3: Internet Shopping and Services Terms

Appendix 4: Notices for Websites and E-mails, Copyright Permission Notices, Disclaimers and Privacy Policies

Acknowledgments

Many writers have provided the inspiration for the legal ideas described in this book. The following have also allowed their copyright material to be included.

Sprecher Grier Halberstam :
Chapter 3   – extracts from various web design contracts
Appendix 2 – web page design contract guidelines
Appendix 4 – terms of use of website and disclaimer
Appendix 6 – legal issues note and E-mail and Internet Guidelines for Employees

Simon Halberstam of Sprecher Grier Halberstam :
Sections in Chapters 4, 9 and 10
Appendix 6 – E-mail, Internet and External Disk Introduction Policy

American Bar Association
(http://www.abanet.org)
Appendix 9 – Standing Committee on Ethics and Professional Responsibility: Protecting the Confidentiality of Unencrypted Email (Opinion 99/413, 10 March 1999)

Clark Holt/Star Internet
(http://www.clarkholt.co.uk and http://www.star.co.uk)
Appendix 1 – Star Internet Ltd contract written by Swindon practice Clark Holt

Desktop Lawyer
(http://www.desktoplawyer.freeserve.net)
Appendix 3 – safe ordering guarantee

Excite
Appendix 3 – terms of service
Appendix 4 – website disclaimer

International Chamber of Commerce, Paris
Appendix 8 – GUIDEC: General Usage for International Digitally Ensured Commerce, a living document. Available from ICC Publishing SA, 38 Cours Albert 1er, 75008 P{aris, France

LawNet
Appendix 4 – copyright notice and disclaimer

Laytons/Richard Harrison
(http://rmh@laytons.com)
Chapter 3 – 'What happens when a hypertext link operates

Pharmalicensing
(http://www.pharmalicensing.com)
Appendix 3 – terms and conditions for subscribers and users of the site

United Nations: UNCITRAL
(http://www.un.or.at/uncitral)
Appendix 7 – Uncitral Model Law on Electronic Commerce with Guide
to Enactment

1 – Getting On-line in Business

'The real scale and profundity of the changes in human life that are in progress . . . the scale of distances has been so altered, the physical power available has become so vast, that the separate sovereignty of existing states has become impossible.'

(H G Wells, 1920)

The Future is E-commerce   [1.1]

E-commerce is the future of world trade. From its humble origins as a cheap and quick means of communication for academics, the internet has become the primary means of communication for many in business. The greatest change has been as the internet moves from being a source of information and communication to a means of doing business – the handling of business transactions. This handbook provides guidance on how to embrace the new technology with enthusiasm and within the law. It is a book about law, albeit the practical aspects of legal matters. Those requiring technical advice need to turn to the many technical experts available.

The overriding message is that there is nothing to fear. The legal risks of E-commerce are no greater on balance than other means of communication. Indeed E-mail has significant legal advantages over paper based methods of communication and greater advantages over an oral arrangement of which there is no permanent record. It is very difficult fully to delete an E-mail. E-mail ensures record keeping is automatically achieved.

This handbook examines current E-commerce legal issues and strives to put these in an international context. National and EU laws will increasingly lose relevance as more business is done electronically. Electronic links mean many can carry on business wherever physically best suits them or where taxes are lowest. The British Government announced in 1999 that it intends to ensure that the UK is the most favoured legal regime for doing electronic business.

1

Despite the international context in which the internet operates, this is a book written by a practising English law solicitor and does not provide advice on all countries' laws in this field. Examples are given where possible of principal States' internet legislation and case law to highlight points made in the text. Advice is also given on how to ensure the preferred laws are imposed (such as English or Scottish law), where possible.

Technological advance is so fast that almost before printing this handbook the technology will have changed again. Therefore, the book also seeks to look at how technology may develop and to offer broad advice which may be applicable to new and emerging technologies.

Scope of This Book [1.2]

This book examines:

- using E-mail to send documents and business communications;
- formation of contracts by electronic means;
- content of E-mails – defamation and liability issues;
- websites – contract and copyright and other intellectual property points;
- employee/employer issues arising from use of E-mail, internet and intranet;
- placing of orders via the internet and related payment issues;
- jurisdiction, choice of law and fora for disputes;
- taxation and customs duties.

Legal Issues [1.3]

The legal issues arising from use of the internet for business purposes are not significantly more complicated than other means of communication. Issues may arise in some countries where a 'signature' is required (E-mail is unsigned under most countries' definitions of a signature). (See further **Chapter 6: INTERNET SHOPPING**.) Some products may not lawfully be sold in some States and their marketing over such an international medium as the world wide web may cause legal difficulties. However, there is no requirement in this jurisdiction for an 'internet' law. One of the principal advantages of the English common law system is that there are few formalities for formation of contracts. Contracts for sale or purchase of goods can be formed by any means provided there is an offer which is accepted, and valuable consideration (normally payment).

Considering Going On-Line? [1.4]

Businesses which have not yet gone 'on-line' will need to consider the advantages and disadvantages of doing so. The following should be considered.

- Will all employees be given access to E-mail? (See further **Chapter 9: EMPLOYER LIABILITY AND DEFAMATION** and the Employee Internet Policy in **Appendix 5**.

- Can the business afford to provide such access?

- Do employees have access to PCs or workstations necessary for such access?

- Will employees be required to communicate with others within the business and/or with suppliers and customers by E-mail, or simply encouraged to do so?

- What security arrangements will be put in place to ensure confidentiality?

- Will customers be able to place orders by E-mail and will E-mail be used for placing orders with suppliers, or will it simply be used as an additional means of supplying information with orders continuing to be arranged in the normal way?

- How quickly will the move to E-mail be made? This will depend on whether or not it is currently in use and how radical a change the business wants to make over a short time period. Most businesses move gradually to E-mail so that employees who are not familiar with it have a period in which to adjust. Decide what to do with employees who will not use computers – some may refuse.

- What use will be made of a website of the business, if a website is to be set up at all. Will this result in other means of advertising or marketing being dropped? Many people do not have access to computers or the internet/E-mail. In most cases adding E-mail as an option can increase business opportunities but to remove other methods of communication entirely could be disastrous.

- Survey staff, suppliers and customers before taking any radical decisions which may have a detrimental effect on the business.

Many businesses are well beyond deciding whether to use E-mail at all. Most are on-line and have websites. This handbook tells them how to avoid the legal risks and minimise loss and damage as well as taking advantage of the legal benefits which flow from these forms of communication. Those who are still undecided about E-commerce should consider the following advantages and disadvantages.

Advantages [1.5]

- Cheap means of communication – costs less than a local telephone call to communicate with supplier or customer or employee on the other side of the world.

- Accessibility – E-mails can be sent during UK office hours to be retrieved by the recipient during their own office hours in a different time zone.

- Speed – an E-mail can be delivered almost instantaneously whereas a courier package could take up to 12 hours to reach its destination and a long fax can take up to an hour or more to print at the recipient's premises.

- Permanence – E-mails are a written record. Commerce done by telephone is harder to prove.

- Environmentally sound – the paperless office saves the destruction of trees. E-mails can be preserved electronically so that no ink or paper is required.

- Saving of paper costs – internal memoranda within a business and information to customers can be sent quickly without the need to print out.

- International – the internet and world wide web enable businesses to reach customers all over the world; world trade links are encouraged; the recipient is given time to consider and translate into their national language the message rather than having to respond immediately to a telephone call.

- Customer preference – the customer can decide if they want access to information; less pressure is brought to bear on a prospective customer and they are less likely to be put off by over-selling.

- Cheap advertising – it is much cheaper to advertise a product on a website than to produce a glossy brochure and post it to China or Japan.

- Research – information about potential customers and suppliers can be ascertained easily from anywhere in the world. Free information of the type previously zealously guarded by various professional advisers and consultants can be obtained quickly and out of office hours. Significant cost savings can be achieved. The amount of information on the internet is enormous and much of it is free.

- Ability to access new markets – UK suppliers without the funds or knowledge to market in far flung countries of the world can obtain access to those markets easily and cheaply.

- Possible saving in rent/office accommodation costs if employees can share office space, hot desk, work from lap tops with internet access, or even work from home.

Disadvantages [1.6]

- Security – sending an E-mail has been likened to sending a post card. However, encryption can ensure messages which are confidential are kept secret and there are security issues with use of the telephone and post too.
- Loss of data – messages are not always sent to the correct recipient, sometimes the links fail. However, similar risks also attach to other means of communication.
- Compliance with all countries' laws – where goods are advertised on the internet and therefore marketed in many countries, compliance with all local laws is normally required. No one can check the laws of all States on particular matters, at least not until the internet collates legal advice of that sort.
- Dissemination of offensive and libellous material – some employees do not think carefully before sending an E-mail. It is easy to inadvertently copy an E-mail to a third party who should not be reading the material. Defamatory material can be sent by accident. Obscene or illegal material can be distributed easily. All these risks can be minimised by careful staff training.
- Old fashioned employees – some staff refuse to become computer literate. The employer may find internal reluctance to move into E-commerce. In some cases this is so ingrained at a high level that the plans have to be scrapped.
- Costs of buying hardware and software and training staff – businesses without PCs or the software needed to support internet access, will need to invest in this area as well as arranging training for their staff. In practice, most businesses have PCs already and there are plenty of offers of free or very cheap internet access. The cost of setting up a website is very small and employees do not require much training to be able to use the world wide web.
- Verification of respondents – there are particular risks with contracts being agreed and orders being placed electronically, including the use of credit cards. For example,

someone could impersonate the card holder but this is also a risk where telephone credit card orders are taken.

- Employees wasting time – whether for work-related searches or using the internet at home for non-work matters. It is estimated that employees waste an average of 30 minutes a day in this way.
- Viruses – use of computers, transferring data and swapping of disks can lead to the transmission of dangerous computer viruses (e.g. the Melissa virus in 1999). There are no such risks with paper based systems. However, risks can be minimised by using virus checkers.
- Legal liability – the ease of copying over the internet or electronically can tempt some into breaching copyright. This legal risk can be minimised by ensuring all employees are educated about such matters.

Increasing Use [1.7]

For most businesses, there is no real choice as to whether or not to use the internet and E-mail. Their competitors are doing so and to prevent their own customers from using the internet to place orders or to find out about the business will result in a loss of sales.

There is little to be gained by dwelling on perceived disadvantages. E-commerce is a reality which businesses cannot ignore.

- Electronic trading was valued in 1999 at US $12 billion per year world wide. By 2002, it will be valued at US $350 billion per year, according to the UK Under Secretary of State for Competition and Consumer Affairs, Dr Kim Howells, MP. Laws that regulate E-commerce will affect almost every business. US on-line retail sales tripled from $2.4bn to $7.8bn in 1998. Internet service provider AOL's 15 million US users spent an estimated $1.2bn on on-line purchases of books, clothing and travel in December 1998. Those holding back will be left behind.
- On-line stockbrokers have an estimated 8 million account holders who make an average of 340,000 trades a day.
- Free internet access began to be offered by providers in 1999 in the UK. Advertising revenues can make this worthwhile for service providers. US business Free-PC has provided US$500 PCs free to buyers in relation for

permanent on-screen advertising space. The Cybergold website pays 1.2m users to allow themselves to be subjected to additional advertising.

- In 1999, the Government announced that it aims to ensure all basic dealings between Government and citizens will be by E-mail by 2008. The proposal is contained in a Modernising Government report issued in April 1999 (www.cabinet-office.gov.uk/moderngov/1999/whitepaper). By March 2001, the Government hopes that 90% of low value Government purchases will be carried out electronically.

- The Lord Chancellor's Department has said that a court service pilot project giving businesses electronic access to bring debt-related cases in the county court, will be extended in 1999.

Minimising the Risks [1.8]

Advice should be sought from technical experts on how to minimise the potential security risks. Each business needs to ascertain whether confidential information will be supplied and, if so, how it can best protect that information. In most cases technology can reduce the risk to an acceptable level.

Improper Use by Employees [1.9]

A study in April 1999 showed that employees surfing the internet were costing large companies £2.5 million a year. The average employee was spending 30 minutes a day browsing the internet. Half of those using the internet at work were viewing pornographic websites in office hours and many used the internet to find a new job.

Of 191 largest international companies 84% gave employees unlimited use of the internet. More than 8 out of 10 employees looked at entertainment, sports news, organised personal finances and booked holidays in working time. Half of those using the internet at work visited chat rooms.

Risks can be minimised by having an internet policy for employees (see further **Chapter 4: SECURITY, CONFIDENTIALITY AND EMPLOYMENT ISSUES** and **Appendix 5**) and by the use of filtering systems and blocking software, which is often free or very cheap, that prevents access to pornographic or other objectionable material.

(Source: InfoSec, computer security organisation.)

Checklist – Going On-line Legally   **[1.10]**

- ● Are we already on-line?
  - ○ Tap existing employee expertise.
  - ○ Find out who is on-line and how it is working within the business.
- ● Are our terms and conditions of purchase and of sale appropriate for on-line commerce?
  - ○ Have them checked by a computer lawyer (list of experts in this field appear at www.chambersandpartners.com) and alter them where needed.
- ● What internet domain name will we pick?
  - ○ Check contracts with employees to see if they cover E-commerce issues.
  - ○ Issue an employee internet/E-commerce guideline document setting out rules and regulations and update it from time to time.
- ● What type of data will be transmitted electronically?
  - ○ Decide if encryption will be necessary.
- ● Does new hardware or software need to be purchased/licensed?
  - ○ If so ensure that the contracts are checked and amended to ensure a favourable legal position.
- ● Who will have internal responsibility for matters such as formation of contracts of purchase, contracts with website designers, monitoring of employee training and use of the internet?
- ● Who will design the website?
  - ○ Decide on the contract terms to be offered to them.
  - ○ Consider who will have liability for the site design.
  - ○ Consider who will be liable for the site content.
- ● What notices or contract terms need to go on the website?
  - ○ Check the ownership of intellectual property rights for designs used on, or material added to, the website.

● How often will the website be updated?

   ○ Allocate responsibility for ensuring that the site is kept up-to-date so that material on it does not breach trade descriptions or price indications or other laws.

● Will orders be taken by E-mail and payments made by credit card details sent electronically?

   ○ If so, check contracts with credit card companies and ensure it is clear where liability lies.

● Will a third party be trusted with taking orders?

   ○ If so check contracts with them in advance.

● Have all necessary *Data Protection Act* registrations been made?

● Might an amendment to a registration be required if personal data will be used for a different purpose from that for which a current registration has been made?

   ○ Take advice on the changes contained in the *Data Protection Act 1998*.

● Will the resultant changes in business practices alter the tax position of the business?

   ○ Consider whether it would make sense from a tax point of view for the business to move.

● Will increased use of E-mail mean fewer employees need to work at the office?

   ○ Examine the legal implications of employees working from home.

   ○ Consider whether workers could be engaged in cheaper parts of the country where wages are lower allowing savings to be made.

● Will existing commercial agreements, such as distribution and agency and other supply agreements, require communication with business partners or other contracting parties by any particular means, which may or may not rule out E-mail.

Exhaustion of Rights: Trade Marks   [1.11]

E-commerce will achieve world free trade through force of technology, rather than the breaking down of restrictive practices by legal means. Although, where goods are protected by trade marks, EU/EEA trade mark owners are entitled to prevent their products being imported into the EU/EEA (following the case of *Silhouette International Schmeid v Hartlauer* [*1998*] *ECR I-4799;* [*1998*] *Tr L R 355*) individual purchases via the internet will be hard to police.

Exhaustion of Rights: Copyright [1.12]

Although the position on international exhaustion of rights and copyright is unclear, unlike that for trade marks, this is even harder to police. If a book, music or computer software can be downloaded from the US supplier by the UK customer who has transacted on-line, it will be hard for local customs officers and UK distributors to know of such a transaction, to levy duty or sue for infringement of copyright or breach by their supplier of their exclusive distribution contract.

Data Protection and Privacy [1.13]

Conversely, if technology develops so that the purchasing by individuals of such items electronically can be monitored for tax and intellectual property purposes, then very full information about who is buying what and when can be ascertained. Just as computers will enable automatic monitoring of those who drive into city centres so that they can be taxed accordingly, so technology run by Government enforcement bodies could check what individual consumers have purchased and tax them accordingly.

The improvement of enforcement through exchange of information electronically by government bodies such as the Inland Revenue, Contributions Agency and Customs & Excise, brings with it substantial data protection and privacy implications. E-commerce can make it both easier and harder to track what someone is doing. Easier in relation to those purchasing legitimately making no effort to hide their identity and much harder where the buyer or seller is able to mask their location and name and operate out of reach of all authorities in the depths of cyberspace.

Single Currency [1.14]

The Euro may be achieving harmonisation of prices within the so-called single market, but internet dollar sales may result in a de-facto world dollar currency. The dollar is already the effective currency in many turbulent markets from Russia to parts of Africa. E-commerce will also consolidate English as the language of commerce. Much of the information on the internet is in the English language. This gives British companies a major advantage which they should seize.

Tax [1.15]

Businesses have a unique opportunity to site themselves in the off-shore jurisdiction which best suits their business and taxation needs. Tax advice should be sought. In 1999, an Institute of Directors survey predicted that the British Government might lose £10 billion of VAT through E-trade.

Opportunities for Small Businesses [1.16]

E-commerce enables the small to compete with the big. Businesses without the resources to advertise outside the UK now have access to customers around the globe. Small businesses should seize the opportunities this brings. Large businesses should be aware of the potential threat to their market share. In particular, larger businesses may take too long to change monolithic structures to enable E-commerce to move forward within their business. Smaller businesses can approve a move to E-mail and use of the internet quickly.

A 'Faceless' Medium [1.17]

E-commerce will be a great leveller. It should result in greater equality and opportunity in many ways, not just as between large and small corporations. No one knows if the recipient of E-mail is disabled, of a particular ethnic origin or female. Examples abound. The writer has a client at school. All his business is done electronically. His limited business' clients have no knowledge that the shareholder and director is a minor. The internet thus can also enhance the rights of children. The writer herself was able to take on new clients abroad days before the birth of her twins and continue to advise them the following week after the birth, seamlessly and, more importantly, completely free of any bias or prejudice they might have otherwise shown had the transactions been other than electronic.

This brings its own risks, however. Sellers may want to know the identity of buyers and vice versa. Although for many getting paid is the only legal issue, most would like to know their goods or services are not being supplied to the mafia or used to prop up an illegal dictatorship. Anonymity has both its advantages and disadvantages.

Change [1.18]

The greatest trend is the increasing pace of change and the difficulty in identifying trends at all. In a relatively short space of time computers have gone from filling entire rooms, such was their size, to being a small business tool which many homes have. Although the trend is likely to be to universal internet use, many people are likely to use TV rather than PCs. This book does not need to predict technological changes but businesses must do so, in consultation with experts or, more cheaply, through searching the world wide web.

Those that have got on-line already are ahead of the pack. Those who have not have not missed the boat, but they need to move quickly. The law will inevitably trail behind, but the flexible and easy legal structure of US and English common law makes it an ideal medium for E-commerce. The opportunities should be seized with enthusiasm.

2 – The Domain Name and Trade Marks

'Generally speaking, there is nothing more valuable than a .com domain name. Combine it with a .co.uk domain and you have staked out a significant piece of cyber-space for your company.'

(Howard Hill, Head of US West Coast Legal Services for NetNames, Electronic Business Law, February 1999)

Executive Summary [2.1]

- Explanation of the domain name system and the various bodies involved.
- Ensure domain names do not infringe registered trade marks.
- Undertake searches in advance at trade mark and other registries.
- The registered trade mark owner normally prevails in any dispute.
- Include appropriate wording on websites.
- Defend and enforce trade mark rights against infringers.
- Using competitors' trade marks – comparative internet advertising.
- Business action plan to avoid trade mark infringement.

Introduction [2.2]

Those considering going on-line for the first time, need to choose the name under which they will operate. This chapter therefore examines legal issues arising from use of business and product names on the world wide web. It does not purport to be an entire summary of trade mark and passing off law. There are many legal textbooks available on such subjects. **Chapter 7: INTERNET ADVERTISING** provides a more detailed look at specific advertising laws.

Businesses need an internet protocol address to which customers, suppliers and others can send their E-mail messages. This makes it easier to contact businesses by E-mail than by telephone. Unless there is access to a telephone directory it is impossible to guess the telephone number of a business, although developments in technology now enable businesses to choose telephone numbers which also follow the alphabetical lettering on the telephone, enabling callers to key in a name rather than a number.

With E-mail addresses the caller may not even need to check the name in advance, though time is saved if the precise address is known. Instead it may be sufficient to assume a leading company 'xyz' will have the domain name 'xyz.com'.

For an individual working within that company often the individual's name is given first such as 'john.jones@xyz.com'.

Such domain names are part of a longer uniform resource locator ('url') such as: 'http://www.xyz.com'. This might be the internet website address where further information about the xyz company would be located.

It is most important for a business to ensure that its domain name is protected. For example, the Financial Times, will want to ensure that when potential customers type 'ft.com' they will access the Financial Times and not Fred Trimble's hi-fi shop in North London!

The Language of the Name [2.3]

International companies generally do not translate their name into the local language before using it abroad or registering a local domain name. Of course, many websites have facilities whereby users can click on to the language of their choice (such as that of the European Commission) and this can help encourage people to buy from the site where they do not speak English. This is a useful marketing tool but a business' image will be diluted if it has a different name in different States. However, in some cases a different name must be chosen because someone else has registered the same name as a trade mark in that State (see further **2.59**).

Many businesses choosing a new name will pick an invented word and undertake searches to ensure it does not have a rude or objectionable meaning in other languages before proceeding. This is just as important with domain names as with any other names.

Registering Domain Names [2.4]

All domain names must be registered with an organisation which can allocate 'top level domains' – the .com or .org etc. part of the names. The US Network Solutions Inc (NSI) body (http://rs.internic.net), administers .com.

NSI had, until comparatively recently, an effective monopoly on registrations of top level domain names. On 4 March 1999, the Internet Corporation for Assigned Names and Numbers (ICANN) agreed a draft set of guidelines to approve new domain name registrars. Clearly criteria are required otherwise bodies could be set up internationally allocating names without proper consideration.

The ICANN board agreed a policy for accreditation for the processing of registrations in the .com, .org and .net 'top level domains'. Accompanying contracts have also been approved. In the same month, the ICANN board also agreed a document setting out the concepts and structure on which the Domain Name Supporting Organisation (DNSO) will be based. This is intended to be an advisory group which is part of ICANN and will recommend policies on the domain name system. It will also choose 3 of the 19 ICANN directors to sit on DSNO's board. ICANN has a conflict of interest policy and procedures for reconsideration of its decisions. Details are on the internet at http://www.icann.org/singaporeresults.html

Previously .com was used for companies and .org for 'not for profit' organisations and .net for internet service providers, but this is becoming diluted and some businesses on learning that their name with .com is already taken will use .org instead.

Countries [2.5]

No particular country is indicated by '.com' and anyone in the world can register an address with that designation. There are at least 200 domain registration bodies in the world all with different requirements for registration. Some require that a business be based in their country before a registration is allowed, others do not. Nominet in the UK does not have a residency requirement in order for a business to register a domain name '.co.uk' (UK company). Nominet can be contacted at http://www.nominet.org.uk.

Nominet in the UK offers names including .co.uk; .org.uk; .ltd.uk and .plc.uk.

ICANN [2.6]

The Internet Corporation for Assigned Names and Numbers (ICANN) was incorporated in November 1998. It has authority to oversee the internet domain and number system. Seven new domains were unveiled:

- .shop
- .web
- .arts
- .info
- .rec
- .firm
- .nom

At the date of writing these have not been activated because of the US Government's proposals that the whole process be re-examined. Those wanting to chart ICANN developments will automatically receive ICANN press releases via the internet if they E-mail 'majordomo@icann.org' and place in the body of their E-mail the message 'subscribe icann-announce'. ICANN's website is at http://www.icann.org. Co-operation between the World Intellectual Property Organisation (WIPO) and ICANN can be viewed at http://www.wipo.org.

Post-testbed Registrars [2.7]

On 25 May 1999, ICANN announced that eight additional applicant companies have met its accreditation criteria and, upon completion of the ongoing testbed program, will be accredited to compete as registrars in the .com, .net, and .org domains. Registration services in the .com, .net, and .org domains are currently provided by Network Solutions Inc (NSI), which has enjoyed an exclusive right to handle registrations under a 1993 co-operative agreement with the US Government. The eight companies joined the five testbed registrars already accredited and the 29 post-testbed registrars that were announced by ICANN on April 21, 1999.

The eight companies named were:

- ABACUS America Inc/A+Net (http://www.abac.com).
- Advanced Systems Consulting Inc (http://www.advsys.com).
- CASDNS Inc (http://www.casdns.net).
- Domain Bank Inc (http://www.domainbank.net).
- Marvin Enterprises Inc/Global Knowledge Group (http://www.gkg.net).
- The Name-It Corporation/Advanced Internet Technologies Inc (http://www.nameit.net).
- NetNation Communications Inc (http://www.netnation.com).
- PSI-Japan Inc (http://www.psi-japan.com).

Further information about these companies is available on the ICANN website. They are added to on a regular basis.

Initial Board [2.8]

On 27 May 1999 in Berlin, the initial board of ICANN formed its Domain Names Supporting Organisation, accepted an application to establish a Protocol Supporting Organisation, considered how to handle some of the intellectual property issues relating to the internet's Domain Name System, reaffirmed its intention to create a system that will permit individuals to select directors as soon as possible and adopted several other operational resolutions.

The first significant decision the initial board took was the provisional recognition of six self-organised constituency organisations representing parties interested in the management of the Domain Name System from six different perspectives. The constituencies, which will elect the Names Council to act as the governing body of the Domain Name Supporting Organisation (DNSO), are the core of the DNSO. The DNSO is one of the three supporting organisations required by ICANN's bylaws (the others are the Address Supporting Organisation (ASO) and the Protocol Supporting Organisation (PSO)).

Like the PSO and the ASO, the DNSO will eventually elect three of the 19 Directors who will constitute ICANN's full board. The DNSO will also prepare recommendations to the initial board regarding ICANN's policy oversight of the Internet's Domain Name System (which translates the internet's numerical addresses into things humans can understand, like www.icann.org). The issues it will eventually be grappling with include the establishment of dispute settlement mechanisms, reconciling the conflicting interests of various domain name holders, and whether, how and when to expand the number of top-level domains (such as .com).

The six recognised constituency organisations represent:

- the registries for country code Top Level Domains (ccTLDs, such as .de, .uk or .jp);
- commercial and business entities;
- the registries for generic Top Level Domains (gTLDs – such as .com, .org and .net);
- intellectual property interests;
- Internet Service Providers (ISPs) and other providers of internet connectivity; and
- registrars – those that register the names under which individuals or businesses wish to be known on the web, such as www.greeneurope.org or www.ibm.com.

The initial board deferred the recognition of the seventh constituency, designed to represent non-commercial Domain Name holders but this was agreed at the ICANN board meeting in Santiago on 26 August 1999. At the same meeting, a uniform dispute resolution policy for registration in the generic top-level omains was agreed.

Two of ICANN's three Supporting Organisations had been formed by May 1999 only the formation of the ASO is outstanding.

WIPO Report [2.9]

In May 1999, the initial board considered a report of the World Intellectual Property Organisation (WIPO) on domain name policy. The report was commissioned by the United States Government in the same white paper that launched the process of setting up ICANN. WIPO was asked to consider the intellectual property issues posed by the first-come, first-served system by which domain names have traditionally been allocated on the internet. While designed to enable users to reach internet resources easily, domain names have acquired a further significance as business identifiers and as such have come into conflict with the system of trade marks that exists in the off-line world.

The initial board considered a number of issues dealt with in the WIPO report, such as:

- how the contact details of domain name holders should be treated and payments collected by registrars;
- payment procedures;
- dispute settlement mechanisms; and
- the policy on 'famous names' and potential new gTLDs.

It noted that the report's suggestions concerning customer payments and the way registrars should treat the contact details of domain name holders are 'closely similar' to what ICANN requires in its accreditation agreement with its accredited registrars, and that it has already scheduled a review of those issues early next year.

ICANN-accredited registrars are being encouraged to develop and voluntarily adopt a model dispute resolution policy. The initial board at ICANN in May 1999 also referred two other important issues: how to treat 'famous names' and whether, how and when to introduce new gTLDs to the newly formed DNSO for analysis and recommendations.

The Advisory Committee recommended that ICANN set up an Independent Review Board empowered to consider complaints that decisions by the ICANN Board violate ICANN's bylaws. Between now and September 2000, ICANN is gradually taking over responsibility for co-ordinating domain name system management, IP address space allocation, protocol parameter assignment co-ordination, and root server system management. Further details on WIPO and the results of the Berlin meetings (including DNSO Constituency Groups, At-Large Membership, and Independent Review) are posted on the ICANN website at http://www.icann.org/berlin/berlin-resolutions.html and at http://www.icann.org/berlin/berlin-details.html.

Doing Your Own Search [2.10]

A business which wishes to arrange its own domain name registration can first search at Network Solutions Inc (http://rs.internic.net) or Nominet (http://www.nominet.org.uk) to check whether its preferred name is already registered. NetNames has search facilities to allow a search to be undertaken for a domain name anywhere in the world (http://www.netnames.co.uk).

What Names to Choose [2.11]

Most businesses will seek to register their name such as 'GHKHoldings.com' or in the UK 'GHKHoldings.co.uk'. Some companies are better known for their initials, e.g. BT rather than British Telecommunications, and will use such an abbreviation instead. In May 1999, a designer E-mail address list was launched. This is the computer equivalent of the personalised number plate and gives anyone with internet access access to a selection of more than 3,500 domain names. They can choose names such as '@greatlove.co.uk' or '@fallinginlove.co.uk'. These names are known as 'Funmail' addresses.

In return for the free service, users have to complete a very detailed form and disclose information about themselves and their interests. That information is then offered to businesses seeking to market their products. 5,000 requests for information about the service were received in the first two weeks of the launch. However, this sort of service is more for the private individual than businesses.

Using Internet Service Providers [2.12]

Most registrations are done by internet service providers (ISPs) rather than individual businesses. Lists of ISPs are at http://www.yahoo.co.uk (under domain names). A typical charge might be about $79 and a payment every year or few years after that.

Company/Business Names [2.13]

UK businesses will already be using a company or business name. If they are incorporated this will be a limited company name registered at Companies House. However, such registration does not confer registered trade mark rights. Just because a business has secured registration of its preferred corporate name does not give it registered rights for trade mark purposes. It should also register as a UK, Community and/or foreign trade mark the names, signs and other devices it uses for marketing its goods or services at the UK Trade Marks Registry and/or the Community Trade Mark Office.

Registration in the UK is under the *Trade Marks Act 1994*. Contact details of the trade marks registries are given at http://www.patent.gov.uk. Where the name is to be used in more than two or three States, it can be cheaper to register a Community Trade Mark rather than paying for registrations in different States.

Domain Names as Registered Trade Marks [2.14]

It may be possible to register a domain name as a registered trade mark but it would only be the original and distinctive parts of the name which could be protected. Thus, a company which had registered virgin.com as a domain name could apply to register the same name at the Trade Marks Registry. Historically most businesses have registered first at the trade marks registry and followed this later with a domain name registration. However, there is no reason why the reverse could not be the case.

Trade mark law protects against use of the same or a similar name and even in relation to non-similar goods or services in certain cases. The trade mark protection would be for the class of goods or services for which an application was made. The parts of the name .com or .org etc. would not be protectable in this way.

Passing Off [2.15]

If a trade mark is unregistered, it may still be protected in the UK by the law of passing off. Passing off is a tort or legal wrong which entitles someone, who has built up a reputation in a particular name or trading style, to prevent others trading off the back of such reputation in misrepresenting themselves as connected with that person. Passing off is much harder to prove than infringement of a registered trade mark and it is essential to show a misrepresentation and damage that has been caused.

Clearing the Name [2.16]

Businesses choosing new trade marks or product names should first do the following.

✓ Undertake a registered trade mark search in the UK – many businesses will use their trade mark agents to do this for them.

✓ Have their advertising agency check that the name is not a rude or objectionable word in the country in which it will be used – with internet use that means an extensive search in all markets where the goods attract potential customers.

✓ Search at Companies House to see if anyone has a limited company of that name.

✓ Undertake an unregistered trade mark search – this is much harder but checks can be made in relevant journals and by asking around in the trade, as to whether anyone else has been trading under the same or a similar name.

✓ Undertake a domain name search (e.g. with net names: http://www.netnames.co.uk).

✓ Take advice on whether the name would be registrable as a trade mark – generally invented names are best. Generic names such as 'bread' to describe a bread product are unlikely to be registrable.

✓ Undertake the relevant registrations, certainly as a trade mark and domain name.

Trade Mark Notices for Websites [2.17]

The web page may well use registered or unregistered trade marks of the business. Ensure that those trade marks where registered appear with an 'R' in a circle: ABC HGY ®

Or use: ABC SDD ™ to indicate an unregistered mark.

Threats Actions [2.18]

It is an offence under the *Trade Marks Act 1994* to threaten another with trade mark infringement where they have not infringed.

Section 21(1) provides that:

'Where a person threatens another with proceedings for infringement of a registered trade mark other than—

(a) the application of the mark to goods or their packaging,

(b) the importation of goods to which, or to the packaging of which, the mark has been applied, or

(c) the supply of services under the mark,

any person aggrieved may bring proceedings for relief under this section.'

The person threatened is entitled to a declaration that the threats are unjustified, an injunction against the threats continuing and damages for any loss suffered. However, it may be possible to show that the trade mark is invalid or liable to be revoked. In addition, mere notification that a trade mark is registered or that an application for registration has been made does not constitute a threat (*section 21(4)*). This section was successfully used in *Prince plc v Prince Sports Group Inc* (unreported, *30 July 1997*) (see **2.30** below).

Claiming Registration Where there is None [2.19]

Section 95(1) of the *Trade Marks Act 1994* makes it an offence to claim a mark is registered when it is not:

'It is an offence for a person—

(a) falsely to represent that a mark is a registered trade mark, or

(b) to make a false representation as to the goods or services for which a trade mark is registered

knowing or having reason to believe that the representation is false.'

For the purposes of *section 95* the use in the UK in relation to a trade mark of the word 'registered' or of any other word or symbol importing a reference, whether this is express or implied to registration, is deemed to be:

'a representation as to registration under this Act unless it is shown that the reference is to registration elsewhere than in the United Kingdom and that the trade mark is in fact so registered for the goods or services in question'.

This is a criminal provision and individuals can be fined as well as businesses. Criminal sanctions are a very helpful weapon for companies to use as many businesses, particularly those seeking to 'cash in' on registration as domain names of other's trade marks, will not be frightened by the threat of civil legal action, but will be concerned about committing a criminal offence. They can easily liquidate their business but a criminal record is a serious matter.

Those involved in advising on intellectual property rights should always consider not only civil proceedings but also whether the criminal law can be used. In addition those with limited funds to cover legal actions may be able to involve local trading standards officers (whose details can be found in the Yellow Pages), in bringing prosecutions in more blatant cases. However, there is no general obligation for them to take up every complaint or case.

Private criminal prosecutions can also be undertaken and solicitors and counsel can advise on whether it is appropriate in certain cases not only to launch civil but also criminal proceedings. It should be noted that the standard of proof required for criminal actions is higher than that for a civil case.

Make sure all those employees and external advertising and computer agency staff working on a business' website or content of E-mail messages/notices etc. are aware that claiming trade mark rights which do not exist is an offence. (See further **Chapter 7: INTERNET ADVERTISING**).

Applications for Registration [2.20]

If an application for registration has been made at the Trade Marks Registry or, for EU-wide marks, the Community Trade Mark Office in Alicante, then the letters '™' must be used until the mark has been granted. Although rights in a mark are not lost if a notice such as this is not used, such a notice is a valuable warning to third parties that the names or devices are protected and should not be copied.

National and International Trade Mark Issues [2.21]

Note that marks obtain protection only in the countries where they are registered. If a business will begin to make sales abroad through the use of the internet, then trade marks should be protected through registration in those markets.

In addition, before supplying any advertising abroad, businesses should carry out a trade mark search to check whether a third party is already using the mark. If they are, then an import, whether through an E-mail order or otherwise, may amount to a breach of trade mark rights of a third party and expensive trade mark infringement proceedings may follow.

Section 10 of the *Trade Marks Act 1994* (and the EU Trade Marks Directive on which it is based) prohibits not only the affixing of a trade mark to goods or their packaging without consent and selling or exposing goods for sale without the trade mark owner's consent, but also importing or exporting of goods under the mark or use of the sign on business papers or in advertising. Note that using a mark on a website is the use of the mark in advertising and that importing foreign goods into the UK through internet purchases is a potentially infringing act.

Liability of Web Page Designers [2.22]

Those who help design web pages or otherwise take control of a business' web page may inadvertently infringe a trade mark under the *Trade Marks Act 1994*.

Section 10(5) makes it an offence to apply a registered trademark to material intended to be used for advertising (or labelling or packaging goods) as that person is treated as a party to the use of the material if it infringes a trade mark if 'when he applied the mark he knew or had reason to believe that the application of the mark was not duly authorised by the proprietor or a licensee'.

Notices for Sales Abroad [2.23]

Cautious businesses may avoid problems by including a notice on their web page stating that orders are accepted only from certain countries (such as those where they know they own the trade mark); or use a different name for sales of products to countries where a third party owns the same trade mark.

An example of such a notice might be:

'We do not accept orders from [Canada]'.

Or a company could say:

'The trade mark [ ] is owned by VVV Corporation in Canada and we do not market our goods under that trade mark in

> Canada. Contact our local dealer by clicking here for further information'.

Exhaustion of Rights [2.24]

Under *Articles 28–30* of the *EC Treaty*, once goods are placed on the market by the owner of the trade mark or other intellectual property rights in the goods, they must be free to circulate around the EU. The rights are said to be 'exhausted' and although most countries' intellectual property laws list 'importing' as an example of an infringing act, once the rights are exhausted in this way, then the goods can be imported even without the trade mark owner's consent. However, this does not apply to counterfeit or pirated products made without the consent of the rights owner.

Neither does this principle apply if there are two trade mark owners of the same name in different territories. In such circumstances they can each stop an import into the other's State even within the EU. Previously, under a principle called 'common origin', if two such trade mark owners formerly held the trade mark in one name and sold it then they could not prevent an import of the goods because it was 'their fault' there were now two different trade mark owners. However, case law abolished this principle in *Hag I & II [1974] ECR 731; [1990] I ECR 371* and *Ideal Standard [1994] 3 CMLR 857*. Where there are two trade mark owners with the same name in the EU they need to ensure that any contract between them which divides the market on geographic or other grounds is checked carefully for compliance with EC competition law under *Article 81* (formerly *Article 85*) of the *EC Treaty*. Under EU case law, any such 'delimitation' agreement must go no further than is necessary to protect the parties' rights. The EC competition law textbooks provide considerable detail on what is and what is not permitted in such contracts.

International Exhaustion [2.25]

Marketing of goods over the internet will involve advertising in every place on earth. In the EU, it was held in *Silhouette Internatioal Schmeid v Hartlauer [1998] ECR I-4799; [1998] Tr LR 355* that the principle of international exhaustion did not apply in relation to trade marks where the goods were imported from outside the EU. This was confirmed when the European Court of Justice reached its decision in *Sebago Inc and Ancienne Maison Dubois et Fils SA v GB-Unic SA* (unreported, *1 July*

1999). However, the English courts in *Zino Davidoff v A&G Import* (*18 May 1999*, unreported, High Court) held that unless a brand owner expressly specifies that his goods cannot be exported to particular States, then the buyer is entitled to resell them where he wishes. The *Davidoff* case has, however, been referred to the European Court of Justice for a final ruling. The English judge was critical of the *Silhouette* case and said:

> 'Silhouette has bestowed on a trade mark owner a parasitic right to interfere with the distribution of goods which bears little or no relationship to the proper function of the trade mark right. It is difficult to believe that a properly informed legislature intended such a result'.

In 1999 there was also intense lobbying from both brand owners and parallel importers for clarificationof the law in this area.

On 29th June 1999, the House of Commons Trade and Industry Committee produced its 8th report *Trade Marks, Fakes and Consumers* which examined this area in detail and which is on the internet at http://www.parliament.uk/commons/selcom/t&ihome.htm. It notes, in relation to the internet at page xxxii, that musical recordings purchased on line over the internet will become increasingly common. The BPI organisation which gave evidence to the committee said it was much easier to use trade mark law than copyright in stopping illegal imports.

> 'To proceed successfully in relation to copyright infringe- ment on parallel importation over the Internet, it is neces- sary to show that the importer is not the consumer, who has a defence because s/he is not importing in the course of a business. The same is not true in relation to trade marks'.

They also said that price differences between the US and UK would level off over 5 years and be within a 10% price range.

Exhaustion and the Internet [2.26]

Where software is supplied on-line, the supplier may not even know the country of destination of the goods ordered. This makes such restrictions on world free trade such as those seen in the *Silhouette* case (see **2.25** above) appear very artificial and in many cases unworkable. The EU case law described at **2.25** above relates only to the *Trade*

Marks Directive. There is no EU or UK case law which holds that there is no international exhaustion of rights for copyright and other intellectual property protected material. However, the legal position is uncertain.

Suppliers using the internet or other means which want to ensure that their buyers do not export the goods elsewhere, should include clear statements about future exports, and will have to seek competition law advice, since many such export bans will be void in any event under various countries' competition laws. In the EU, where an agreement falls within the *Distribution Block Exemption Regulation 1983/83*, then the supplier is entitled to prohibit the buyer from advertising outside its territory, but cannot impose an absolute export ban. If such a ban were imposed then it would be void under *Article 81* of the *EC Treaty* and the supplier would risk a fine of up to 10% of worldwide group turnover.

In 1998, the Publishers Association were reported in the press to be arguing that the import of books from the US via internet sales sites amounted to a breach of UK copyright, as indeed on the face of the *Copyright, Designs and Patents Act 1988*, it would be. However, if international exhaustion of rights applies, then the US suppliers, whose books are not counterfeit and have been made with the permission of the rights owner, would be free to export them to the UK. Under earlier UK case law it was established that if the goods to be imported were, despite being genuine products, of poorer quality, such as the lower quality Colgate toothpaste sold for South America in *Colgate Palmolive v Markwell Finance [1990] RPC 197*, then the UK trade mark owner could prevent an import on the grounds that the UK public would be confused and would expect the product to be of the same quality as that brand of paste as sold for the UK market.

However, cases such as *Colgate* have to date solely been confined to trade mark matters. It may be possible to argue that UK buyers of books would expect English spellings or some other quality issue but that is unlikely to succeed. A test case on international exhaustion of rights and copyright is urgently required to clarify the legal position.

UK Case Law [2.27]

Case examples show the current difficulties businesses have had in establishing their own domain names and enforcing their rights in them.

Harrods [2.28]

On 6 December 1997 the UK High Court found in favour of Harrods in a case involving use of the 'Harrods' name (*Harrods Ltd v UK Network Services Ltd [1997] 4 EIPR D-106*). Harrods objected to the registration of 'harrods.com' by unauthorised persons. Harrods had registered 'harrods.co.uk' as its internet address. The defendants had registered at least 54 other 'famous' names. The judge, Lightman J, held that the registration 'clearly constituted infringement of Harrods' registered trade marks and passing off'. Harrods successfully obtained an injunction and the defendants were ordered to take all steps necessary to hand the name over to Harrods.

Pitman [2.29]

Less clear is the position where two businesses use the same trading name. This is never recommended as a business practice because of the confusion it can cause. However, sometimes the use of a similar or identical name happens by accident or perhaps two businesses in very different trading areas use the same name and find later that their trades begin to overlap. In *Pitman Training Limited and PTC Oxford Ltd v Nominet UK and Pearson Professional Limited ([1997] FSR 797)*, the High Court considered an interlocutory (emergency) application for an injunction pending a trial, concerning two companies using the name Pitman. This was a case where both companies used to be part of the same group but were then split into two in 1985.

The claimants in the case received the training and examinations section of the business and the publishing part went to Pearson Professional Ltd, the defendant, which owns the Financial Times newspaper. Pearson applied to register 'pitman.co.uk' as an internet site in February 1996 but as it did not have immediate plans to use the name, it did not publicise the site straight away. The website was then designed and gradually the address was put on advertisements.

In December 1996, Pearson was ready to use the registered address but found that PTC Oxford Ltd had had the name assigned to it, even though Pearson had registered the name first. This is not supposed to happen on the first come, first served basis of current internet registrations. Pitman Training (PTC) began using the name in July 1996. Pearson's solicitors threatened legal action so the name was transferred back to Pearson. PTC then sued but did not win.

The case is different from *Harrods* (see **2.28** above) because it seemed that at the time neither party had a registered trade mark. The judge refused an injunction in *Pitman* because PTC had hardly used the website address at all. There was no association in the mind of the public of the address with PTC. PTC had only had two E-mail responses to its advertisement giving the internet address. PTC had also said that the action of Pearson in trying to persuade Nominet to hand the name back to Pearson was an abuse of the process of the court – a sort of threats action. However, the judge said as legal action had not been started this could not be the case.

Prince [2.30]

Prince plc v Prince Sports Group Inc (unreported, *30 July 1997*) was a High Court decision in this area. Prince Sports Group Inc is well known as a seller of sports equipment in the USA. In 1995, Prince plc, a UK IT services provider, registered 'prince.com' as its domain name and used that name. Prince Sports applied to register its name and found out Prince plc had got in first. On 16 January 1997, Prince Sports' US lawyers wrote to Prince plc alleging infringement of UK registered trade marks through Prince plc's domain name having been registered and used. Prince plc sued Prince Sports for unjustified threats of trade mark infringement. The UK High Court, Neuberger J, held that the threats in the US lawyers' letter did breach the *Trade Marks Act 1994, s21* (see **2.18** above).

The claimants, Prince plc, had also asked the judge for a declaration that use of its domain name did not infringe Prince Sports trade marks. The judge would not grant that declaration. Prince Sports sued Prince plc in the US over ownership of the domain name.

Mecklermedia v DC Congress (High Court, 6 March 1997) [2.31]

Mecklermedia publish a magazine called Internet World in the UK and abroad under a licence from VNU. It also runs trade shows in the UK under that name (having done so since 1994) and abroad. It has a popular website www.iworld.com. Mecklermedia sued DC Congress (DC) who organises German trade shows. In 1996, one of DC's shows was called 'Internet World'. To promote the show it did a mailing in the UK including to Mecklermedia's customers and set up a website using the name Internet World. Mecklermedia objected and sued DC in the UK. DC had the name registered as a trade mark in Germany and was based there. It applied to strike out Mecklermedia's case because of these jurisdictional issues. The judge said:

> '[w]hen an enterprise wants to use a mark or word through-
> out the world (and that may include an internet address or
> domain name) it must take into account that in some places,
> if not others, there may be confusion. Here it is clear DC
> Congress knew that Mecklermedia used the name 'Internet
> World' and I do not think it is surprising that [DC
> Congress] is met with [legal] actions in places where
> confusion is considered likely'.

The decision means that those advertising over the internet need to check in all relevant jurisdictions that they do not breach trade mark law. The fact that a UK business has a UK trade mark, does not mean it avoids infringement of identical trade marks registered in the names of other businesses abroad.

Avnet   [2.32]

Avnet Inc v Isoact Ltd [1997] 8 ETMR (26 July 1997). The plaintiff was the registered proprietor of a trade mark registered in class 35 for advertising services. The defendant was an internet service provider involved in the aviation field and used names Aviation Network and Avent in its business. It offered its members E-mail addresses, construction of websites and advice on technology in the normal way of internet service providers.

Avent Inc did not succeed in its application for summary judgment. The registered trade mark was registered for advertising and promotional services. This was not what the defendant was using it for. In any event those services offered by Isoact were not in class 35.

One in a Million   [2.33]

In *BT, Virgin, Sainsbury, Ladbroke and M&S v One in a Million* the court had to consider various passing off and trade mark issues.

The High Court Decision (The Times, 2 December 1997) **[2.34]**

The High Court, on an application for a summary (or quick) judgment, held that these famous claimants could force One in a Million, which had registered their names as internet domain names, to hand them over to the rightful owners. The names which had been registered were trade marks of the plaintiffs and had only been registered by the defendant in order to make money out of them. The plaintiffs sued for passing off and trade mark infringement.

In his judgment, the judge first explained the use of domain names in this field. He said Marks & Spencer had a number of domain names including 'marks-and-spencer.co.uk', 'marks-and-spencer.com' and 'stmichael.com'. The domain name 'marks-and-spencer.co.uk' enables it to have an E-mail address such as 'johnsmith@marks-and-spencer.co.uk' and a website address of 'http://www.marks-and-spencer.co.uk'. The most obvious use for registration of such famous names is to sell them to the business whose name they are. It may also be sold to a business unconnected with the name, that thinks it can sell it to the true owner for a profit. Thirdly, it might be sold to someone of the same name – such as a Mr John Sainsbury. Fourthly, it may be retained and not sold in order to block registration by the true owner.

The judgment reports that one of the individuals behind the defendant wrote to Burger King, after acquiring 'burgerking.co.uk'. Burger King had already registered burger-king.co.uk. He wrote:

> 'Further to our telephone conversation early this evening, I confirm that I own the domain name burgerking.co.uk. I would be willing to sell the domain name for the sum of £25,000 plus VAT. In answer to your question regarding as to what we would do with the domain name should you decide not to purchase it – the domain name would be available for sale to any other interested party.
>
> As I am sure you are aware the Internet is an extremely fast growing medium, and the standard convention for Domain name for company name of more than a single word is to have no hyphens in the domain name. Although you currently have burger-king.co.uk this would not be the most obvious first choice for any individual to use, should they be speculatively looking for your UK website.'

The decision also referred to a similar letter sent to BT asking for £4,700. The judge refers to similar cases such as *Direct Line Group*

Limited v Direct Line Estate Agency [1997] FSR 374. In that case an injunction was granted to Direct Line to prevent two individuals incorporating a large number of companies with Direct Line in their names. In *Glaxo Plc v Glaxowellcome Ltd [1996] FSR 388* the court stopped the registration of someone who had registered Glaxowellcome Ltd just after the merger of Glaxo and Wellcome was announced. In that case Glaxowellcome had not then started to trade but the judge decided it was likely it would in future. The judge in *Glaxo* said:

'The court will not countenance any such pre-emptive strike of registering companies with names where others have the goodwill in those names and the registering party then demanding a price for changing names. It is an abuse of the system of registration of company names. The right to choose the name with which a company is registered is not given for that purpose'.

A similar case, also quoted in *One in a Million*, was *Direct Line Group Limited v Direct Line Estate Agency Ltd [1997] FSR 374.* There was a registered company name at issue in that case also, and not a domain name. The registration by the defendant had been solely subsequently to attempt to sell the name to the true 'Direct Line'. The judge said that the courts would not permit this. An injunction was granted pending trial even though the defendants had not traded under the name.

The problem in these internet and other name cases is that to sue for passing off, it normally has been necessary to show that the person misusing the name is using it in the course of trade. Simply to register an internet address but not to use it may not satisfy this requirement.

In *One in a Million* the judge said it was not 'passing off' to go equipped to undertake this activity. However the judge said it was clear that the plaintiff's rights would be infringed in the future as there was no other reason why the defendants had chosen marksandspencer as an internet address. The following passage from the judgment makes the legal position quite clear:

'Any person who deliberately registers a domain name on account of its similarity to the name, brand name or trade mark of an unconnected commercial organisation must expect to find himself on the receiving end of an injunction to restrain the threat of passing off, and the injunction will be in terms which will make the name commercially useless to the dealer'.

It was also held to be trade mark infringement, since M&S had a registered trade mark. The use of a trade mark in the course of the business of a professional dealer for the purpose of making domain names more valuable and extracting money from the trade mark owner, is a use in the course of trade for trade mark purposes. The definition of such use is also elaborated upon in the decision *British Sugar plc v James Robertson & Sons Ltd [1996] RPC 281.*

The judge thought no one would use the name 'marks and spencer' or 'cellnet' unless they were trying to trade off their reputation. However, the same might not be true in relation to names like Sainsbury, Ladbroke, Virgin and BT. The judge found that the defendants had made a deliberate practice of registering such famous names for the purposes of sale and the registrations were therefore not innocent. The defendants were ordered to transfer the names to the plaintiffs.

Court of Appeal [1998] FSR 265; [1998] Tr LR 333   [2.35]

In *British Telecommunications plc, Virgin Enterprises Ltd, J Sainsbury plc, Marks & Spencer plc, Ladbroke Group plc v One in a Million Ltd and Others* the Court of Appeal examined the same issues as in **2.34** above. The judgment is also on the internet at http://www.nic.uk/news/oiamappealjudgment.html. On appeal it was held that:

- registration of a third party's distinctive name as a domain name can amount to passing off;
- trade mark infringement was also found through such registration as domain names which were designed to take advantage of the distinctive character and reputation of trade marks in an unfair and detrimental way; and
- the summary judgment of the High Court would stand and the appeal was dismissed with an order that the defendant pay the costs.

Leave to appeal to the House of Lords was refused. The court examined whether there was a tort or legal wrong of going equipped to 'pass off'. The court said it would intervene in cases of this type where passing off is established or threatened, where the defendant is jointly involved with another in passing off which is either threatened or actual and also where the defendant equips himself with an instrument of fraud.

The court thought that registering 'marksandspencer' was clearly an instrument of fraud whereas some of the other names were different.

'The placing on a register of a distinctive name such as marksandspencer makes a representation to persons who consult the register that the registrant is connected or associated with the name registered and thus the owner of the goodwill in the name'.

Looking at registered trade marks, the court found that an internet domain name was an indication of origin and that was why the names were registered.

Practice Issues [2.36]

✓ Those registering internet domain names should undertake registered trade mark searches and searches in any registries and trade presses which might throw up unregistered use of the name chosen.

✓ Seek consent from trade mark owners in cases of doubt, or alternatively alter the name. Do this early on before costs are incurred.

✓ Do not give in to blackmail by those who have registered a name. Instead threaten to sue them (take legal advice first though because unjustified threats of trade mark infringement are an offence under the *Trade Marks Act 1994* – see **2.18** above).

✓ In theory, carry out trade mark searches in all countries where the mark will be used. In practice this is very difficult and too expensive for many businesses. If goods will be sold using the domain name/site and someone else owns the name abroad, putting a notice stating that orders are not accepted from other countries specified (see **2.23** above) may assist but it still may not prevent a legal action. Consider in such cases agreeing with the other party who uses the same name terms on which each party will use the name, as is common with split trade mark ownership cases already throughout the world.

US Cases [2.37]

Brookfield Communications Inc v West Coast Entertainment Corp (1999) US App LEXIS 7779, 9th Cir. 22 April 1999 [2.38]

The US 9th Circuit held that mere registration of a domain name for a website does not give legal rights in the name as a trade mark. Registration is not sufficient 'use' under the US Langham Act. Since 1986 a chain of video rental stores had traded under The Movie Buff's Movie Store and they registered it as a trade mark in 1991 and in February 1996 registered moviebuff.com. In August 1997 Brookfield filed a trade mark application of MovieBuff and announced plans in November 1998 to launch an entertainment industry database on its website. Since 1993 Brookfield had sole software under the moviebuff logo and since 1997 had offered it over its website.

Brookfield sued West Coast for trade mark infringement and unfair competition. On appeal the 9th circuit held that Brookfield had senior rights and there was unlikely to be confusion. Brookfield filed its trade mark application for MovieBuff before West Coast publicly announced its website so Brookfield acquired priority. West Coast's use of the MovieBuff name in its website metatags and in hidden codes was also trade mark infringement.

Playboy Enterprises v Chuckleberry Publishing, 19 June 1996 [2.39]

This case concerned the use of the 'Playman' trade mark on an Italian internet website. The US courts held that this amounted to breach of a US court injunction which restrained use of that name in the US (because it was too similar to the Playboy mark). Use in Italy was not prohibited. The Italian courts had permitted the Playman mark to be used in their State.

Panavision International LP v Toeppen (141 F 3d 1316 (1998)) [2.40]

Dennis Toeppen of Illinois registered with the US Internet registrar (Network Solutions Inc) over 100 domain names.

These included well known US company names and trade marks such as 'Panavision.com'. On his website he displayed photographs of the Illinois city of Pana. This led to Panavision International sending him a lawyers' letter. He offered to 'settle' the matter for $13,000. Panavision refused. Toeppen then registered the domain name Panaflex.com. Panaflex was one of Panavision's trade marks. This website simply contained the word 'Hello'.

Panavision sued in California for trade mark dilution. Toeppen contended that the Californian court had no jurisdiction over him. The court disagreed and granted Panavision summary judgment. Toeppen appealed.

This judgment was affirmed by the US Court of Appeals. On the issue of jurisdiction, the Court stated that, as a general rule, the mere registration of another's trade mark as a domain name, in the US, even if combined with its use on a website, would not be enough to subject someone domiciled in one State to jurisdiction in another. However, here there was something extra. Toeppen had tried to extort money from Panavision causing injury in California. Therefore, he was within the Californian court's jurisdiction.

The Court also found that there had been dilution of Panavision's trade mark. Toeppen's business was registering trade marks as domain names and selling them to their rightful owners. This reduced Panavision's ability to identify its goods and service on the internet and jeopardised its reputation in its name. It would also make it difficult for potential customers to find its real website.

KCPL Inc v Nash 1998 US Dis. Lexis 18464 1998 WL 823657 (SNDY 24 November 1998) [2.41]

Nash registered the domain name 'reaction.com'. KCPL sold luggage, footwear and clothing using trade marks 'Reaction' and 'Kenneth Cole Reaction'. Nash was resident in California and KCPL sued in the

Southern District of New York for trade mark infringement, dilution and unfair competition. KCPL said Nash had demanded money for the rights to 'reaction.com', though he had not constructed a functioning website – his site just said 'under construction'. KCPL asked the court to follow *Panavision v Toeppen* (see **2.40** above).

The New York court refused. It said its legislation was narrower than that in California and did not extend outside its jurisdiction in the same way. Nash did not 'transact business' or commit a tortious act in New York.

Data Concepts Inc v Digital Consulting Inc No 97-5802, 1998 Fed App. 0241P, 47 USPQ 2d 1672 (6th Cir 5 November 1998) [2.42]

Digital Consulting Inc began proceedings with Network Solutions Inc to have the name 'CDI.COM' transferred to it. CDI.COM was registered by Data Concepts Inc. Data Concepts Inc sued for a declaratory judgment of its entitlement to the name. Data registered the domain name in 1993. Digital had registered the name as a federal trade mark in 1987.

Digital was granted a summary judgment and injunction stopping Data using DCI.COM. However, this was reversed by the court on appeal (to the Sixth Circuit). They said there was a triable issue and the matter must go back to the court for reconsideration, though they did think that Digital had the senior use of the mark.

Conseco Inc v Hickerson 698 NE 2s 816 (Ind Ct App 14 August 1998) [2.43]

A Texan resident, Mr Russ Hickerson wanted to find details of anyone who had been treated unfairly by Conseco or any of its subsidiaries, so he set up a website. The website did not advertise or sell any products but it did use Conseco's trade mark: 'Conseco inc'.

Conseco sued Mr Hickerson for trade mark dilution and infringement, commercial disparagement, defamation and tortious interference with contractual relationships arising from the website. The company was granted a temporary restraining order but refused a temporary injunction. On appeal, the Indiana court of appeals examined jurisdictional issues only. The court said it had no jurisdiction over Mr Hickerson and followed an earlier case *Cybersell Inc v Cybersell Inc (130 F3d 414 9th cir 1997)*. That case had held that an internet advertisement was not sufficient to support personal jurisdiction over a non-resident. The defendant must direct his activity at a particular State which Hickerson did not do. He had no direct advertising and did not send E-mails, letters or make calls to Indiana. Simply discussing Conseco was not enough to allow Indiana to have jurisdiction over him.

French Cases [2.44]

More than a dozen cases concerning domain names were decided in France towards the end of 1998. It appears that the French courts are applying traditional trade mark principles to domain name cases. French courts also consider that they are the proper forum for all litigation arising from domain names accessible on a computer screen located in France.

SG2 v Brokat [2.45]

In the decision of 13 November 1997 in *SG2 v Brokat*, the District Court of Nanterre ruled on an application for an injunction that Brokat, a German company that used the domain name 'payline' on the internet in Germany, was infringing the trade mark 'payline' registered in France by SG2. The President of the District Court of Nanterre considered that the infringement was committed in France by the mere appearance of the word 'payline' on the screen.

The trade mark infringement also occurred by the distribution by Brokat at a conference held in Paris of a brochure on which the domain name was printed.

Identical Web Page Presentation [2.46]

In *Cybion v Qualisteam*, the Court of Commerce of Paris ruled, on 9 February 1998, that a web page that reproduced the presentation (look and feel) and the main information contained in another web page, infringed the rights in that other web page. Damages awarded were minimal (50,000 francs, US$8,000) since the defendant had modified his web page immediately after being sued.

Spanish Cases [2.47]

SERTEL [2.48]

The *SERTEL* case involved the claimant's ownership of the registered trademark 'SERTEL'. It was a decision in the First Instance Court of Palma de Mallorca. The claim was for unfair competition and breach of trade mark when the defendant registered the domain name 'sertel.es'. ('ES' stands for 'Spain' – 'Espana'). The defendant gave in on many issues and agreed to transfer the name to the claimant after a temporary period so there was no detailed analysis of the law.

OZU [2.49]

In *Ozu*, both claimant and defendant wanted to register the name 'OZU' as a domain name in Spain. It was a registered trade mark of the claimant already and the defendant registered it at InterNIC as 'ozu-com'. The registered trade mark owner won an interim order.

Trends [2.50]

In general, the cases above are consistent, whatever the jurisdiction. The trend is as follows.

> ✓ Those registering famous names to sell them to the rightful owner are not supported by the courts. They could infringe trade marks. It remains a practical reality that because of court costs though it can be cheaper to buy them off in some cases. However, this can set a bad precedent.
> ✓ The earlier use of the trade mark will prevail. Therefore, if A registers a trade mark before B registers a domain name, then A is likely to win in any dispute.
> ✓ Most courts will need to find a connection with the State in which the proceedings are brought, before it will allow an action for infringement.

International Co-operation [2.51]

Internet domain names are international. The most sensible future arrangements will be internationally agreed. In May 1999, the World Intellectual Property Organisation (WIPO) put forward proposals to ICANN, (see **2.9** above) the internet international body, with the aim of stopping 'cybersquatting' and other breaches of trade mark rights, many of which are the subject matter of some of the cases detailed in **2.25** *et seq.* above.

The abuses WIPO hopes to prevent include:

● registration of internet addresses or domain names of well known trade marks in order to sell them back to their owners at a high price;

● registering names closely resembling a trade mark to gain business from accidental visitors to the official site; and

● registration of domain names to prevent competitors having the name or to enable negative information about a business' products, or the business itself, to be disseminated.

WIPO's recommendations concern registrations in the three top open generic level domains (gTLDs) .com, .net and .org.

WIPO's Proposals [2.52]

WIPO has made the following proposals.

● Those applying to register would have to agree to their contact details being public and those who had untraceable sites would be deregistered. WIPO has drawn up a list of minimum 'best practice' registration procedures for gTLD registrars.

● A uniform and mandatory system of arbitration allowing recognised trade mark owners to force cybersquatters to give up sites which they acquired for abusive use. There would be no targeting of legitimate registrants.

● Owners of well known marks could obtain exclusions preventing others registering them – a WIPO panel would decide on exclusion applications.

WIPO has also argued for slow consideration of any future gTLDs and only after much consideration should they be introduced. On 26 August 1999, the ICANN board passed a resolution adopting a uniform dispute resolution policy for registrars in the generic top-level domains. The resolutions are at http://www.icann.org/santiago/santiago-resolutions.htm.

The proposals above are correct at the date of writing but in such a fast moving field the latest position should always be checked.

Comparative Advertising [2.53]

Using a competitor's trade mark on an internet website can amount to breach of trade mark. There are many UK cases on 'comparative advertising'.

Cases include *Emaco Ltd and Another v Dyson Appliances Ltd* (*The Times, 8 February 1999*), under which rival vacuum cleaner manufacturers sued each other for breach of trade marks and malicious falsehood revolved around comparative advertising.

The *Trade Marks Act 1996* permits the use of a trade mark except where it is 'otherwise than in accordance with honest practices in industrial or commercial matters' (*section 10(6)*). In this case, the High Court dismissed the reciprocal malicious falsehood claims on the grounds there was no malice. However, as the documents published were misleading and contained false representations about a competitor's product, there was breach of trade mark rights. *Vodaphone Group plc v Orange Personal Communications Services Ltd* [1997] *FSR 34* and *Cable and Wireless plc v British Telecommunications plc* [1998] *FSR 383* were followed. Comparative advertising has considerable persuasive power with consumers but often leads to litigation.

Note that these cases related to normal rather than internet advertising but there is no reason why use of a trade mark on a website would not be treated in the same way as use of a trade mark in a journal for these purposes.

Guidelines for Comparative Advertising [2.54]

Comparison with a competitor's products is one of the most convincing means of showing a customer why the advertising business' products are best. However, many businesses have regretted this form of advertising and it can result in very public disputes about the product concerned with rival experts' reports being used in evidence. Therefore, businesses should consider the following.

✓ Only engage in comparative advertising after having taken legal advice.
✓ Using a competitor's trade mark on an internet website is likely to lead to greater risks than use in other media because it will be broadcast in other jurisdictions. This means the damaged party can pick the country where such advertising is prohibited and avoid suing in countries such as the UK which have a relative benign regime.
✓ Only use scrupulously fair comparisons and avoid any comparison which is in anyway inaccurate.
✓ Compare like with like.

EU Comparative Advertisement Directive   [2.55]

EU *Directive 97/55*, which amends *Directive 84/540* on *Misleading Advertising* so it covers comparative advertising, was published in the EU's official journal in 1997 (*OJ 1997 L290/18*). It must be implemented by all Member States by 6 April 2000.

The Directive defines comparative advertising as 'any advertising which explicitly or by implication identifies a competitor or goods or services offered by a competitor'. Comparative advertising is permitted if it:

- is not misleading;
- compares goods or services meeting the same needs or intended for the same purpose;
- objectively compares one or more material, relevant, verifiable and representative features of those goods and services, which may include price;
- does not create confusion in the market place between the advertiser and a competitor or between the advertiser's trade marks, trade names other distinguishing marks, goods or services and those of a competitor;
- does not discredit or denigrate the trade marks, trade names, other distinguishing marks, goods, services, activities or circumstances of a competitor;
- relates in each case to products with the same designation, for products with designation of origin (this covers items such as Champagne emanating from the Champagne region of France);

- does not take unfair advantage of the reputation of a trade mark, trade name or other distinguishing marks of a competitor, or of the designation of origin of competing products; and

- does not present goods or services as imitations or replicas of goods or services bearing a protected trade mark or trade name.

Under the Directive, if a comparison with a special offer is made then this must indicate, in a clear and unequivocal way, the date on which the offer ends or if it is subject to the availability of other goods or services.

The advantage of this legislation (which is not yet implemented in the UK at the date of writing) is that it is pan-EU/EEA so at least in those EU/EEA states the advertiser over the internet will know what the harmonised legislation says.

Business Practices [2.56]

Assuming a business has decided to use the internet and E-mail, it then needs to decide what names to register as domain names. It may simply have one trading name which it registers as xyz.com. However, it may market and sell a wide variety of products under a number of different product names. It will need to decide which, if any, to register. The business should also check it has undertaken all the trade mark registrations it should have done. Some businesses have decided to register their name as a domain name in all countries in which they operate. Others have made only a very few registrations.

For example, Ford, the motor company, has gone for the thorough approach. Its main web page is www.ford.com. From there a surfer can move to the UK company at www.ford.co.uk. This approach requires a number of different domains to be registered and paid for.

An alternative to this approach is to register one domain and then have a third level designator for products with designation of origin – such as uk.xyz.com.

Checklist – Avoiding Infringement and Reducing

Risks [2.57]

✓ Pick invented words which are acceptable in all major languages.

✓ Do full searches first.

✓ Outsource responsibility for the choice to a large entity with insurance cover.

✓ Ensure that the business has intellectual property litigation insurance cover.

✓ Include notices on websites.

✓ Take firm, quick action against infringers.

✓ Do not give in to domain name blackmailers.

✓ Exploit domain name bodies' registration appeals procedures rather than the courts. Courts are expensive.

✓ If a name is someone else's in another State, note this on the website and do not take orders under that name from that jurisdiction.

✓ Obtain intellectual property indemnities and warranties from suppliers and designers where possible.

✓ Educate staff in trade mark matters.

Grey Areas [2.58]

Trade marks provide protection principally in the category of goods for which they are registered. As the cases section above (see **2.27** *et seq.*) shows, often two businesses will own the same trade mark but either in relation to different goods, or in different countries.

Same Mark or Similar Mark – Same

Goods/Services [2.59]

Where two businesses own the same mark or a similar mark for the same goods in different States, neither breaches the law until they start importing their goods into the country of the other party.

There is a significant body of case law in relation to the EC competition rules which is relevant here.

In practice, the sensible solution is to agree between the potential litigants the terms on which they will each use their trade mark. Such agreements have a great propensity to divide the market. For example, the owner of a UK trade mark could agree with the French holder of the same mark to only use the mark in the UK, if the Frenchman agrees to stick to France. Such efforts to divide the EU market on geographical grounds can infringe *Article 81* of the *EC Treaty* which prohibits anti-competitive agreements which affect trade between EU Member States. Specialist competition law advice should be taken on this area.

There used to be a legal principle under EU law called the 'common origin' doctrine, whereby if a trade mark used to be in the same hands but ownership was then split, such as through a sale or because of State confiscation, then the trade mark owners could not prevent goods under the rival mark being imported into their country. However, this doctrine was abolished. Therefore, it is now even more important to consider all the legal implications carefully before selling off a business with its trade mark in one State where that mark is used by a business in another State where the mark is retained.

The use of the internet and growth of world trade means that the risk of confusion is much greater. The easier cases are where someone unrelated to a mark registers it as a domain name and then seeks to sell it to the true owner. Much more difficult are the cases where there are owners of two names in different States for the same goods. In practice they will need to make this clear on their web pages and may need to reach an agreement between themselves which is thoroughly vetted under all relevant competition laws, to determine how they will use the mark so that it is not confusing to customers.

Same or Similar Mark – Different
Goods/Services [2.60]

Trade marks are registered for particular classes of goods and services. Although the *EU Trade Marks Directive* and the *Trade Marks Act 1994* do permit litigation where use is made in a different class by an 'infringer', this is only in limited circumstances. *Section 10(3)* of the *Trade Marks Act 1994* provides that this is where the trade mark:

'Has a reputation in the UK and the use of the sign, being without due cause, takes unfair advantage of, or is detrimental to, the distinctive character or the repute of the trade mark.'

Where two legitimate traders both with registered trade marks for the same or a similar name in the one State, attempt to register their name as a domain name, they cannot thereby register only for the types of goods in which they trade. Therefore, the business which applies first will obtain the registration. There may be cases where an action for breach of trade mark or passing off will succeed. For example, a small shop trading as 'Virgin Gardenware' which sought to register an internet name 'virgin' may be challenged. However, in many cases there will be two equally as well known marks for which registration as a domain name is sought. Sometimes one party can buy the domain name from the other. Often a business with a trade mark registration will not be interested in owning a domain name in any event.

The registration bodies (see http://www.icann.org/santiago/santiago-resolutions.htm) have their own dispute resolution procedures which can be invoked and are cheaper than resorting to court litigation.

Response to a Domain Name 'Blackmailer'   [2.61]

The wording below is designed to be used where a letter or other communication is received by a business seeking to persuade a trade mark owner to purchase its own name. It is not a substitute for legal advice. In particular, those sending such letters always need to consider all the circumstances. There may be several owners of the same mark as considered in **2.59** above.

It is important to ensure that any such letter does not breach the provisions of *s21* of *the Trade Marks Act 1994*, which prohibits the making of groundless threats of infringement proceedings (see **2.18** above). It is generally a good idea not to publicise the text of such a letter, as the risk of a threats action is increased.

[On headed notepaper]

Date . . . . . .

We have received your letter of [*date*] offering us the right to purchase domain name [ ] which you have registered in [ ].

This name is our registered trade mark no. [ ] [*or – is confusingly similar to our registered trade mark no.*]. Your exploitation of this name amounts to breach of our trade mark and passing off.

We require that you undertake within 7 days of the date of this letter to:

(1)   transfer the domain name to us;
(2)   confirm in writing that you have registered no similar names or other names of ours as domain names, company registered names or registered trade marks and are in no other way are breaching our trade marks or passing your business off as ours;
(3)   pay us damages of a sum to be agreed; and
(4)   pay our legal costs.

If we do not hear from you within 7 days of the date of this letter we shall have to instruct our solicitors to proceed.

Yours faithfully,

Note that:

●   where the letter is to be a formal final letter before action then the final paragraph should state legal proceedings will be issued if the response is not received;

●   many businesses will want their solicitors to send such a letter rather than doing so themselves;

●   the letter is an 'open' letter and therefore is not intended to be or to be marked 'without prejudice'; and

●   under the *Civil Procedure Rules 1998*, there is a stringent duty on litigants and their legal advisers to attempt to settle disputes before resorting to litigation. Efforts should therefore be made to have the matter mediated or settled by agreement between the parties. A Part 36 claimant's offer may often be recommended. Take legal advice.

●   Consider whether any criminal proceedings can be brought. These can be a more effective deterrent.

Decisions on International Exhaustion of Rights and Trade Marks [2.62]

   Silhouette International Schmeid v Hartlauer [*1998*] *ECR I-4798;* [*1998*] *Tr LR 355.*

- *Sebago Inc and Ancienne Maison Dubois et Fils SA v GB-Unic SA* (unreported, *1 July 1999,* (ECJ)).
- *Zino Davidoff v A&G Imports* (unreported, *18 May 1999,* (High Court)).

Further Information on Trade Marks and Domain Names [2.63]

American Intellectual Property Law Association (AIPLA): http://www.aipla.org.

Benelux Trademark and designs Office: http://www.bbtm-bbdm.org.

Community Trade Mark Office (OHIM): http://europa.eu.int/agencies/ohim/ohim.htm.

European Communities Trade Mark Association (ECTA): http://www/ecta.org.

European Patent Office: http://www.european-patent-office.org.

ICANN March 1999 results and documents http://www.icann.org/singaporeresults.html and August results http://www.icann.org/santiago/santiago-results.htm.

International Trade Mark Association (INTA) http://www.inta.org.

Netnames – for search of domain names anywhere in world: http://www.netnames.co.uk. Nominet: http://www.nominet.org.uk.

Network Solutions Inc, Secure Administration and Competition in Domain Naming Services: http://www.netsol.com.

UK Trade Marks Office: 01633 814000. Website: http:/www.patent.gov.uk.

WIPO general site which links to national and regional intellectual property office: http://www.wipo.int.

Administrative Domain Name Challenge Panels, Substantive Guidelines Concerning Generic Top Level Domain, Memorandum of Understanding Page http://www.gtld-mou.org.

Internet Domain names, Comments on the Registration and Administration of, National Telecommunications and Information Administration, http://www/ntia.doc.gov/ntiahome/domainname.

Memorandum of Understanding between the US Commerce Department and Internet Corp. for Assigned Names and Numbers (ICANN), http://www.ntia.doc.gov/ntiahome/domainname.

Californian trade mark legal enforcement service is at: http://www.imagelock.com.

Recommendations for Administration and management of gTLDs, Final Report of the International Ad Hoc Committee, Internet International Ad Hoc Committee, http://www.iahc.org/draft-iahc-recommend-00.html.

Technical Management of Internet Names and Addresses, National Telecommunications and Information Administration, http://www.ntia.doc.gov/ntiahome/domainname.

Trademark Examination of Domain names, US Patent and Trade Mark Office: http://www.uspto.gov/web/offices/tac/domain/tmdomain.htm

Training Materials for Applying Computer Protection of Trademarks on Internet: http://www.uspto.gov.

3 – Copyright and Database Right

'For a company that depends upon intellectual property for its livelihood, such as a software company or an internet-based publisher, copyright law provides a framework that ensures that the company can compete in the marketplace'.

Jonathan Rosenoer, CyberLaw – The Law of the Internet

Executive Summary [3.1]

- Copyright protects most materials on the internet. It is an unregistered right which arises as soon as it is created.
- It protects computer software and its source code, screen displays and other literary, musical and artistic works on the internet.
- In the EU, database right is a lesser right than copyright which may be the sole protection for some new databases which lack individual creativity.
- Downloading material from the internet may involve breach of copyright.
- Hypertext links with other websites are normally permissible.
- Copyright material placed on the internet should include appropriate copyright notices.
- Contracts with web page designers should be carefully drafted by lawyers.

This Chapter examines copyright and the internet. It shows how computer programs and website materials are protected by various forms of copyright and the implications of this. It also examines typical contracts for the design of websites. **Chapter 6: INTERNET SHOPPING** examines licensing copyright material via the internet. It also examines 'database right' and gives some examples of web copyright issues such as hypertext links and messages to bulletin boards and describes their status under the law.

Copyright is a useful right for the IT sector. It could almost have been designed with computers and the internet in mind, were it not for the fact that it owes its origins to legislation concerning printing. A 1483 Statute of Richard III in the UK encouraged the printing of books and other legislation quickly followed, particularly to prevent importation of materials deemed undesirable.

Copyright:

- requires no registration (in the UK);
- arises as soon as a work is produced;
- costs nothing to obtain protection; and
- lasts for a lengthy period without any requirement for renewal – life of the author plus 70 years in the EU.

It is flexible, simple and easy to apply. However, the right is only breached where copying can be shown to have taken place. It is not as broad as a registered patent protecting an industrial invention. Patents are infringed even if a defendant originated an invention independently without knowledge of the patent.

Before printing was invented, there was little need for copyright protection, hence the lack of UK legislation until about 500 years ago. The law has, therefore, generally followed technological developments and the IT/internet sector today is no different in legal impact than changes in the 1400s. The beauty of English, and indeed US common law, is that generally the legislation as it stands can be extended to new media.

Computer Programs [3.2]

Copyright protects computer programs as literary works. Even before the *Copyright (Computer Software) Amendment Act 1985* was introduced, this was almost certainly the position under the *Copyright Act 1956*. The *Copyright, Designs and Patents Act 1988* further consolidated the position.

Software Directive [3.3]

The *Copyright (Computer Programs) Regulations 1992 (SI 1992/3233)* implemented the *EU Software Directive* in the UK (*Directive 91/250 (OJ 1991 L122/42)*) from 1 January 1993. The *Software Directive* required that all Member States must protect computer software by copyright.

This was already the case in the UK and therefore no major change in the law was required. The Directive also included a right:

● to make back up copies where necessary for lawful use;
● for licensees to repair software of which they are licensed (unless their licence contract prohibits this – most do);
● to study the functioning of the program – though not to use the information so discovered for any other purposes; and
● to decompile the software to write interoperable programs – which is of such limited scope it rarely applies.

Refusals to License and Abuse of Market Power [3.4]

Any clause in a contract restricting these rights, will be void in the EU except for any restriction on repairs. In certain cases a refusal to allow a licensee a license of copyright to effect repairs may amount to an abuse of a dominant position contrary to *Article 82* (formerly *Article 86*) of the *EC Treaty* or its equivalent – the Chapter II Prohibition in the Competition Act 1998 in the UK (from 1 March 2000). However, this would only be where the refusal prevented a new product emerging for which there was consumer demand, or where the supplier itself was refusing to repair (e.g. as in the *Volvo v Veng* decision [*1988*] *ECR 6211*; [*1989*] *4 CMLR 122* and *RTE v Commission* [*1995*] *I ECR 743*; [*1995*] *4 CMLR 718*.

Despite these legislative provisions, the basic principle in most States is that there is no obligation to license copyright or indeed any other intellectual property right to third parties. Licences are not available to all comers. The owner of a right or indeed any other property is entitled to do nothing with it and not to permit others to use it either, if they so wish. There are exceptions such as compulsory patent licence legislation and the risks run by trade mark owners to have their right challenged if they do not use the mark for a certain period, often 5 years. In most cases, therefore, the rights are inviolate. Indeed, the *EC Treaty* enshrines ownership of intellectual property rights in its provisions. Copyright is one of the so-called 'intellectual property rights' which also include trade marks (see **Chapter 2: THE DOMAIN NAME AND TRADE MARKS**) and designs.

UK Law [3.5]

Section 3 of the *Copyright, Designs and Patents Act 1988* protects computer programs as literary works. Copyright does not subsist until the work is recorded in writing or otherwise. 'Or otherwise' includes electronic media. *Section 17(2)* provides that copying includes reproducing the work in any material form and 'storing the work in any medium by electronic means'. *Section 17(6)* states that copying includes 'the making of copies which are transient or are incidental to some other use of the work'.

This has been established law for some years and is described in detail in the standard software licensing and computer law textbooks and will not be repeated here.

Copyright and the Internet [3.6]

Copyright works of many different kinds appear on the internet including:

● information on internet web pages – these might be artistic works, drawings and designs, business brochures, product specifications;
● information which can be downloaded from web pages – such as music or computer software or literary, artistic or other works;
● computer software which is protected by copyright itself and which enables the software and systems to work; and
● postings to bulletin boards and newsgroups by individuals.

These are considered in more detail at **3.51** *et seq.* below.

Copyright Term Directive [3.7]

EU Directive 93/98 (OJ 1993 L290/9) (a copy of which appears on the EU Commission's website at http://www.europa.eu.int/eur-lex) provides that all EU Member States must protect copyright for the life of the author plus 70 years. In the UK this was previously the author's life plus 50 years.

Draft EU Copyright Directive [3.8]

On 10 December 1997, the European Commission proposed a Directive on the harmonisation of aspects of copyright rules and related rights in the information society. It would harmonise rights of reproduction, communication to the public (including making protected material available on demand over the internet), distribution right and the legal protection of anti-copying systems and information for managing rights. It would also implement obligations in the December 1996 World Intellectual Property Organisation (WIPO) treaties (http://www.wipo.org). The latest version (25 May 1999) is at OJ 25 June 1999 C180/6 and on the Commission's website.

Web Caching and the Draft Directive   **[3.9]**

At the date of writing, the Directive had still not been agreed. Recital 23 of the May 1999 version of the draft *Copyright Directive* would make an exception from the exclusive rights of copyright owners for 'acts of caching or browsing'. *Article 5* provides that temporary acts of reproduction such as:

> 'transient and incidental acts of reproduction which are an integral and essential part of a technological process, including those which facilitate effective functioning of transmission systems, whose sole purpose is to enable use to be made of a work or other subject matter and which have no independent economic significance'

are permitted (i.e. not included within the exclusive rights of the copyright holder). The draft Directive also includes a right for individuals to copy for private purposes. Under current English law, the making of a temporary copy is stated clearly to be a breach under the *Copyright Designs and Patents Act 1988*. Under this Act, it is clear that even just copying a disk to a hard drive for a very short period is breach of copyright where no licence exists.

Ownership   **[3.10]**

In the UK, copyright is owned by the author – *section 9* of the *Copyright, Designs and Patents Act 1988*. There are special rules for sound recordings, films, broadcasts, cable programmes and typographical arrangements of published editions.

Section 11(2) of the *Copyright, Designs and Patents Act 1988* provides that where a literary, dramatic, musical or artistic work is made by an employee in the course of their employment, their employer is the first owner of the copyright 'subject to any agreement to the contrary'.

Commissioned Works [3.11]

In the UK, works which are commissioned are common, particularly for the design of web pages. Copyright issues arising from commissioning of websites are examined in more detail at **3.74** below. The important issue for those commissioning any copyright work is to ensure that a contract sets out who will own the copyright or any other intellectual property rights in the works produced. If the person paying for the work does not agree otherwise, then the copyright will remain with the author, or the author's employer, and all the commissioner receives is a right to use or non-exclusive licence. This may be sufficient and indeed with many copyright agreements a higher fee is obviously paid for ownership rights, but the issue should be considered and addressed in all cases.

Laws abroad may well vary so ensuring a written agreement is in place is essential.

In the UK where designs (whether an unregistered design right or copyright) are commissioned, the default position is the opposite to that which applies in relation to copyright. For designs, the commissioner owns the rights unless there is agreement to the contrary.

Some of the rights described here differ depending on the format in which the work is reproduced. It is not entirely clear in law whether material disseminated over the internet is a 'film' or sound recording. If the picture is moving it may well be a film and when sounds are broadcast over the internet then a sound recording may be involved. There have been public disputes in various jurisdictions between broadcasting regulators and telecommunications regulators as to which should be regulating the internet. What is clear is that the convergence of media means that areas of law which were previously discreet, have now themselves converged and those advising in this field need a broad knowledge of both media, telecommunications and computer law.

Employee Works [3.12]

In the UK, works produced by an employee in the course of their employment are owned by the employer (*Section 11(2)* of the *Copyright Designs and Patents Act 1988*). The parties to an agreement of employment can agree otherwise if they wish. Note that the question of on whose time a work was produced and on whose computers, does not affect the position of ownership. For example, an employee may have breached his employment contract in writing a novel at work but that does not mean his employer owns the copyright and is entitled to claim the employee's earnings.

Contractors [3.13]

Many workers are not 'employees' in the strict legal sense. Even though a number of recent UK employment law measures (such as some provisions of the *Working Time Regulations 1998 (SI 1998/1833)*) extend beyond employees to 'workers' and thus catch the self employed and some contractors, for copyright purposes the distinction is absolute. Therefore, all those using staff hired from agencies, workers with their own limited companies and other 'self employed' staff should not rely on *section 11(2)* to ensure their rights. In the IT industry, the use by individuals of their own limited companies is prevalent, often so the individuals find it easier to maintain that they are self-employed, with the tax advantages that brings.

Disguised Employment [3.14]

The 1999 UK budget announced that those in 'disguised employment' would be taxed as if they were employees. 'Disguised employment' refers to employment where the contractor uses the device of a limited company to provide his services to one client only and the contractor is therefore in reality really an employee but is using the company to ensure he/she benefits from the tax advantages of contracting through a company. The proposals led to much criticism and may be watered down after many IT contractors threatened to leave the country. Businesses need to chart the progress of such legislative change carefully and amend contracts with contractors accordingly, depending on what any new legislation says.

Wording to use with Contractors [3.15]

Those commissioning works may use wording such as the following.

'All intellectual property rights in works you produce for us in the course of this assignment shall be owned by us. You will sign all documents needed to assure us of these rights and warrant the works are your original works and not those of a third party. You will indemnify us for any breach of this warranty. You waive all moral rights in such works and will only use them for the purposes of this assignment. Such works will be regarded as our confidential information'.

The wording above covers not just ownership of rights but also includes a warranty and indemnity concerning intellectual property rights which can also benefit the commissioner. It makes it clear to the author that he may only use the work to perform the contract (and not, therefore, with other clients) and that the information is confidential. In some cases the works produced will be published and in those circumstances the courts would not protect them as confidential information whatever such a clause as that above might say. As to the waiver of moral rights – see **3.21** below.

Moral Rights [3.16]

Moral rights were introduced into English law for the first time when the *Copyright, Designs and Patents Act 1988* came into force.

Right to be Identified as Author [3.17]

The first moral right is the right to be identified as the author of a work. Thus, someone who has written a work is entitled to have their name appear on it even if the ownership of the work is with someone else. However this right (under *s77* of the *Copyright, Designs and Patents Act 1988*), only applies if the author 'asserts' the right by saying they want it to apply. It is standard practice when commissioning copyright works in many sectors to have the author 'waive' their moral rights as in the example at **3.15** above.

Right to Object to Derogatory Treatment [3.18]

Under *section 80* of the *Copyright Designs and Patents Act 1988*, there is a right to object to derogatory treatment of a work. For example, an artist producing a website design could prevent it from being altered in a derogatory way. Treatment under *section 80* includes the addition to, deletion from, alteration to or adaptation of the work.

False Attribution [3.19]

Section 84 of the *Copyright Designs and Patents Act 1988* provides that every author has the right not to have a work falsely attributed to them as author. This right lasts for up to 20 years after the death of the person concerned (*section 86(2)* of the *Copyright Designs and Patents Act 1988*).

Privacy of Photographs and Films [3.20]

Section 85 of the *Copyright Designs and Patents Act 1988*, allows those who have had a photograph or film made 'for private and domestic purposes' under a commission, to stop the work being made public or shown in public or included in a broadcast or cable programme service (see the *Shetland* case at **3.22** below, where it was suggested that an internet web page could be such a cable programme).

Waiver [3.21]

These moral rights can be waived (*section 87* of the *Copyright Designs and Patents Act 1988*) or, if someone consents then they do not apply. For example, if someone put their photograph on their own personal web page then their right of privacy of photographs would be waived. However, the issue would still remain as to copyright in the photograph. Copyright in photographs normally remains with the person taking the photograph. Therefore, if the subject broadcast the photograph on their internet website, they may breach the copyright of the photographer. In any event; they would probably by implication have waived the *section 85* right; and they could not prevent further dissemination by the photographer.

The Shetland Case [3.22]

In the Scottish case of *The Shetland Times* (which eventually settled on 14 November 1998 in the Court of Session) the court, on an application for an interim interdict (Scottish emergency court order), had granted a restraining order preventing the reproduction of newspaper headlines on one page from being copied to another. The pursuers (claimants) had maintained that the headlines on their website were cable programmes under *section 7* of the *Copyright Designs and Patents Act 1988*. They said that the defenders were making cable programme services available in breach of *section 20* of the *Copyright, Designs and Patents Act 1988* in infringement of copyright.

The facts were that The Shetland Times put their news out on the internet at www.shetland-times.co.uk. The Shetland News, a rival newspaper, set up a website at www.shetland-news.co.uk. Shetland News linked directly to news stories published by the Shetland Times using the headlines created by the Shetland Times for those stories. Thus anyone accessing the Shetland Times via the Shetland News' site could move straight to the Shetland Times news stories. If they went straight to the Shetland Times page they would first have to read the front page and advertising for which advertisers had paid. Shetland Times wanted readers to read the advertising and wanted to prevent there being a hypertext link to their site.

On the cable programme point the court decided that it was a cable programme under *s7*, even though those viewing the site obtained access through their own efforts. The court said that the information was 'sent' as it was put out on web page.

This was just an interim decision and the case finally settled without coming to a court hearing and is not binding precedent in England.

The initial interdict decision is reported at *Shetland Times Ltd v Dr Jonathan Wills and Another* [*1997*] *Tr L R 158*. The settlement is mentioned at IT Law Today January 1998 issue and see also [*1997*] *FSR 604.*

No Moral Rights in Computer Software [3.23]

There are no moral rights in computer software by virtue of *section 79(2)(a)* of the *Copyright Designs and Patents Act 1988*, nor to computer generated works (*section 79(2)(c)*). However, the appearance of a website is an artistic work in which moral rights exist. Therefore, the website design contract should ideally (from the point of view of the buyer) waive the moral rights of the designer and/or employees who are employed by a corporate designer. In practice, those employees should also sign waivers of their moral rights as they will not have contracted with the client directly.

The underlying software which runs a program or website is a copyright work in which there will be no moral rights because of the provisions of *section 79* of the *Copyright Designs and Patents Act 1988*.

The moral rights cannot be assigned (*section 94*) but they can be passed on death to heirs of an estate (*section 95*).

Computer Generated Works [3.24]

Where a work is computer generated, the author is the person 'by whom the arrangements necessary for the creation of the work are undertaken' (*section 9(3)* of the *Copyright Designs and Patents Act 1988*). Few works qualify as computer generated work, as to be this they must have no known human author.

Infringement [3.25]

Section 17 of *the Copyright, Designs and Patents Act 1988,* sets out the situation when copyright will be infringed. There are many detailed copyright textbooks available such as *Copinger and Skone James on Copyright* to which reference should be made if a copyright dispute arises, as this book does not attempt to cover the entirety of copyright law. Copying means reproducing a work in any material form and this includes expressly storing the work in any medium by electronic means. *Section 17(6)* provides that this includes transient or temporary copies.

Every time software is loaded on to a computer an act of copying occurs. It is for this reason that the software industry is able to control so strictly the uses to which programs can be put. If a book is bought, the owner of the paper in the book does not need a licence of the copyright in the words. If he wants to copy the book he would have to obtain consent, but he can read the book without any copying. If instead he takes a licence of copyright in a computer program, every time the programme is used there will be an act of copying for which a licence is required.

That licence may legitimately restrict the use of the program to one named individual at one location on one computer for one period such as a year or less. In most cases the owner of copyright has no obligations to grant licences at all so any licences granted can be as limited as the owner wishes (but see the references to abuses of dominant position under *Article 82* (formerly *Article 86*) of the *EC Treaty* and refusals to license at **3.4** above).

Infringement also occurs in some circumstances where a copyright work is issued to the public. This includes putting copies into circulation – which may include broadcast on the internet (*section 18* of the *Copyright Designs and Patents Act 1988*). Playing the work in public may also infringe under *section 19* – again this may include playing over the internet. If apparatus is used for receiving visual images or sounds conveyed by electronic means, 'the person by whom the visual images or sounds are sent, and in the case of performance the performers, shall not be regarded as responsible for infringement' (*section 19(4)*). Thus, BT would not be liable if someone used a telephone to broadcast a work in breach of copyright under this provision.

This is relevant to the issue of liability for internet service providers – see **Chapter 10:** DATA PROTECTION, HACKING, SECURITY AND ISP LIABILITY.

Software Copyright – Case Example [3.26]

There have been few cases in the English courts concerning copyright protection for software. Copyright, in its early days, was not developed with computer software in mind. The decision in *Cantor Fitzgerald International and Another v Tradition (UK) Ltd and Others* (*The Times, 19 May 1999*), examined what 'copying' means in relation to computer software. The claimants were Cantor Fitzgerald International (CFI). They carried on a business as inter deal brokers in bonds. Tradition (UK) Ltd and the other defendants were also in the same business. CFI sued for breach of copyright in computer programs which were part of a bond-broking system. They also sued for breach of confidentiality in relation to those programs.

The defendants' programmers admitted that 2,952 lines of source code of the defendants' system had been copied. This was out of a total of 77,000 lines. Under the *Copyright, Designs and Patents Act 1988*, there is only breach of copyright where a substantial part of a copyright work is copied. The main expert witness of the defendants, a Dr McKenzie, identified a further 1,964 lines of code which may have been copied too, though this was not certain. Most of the modules which the court was considering had been individually compiled and after that linked into a small number of programs which could have been compiled from a single file source.

The judge confirmed that computer programs are protected by copyright as literary works by *section 3(1)(b)* of the *Copyright, Designs and Patents Act 1988*. However, he said that there was a risk of mistakes being made if well known principles developed for copyright literary works were applied to computer programs without proper consideration by the court.

No Errors [3.27]

If a computer program is to work properly, then it must contain no errors of syntax in computer language (which would prevent it from compiling) and no semantic errors. The computer cannot work out what is wrong if such mistakes are present. The judge said that copyright is designed to protect the skill and labour expended by the author on the work. If someone copies a part of a work on which the author has expended substantial skill and labour then there would be breach of copyright. Even betting coupons have been held protectable as copyright works as in the *Ladbroke (Football) Ltd v William Hill (Football) Ltd [1964] 1 WLR 273*. This was quoted in the Cantor Fitzgerald case:

> 'Whether a part is substantial must be decided by its quality rather than its quantity. The reproduction of a part which by itself had no originality will not normally be a substantial part of the copyright . . . It is when one is debating whether the part reproduced is substantial that one considers the pirated portion on its own.'
>
> (From *Ladbroke* as quoted in *Cantor Fitzgerald*)

A lot of the work which had gone into the original program had been very mechanical labour. Was that relevant in deciding if there was originality in the copyright sense? Only original works are protected by copyright.

The architecture of a computer program meant the overall structure of the system at a very high level of abstraction or the structure of the program itself. This had been considered in the earlier case of *Ibcos Computers Ltd v Barclays Mercantile Highland Finance Limited [1994] FSR 275*. This architecture was protected if a substantial part of the programmer's skill, labour and judgment went into it.

Here, as in the *Cantor Fitzgerald* case, 2,952 of 77,000 lines of codes were admitted by the defendants as having been copied. Had there been substantial copying?

The court said that the test was not whether the system would work without the copied code. Nor was the issue the amount of use the system made of the code. Instead the test was a comparison of the collection of modules viewed as a whole in the light of the skill and labour in design and coding which went into the piece of code which was copied.

The claims of the claimants were allowed in part. In practice clients often ask how much they can copy from a computer program or indeed any other copyright work without breaching copyright. There is no fixed percentage in law, as this case makes clear. Although earlier copyright cases have held that 'if it is worth copying it is worth protecting' and not much needs to be copied for a breach to be found, there is a base line limit. There are also fair use provisions of the *Copyright, Designs and Patents Act 1988*, which provide a defence to infringement.

Ideas and their Expression [3.28]

There is no copyright in ideas, just in their expression. So if someone wants to design a computer program which will achieve the same objective as another program, subject to the laws of confidentiality, any contract in place or there being any patents, they normally are free to do so. However, if they use the first program as a base and copy codes from it, even small parts proportionally as in this case, they risk a copyright infringement case.

Confidentiality [3.29]

The programmers had written a complex set of programs whilst working for Cantor. In 1992 the programmers moved to Tradition and set up a similar system at that company. At Cantor they had used the VAX VMS system to develop a method of inter-process communication by 'locking'. Cantor said this was their trade secret. The judge said it was not confidential as it had been the subject of various articles in Digital Equipment manuals. He also said that this locking as a form of inter-process communication was 'firmly in the category of useful techniques or wrinkles which an ex-employee will not be prevented from using' once he has left his employment and gone to work for another. It was a programming technique and an employee could only be prevented from using it by a restrictive covenant and there were no covenants in this case.

There are three levels of information:

- public domain information which anyone can use;
- confidential information which form part of the skills and knowledge of the employee and which can only be restrained by a restrictive covenant and then only for a limited period such as six months after termination of the employment contract; and
- secrets – use of which the employer can always restrain.

This Chapter examines the law of copyright. The common law of confidentiality is, however, often used in litigation in conjunction with a breach of copyright claim. Any information on the internet is not of course confidential as it has been published and the courts will not restrain the further dissemination of information under the laws of confidence, which has already lost its confidential nature once published. One scientist E-mailing a new invention to another, where there is not a confidentiality agreement in place, would amount to such publication. Therefore, those in businesses advising technical staff should ensure that the staff are aware of the laws in this field, particularly where the invention may, unlike much software, be patentable. No registered patent can be obtained under the *Patents Act 1977* for computer programs and most other States' patents laws where the invention is part of the state of the art and has been published before the application is made.

Database Law [3.30]

Examples of databases on the internet include alphabetical lists of names and addresses and lists of hypertext links and website addresses. Such collations of data may not be sufficient to amount to separate copyright works under the *Copyrights, Designs and Patents Act 1988* where created after the EU *Database Directive 96/9* (*OJ 1996 L77/20*) came into force. Earlier works, at least in the UK, continue to attract copyright protection.

The *Copyright and Rights in Databases Regulations 1997* (*SI 1997/3032*) came into force on the 1 January 1998 when the EU *Database Directive* was implemented in the UK. The aim of the Directive was to ensure all EU Member States have the same laws on copyright protection for databases. The regulations make changes to the *Copyright, Designs and Patents Act 1988*.

Section 3A(1) of the *Copyright and Rights in Databases Regulations 1997* defines a database as:

'. . . a collection of independent works, data or other materials which—

(a)   are arranged in a systematic or methodical way, and
(b)   are individually accessible by electronic or other means'

The Regulations therefore apply not just to traditional databases on computers but also to items such as directories in paper form or tables in a book, as they refer to the material being accessible by electronic 'or other means'.

Section 3A(2) states that a database will be original:

'if and only if by reason of the selection or arrangement of the contents of the database the database constitutes the author's own intellectual creation'.

Under the old law, there was no requirement that in order for databases to be copyright protected they had to be works of intellectual creation. Now there is. However, those databases which now do not meet that standard get a lesser right called database right. Most of the provisions in the *Copyright and Rights in Databases Regulations 1997* relate to this new database right.

Database Right   [3.31]

Regulation 29 of the *Copyright and Rights in Databases Regulations 1997*, provides that where a database was created on or before 27 March 1996 (when the EU *Database Directive* came into force) and it did have copyright under English law when created, then it carries on having copyright until the end of the copyright term. This period is normally the life of the author plus 70 years. Whereas the database right lasts for just 15 years.

However, some databases created before that date did not benefit from copyright under the old English law. These might include a mere alphabetical list with no order or structure to their contents other than the use of the alphabet. Indeed, in practice, it was often hard to know which databases were protected under old English copyright law. *Regulation 30* of the *Copyright and Rights in Databases Regulations 1998* provides that if a database were made on or after 1 January 1983 and had it been created after 1 January 1998 database right would apply to it then there will be database right from 1 January 1998.

The remaining category is databases created before 1 January 1983 which did not have copyright protection (many would have done and they keep their copyright). Those older databases – which may include old static (i.e. unchanging) databases in archives – which are not works of intellectual creation or 'original' under the old provisions of the *Copyright, Designs and Patents Act 1988*, would have no protection under the new law. As they had no copyright protection under the old law anyway the fact they are not protected under the new provisions does not matter.

The *Copyright and Rights in Databases Regulations 1997* do not define what a work of intellectual creation is, so it is not immediately apparent which works will obtain copyright protection and which will not. The distinction between copyright and database right is not of major importance. Although database right just lasts for 15 years in practice the period is extended under the legislation by changes to a database and secondly the long copyright period is often unnecessary because works are no longer commercial after a decade or so.

Databases which have copyright protection will automatically have the lesser database right too. In practice, if a database has both rights the lawyers would use the stronger right in litigation. Database right exists in databases as defined above where 'there has been a substantial investment in obtaining, verifying or presenting the contents of the database'. So it can be seen that there is no requirement for creativity or intellectual elements. It is enough if work has been put in. This can be in terms of checking the contents or finding the information (such as walking the streets of London to prepare a street map) or putting it together in an attractive or useful way with helpful headings. These rights protect the database, not the computer software which runs it (that has its own copyright) nor the information which might be a copyright work on the database. For example a database of musical works accessible remotely by modem will have copyright protection as musical works of the music on the database (which is not covered by these regulations) but may also have database right in the database structure, headings, methodology etc. To complicate matters further protection of compilations such as a records chosen for a CD continues under the *Copyright, Designs and Patents Act 1988* as before.

The Maker of the Database   **[3.32]**

The maker of the database is the person who takes the initiative in obtaining, verifying or presenting the contents of the database and assumes the risk of investing in it. However, if a database is made by an employee in the course of his employment, the employer is regarded as the maker of the database. This is the same as for copyright – see **3.12** above. The 'maker' is the first owner of the database right.

Here copyright and database right law appear to diverge. It appears that someone paying someone else to produce a database for them (i.e. someone commissioning a database) will automatically own the database right. However, under the *Copyright, Designs and Patents Act 1988*, they will not own the copyright in that database. The general rule is that, in the absence of agreement to the contrary, someone paying a third party to produce a copyright work simply obtains a licence to use the rights and not ownership of the copyright, as was seen at **3.11** above.

So if A commissions B to produce a database for him and they have no written contract, B will own the copyright and A the database right. The anomaly is easily avoided in practice by ensuring there is a written agreement which says one or other party owns both rights.

Infringement of Database Right [3.33]

Database right is infringed if someone extracts or re-utilies all, or a substantial part of, the contents of the database. Repeated and systematic extraction or re-utilisation of insubstantial parts of the contents of a database may amount to extraction and re-utilisation of a substantial part of the contents. *Regulation 19* of the *Copyright and Rights in Databases Regulations 1997* expressly states that there will be no infringement when an insubstantial part is taken, provided that the database has been made available to the public. However, in practice users of databases will be fearful of falling foul of the wrong side of this rather tenuous line so it is not clear what additional user rights they are given, if any by the legislation. Indeed, *Regulation 19* provides that where under an agreement someone has a right to use a database protected by database right which is made available to the public, any term or condition in the agreement shall be void in so far as it purports to prevent that person from extracting or re-utilising insubstantial parts of the database for any purpose.

A substantial part may be used for illustration for teaching or research, provided the source is indicated. This is a 'fair dealing' right which already exists with copyright works. Note that this is subject to the use being other than for commercial purposes.

If the identity of the database maker cannot be ascertained and it is reasonable to assume that a database right has expired, then substantial parts can be copied under *Regulation 21* of the *Copyright and Rights in Databases Regulations 1997*. This of course will not be for at least 15 years except perhaps in relation to some old static archival databases not protected by copyright and made many years ago.

Term of Protection [3.34]

Database right lasts for 15 years from the end of the calendar year in which the database was completed. For example, imagine a genealogist putting together a list of the names and addresses of all people called 'Jenkins' in the UK for marketing purposes. It is unlikely his database will have copyright protection if it is just alphabetical and he is making it after the *Copyright and Rights in Databases Regulations 1997* came into force. However, it is likely to have database right protection if substantial investment has gone into making it. It is interesting to consider who has to make the substantial investment. If the genealogist pays British Telecom or someone else to supply him with the data and he is paying for it, is there a financial figure below which the 'investment' is not substantial enough to result in the 'work' being classed as a database capable of protection? If the work is made in two seconds because of a brilliant computer program is the person using the program creating a work with database right in it?

Changes Extend Term of Protection [3.35]

Looking at the term of protection issue, the database will be protected (if made in 1999 and made available to the public in the same year) for 15 years – i.e. to the end of 2016. However, *Regulation 17(3)* of the *Copyright and Rights in Databases Regulations 1997* provides that any substantial change to the contents of the databases:

> 'resulting from the accumulation of successive additions, deletions or alterations, which would result in the database being considered to be a substantial new investment shall qualify the database resulting from that investment for its own term of protection'.

This means that if substantial changes are made, the period effectively rolls on for another 15 years.

Notices on the Database [3.36]

There is a provision in the regulations to make it clear that if a name purporting to be that of the maker of the database appears on copies of the database then, until the contrary is proved, that person is assumed to be the maker.

Website Notices and Database Rights [3.37]

Where a website contains information which may be protected by database right, a notice should appear to benefit from the provision described above at **3.36** such as:

'Database Right: XYZ plc 1999'.

Property Right [3.38]

The database right, like copyright, is a 'property' right in law.

Other Provisions [3.39]

Schedule 1 of the *Copyright and Rights in Databases Regulations 1997* contains a long list of exceptions to database right for those involved with public administration. *Schedule 2* of the *Copyright and Rights in Databases Regulations 1997* sets out details of public licensing schemes for database right along the lines of the schemes to which businesses can pay annual fees for rights to copy certain copyright works.

Other Areas [3.40]

Copyright and database rights have been described above, particularly how they apply to the internet. It is likely that many new initiatives, not just at EU level but also internationally, will occur in the short term relating to the internet and the legal position should therefore be followed closely.

3 – Copyright and Database Right

EU Green Paper and IT [3.41]

The European Commission has adopted a Communication reporting on the results of the public consultation on the Green Paper on the convergence of the telecommunications, media and information technology sectors. This led to a number of measures including the draft Copyright Directive (see **3.8** above). Such convergence is much in evidence on the internet. The results were announced on 10 March 1999 and details are on the internet at http://www.ipso.cec.be/convergencegp/ip164en.html.

The Green Paper was originally published on 3 December 1997. It drew attention to the implications of convergence in relation to economic development, job creation, cultural identities and social impact. 270 written responses were received during the first stage of the consultation to May 1998. The principal conclusion was that the convergence of technological platforms and network infrastructures was a reality and that similar regulatory conditions should apply to all infrastructures whatever services they carried.

The European Parliament, Economic and Social Committee and Committee on the Regions issued favourable opinions on the Green Paper.

A second stage public consultation took place on three key areas:

● access to networks and gateway facilities;
● investment, innovation and content production; and
● balancing regulation between public interest and competition considerations.

80 organisations commented in this second stage consultation exercise.

Key Messages [3.42]

The key messages arising from the consultation are that:

● with regard to regulation, there is a continuing need to meet a range of public interest objectives whilst recognising the need to promote investment, particularly in new services;
● there is a need for clarity and proportionality in rules and regulations imposing obligations in the public interest, sector-specific regulation complementing case by case application of competition rules and promotional measures ensuring outcomes according to specific policy objectives.

- transport and content regulation should be seperated, recognising that links between the two could cause competition law problems. There should be a more horizontal approach to regulation with:
  - ○ homogenous treatment of all transport network infrastructure and associated services, whatever services are carried;
  - ○ the need to ensure content regulation accords with the specific characteristics of the content services and with the public policy objectives associated with those services;
  - ○ the need to ensure content regulation looks at the audiovisual sector in particular; and
  - ○ application of an appropriate regulatory regime for new services which recognises the large initial investments which must be made before a launch, though also protecting consumers.
- a balanced solution is needed on public broadcasting. This would examine how public broadcasting could be integrated into the new environment to respect Member States' competence in defining the remit of public service broadcasting in accordance with *Protocol 9* of the *Amsterdam Treaty*;
- competition laws should be applied effectively with a gradual phasing out of sector-specific regulation as the market becomes more competitive; and
- action should be taken to promote European content on the internet rather than that of foreign authors.

Progress [3.43]

The Commission's 1999 draft *Copyright Directive* (discussed at **3.8** above) has emerged from this review and other legislation is likely.

Copyright Practical Points [3.44]

In legal practice the same copyright issues arise again and again. The statements below are ALL UNTRUE but are commonly believed.

We paid for the work so we own the copyright.

The author retains copyright unless an agreement says otherwise or unless they are an employee. The commissioner (person paying) simply obtains a licence to use the rights. This is not the same as ownership.

The main difference is that it is the owner who normally decides what further licences can be granted and makes money from them.

It is in the public domain so it is not copyrighted.

As most readers will know lots of information in the public domain is protected by copyright, from newspapers (in relation to which there is a Newspaper Licensing Agency scheme available for those who make regular copies) to books. Just because those works can be purchased they are not therefore free of copyright restrictions and the same is true of copyright on the internet.

The important point about public domain is that information in the public eye in this way cannot be protected by the courts as secret or confidential information. That is because it is not secret. However, the law will restrain it being copied without a licence.

We have no protection as we have not registered our copyright

No registration is possible in the UK. Copyright is an unregistered right. Some authors send themselves copies of their works and leave the package unsealed or they lodge it with a third party to prove their copyright. This is only one means of proving the date of the work and is not a method enshrined in any statute.

Registration of Copyright [3.45]

In the US, it used to be a requirement that a copyright notice be included on a work before it was protected by copyright. However, when the US joined the Berne Convention, this changed. The Berne Convention does not require notices to appear for protection to be available. However, in practice, it is sensible to warn potential infringers of rights by putting a notice on copyright works. Not all countries are signatories of the Berne Convention and given that web pages will be seen all over the world it is a sensible precaution to include a copyright notice on any copyright material placed on the world wide web – examples of such notices appear at **3.46** below and **Appendix 3** below.

For example, registration in the US is with the Copyright Office. There are registration fees to pay. If a work is registered then statutory damages of between $500 and $20,000 for each work which is copied and up to $100,000 for knowing breaches can be obtained, as well as recovery of lawyers' fees. A registration certificate is obtained and this is good evidence of ownership of rights. Works to be protected from first publication must be registered in the US within 3 months of creation and can be registered by the owner or exclusive licensee. The work must then be deposited with the Copyright Office.

Many of the works put on the internet are simply copyright in a web page or marketing material and registration may be unnecessary. However, much depends on the works concerned and all businesses, whether using the internet or not, need to ascertain whether a registered copyright in a jurisdiction such as the US is useful to them or not.

Copyright Notices for Websites [3.46]

A copyright notice (e.g. © E S Singleton 2000), although not necessary to obtain copyright in all countries, is essential in others and as the work on the internet will be seen everywhere without limit, a notice should, therefore, be included. It is wise to include a contact name and address too, in case someone seeks copyright permission later.

Some countries' laws require the wording: 'All Rights Reserved' and it is therefore sensible to include this wording too.

In the US case of *Religious Technology Center v Netcom On-Line Communications Serv* (*907 F Supp 1361, ND Cal 1995*), the US court held that if a notice is included this may be enough to support a demand that an internet provider or bulletin board service operator remove an infringing copy of a work from its system to stop its being transmitted over the internet. The court said that 'Where works contain copyright notices within them, it is hard to argue that a defendant did not know the works were copyrighted'.

In practice, any information which is valuable should not be placed on the internet where it can be copied, as legal prevention can be difficult and expensive.

Export of Copyright Material [3.47]

Where the 'goods' sold are themselves copyright works then special issues arise. As was seen in **Chapter 2: THE DOMAIN NAME AND**

TRADE MARKS, export of copyright works without the consent of the copyright holder may amount to a breach of copyright except where the owner has given their consent. However, under *Articles 28–30* of the *EC Treaty*, sometimes the rights are said to be exhausted because the seller has consented to the sale in which case the seller cannot invoke national copyright law to prevent the import of the goods concerned into the territory to which it objects. Those marketing goods on the internet which are protected by copyright or computer software should state clearly any export restrictions, having ensured first that such restrictions do not breach any relevant competition laws and that the export restriction can be seen by all subsequent sublicensees/buyers. The trade mark implications in this field and in particular the *Silhouette*, *Sebago* and *Davidoff* cases are examined at **2.25**.

Internet Works and Copyright [3.48]

Posted Messages [3.49]

Many people contribute to newsgroups on the internet. The messages they send remain their copyright subject to agreement to the contrary and subject to those messages being sufficiently substantial to comprise a copyright work. In the UK, works which are just a few lines long, like some of the code in the *Richardson v Flanders* decision [*1993*] *FSR 497* which was very short, will not merit copyright protection. One website address is not a copyright work though it may be registrable as a trade mark and/or be protectible by the law of passing off (see **Chapter 2: THE DOMAIN NAME AND TRADE MARKS**).

In *Exxon Corporation v Exxon Insurance Consultants Ltd* [*1982*] *Ch 199*, the Court of Appeal held that the word 'exxon' was too short to be a copyright work. There are also exceptions to copyright for fair dealing such as criticism or review. There will be no breach of copyright unless a substantial part of a work has been taken. The example below illustrates the application of this concept.

Examples

Jo sends a message to Jane on a public bulletin board:

> 'I saw his eyes, blue as dark sea towards night, gazing
> in wonder, drinking in sight of me, I, the so familiar
> one who would always love him, no matter what'.

Jane promptly includes the words as her own in a book or article. Has she breached copyright?

The passage is probably not long enough to comprise a copyright work. The title of the song 'The Man who broke the bank at Montecarlo' was held not to be sufficiently long in one case, though other cases have taken the view that if it is worth copying it is worth protecting. With a statement of some purported literary merit, there may be more likelihood of protection than an E-mail such as 'I saw him giving a talk last year in Mexico and he is not worth going to see. The hotel's good though.' The sentences are almost the same length but the effort and thought gone into one may be more than the other. A third example might be a prosaic but lengthily researched posting such as:

'See *R v Thomas*. I have looked up the references (it took an hour and I hope you are grateful). They are [1998] 2 AXE 566 . . . etc. A summary of the case is that there is tortious liability for negligence in your example 1 but not in 2'.

The issues are length, effort and results. There is no copyright in ideas, just in their expression. In the last example if a string of references is given they together may obtain database right (see above) even if the short posting itself does not obtain copyright.

Is there breach of moral rights?

The author has not asserted his right to be identified as author. However there has been a false attribution of authorship but only if the work is a copyright work in the first place. If it is not then there is no breach of moral rights. Secondly there are no moral rights in database right protected works which do not merit copyright protection so if the statement were only protected by database right, such as in the second example if it listed many cases then no moral rights would exist.

Has there been a substantial taking of the work?

Yes, if all of it has been copied. It is the importance of what is taken rather than the percentage of the words taken which is important. If Jo rewrote the item in his own words he would not breach copyright at all.

Were there any conditions to which Jo agreed when signing his contract with the internet service provider or when posting messages?

If there were such conditions, they may provide that others can copy the work. It is highly likely that everyone who posts a message to such a bulletin board is at the least granting an implied licence for others to copy the message to their computer and to print it and also to copy it and paste it in the usual way into their reply message which is standard procedure to show the readers of the response to what the second commentator was responding.

Newspaper Letter Analogies **[3.50]**

It is well recognised under copyright law that those sending a letter for publication to a newspaper are impliedly consenting to its being printed in that newspaper. These days they probably also impliedly consent to the letter appearing in the electronic version of the newspaper too. They do not necessarily impliedly consent to its appearing in a book of 'Best letters from the AD Times' which is then sold by the publisher.

The sender of the letter is giving a licence to publish the letter and not ownership of copyright. Thus the letters Diana, Princess of Wales allegedly wrote to James Hewitt are copyright works in which the copyright remains with her estate for the benefit of her heirs. The paper on which they were written is owned by the recipient of the letters who has the right to read them and undertake any acts in relation to the paper except any which may amount to copying of the copyright works in them.

Wording for Bulletin Boards **[3.51]**

Those hosting discussion groups etc. may like to include wording such as:

'By sending messages to this group you consent to your messages being read, downloaded and printed and copied into other messages. However, users may not reproduce such messages in any other form nor commercialise nor otherwise publish them nor forward them outside the group.'

An alternative would be to state that posting of the message implies assignment of the copyright. This is unlikely to work in law as copyright assignment can only be by agreement 'signed' by the assignor. English law in most cases does not require signatures for contracts. Oral contracts and electronic contracts are enforceable – see **Chapter 6: INTERNET SHOPPING**. However, assignments of copyright must be signed and signatures are not possible over the internet. The UK and EU may change the law in this area.

If the service provider hosting the bulletin board wants to avoid the assignment problem it could instead provide that:

> 'By sending messages to this group you license all forms of copying of your message and waive all moral rights. You undertake to ensure that you do not send material in breach of the rights of others'.

Hypertext Links [3.52]

Linking one web page to another does not involve making a copy in the usual copyright sense. One analogy is with a 'further information' section at the end of a book telling the reader what other papers or sources are available.

In practice most websites contain hypertext links to other sites and no adverse legal consequences follow. Many specifically have a useful 'links' section. A website linked to many others is much more likely to be effective as a commercial tool and any legal risks which flow from that are outweighed by the commercial advantages of the link. Unless and until legal precedent establishes a major legal difficulty with linking, businesses should continue to use it. However, problems may be more likely to occur with the links detailed in **3.53–3.59** below.

Linking to Critical Sites [3.53]

Providing critical material about a business, perhaps registering it as a company name followed by 'sucks.com' (see **Chapter 2: THE DOMAIN NAME AND TRADE MARKS**) and then linking to its site – even if the material is accurate and not defamatory, in practice the linked business may try to take legal action.

Linking to Confusingly Similar Trade Marked Domain Name Sites [3.54]

Registering a confusingly similar domain name to one already registered may therefore be a breach of trade mark or amount to passing off and then linking to the legitimate one – even if simply to warn people of the similarity For a US case in this area see **2.37**. However, where two businesses can rightfully claim a same or similar name, then reaching agreement as to how consumers will not be confused, such as by agreed wording on the website and hypertext links to the other's site, can assist. Ensure any such delimitation agreements do not breach competition law if they divide any markets.

Linking to Illegal or Disreputable Sites [3.55]

Linking an illegal material site to a reputable business' site – e.g. a manufacturer of toy dolls would not look kindly on a distributor of pornographic comics featuring the doll's lookalike linking to its site.

Linking to More Expensive Suppliers' Sites [3.56]

Linking a supplier of cheaper versions of the same product's site to the more expensive supplier's may cause problems. For example, a supplier of very expensive T shirts may find its site used for comparative advertising purposes on the website of a cheaper supplier. Assuming that the products are not counterfeit and there are no trade mark or other legal problems then such a link may be lawful. A discussion of the legality of comparative advertising under UK and EU law is given at **2.53**. The mere linking without reproduction of the trade mark may itself amount to comparative advertising. Comparative advertising is generally permissible as long as it is fair and does not misrepresent the facts or be dishonest. It is doubtful that saying 'Details of our main competitors' products can be seen on the following web pages. Check out their prices and return to us. www.abc.co.uk; xyz.com' would be permitted.

If abc and xyz are not themselves trade marks then it is submitted that there is no 'use of the trade mark' in any sense. Instead all the web page advertiser is doing is the internet equivalent of stating that the catalogue of competitors can be obtained from particular telephone numbers. If instead the names of those businesses are also their web addresses (as is often the case), then the mere reference to them could amount to trade mark use. However, under UK and EU law this is permitted as legitimate comparative advertising. Therefore such linking, even of website addresses which are registered trade marks, is allowed (in the EU). Jurisdictional issues are dealt with in **Chapter 10: DATA PROTECTION, HACKING, SECURITY AND ISP LIABILITY**.

Taking Viewers Beyond an Initial Advertising Page **[3.57]**

Where a link takes viewers to another site but avoiding page 1 of the site where advertising appears for which advertisers have paid substantial sums of money. This was part of the problem in the *Shetland Times* case, see **3.22**.

Passing off Linked Site as being Generated by the Same Site **[3.58]**

Anyone who suggests that the site to which they are linking theirs is generated by themselves, could be sued for passing off in the UK. Such suggestion may be made through use of a same name or image, or appearance of the site or through the wording used.

Using Headings or Headlines of Another Site in Making the Link **[3.59]**

Under the *Copyright, Designs and Patents Act 1988*, newspaper headlines such as those which were the subject of the *Shetland* case (see **3.22**), can be separate copyright works. In *Shetland* it was conceded that headlines were literary works by both sides, though in practice short titles are not copyright works. The compilation of many headlines together is highly likely, however, to be a copyright work or at least protectable by database right (see **3.30** above). A short headline like the Sun's infamous 'Up Yours Delors' is therefore unlikely alone to be a copyright work but if someone where to copy every headline in the Sun over a particular period then they may be a copyright breach. If the person doing the copying makes the compilation, they may in fact obtain their own copyright (or more likely database rights) arising from the effort they have put into creating the compilation under tha database and copyright legislation and if the individual headlines are not copyright works the newspaper could not prevent the dissemination of copyright grounds of the compilation of headlines. If instead the newspaper produced its own compilation of headlines it would be breach to copy it.

Operation of Hypertext Links [3.60]

The author of a web page who links it to another page does not copy and publish in the conventional sense. The internet is based on the copying of digital information, divided into packets, and reassembled after transmission through numerous ratruns in networks around the globe.

The final copy of the displayed web page is based on what is assembled by the viewer's browser in response to commands given to it by the author's HTML file whose address he has asked the browser to find. The HTML file contains various elements, including:

- text and its formatting;
- the URLs of any external information and instructions for incorporating that information; and
- links to other files which it might be helpful to display.

When the third party operates the link, as suggested by the author, the original owner's page may be displayed on the third party's screen. It can be displayed as a result of choice by the viewer (the clicked on hyperlink) or automatically (the displayed image). Thus, albeit prompted by the author, it is the third party viewer whose machine requests copies of the original site owner's Web resources and displays them.

This is not conventional copyright analysis. What is happening is that the author is putting the means to make copies of the owner's work into the hands of the viewer. There is, nevertheless probably infringement somewhere.

From 'Unacceptable Linking . . . is Shetland Relevant' by Richard Harrison, Partner, Laytons, rmh@laytons.com. Reproduced with permission.

Notices on Linking [3.61]

Businesses which do not want their sites to be linked with others should say so. They may by contract law be able to prevent this, though in practice it could be difficult. The mere fact of having a website involves giving an implied licence to those who use the internet to view it. Some businesses have code words and charge fees for those wanting to access valuable parts of their website. Clearly, in those circumstances the licence is only granted to those who pay and use the code. On other sites there are no such restrictions and the very minimum must be an implied licence to view and probably also to print. No licence to incorporate the material in any other document is likely to be implied unless the site suggests otherwise.

Such a notice may say:

> 'Although we are keen to increase usage of this site we do not authorise any linking with other sites without our prior E-mailed approval. E-mail us with full details of your proposed linked site and we shall notify you if we consent to the creation of the relevant link.'

For example a business putting forms on the internet may thereby impliedly license use of the forms in business; though a notice on the site may state otherwise. Increasingly businesses operating over the internet prohibit unauthorised links.

Practice Point   **[3.62]**

In practice, the aim is to have the site linked to as many other sites as possible. Even negative publicity can generate sales as all advertisers know. Most suppliers do not object to linking, unless it falls within one of the categories listed at **3.57–3.60** above and there are therefore few risks involved in arranging a link. The following series of steps could be taken by the cautious supplier.

> ✓ Look at the site to which a link will be made – check it is suitable and helpful to the customer. It may be irrelevant and annoy the customer. For example, someone searching for information items for dolls' houses will not be pleased if they are persuaded to waste time moving to a site about the construction of high rise blocks of flats.
>
> ✓ Keep the links under review. Often sites are removed or changed and it annoys customers and wastes their time if the links are out of date or unobtainable.

✓   Ensure the link is not to a site that will take a very long time to download and annoy customers because of the delay. There may be some graphic sites with sound which are excellent but very slow. Consider saying before the link that the site to which reference is made will be slow to access.

✓   Check that the other site is lawful. Although this is not always clear, sometimes simply checking the site will show a problem such as illegal content or even just poor taste advertising. A business marketing thermal underwear to the over 70s may annoy some of its viewers if it linked to its lingerie catalogue or that of another supplier.

✓   Ensure a contract with any business involved in assisting the supplier with its internet links contains appropriate restrictions on to where links can be placed – incorporating some of the points above – such as an obligation on the designer/business to ensure that links are kept up-to-date and are only to legitimate sites.

US and Hypertext Links [3.63]

In *MAI Systems Corporation v Peak Computer 991 F2d 511 (9th Cir 1933)*, the US court held that a copy of a work in RAM is a 'copy' for copyright purposes in the US and therefore a link could be a breach of copyright. However, US lawyers do not necessarily agree a breach of copyright occurs. Mr J Rossenoer in *'Cyberlaw The Law of the Internet'*, a book on this subject writes that 'But because the World Wide Web is, in essence, a protocol that exists only to link sites to each other, it is hard to see how anyone could claim the right to restrict site access only to those receiving specific permission to do so'. A list of website addresses however may itself be a copyright work or in the EU be protected by database right.

Meta-tags [3.64]

Meta-tags are keywords picked up by search engines making lists of websites relevant to a search request. Some businesses will include words relevant to a competitor's product only in their own website to ensure searches also take the viewer to their site. In the US case of *Niton Corporation v Radiation Monitoring Devices Inc (US District Court – Massachusetts, 18 November 1998)* Niton said Radiation Monitoring had put meta-tags on its website with the Niton name and the name of a

Niton product. The judge granted a preliminary injunction requiring modification to be made to the site. See also the Brookfield US case at **2.37**.

Notice to Protect List of Websites [3.65]

A business providing a list of website addresses, either on its website or elsewhere, could draw attention to the copyright nature of the list with words such as:

> 'This list is protected by copyright and database right © XYZ Ltd 2000, All Rights Reserved. Although the sites may be accessed from the list no copying of the list is permitted whether in electronic or other form.'

Content [3.66]

The works on the website may be:

- trade marks – protected by trade mark law and passing off (see **Chapter 2: THE DOMAIN NAME AND TRADE MARKS**);

- descriptions of products – literary works and possibly software available as freeware or shareware;

- artistic works such as drawings, designs, screen displays – this is protected in the same way as a painting. There is little case law in the UK over protection for the look and feel or user interface on a computer screen though the US *Apple v Microsoft* dispute in the US over the appearance of the Windows software (*821 FSupp 616 (ND Cal 1993)*) is of persuasive force in the UK; or

- computer software – literary work.

Copyright law and the internet has been summarised at **3.6** above. In the UK there are few special laws which apply and in principle the test of protection and infringement and indeed ownership are much the same whatever the form of the work concerned and whether internet related or not. Where a copyright dispute does arise, it is sensible to seek advice from specialist computer lawyers early in the dispute so that hopeless cases are not pursued at great expense.

Website Specification Agreements [3.67]

Many buyers in the IT field have discovered to their cost the risks of proceeding with a project before they and the supplier know what is required. It is therefore often sensible and cost effective first to contract with a supplier to produce a specification for the work to be done. This surprises many business people who are familiar with the 'free estimate' provided by suppliers. The difference arises from the fact of the complexity of the services to be provided. Sometimes a user will draw up their own statement of user requirements instead or if the contract to design the website is big enough, an invitation to tender.

Possible Clauses [3.68]

The principal clauses to include in such a specification agreement are given below. They are extracted from Sprecher Grier Halberstam contracts. In addition, **Appendix 1** includes a:

- short web page design agreement drafted from the point of view of the supplier;
- contract with a sub-contractor of the designer;
- contract for the supply of software to be used on the site and for ongoing services; and
- longer form contract, from the supplier's point of view, for the commissioning of general software.

> '2.   THE AGREEMENT
> 2.1   In consideration of payment of the Fees, the Designer will draw up the Specification for the Client.
> 2.2   If the Client requests the Designer to perform any services not expressly covered by this Agreement, such services shall be provided at the Billing Rates.
> 2.3   In the event that the Designer develops the Website for the Client, the Designer will give a credit to the Client in respect of fees due for the development of the Website equal to the Fees paid pursuant hereto.'

The aim here is to ensure that the designer prepares the specification for the website with sufficient effort and skill and does a proper job of it. If the designer knows it will be paid whether or not the client decides to proceed then a better job will be done. The provisions of clause 2.3 mean that if the job is then placed with the designer the client will receive a credit for any payment made.

> '3.   CLIENT'S OBLIGATIONS
>
> 3.1   The Client undertakes to secure copyright and other appropriate licences or consents where necessary for the inclusion of all material, data and information provided to the Designer pursuant hereto to enable the Designer to incorporate such material, data and information into the Specification.
>
> 3.2   The Client undertakes that it will provide or procure the provision of the information, data and material required for the provision of the Specification by the Designer in whatever formats and timescales set by the Designer.'

It is important that both parties agree which will be responsible for obtaining copright clearances for materials used in the specification. The contract should also include a clause dealing with ownership of intellectual property rights.

> '5.   PAYMENT
>
> 5.1   Subject to contrary provision in the Schedule, the Client agrees to pay any invoice arising from this Agreement within 14 days of the invoice date.
>
> 5.2   If the Client fails to pay any invoice in accordance with Clause 5.1 above, the Designer shall be entitled to charge interest on a daily basis on any sums outstanding from the invoice date until payment (both before and after judgement) at an annual rate 4% above the Base Rate for the time being in force of Barclays Bank Plc or at the statutory judgement rate as applicable.
>
> 5.3   For the purposes of this Agreement, time of payment shall be of the essence.'

The payment clause should reflect the commercial terms agreed. Here the client is to pay within 14 days. In certain cases the *Late Payment of Commercial Debts (Interest) Act 1998* will entitle the designer to charge interest automatically on overdue debts.

> '6.   LIMITATION OF LIABILITY
>
> 6.1   The Designer is not liable for any indirect loss or consequential loss (including but not limited to, in respect of both indirect and consequential loss, loss of profits, revenue, data or goodwill) howsoever arising suffered by the Client and

> arising in any way in connection with this Agreement or for any liability of the Client to any third party.
>
> 6.2 The Specification will be created as a basis for the development of the Website by the Designer for the Client. No liability whatsoever is accepted by the Designer for any use of Specification by the Client or any third party.
>
> 6.3 None of the clauses herein shall apply so as to restrict liability for death or personal injury resulting from the negligence of the Designer or its appointed agents.
>
> 6.4 No matter how many claims are made and whatever their basis, the Designer's maximum aggregate liability to the Client under or in connection with this Agreement in respect of any direct loss (or any other loss to the extent that such loss is not excluded by Clause 6.1 or 6.2 above or otherwise) whether such claim arises in contract or in tort shall not exceed a sum equal to twice the amount of the Fees paid pursuant hereto.
>
> 6.5 The Client agrees that it is in a better position than the Designer to foresee and estimate any loss it may suffer in connection with this Agreement and that the Fees have been set after taking full account of the limitations and exclusions in this Clause 6.'

The respective liabilities under the contract should be clear. Clause 6.3 reflects the provisions of the *Unfair Contract Terms Act 1977* which precludes exclusion of liability for death or personal injury. If such a provision is not included then the entire clause may be void and unenforceable. Having a total limit on direct loss in Clause 6.4 is also sensible from the designer's point of view. However, the buyer would prefer a clause which:

● does not exclude terms implied by law which often would be excluded by designers in their limited warranty clause;

● does not limit total liability or instead includes a high limit such as a level linked to the designer's insurance cover; and

● provides that the designer is liable for all reasonably foreseeable losses arising from any breach of contract.

Warranties [3.69]

Due Skill and Care [3.70]

The designer may offer a warranty to use due skill and care in performing the services.

Confidentiality **[3.71]**

The designer is likely to be given access to confidential information when designing the site and drawing up the specification, so clauses should be included which require such information to be kept strictly confidential.

General **[3.72]**

General clauses such as those stating whether this is the entire agreement between the parties, which country's laws apply etc. should be inserted.

Schedule **[3.73]**

A Schedule should set out the fees which will be paid and when they will be paid. In some cases stage payment will be appropriate.

Smaller businesses may not need a contract to draw up a specification for the site but for larger businesses spending money on the specification can significantly reduce the risk of disputes arising later over exactly what work was contracted to be done.

Website Design Agreements **[3.74]**

Although in many cases a separate agreement for the drawing up of a specification such as that considered at **3.67** *et seq.* above will not be required, it will always be essential to have written terms for the drawing up of a website. English law will enforce verbal agreements in these matters but an oral arrangement would not cover a wide range of important legal issues detailed below.

Definitions **[3.75]**

The Agreement would define terms used in the contract. A definition of a website might be as below.

'Website' – a compilation of one or more webpages being a combination of text, data, sound, images or other material accessible through WWW to be developed by the Designer pursuant to the Specification.'

Work to be Done [3.76]

A clause should be inserted stating that the designer will provide services described in a schedule and that the client will then pay the price set out in the agreement for this work.

Wording for Designers [3.77]

The wording below concerning payment protects the position of the designer very well. Buyers of such services would want a less onerous clause.

'3. PRICE PAYMENT AND CANCELLATION

3.1 Project Price is exclusive of VAT.

3.2 Any products or services not expressly provided for in this Agreement (including but not limited to making the Website available for access and the maintenance of the Website) shall be chargeable on a time and materials basis in accordance with the Billing Rates.

3.3 Subject to contrary provision in the Schedules, the Client agrees to pay any invoice arising from this Agreement within 30 days of the invoice date.

3.4 If the Client fails to pay any invoice in accordance with Clause 3.3 above, the Designer shall be entitled to charge interest on a daily basis on any sums outstanding from the invoice date until payment (both before and after judgement) at an annual rate 4% above the Base Rate for the time being in force of Barclays Bank plc or at the statutory judgement rate as applicable.

3.5 Non-delivery or non-performance of services by any third party other than the Designer's agents in relation to the Project or any part thereof shall not give the Client any right to delay any payment to the Designer or to make any claim whatsoever against the Designer.

3.6 In the event that the Client wishes to cancel this Agreement at any stage, the Cancellation Fee shall become immediately payable.

> 3.7 The Designer shall be entitled to suspend the Project or any part thereof until arrangements as to credit or payment to the satisfaction of the Designer have been made.
>
> 3.8 The Designer shall be entitled to treat the Agreement as having been repudiated by the Client in the event that:
>
> O payment of any element of the Project Price is not received by the due date; or
>
> O the Client fails to pay any other sum due to the Designer under this Agreement or any other agreement; or
>
> O an order is made or a resolution is passed for the winding up of the Client; or
>
> O a provisional liquidator is appointed in respect of the Client; or
>
> O an administration order is made in respect of the Client; or
>
> O a receiver is appointed in respect of the Client or all or any of its assets; or
>
> O the Client is unable to pay any of its debts within the meaning of Section 123 of the Insolvency Act 1986; or
>
> O a voluntary arrangement is proposed under Section 1 of the Insolvency Act 1986 in respect of the Client; or
>
> O the Client breaches a term of this Agreement and such breach is irremediable, or, if remediable, is not remedied to the Designer's satisfaction within 7 days of notice to remedy such breach.
>
> 3.9 For the purposes of this Agreement, time of payment shall be of the essence.'

See further **Appendix 2**.

Issues for Buyers [3.78]

The clause at **3.77** above is drafted from the point of view of the designer. Buyers of such services would want to reverse a number of the provisions above. For example, they would not want time to be of the essence for payment but would want time limits for delivery of the website on the same basis. If there is a new product launch with advertising over a number of different media, having a website ready on time could be crucial and if other marketing material gives the website address and it is not ready on the launch date, substantial loss could follow. All buyers should, however tough their contractual delivery times, add a margin for delay into their timescales and also ensure that if they change their requests and any delay therefore results, that this is allowed for in any product launch.

'4.   THE CLIENT'S OBLIGATIONS

4.1   The Client undertakes to secure copyright and other appropriate licences or consents where necessary for the inclusion of any material, data and information provided to the Designer pursuant hereto to enable the Designer to incorporate such material, data and information into the Website.

4.2   The Client undertakes that it will provide or procure the provision of the information, data and material required for the purposes hereof by the Designer in whatever formats and timescales agreed by the parties and set out in the Specification.

4.3   The Client undertakes to pay all taxes, fees, levies and duties whether for import or otherwise arising in any part of the world in connection with the Website.

4.4   The Client undertakes to keep secure from third parties any passwords issued to the Client by the Designer in connection herewith.

4.5   The Client undertakes fully to virus-check all data supplied to the Designer pursuant to this Agreement.

4.6   In the event that the Client wishes to enter into a maintenance agreement with a third party after completion of the Website, the Client undertakes to enter into appropriate licences with owners of Third Party Copyright as notified by the Designer and to meet associated costs.

4.7   The Client undertakes that during acceptance testing of the Website it will conduct all such tests as are necessary to satisfy itself that the Website conforms to the Specification.'

The client may conversely wish to foist responsibility for some of the clearances required in this provision on the designer, however, in areas such as the material to be placed on the site, it is the client who will be passing this to the designer and in most cases the client is in the best position to check that all rights are cleared. Some designers may use art work of a third party on a site for a client or musical works. The contract should clarify which party will obtain the clearances required.

Intellectual Properties and Indemnities [3.79]

A clause should be inserted stating whether the client or the designer will own intellectual property rights in the site. There may be elements of copyright works which the designer uses on all websites for clients in which it wishes to retain copyright and separate new works created for that client, in which it is happy to transfer copyright. The contract should make the division between such rights clear.

The designer will want the protection of a clause requiring the client to tell the designer if any disputes over intellectual property rights arise and the client should also notify the designer as to whether material passed to the designer to incorporate in the website is the copyright of a third party. Similarly, the designer should be obliged to notify the client of the same issue. For example, the designer may take art work from a software programme which in fact does not authorise such use and then the client is at risk of being sued, but had assumed the designer would have cleared all the rights issues. The client will impliedly be allowing the designer to use its intellectual property rights, copyright and trade marks on the site and it is better if this is expressed in the contract by way of an express clause.

Limitation of Liability [3.80]

A designer may try and introduce the following clause.

> '6.1 It is the Client's exclusive responsibility to ensure that the parameters of the Project are fully reflected in the Specification. The consequences of any failure so to do, financial or otherwise will be for the sole account of the Client.
>
> 6.2 The Designer is not liable for any indirect loss or consequential loss (including but not limited to, in respect of both indirect and consequential loss, loss of profits, revenue, data or goodwill) howsoever arising suffered by the Client and arising in any way in connection with this Agreement or for any liability of the Client to any third party.
>
> 6.3 The Website will be created with a view to ongoing operation and maintenance by the Designer. If the Website is not being operated and maintained by the Designer, no liability whatsoever is accepted by the Designer for any use of the Website by the Client or any third party.

> 6.4 The Designer shall have no responsibility whatsoever for the consequences of the Client's failure to comply with Clause 4.7.
>
> 6.5 The Designer is not liable for any viruses uploaded to the Website by third parties or the Client's employees or agents.
>
> 6.6 The Client alone is responsible for virus-checking any programs, macros, data files or other material accessed through the Internet.
>
> 6.7 The Designer is not liable for any failure in respect of its obligations hereunder which result directly or indirectly from failure or interruption in software or services provided by third parties.
>
> 6.8 None of the clauses herein shall apply so as to restrict liability for death or personal injury resulting from the negligence of the Designer or its appointed agents.
>
> 6.9 No matter how many claims are made and whatever the basis of such claims, the Designer's maximum aggregate liability to the Client under or in connection with this Agreement in respect of any direct loss (or any other loss to the extent that such loss is not excluded by Clause 6.1–6.7 above or otherwise) whether such claim arises in contract or in tort shall not exceed a sum equal to twice the amount of Project Price which the Client has paid at the time such claim arises.
>
> 6.10 The Client agrees that it is in a better position than the Designer to foresee and estimate any loss it may suffer in connection with this Agreement and that the Project Price has been set after taking full account of the limitations and exclusions in this Clause 6. The Client is recommended to effect suitable insurance having regard to its particular circumstances and the terms of this Clause 6.'

Conversely, a buyer would prefer:

> 'The Designer shall be liable for all reasonably foreseeable loss and liability arising from its breach of this Agreement and obligations implied by law. The Designer warrants that it has professional indemnity insurance cover to the level of £[ ]. [The Designer's total liability to the Client shall not exceed such level for each and every claim], provided that nothing in this agreement shall limit or exclude the liability of the Designer to the client for death or personal injury caused through negligence.'

Testing and Acceptance of Website [3.81]

A clause should be added giving the client the right to monitor the development of the site and check work is going to plan and in accordance with the agreed timescale. Once it reaches particular milestones or is finished in the opinion of the designer, then there should be provisions for testing the site. Acceptance tests could be agreed in writing preferably before the design contract is signed, perhaps as part of the specification phase. In practice, the tests are often developed once the project has begun. This carries with it certain legal risks because the parties may not agree as to what those tests will be.

Most contracts would include an obligation on the designer to produce a website which matches the specification. If it does not normally there would be an opportunity within a defined timescale for the designer to go away and correct the site. The wise buyer will ensure that there is an ultimate time limit on fixing the site to ensure it meets the specification.

If it fails within the final timescale, then the buyer will reserve the right to reject the site and not make any further payments due and possibly receive a refund of monies which have been paid.

Warranties [3.82]

An example of warranties from the perspective of the designer might be as follows.

> '8.1   For 90 days after acceptance, the Designer warrants the Website will perform in all material respects in accordance with the Specification. If the Website is modified in any way by any entity other than the Designer, this warranty will immediately lapse.
>
> 8.2   The Designer warrants that the Website will be virus-free at the time the Client is given the opportunity to test the Website pursuant to Clause 7.2 above.
>
> 8.3   The Designer makes no warranty that operation of the Website will be uninterrupted or error-free, nor that the Website will be compatible with any particular browser or other software other than any specifically identified as suitable in the Specification.
>
> 8.4   The warranty set out in Clauses 8.1 and 8.2 are exclusive of and in lieu of all other conditions and warranties, either

> express or implied, including without limitation those relating to satisfactory quality or fitness for purpose.
>
> 8.5 The Client hereby warrants that it has not been induced to enter into this Agreement by any prior representations whether oral or in writing except as expressly contained in this Agreement and the Client hereby waives claim for breach of any such representations which are not so expressly mentioned.'

Most clients would require a warranty for longer than the period set out above.

Confidetiality Clause [3.83]

Most website designers will be working closely with the client and will have access to confidential information about the business or clients of the client and should therefore be restricted by contract from breaching that confidentiality.

Change Control Clause [3.84]

As with any software design project, change control provisions are necessary as the requirements of buyer and seller are often not clear until the work is begun. The important legal point is to ensure that there is a formal written procedure whereby each party must agree to a change in writing and any cost implications of such changes are agreed before the work is done. Many software disputes arise where one party is not advised properly of a change and its consequences.

Boilerplate Clause [3.85]

Standard clauses such as choice of law and jurisdiction, status of headings, entire agreement, notices, severance and personal performance/assignment should be included too.

Schedules [3.86]

Every web design contract is difference and therefore much of the detail will be included in Schedules.

Website Maintenance and Operation

Agreement [3.87]

Once a website has been designed, a contract will be required for its maintenance and operation. This will often be a contract with the designer or can be with a third party. The extracts from a contract considered below are simply an example of one contract drafted from the point of view of a designer/host of the website. The buyer will want stronger provisions to protect its position. Notes on this contract appear in **Appendix 2**. Also contained in **Appendix 2** is a short set of conditions given as an example used for contracting with an Internet Service Provider (ISP). The notes in **Appendix 2** relate to the Sprecher Grier Halberstam website maintenance and operation agreement, extracts from which appear below.

Services [3.88]

An effective clauses stating that one party will maintain and operate the site for the other should be included.

The types of services to be provided might include:
  '● installation and operation of the website on the Operator's server as described in Sch [ ];
  ● facilitating and maintaining public access to the website;
  ● registering and marketing the website as specified in Sch [ ];
  ● updates limited to the extent specified in Sch [ ];
  ● monitoring the operation of the website;
  ● provision of log reports on website activity as described in Sch [ ], including access, download and upload statistics;
  ● provision of telephone support to the client representative during the hours specified in Sch [ ];
  ● efficient and reasonable categorisation of problems;
  ● acknowledging the existence of problems in accordance with the timescales indicated in Sch [ ];
  ● rectification of problems within the timescales indicated in Sch [ ];
  ● provision of a secure method for the client to transact business on the website as indicated in Sch [ ];
  ● provision of a mirror server;
  ● back up and off site storage of the website and transactional data as set out in Sch [ ];

● the provision of access to the internet for the client;
● nomination or registration of a WWW domain name for the website on behalf of the client to the extent specified in Sch [ ]'.

This clause envisages considerable detail appearing in various schedules.

Fees [3.89]

A clause will be required stating what fees will be paid. There is likely to be a maintenance fee payable. The contract should state when it is paid. In practice, some suppliers require payment annually in advance. Buyers should seek to negotiate monthly or quarterly fees instead.

Rights to charge interest on overdue money are common. Many buyers will negotiate fixed fees for a particular period for maintenance of the website, with rights for the fees to be increased after a particular period.

Website Content [3.90]

An example of a clause favouring the operation of the site in relation to website content is given below.

'5.1 The Client recognises and accepts that it bears sole responsibility for the content of all Material on its Website. For the avoidance of doubt, this clause shall apply to all Material, whether posted on the Website by the Client itself, or on the Client's behalf by another person (whether Operator or a third party).

5.2 Operator shall retain the right at all times to refuse to post any Material (where the Client requests its posting) and to suspend availability of the Website, place a prominent notice on the Website where an allegation of defamation or Intellectual Property Right infringement is made by a third party or place a link on the Website to another Website containing the alleger's version of events and/or to remove any Material already appearing on a Website which, in the opinion of Operator may under the laws of any jurisdiction from which it is possible to access the relevant Website:

> (a) be illegal, illicit, indecent, obscene, defamatory, infringing of third party rights (of whatever nature and including, without limitation, any Intellectual Property Rights);
>
> (b) be in breach of any applicable regulations, standards or codes of practice (notwithstanding that compliance may not be compulsory);
>
> (c) harm the reputation of Operator in any way.
>
> 5.3 Operator's rights to suspend the Website and/or remove content under Clause 5.2 above shall be without prejudice to the sole responsibility of the Client for content of the Website under Clause 5.1 and to the warranties given by the Client relating to that content in Clause 5.4 below. Posting of Material by Operator on the Website shall not under any circumstances constitute a waiver of any of its rights in relation to such Material or of any breach of the Client's obligations under this Agreement.
>
> 5.4 The Client warrants, represents and undertakes in relation to all Material (including, for the purposes of this Clause 5.4, any Material which it requests Operator to post on a Website) that:
>
> (a) no such Material shall be obscene, indecent, defamatory of any persons or otherwise illegal or unlawful under the laws of any jurisdiction from which the Website may be accessed; and
>
> (b) the Client either has sole ownership of all Intellectual Property Rights in such Material in each jurisdiction from which the Website may be accessed and/or has obtained full and effective licence(s) from all relevant third parties allowing the Client to use relevant Material and to permit its dissemination worldwide by Operator hereunder.'

Where the operator will be putting forward material itself on the website, the client will want equivalent warranties to some of those listed above.

Change Control [3.91]

Websites vary over time and most clients will want to ensure that the contract will accommodate such changes. A change control clause will usefully be included. An example of such a clause is given below.

'6.   CHANGE CONTROL

6.1   If at any time, the Client wishes the Operator to effect any Enhancements, the Client shall supply to the Operator full written particulars of any desired Enhancement.

6.2   The Operator will then quote for such Enhancement in accordance with Clause 4.8 above.

6.3   If the Client accepts the quote, full particulars of the Enhancement including pricing and time of payment are to be recorded in an Enhancement Specification to be signed by both parties and appended to this Agreement.

6.4   If the Enhancement is to be carried out, the Client undertakes to secure copyright and other appropriate licences or consents where necessary for the inclusion of all Material, data and information provided to the Operator pursuant hereto to enable the Operator to incorporate such Material, data and information into the Website.

6.5   The Client undertakes to obtain all necessary consents for the Operator to incorporate into the Website Material and information provided by or on behalf of the Client to the Operator.

6.6   Once an Enhancement has in the opinion of the Operator been completed, the Operator will notify the Client in writing and provide the Client with an opportunity to test the Enhancement in the manner set out in Schedule 5. The Client shall be deemed to have accepted the Enhancement unless within 14 days of the date of such notification, it notifies the Operator to the contrary in writing and specifies in such notice the grounds for not accepting the Enhancement. The Client shall not refuse to accept the Enhancement unless it substantially fails to conform to the Enhancement Specification referred to in Clause 6.3 above.

6.7   If the Enhancement does not comply with the Enhancement Specification, the Operator agrees to carry out any necessary modifications without extra charge. On completion of such modifications the procedure set out in Clause 6.6 will be repeated.

6.8   Unless otherwise agreed in writing by the parties, after acceptance of the Enhancement and payment of all sums due by the Client, the Operator agrees to assign in writing copyright in the Enhancement to the Client with the exclusion of:

(i)   Retained Copyright which will be licensed to the Client in return for a licence fee determined by the Operator; and

(ii)   Third Party Copyright.

6.9   Subject to contrary agreement by the parties in the relevant Enhancement Specification, Enhancements will be invoiced and payable in accordance with the terms of this Agreement.

6.10 Without prejudice to Clause 6.11, in the event that the Client cancels a requested modification at any time between signing of the Enhancement Specification pursuant to Clause 6.3 and notification of readiness of the modification for acceptance testing pursuant to Clause 6.6, a payment shall become immediately due to the Operator equal to fifty percent of the fixed price if a fixed price has been agreed or otherwise on a time and materials basis in accordance with the Billing Rates.

6.11 In the event of cancellation by the Client, goods, services and licences already contracted for by the Operator in relation hereto must be paid for by the Client.'

Obligations of the Client [3.92]

The operator will need to know the point of contact with the client on the website. The agreement is also likely to provide that the client not the operator is responsible for ensuring copyright compliance and clearances. In addition, it is common to include a clause stating that the client will be responsible for payment of all relevant taxes arising from the running of the website.

Archiving the Web Pages [3.93]

It may become necessary to refer to an earlier version of a web page in litigation. Not all users will keep old copies but the contract should state which party has responsibility for this. For example, actionable representations may have been made on the website and a case built on the basis of the statements given there. Some businesses have effectively rewritten their corporate history as can be seen when their changing websites are examined. The archived copies should be kept ideally in paper and electronic form and be dated.

Intellectual Property Rights [3.94]

A clause stating which party owns intellectual property rights in the website should be included. Many operators will require the client to indemnify them against intellectual property actions brought against them. Where the operator is providing works or materials in which intellectual property rights reside, a warranty and indemnity from operator to client should be negotiated.

Limitation of Liability [3.95]

A clause similar to that for the web design contract above (see **3.80**) should be included.

Term and Termination [3.96]

The client may not wish to use the services of the operator forever in relation to operation of the website. Nor will the operator always want to be obliged to provide the services. A clause such as the following can be included.

'10.   TERM AND TERMINATION
10.1 This Agreement shall continue for an initial term of 12 months and thereafter from year to year unless and until terminated in accordance with the provisions hereof.
10.2 Either party may terminate this Agreement with immediate effect by written notice to the other in the event that the other party:

○   fails to pay any amount due hereunder;
○   breaches any term of this Agreement and such breach is incapable of remedy or if the breach is remediable, it continues for a period of 30 days after written notice requiring the same to be remedied has been given to the party in breach;
○   an order is made or a resolution is passed for the winding up of the other party; or
○   a provisional liquidator is appointed in respect of the other party, an administration order is made in respect of the other party, a receiver is appointed in respect of the other party or all or any of its assets or if the other party is unable to pay any of its debts within the

> meaning of section 123 of the Insolvency Act 1986, or if any voluntary arrangement is proposed under section 1 of the Insolvency Act 1986 in respect of the other party.
>
> 10.3 Either party may give at least 30 days' written notice to expire on an anniversary hereof of its decision not to renew the Agreement for a further year.
>
> 10.4 Termination of this Agreement shall be without prejudice to any other rights or remedies of either party.
>
> 10.5 In the event of termination other than for breach by the Operator, goods, services and licences already contracted for by the Operator in relation hereto must be paid for by the Client.
>
> 10.6 In the event of termination of this Agreement other than for breach by the Client or termination pursuant to Clause 10.2, the Operator undertakes to facilitate the transfer of the Website in accordance with Clause 4.9 and to license the Retained Copyright to the Client in return for a licence fee to be determined by the Operator.
>
> 10.7 In the event of termination the Client will be responsible for entering into appropriate licences with Third Party Copyright owners and meeting the costs thereof.'

The clause above refers to 'retained copyright' – this will be appropriate in cases where the operator keeps copyright in material which it is using. It also refers to third party copyright. This is copyright material in which a third party owns the rights and again should be addressed in the agreement.

Warranties [3.97]

The contract of an operator and a client will differ substantially in the area of warranties. The operator will wish to warrant as little as possible. The client will want the website to always be up and running and working properly. The standard contracts of many operators are very one sided and most clients have to live with very little protection and no guarantee of the website's universal availability. It is not uncommon for websites to be out of operation for technical reasons. Many operators will specifically state that they do not warrant that the provision of the services will be uninterrupted or error-free.

Other Clauses [3.98]

Other clauses requiring that the operator provide personal services and not assign the contract and the standard boilerplate wording in contracts of this sort should be included.

Further Information [3.99]

Many useful computer/IT and software agreements and precedents and commentary appear in Butterworths' Encyclopedia of Forms and Precedents.

Compilations as copyright works: *Ibcos Computers Ltd v Barclays Mercantile Highland Finance Ltd [1994] FSR 275.*

Whether a computer program was copied: *Richardson v Flanders [1993] FSR 497*

Confidentiality and taking substantial parts of computer programs: *Cantor Fitzgerald International and Another v Tradition (UK) Ltd and Others (15 April 1999, Times Law Report 19 May 1999).*

Websites [3.100]

The EU directives on copyright law appear on the European Commission's website: http://www.europa.eu.int.

The EU initiatives on convergence are at http://www.ipso.cec.be.

Trade marks websites are listed at the end of **Chapter 2: THE DOMAIN NAME AND TRADE MARKS.**

The Weblaw site: http://www.weblaw.co.uk.

4 – Security, Confidentiality and Employment Issues

'Privacy considerations suggest not to limit the use of cryptography as a means to ensure data security and confidentiality. The fundamental right of privacy has to be ensured, but may be restricted for other legitimate reasons such as safeguarding national security or combating crime, if these restrictions are appropriate, effective, necessary and proportionate in order to achieve these other objectives.'

(European Commission Communication '*Ensuring Security and Trust in Electronic Communication*')

Executive Summary [4.1]

- Customers will only purchase on-line and use E-mail for communications where security is ensured.
- Wording should be placed on E-mails to protect against security breaches.
- Various technological devices can be used to provide levels of assurance.
- Various legislative proposals are relevant in this field including the UK 1999 Electronic Communications Bill and EU draft *Electronic Signatures* and *Electronic Commerce Directives*.
- Employees should be informed about how and when they can use the internet and E-mail at work.
- Contracts can include clauses setting out how E-mail and other electronic links will be used in performance of the contract as in **Appendix 5**.
- An E-mail policy such as those in **Appendix 6** can be used.
- Professionals such as solicitors should be careful in using E-mail but are not prohibited from its use. The American Bar Association's 1999 Opinion on this topic is in **Appendix 9**.

This Chapter describes the principal security issues relevant to E-commerce and provides guidance on ensuring employees do not abuse their use of the internet and E-mail at work. It does not provide a technical guide to security issues, which should be obtained from the experts, not the lawyers.

E-mails [4.2]

Sending an E-mail has been described as being akin to sending a postcard. Many commercial communications are not confidential and there is therefore no difficulty with their being sent in such format. In other cases it is crucial that appropriate security measures are taken.

Confidentiality Notices on E-mails [4.3]

If an E-mail goes to the wrong recipient in many cases there is no legal difficulty. However, if it contains confidential information then the sending of it in error to the wrong recipient can be disastrous. For example, the E-mail may be inadvertently 'CCed'.

A sends an E-mail to B and copies C with a request for information about B's products. B sends an E-mail back to A giving the information and saying 'we do not know why you are keeping C informed about this. Their products are seriously deficient and held in very low standing in our business area'. B forgets to delete C as the recipient of the information. C receives the E-mail which for argument's sake here is assumed to be libellous and sues. (Defamation is addressed in **Chapter 9: EMPLOYER LIABILITY AND DEFAMATION.**)

It is for these reasons that normally E-mails from larger companies and lawyers contain notices such as the following. The words are often similar to those on fax cover sheets.

> 'This message may be confidential information and will be protected by copyright. If you receive it in error, notify us, delete it and do not make use of, nor copy, it.'

Under the common law of confidentiality, information will lose its confidential nature unless it is only disclosed to others who are told that it is confidential. Although it is best practice to have others sign confidentiality contracts before disclosure of the confidential information, confidentiality can be imposed verbally where necessary or by a written notice or by E-mail.

A larger number of examples of words for E-mail notices are given in **Appendix 4**. Some from law firms go as far as to say that data may be corrupted and reliance should only be placed on a hard copy. It is wise to tell the recipient what to do if the E-mail is received in error – such as to notify the sender by a given telephone number.

The words above do not state that the E-mail is definitely confidential information because often E-mails will not be. For example, a public notice of an annual general meeting is not confidential information. It would therefore appear silly to state that all E-mails were confidential. Virtually every E-mail would be protected by copyright however, so the notice makes that clear. Lawyers' notices should also refer to the fact that the advice or information may be privileged – protected by solicitor and client privilege.

Copyright [4.4]

Confidentiality notices also normally state that the material in the E-mail is copyrighted so that anyone receiving it in error, or indeed the intended recipient, is aware that the words are a copyright work. (see further **Chapter 3: COPYRIGHT AND DATABASE RIGHT**).

Notifying Sender [4.5]

The notice would also ask the recipient of the message received in error to notify the sender that it has been so received.

The sender cannot force a recipient to notify the sender of a message received in error. In the UK, under the *Unsolicited Goods and Services Act 1971*, if goods are received where they were not ordered the recipient is under no duty to notify the sender and indeed may keep the goods as their own property after six months. Similarly, where junk mail is sent the recipient may either keep the paper or throw it away. It is deemed to be given by the sender to the recipient. An unsolicited E-mail message sent in error cannot therefore be required to be returned.

However, if the message is protected by copyright and if its confidential nature is clear to the recipient because of a notice, the nature of the information or because each electronic page has 'confidential' marked on it, then the recipient is still restrained in law about what they can do with that information. They could not, for example, publish it or send it to someone else. The sender could obtain a court injunction restraining such copying or misuse under the laws either of confidentiality or copyright. Those laws apply whether or not there is a contract in place between sender and recipient and, therefore, can be used where a message is sent in error.

One of the risks with E-mail is that messages will be sent to many recipients where only one was intended. All staff should be educated to think carefully before sending an E-mail. It is very easy to return a message which the sender had copied to a third party where the return message should not appropriately be sent to that party.

Establishing an E-mail link with a Customer or Contact [4.6]

Not all businesses are on line. Where a business wants to begin an E-mail relationship with a contact, it first needs to be established whether they are happy to communicate, or even trade, in that way. Internet transactions are dealt with in **Chapter 6: INTERNET SHOP-PING** as are issues such as incorporating terms and conditions into contracts. Electronic payment is covered in **Chapter 8: PAYMENT FOR GOODS AND SERVICES.**

However, in relation to security, the person wanting to use E-mail should first establish if this is acceptable to the other person. They may believe that the nature of the communications will be too secret to justify the risks of E-mail. They may want encryption to be used. Where a business wishes to assume E-mail is acceptable, it could write to the customer/supplier in the following terms.

'We prefer to communicate with our customers and suppliers by E-mail as this is efficient, quick and saves costs. However if you wish us not to do so please notify us in writing right away and we will not do so. If we do not hear from you to the contrary we will assume you are happy for us to do so and we will correspond to the E-mail address you have supplied to us. If you ever want to change this then please write and E-mail us for security reasons. If you require us to use any encryption software for ordinary business communications between us please let us know.'

Some businesses will have their own security procedures in place of which they would obviously notify all suppliers and customers in any communication such as that above.

Ideally the computer system would generate the relevant message whenever an E-mail was sent rather than requiring the employee to generate it themselves each time an E-mail is sent. Stating a contact address and telephone number and fax are a good idea too, as it will retain business and it shows that a business is identifiable and not a 'fly by night' operation which could not tracked down. Law firms for example will often state that details of partners are available at a particular address – see the example in **Appendix 4**.

Terms for Contract Performance and Communication [4.7]

An example of contract terms setting out how parties to a long term supply contract may operate E-mail and electronic communications can be found in **Appendix 5**. These are detailed terms for major contracts.

In other cases a more simple form of wording may be used such as:

> 'Communications under this contract may be made by E-mail and will not be encrypted or otherwise sent in any special form unless one parties notifies the other of a special such requirement and pays the additional costs of such a requirement'.

In the example in **Appendix 5**, the terms go as far as stating what information must appear on an E-mail – such as the name of the sender and the date.

Notices clauses in contracts often contain formal requirements for services of notices under agreements. Lawyers debate whether fax should be permitted for such notices and often clauses do allow such form provided the fax is confirmed by post. The same can be said of E-mail. An E-mail notice could be sent which is then confirmed by registered post. The types of notices in relation to which such clauses apply are termination of the contract or service of notice of breach etc. These are important legal notices and should be assured of delivery.

The clause would then normally state when delivery was deemed to have been effected. With E-mail this is not necessarily instantaneous. Some businesses' internal systems involve routing to several places first.

Standards for Security [4.8]

Standards are changing quickly in the E-commerce field so always check the latest position. British Standard BS7799 is the *British Standard for Information Security Management*. In 1999, the British Minister for Small Firms handed out the first 'c: cure' certificates to organisations which had complied with BS7799. C:cure enables businesses to compare their information security management systems against best practice as shown in the standard.

Some businesses add a clause to contracts requiring compliance with particular standards or set this out in invitations to tender documents. Where the EU public procurement rules apply, however, EU standards rather than British standards should be picked wherever they exist to avoid breach of the directives and UK implementing regulations in this field. The EU policy guidelines on the obligation to apply EU standards is published at *OJ 1989 L40/12*. There are few IT EU standards except those on ergonomic and health and safety matters, electrical safety or electromagnetic compatibility. There are not many EU standards on services. The European standardisation bodies are CEN, CENELEC and ETSI and the international bodies are ISO and IEC.

Although there is a dearth of EU standards in the IT field, there are many at international level, particularly concerning OSI – standards for open systems interconnection and these deal with lots of areas of IT specifications, design, development, networking and applications. The standards must be purchased and are not available over the internet though all the standards bodies have websites.

Solicitors and E-mails [4.9]

Some business relationships automatically impose strict obligations of confidentiality. For example, solicitors are under a rightfully onerous duty of confidentiality to their clients. This does not preclude the use of E-mail but it certainly means the firm must be particularly careful about its use. By August 1999 the Law Society did not have special rules for E-mails, but recommend that if particularly sensitive documents are to be despatched by this method, the client is told and warned and perhaps advised that the document should go in the post instead. They also do not regard E-mails as professional stationery on which the full firm details must appear. If an E-mail is sent to a third party rather than the client then the full address, telephone number, fax and other contact details should ideally appear.

US Ethics Opinion and E-mails [4.10]

In 1999 the US American Bar Association's standing committee on ethics and professional responsibility determined in an opinion that lawyers do not violate client confidentiality by transmitting documents by unencrypted E-mail. It held that lawyers have an obligation to take reasonable steps to protect client secret information against unauthorised use or disclosure but this does not extend an absolute expectation of privacy in a communications medium. Lawyers should consider with the client whether information is particularly sensitive. The opinion is in **Appendix 9** and on the Internet at http://www.abanet.org/cpr/fo99-413.html.

Addresses and Corporate Names on E-mails [4.11]

As to the requirements of legislation and information to appear on 'notepaper' and other business stationery, reference should be made to **Chapter 6: INTERNET SHOPPING**. In practice, businesses are advised for commercial reasons even if there is legal uncertainty on the point, to show their full corporate details on E-mails. This enables the client more easily to telephone or send them a fax and looks more professional. It also enables the customer or supplier to ascertain the trading entity, full corporate name etc. of the business with which they are dealing.

The person signing the E-mail should also give their full name including surname even if they put their first name where a signature would go in a letter first and their status as on a business letter. These details can be very useful indeed both in subsequent litigation and in showing to whom a document was addressed or intended to be addressed.

Other E-mail requirements – Dos and Don'ts [4.12]

Do

✓ DO think before writing. Grammar and spelling mistakes look just as unprofessional on screen as they do on paper.

✓ DO be courteous – and remember that face to face humour may not work electronically.

✓ DO be relevant. It is all too easy to push the 'all' button! Being selective is the secret of success.

✓ DO check you are sending it to the right destination before you send it – once it is gone you can't get it back.

✓ DO reply to messages straight away so the sender knows you did receive the message.

Don't

✗ DON'T carry out sensitive management tasks by E-mail. It can make people feel alienated if information about matters such as salary reviews or major organisational changes arrive on screen and they don't have an opportunity to discuss it face-to-face with anyone.

✗ DON'T play politics on E-mail; using the 'cc' button to land colleagues in trouble or shift blame is not likely to build good relationships.

✗ DON'T send messages that are so long and complex that the only way for the receiver to deal with it is to print it out – this defeats the object of E-mail! No one will thank you for huge attachments which take hours to download either.

✗ DON'T air controversial and inaccurate views on E-mail – it is subject to the libel laws and you could be sued for defamation!

✗ DON'T print off your E-mails to file them – create a computer filing system for them instead.

The above advice is based on data gathered for a report called 'Teleculture Futures' produced by the Henley Centre for BT National Business Communications division. BT offers a helpline for those needing assistance in how they can 'change the way they work'. Tel: 0800 800 800.

Despite the advice above as to not to print off and file in paper form E-mails, many people do find this helpful and solicitors for example with a paper file may find it easier to retrieve the entirety of correspondence from one paper file later so may prefer, and indeed be advised, to print out the E-mails and file them.

Internet Fraud [4.13]

Internet fraud takes many forms. The law as it stands prohibits most of the common forms of such fraud whether they relate to the internet or other more traditional forms of deception. However, it is in the application of the law and its enforcement that the principal difficulties arise.

Obtaining Goods by Deception [4.14]

In addition the obtaining of services, rather than goods, by deception has not been a specific offence under English law and does not breach the *Theft Act 1968*. Therefore, where a fraud relates to the provision of services rather than sale of goods over the internet, then the existing criminal law is not as easy to apply. In 1999 the UK Government proposed extending the legislation in this field to cover services.

Examples of Internet Fraud [4.15]

US internet fraud rose by 600% from 1998/9. The statistic is from the US National Consumers League and showed an increase in internet fraud cases reported to them from 1,280 to 7,752.

Pairgain Technologies [4.16]

A scam, whereby a small high-tech company was tipped for a false takeover, resulted in huge increases in the share price in 1999. The 'story' portrayed on an internet website looked identical to an official Bloomberg news story and concerned Pairgain Technologies, a Californian company which was allegedly to be taken over by ECI Telecom. The share price surged from $8.50 to $11. Even after the story was retracted the share price stayed high. The US Securities and Exchange

Commission has stepped up its investigations of internet fraud and has a new division within its agency. It brought more than 60 cases in this field in 1998/9.

Credit Development International [4.17]

One alleged pyramid scheme made false promises that those who joined would receive an unsecured Visa or MasterCard with a US$5,000 limit and a low rate of interest and the chance to receive a monthly income of US$18,000. The Federal Trade Commission in the US obtained an injunction and estimated that over 30,900 US consumers had lost a total of US$3m – 4m.

Fortuna Alliance [4.18]

One internet scam involved promises to consumers that if they paid US$250 they would receive profits of over $5,000 per month. More than 95% of those joining would not make more than they paid in. In June 1998, the Federal Trade Commission obtained a court order prohibiting the scheme involving Fortuna Alliance until US $2m plus interest owed to consumers had been paid.

Beanie Baby Fraud [4.19]

Two US citizens were alleged to have offered rare Beanie Babies (beanbag toys) for sale over the internet. Sums of up to $400 per Beanie Baby were paid by 13 people but the goods were never received.

Top 10 [4.20]

The top ten reported internet frauds are:

1. web auctions resulting in fraud (68%) – of course many web auctions are perfectly legal and reputable;
2. general merchandise sold but goods never sent (18%);
3. hardware/software which is never sent (3.5%);
4. charging for services that are supposedly free (3.4%);
5. materials and equipment sold to those who are promised work they can do at home which does not materialise;

6. business opportunities/franchises which involve deception (many business opportunities and franchises over the internet are perfectly genuine);

7. pyramid/multi-level marketing schemes;

8. offering credit cards to bad credit risk people for up front fees;

9. advance fee loans – loans if large fees are paid which are not then provided; and

10. job offers and overseas work – fees paid for possible jobs which do not emerge.

These examples are not particularly different from the general fraud/scams reported in all business sectors. In most cases the existing law will apply.

Application of English Law [4.21]

Most UK legislation relating to unfair or unlawful trading applies equally to internet as to any other form of advertising.

● Trade descriptions – the *Trade Descriptions Act 1968*, for example, prevents a false trade description being applied to goods.

● Misleading advertising – see **Chapter 2: THE DOMAIN NAME AND TRADE MARKS**.

● Infringement of trade mark – marketing of counterfeit and pirated goods is common over the internet, such goods may breach trade mark or other intellectual property rights, see **Chapter 2: THE DOMAIN NAME AND TRADE MARKS**.

It can be significantly harder to track down the perpetrators of the worst internet frauds because of the global nature of their business and their ability to mask their identity over the internet. That has not stopped the UK and US and other authorities seeking to track down such persons.

Security Steps for Consumers Buying On-line [4.22]

Consumers concerned about the legal risks of buying on-line can, depending on the type of internet browser they use, see a broken key or closed padlock sign to indicate that the site is secure. They should also ascertain whether the website address begins https:// and not the more normal http:// as the extra 's' signifies a secure site.

Where a supplier is new to them a business can make further enquiries before a purchase takes place – e.g. the consumer can telephone the provider to check they are bona fide.

Where the business is dealing in the financial area then a check can be made as to whether or not it is registered with the Financial Services Authority (http://www.fsa.gov.uk).

Payment issues are addressed in **Chapter 8: PAYMENT FOR GOODS AND SERVICES**.

Data Protection [4.23]

Another important security issue is that of personal data and its processing on the internet. This is dealt with in **Chapter 10: DATA PROTECTION, HACKING, SECURITY AND ISP LIABILITY**, including liability under the *Data Protection Act 1998*.

Security and the UK Proposals [4.24]

In 1999, the UK Government proposed new legislation to address security issues arising from the use of E-commerce. It is doubtful if they will be enacted in their entirety, however they provided a useful summary of the legal position and so are set out here. The consultation document was *Building Confidence in Electronic Commerce – a Consultation Document* (URN 99/642) (5 March 1999). The DTI Electronic Communications Bill Team can be contacted on tel: 020 7215 1435, fax: 020 7931 7194. The paper is available at http://www.dti.gov.uk/cii/elec/elec_com.html.

The aim was to build a voluntary licensing system for providers of cryptographic services and to provide for legal recognition of electronic signatures. The Consultation document followed the Government's White Paper 'Our Competitive Future: Building the Knowledge-Driven Economy' (www.dti.gov.uk/comp/competitive). The government had earlier set out its broader electronic commerce agenda in 'Net Benefit: the electronic commerce agenda for the UK' at www.dti.gov.uk/cii.ecom.htm.

The document explains the Government's proposals for legislation to promote electronic commerce. The policy is based on the:

- Government's intention to put in place a policy and legal framework to promote electronic commerce;
- need to promote users' confidence both in the technologies which allow integrity and confidentiality and in the providers of cryptography services;
- fact that the law should, as far as possible, be technologically neutral;
- intention that licensed Certification Authorities would be in a position to offer certificates to support electronic signatures reliable enough to be recognised as equivalent to written signatures;
- recognition that clear differences in approach need to be afforded to the development of electronic and digital signature services and to encryption services;
- need for new powers for law enforcement agencies to gain legal access, under proper authority and on a case by case basis, to encryption keys or other information protecting the secrecy of stored or transmitted information so as to maintain the effectiveness of the existing legislation designed to protect the public from crime and terrorism in response to new technological developments.

OEDC Guidelines on Cryptography Policy [4.25]

The UK Government hopes to ensure consistency between the proposed UK and EU laws on cryptography. Of particular note are the OECD Guidelines on Cryptography Policy (available at http://www.oecd.org).

OEDC held a conference on E-commerce in October 1998. Ministers representing 29 countries at the conference signed a declaration on the need for governments to adapt legislation to allow electronic signature services to flourish on a global basis and stressing the need for protection for user data under data protection and privacy legislation.

The Guidelines state:

> 'National cryptographic policies may allow lawful access to plaintext or cryptographic keys of encrypted data ... Where access to the plaintext or cryptographic keys, of encrypted data is requested under lawful process, the individual or entity requesting access must have a legal right to

the possession of the plaintext, and once obtained the data must only be used for lawful purposes.'

International Chamber of Commerce – Digitally Assured Commerce [4.26]

The International Chamber of Commerce has run an Electronic Commerce Project. It has published its General Usage for International Digitally Ensured Commerce (GUIDEC) at http://www.iccwbo.org/home/guidec/guidec.asp. This document was drafted by the ICC information security working party. It covers issues such as electronic data interchange (EDI) trading agreements, civil and common law matters, the Uncitral model law (see **4.27** below) and certification. It also includes a very useful glossary. A copy appears at **Appendix 7**.

United Nations Commission on International Trade Law and Model Law [4.27]

Reference should also be made here to the United Nations Commission on International Trade Law (UNCITRAL) and its model law on electronic commerce (at http://www.un.or.at/uncitral/english/texts/electcom/ml-ec.htm and in **Appendix 7**.

UNCITRAL is the UN body which deals with electronic commerce. In 1996 it finalised its model law which is aimed at governments in the hope they will bear its provisions in mind when enacting legislation in this field. Singapore was the first country to enact this law into its own national law. UNCITRAL also has a working group working on detailed Uniform Rules on electronic signatures and certification authorities.

Changing UK Law [4.28]

As discussed at **4.25** above, the UK Government is proposing to change the law to ensure that electronic signatures are recognised by statute. It may examine every statute that requires a document or signature to be written or adopt a more global approach.

It is also considering a voluntary licensed certification authority scheme whereby those businesses which offer certificates to support electronic signatures can be regulated. There is a considerable amount of detail in the consultation paper about these issues.

However, the Government will not require that all electronic signatures are verified by such bodies before they are valid. The approach will be a voluntary scheme. They have no intention of disturbing existing use of electronic messages between parties such as within closed user groups. The use of electronic data interchange and other methods for messaging, invoicing and ordering goods will continue without new regulation.

Reference is also made to a separate exercise by the DTI on company law proposals which may lead to companies being able to deliver communications to shareholders by electronic means. The Government is also considering whether it should legislate to stop unsolicited E-mails known as Spam. Measures already in place include the following.

- Most internet service providers have systems to combat unsolicited mails which they operate on a voluntary basis. The London Internet Exchange (LINX) intends to finalise best practice guidelines for how providers should deal with spam later in 1999.

- The Direct Marketing Association is working with the US DMA to develop a world-wide E-mail preference scheme so that those who do not want unsolicited E-mail can register and thus ensure they do not receive it (the DMA won the tender to run in 1999 the UK's first preference scheme for faxes – see http://www.dma.org.uk).

- Some service providers offer opt-in schemes to gain commercial advantage.

Trusted Third Parties [4.29]

Annex A to the 1999 electronic commerce white paper sets out the proposed conditions which must be met for a body to be authorised as a trust service provider. The paper explains how cryptography keys can be used as a signature. One way of providing electronic signatures is to make use of what is known as 'public key or asymmetric cryptography'.

Public Key Cryptography [4.30]

Public key cryptography uses two keys, also known as a 'key pair'. These keys are both large numbers with special mathematical properties. When this technique is used for signatures, the private key (which is only known to its owner) is used to transform a data file by scrambling the information contained in it. The transformed data is the electronic signature and can be checked against the original file using the public key of the person who signed it. Anyone with access to the public key which might for example be available on a website, can check the signature. This allows them to verify that it could only have been signed by someone with access to the private key.

Where the only person with access to the private key is the owner then the owner must have signed the message and cannot later deny having signed it (repudiation). If a third party altered the message, the fact that they had done so would be easily detectable.

Licensed Certification Authorities [4.31]

The UK Government in its 1999 white paper proposed that Licensed Certification Authorities would be authorised. They will not be allowed to store the private key of a key pair. The private key will be kept by the individual only. An alternative to the use of a trusted third party and key escrow is the use of encryption products which support key recovery or key encapsulation. Illustrative examples of the products on offer are given in the white paper.

New Offence Not to Decrypt [4.32]

There will be a new offence of not decrypting enciphered material when demanded, not to provide requested keys needed to decipher files or messages or not to state where keys are hidden. This will be under the *Police and Criminal Evidence Act 1984*.

Interception of Communications Act 1985 [4.33]

Other issues are law enforcement such as when police should be allowed access to encrypted messages in investigating crimes. The *Interception of Communications Act 1985* is due to be revised (see http://www.homeoffice.gov.uk).

The Electronic Communications Bill [4.34]

The DTI published its consultation on an Electronic Communications Bill in July. It can be bought from the Stationery Office for £9.70 (Cm 4417; tel: 020 7873 9090) or downloaded from the internet (http://www.dti.gov.uk/cii/elec/ecbill.pdf).

Three documents were published.

● Consultation Document and Government's Response to the Trade and Industry Committee's Report.
● Explanatory notes to the Bill.
● Electronic Communications Bill.

Other measures in the Bill include:

● licensing of new radio spectrum for broadband wireless services;
● opening up BT's local network for broadband services; and
● introduction of the third generation of mobile phones, giving mobile access to the internet.

The Bill aims to ensure people and businesses can where they prefer communicate electronically with Government rather than on paper. It provides a legal framework for the use of electronic signatures so people 'can be sure about the origin and integrity of communications'. It also allows trust to be placed in providers of cryptography services by introducing a voluntary 'approvals' scheme. It will help prevent the Government's law enforcement powers being eroded through the criminal use of encryption but without requiring the storage of decryption keys with third parties. It also simplifies the process under which existing Telecommunication Act licences can be amended.

Register of Approved Cryptography Service Providers [4.35]

Part I of the Bill provides for the setting up of a register of approved cryptography service providers. *Part II* is particular relevant for those drafting contracts. *Section 7* states:

> 'In any legal proceedings (a) an electronic signature incorporated or logically associated with a particular electronic communication, and (b) the certification by any person of such a signature, shall each be admissible in evidence in relation to any question as to the authenticity of the communication or its integrity'.

Electronic Communications **[4.36]**

Section 8 gives ministers powers to change legislation to allow for electronic communications. For example copyright can only be assigned by a document signed by the assignor (though a contract which provides that when copyright is created it will vest in someone else does not need such a requirement as vesting of rights on creation is different from assignment). Ministers may choose to introduce a law allowing an electronic signature for assignment of copyright in this way.

The explanatory notes section of the Bill commenting on *section 8* states:

> 'Some businesses have contracted with each other on paper about how they are to treat each other's electronic communications. Clauses 7 and 8 do not cast any doubt on such arrangements'.

Part III provides for investigation of protected electronic data – the duty to disclose encryption keys to Government agents for example is contained in this part of the Bill. *Part IV* deals with telecommunications licences.

The explanatory notes which go with the bill contain many useful references to other relevant web sites which will aid those involved with researching this area.

The Bill at the date of writing is still a draft. This is an area to watch closely.

Electronic Commerce Draft Directive **[4.37]**

The European Commission proposed a draft Directive on 18 November 1998 on *Electronic Commerce*. A copy of the Directive is on the DTI website at http://www.dti.gov.uk/cii/ecomdirective/ index.htm (hard copies from DTI by fax on 020 7215 4161) and at http://www.ispo.cec.be/E-commerce/docs/legalen.pdf. The draft Directive addresses issues such as formation of contracts and liability of service providers (see **Chapter 10: DATA PROTECTION, HACKING, SECURITY AND ISP LIABILITY**).

Electronic Signatures Draft Directive [4.38]

In May 1998 the Commission also adopted a draft *Electronic Signatures Directive* (DTI contact nigel.hickson@ciid.gov.dti.uk). In the same month the Justice and Home Affairs Council of the Commission adopted formal consultation on encryption and law enforcement (European Council Doc. No 8856/98 (PRESSE 170/G)).

The draft *Electronic Signatures Directive* was published at *OJ 1998 C323/5*. January 1999 amendments before the EU Parliament were made and published at *OJ 1999 C104/49*. Both the original text and amended draft can be accessed at http://www.ispo.cec.be/E-commerce/legal.htm. This website is one of the most comprehensive for showing latest EU electronic commerce legal developments and also provides links to sites such as that of UNCITRAL.

The draft Directive covers the legal recognition of electronic signatures and establishes a legal framework for certain certification services to be made available to the public. The UK Government, in its consultation on E-commerce stated that an electronic signature can provide a far higher level of assurance than a manual signature. The electronic signature identifies the signatory and, if properly implemented, is much more difficult to forge than a manual signature. It also can be used to show whether a document has been altered since it was signed. This cannot so easily be checked with a manual signature.

Article 3 of the draft Directive states that Member States may introduce voluntary accreditation schemes. *Article 5* provides that Member States must ensure that an electronic signature is not denied legal effect solely on the grounds that the signature is in electronic form or not based on a qualified certificate or a certificate issued by an accredited certification service.

Those certification service providers issuing qualified certificates would have to accept liability for accuracy of information unless the certificate said otherwise, compliance with the Directive's requirements and the certificate would provide an assurance that the person identified in the certificate is who they are alleged to be at the time the certificate is issued. An Electronic Signature Committee would be set up to assist the Commission in this field. The Directive would be required to be implemented by 31 December 2000 though as this is in a draft Directive it may be delayed.

An electronic signature would be defined in the draft Directive as 'a signature in electronic form in, or attached to, or logically associated with, data which is used by a signatory to indicate his approval of the content of that data and it is:

- uniquely linked to the signatory,

- capable of identifying the signatory,

- created using means that the signatory can maintain under his sole control, and

- linked to the data to which it relates in such a manner that any subsequent alteration of the data is revealed.'

Requirements for Qualified Certificates [4.39]

Qualified certificates must contain:

✓ the identifier of the certification service provider issuing it;

✓ the unmistakable name of the holder or an unmistakable pseudonym which shall be identified as such;

✓ a specific attribute of the holder such as the address, the authority to act on behalf of a business, the credit-worthiness, VAT or other tax registration numbers, the existence of payment guarantees or specific permits or licences;

✓ a signature verification device which corresponds to a signature creation device under the control of the holder;

✓ the beginning and end of the operational period of the certificate;

✓ the unique identity code of the certificate;

✓ the electronic signature of the certification service provider issuing it;

✓ limitations on the scope of use of the certificate, if applicable; and

✓ limitations on the certification service provider's liability and on the value of transactions for which the certificate is valid, if applicable.

Requirements for Certification Service

Providers [4.40]

There are a number of requirements which certification providers must satisfy as detailed below.

Certification providers must:

✓ Demonstrate the reliability necessary of offering certification services.

✓ Operate a prompt and secure revocation services.

✓ Verify, by appropriate means, the identity and capacity to act of the person to which a qualified certificate is issued.

✓ Employ personnel who possess the expert knowledge, experience and qualifications necessary for the offered services, in particular competence at the managerial level, expertise in electronic signature technology and familiarity with proper security procedures. They must also use electronic signature products that ensure the technical and cryptographic security of the certification processes supported by the products.

✓ Use trustworthy systems, and use electronic signature products that ensure protection against modification of the products so that they cannot be used to perform functions other than those for which they have been designed. They must also use electronic signature products that ensure the technical and cryptographic security of the certification processes supported by the products.

✓ Take measures against forgery of certificates and, in cases where the certification service provider generates private cryptographic signature keys, guarantee the confidentiality during the process of generating those keys.

✓ Maintain sufficient financial resources to operate in conformity with the requirements laid down in this Directive, in particular to bear the risk of liability for damages, for example, by obtaining the appropriate insurance.

✓ Record all relevant information concerning a qualified certificate for an appropriate period of time, in particular to provide evidence of certification for the purposes of legal proceedings (such recording may be done electronically).

> ✓   Not store or copy private cryptographic signature keys of the person to whom the certification service provider offered key management services, unless that person explicitly asks for it.
>
> ✓   Inform consumers before entering into a contractual relationship in writing.

Distance Selling Directive   [4.41]

The EU *Distance Selling Directive (97/7)* contains provisions which require Member States to change laws to allow consumers to register their objection to receiving unsolicited E-mails sent for distance selling purposes. It does not apply to business to business transactions, only transactions involving a consumer. The UK must implement this Directive by 4 June 2000 but has still not drafted the UK regulations. Details can be found on the DTI website (http://www.dti.gov.uk) by searching for 'Distance Selling Directive'. The *Telecoms Data Protection Directive (97/66)* (which was implemented in the UK on 1 May 1999 in part) does not apply to E-mail.

The benefits to consumers through having independent intermediaries acting in the electronic marketplace, are set out in the White Paper. These include guarantees of order fulfilment and management of commodity prices. In 1999, a new draft directive on distance selling of financial services was debated which had not yet been agreed at the date of writing. This would specifically cover internet marketing as well as telephone and other distance methods. It proposes a 30 day cooling-off period.

Employees and Security   [4.42]

Closely related to the security issues mentioned above are the risks which employees can bring to a business through their use of E-mail.

Employees should be given guidance on what is and is not permissible in the office in relation to the use of E-mail. One issue is whether it is acceptable to use the corporate E-mail system for private messages. A total prohibition against private use may protect the business from liability for individual abuses. However, if private use is allowed, then an authorised act done in an unauthorised way may leave the business exposed to liability.

The key to avoiding liability without hindering effective use of the technology available to business is through enhancing staff understanding of the many implications (including legal ones) stemming from their acts whilst using the internet or E-mail. Through such education, effective risk management can be achieved. **Appendix 6** includes a set of employee guidelines.

Two thirds of websites disclose their privacy policy and information practices. The annual US report on the Emerging Digital Economy looks at these issues in detail and provides a huge amount of information on E-commerce – see http://www.doc.gov. The June 1999 version is the latest example.

---

1. A survey by InfoSec, a computer security firm, in April 1999 found that a third of companies did not have a policy on the use of the internet at work.
2. Half did not have policies for controlling use of external E-mails – causing risks of viruses.
3. Two out of five companies had discovered a serious incident of improper use of the internet.
4. Of the two companies finding a serious incident only 21% of cases resulted in disciplinary action.
5. Half the incidents were discovered by use of monitoring software.
6. One in five incidents were found by chance.
7. One in 10 incidents were reported by a work colleague acting as informer.
8. Eight out of 10 employees at work use the internet for matters such as reading sports news and organising personal finance, arranging holidays, looking at entertainment.
9. Half of those using the internet at work used chat rooms.

By instituting a policy so that employees know where they stand, some of the activities above can be avoided. **Appendix 6** includes a general E-mail policy for a solicitors' practice (Sprecher Grier Halberstam) and a disk introduction policy, preceded by a general note for employers. However, each business' needs and E-mail /internet use differ substantially so any example should just be used for reference rather than assumed to be appropriate for every case.

Confidentiality [4.43]

(Paras **4.43** – **4.59** were written by Simon Halberstam)

Businesses need an E-mail user policy showing the need for confidentiality notices on E-mails sent to external bodies and clients, and disciplinary measures being included in employee contracts. The ability of a disaffected employee, or someone who is soon to leave the business, to send large quantities of confidential information by E-mail – whether it be trade secrets, client lists, technical and know how information, in short anything valuable – to either a personal external E-mail address or to a competitor, should be a matter of real concern.

Monitoring [4.44]

To safeguard against confidentiality breaches and employee abuse, high profile monitoring of both E-mail and web use, should be a priority. Whilst such measures will not prevent such disclosures, they may deter them.

Similarly, publicising and including the right for the business to monitor such use in employees' contracts will safeguard the business from complaint. The Sprecher Grier Halberstam example of such a policy is given in **Appendix 6**.

Distinguishing Private and Corporate E-mails [4.45]

Some thought should be given to the form of signature, which should be attached to E-mails which identify it as emanating from the business, similarly if private use is allowed, a separate signature should be used to distinguish corporate E-mails from personal ones. This may be particularly pertinent if employees post messages to newsgroups.

Maintenance of Records [4.46]

Another issue, which appears to have received scant attention is the maintenance of records, which is a legal obligation covering many types of business communications. A business' policy in respect of the storing or destruction of documents should be extended to take account of E-mail use in the business process. This may also have ramifications in respect of any litigation involving the business, as

E-mail will be subject to the discovery process obliging all relevant documents (including E-mails) to be made available to the other party.

Defamation [4.47]

The ability to send abusive, harassing and offensive material via E-mail can have serious consequences for a business which may be liable if effective steps to prevent such activities are not put in place and maintained. Defamation is covered in **Chapter 9: EMPLOYER LIABILITY AND DEFAMATION**.

Proving Identities [4.48]

As the identity of the sender can be manipulated, it is possible to appear to be someone else and use this for nefarious purposes such as sending abusive E-mail in the name of others. It may be difficult for a particular employee to prove that the E-mail did not emanate from him/herself.

Practical Time Saving [4.49]

For some employers, the best way of ensuring employees do not waste time on the internet is to forbid them to use it at work whether on the business' computers or on their own laptops. Other tips include:

● having one stand alone system with access only in the office which is overlooked by the boss;

● having a written log of time used which employees must complete;

● providing them with helpful advice such as making sure they write a list of what they are looking up in advance and that they do not depart from that by being distracted by other things; and

● using bookmark facilities so that sites can be noted and easily found on subsequent occasions – but do not over use this facility and have an unwieldy bookmarks list. It may be better to make a written notes of the popular sites.

Employee Dismissal [4.50]

On 15 June 1999, a Liverpool tribunal ruled that an information technology manager who surfed the Internet in working hours to check holiday bookings, had been fairly sacked. Lois Fraxhi had worked for Focus Management Consultants in Alderley Edge in Cheshire and brought an unfair dismissal claim after she was sacked. The tribunal held that she was guilty of misconduct in using the Focus Management Consultants' computer.

She was dismissed in July 1998 after working for over two years at the company. She alleged she had been sacked because of her pregnancy. Stephen Jones, a director, said her sacking was because of her use of the internet and the fact that she had lied about it. Such surfing at work is estimated to cost British companies £2.5 million a year.

Internet and Intranets [4.51]

Many larger businesses have internal intranets where messages can be exchanged within a more secure environment than over the internet generally. Each business will need to take technical advice on whether an intranet is appropriate to them. From a legal point of view, the issues are no different save that where access to an intranet is appropriately restricted just to employees, they all operate under the umbrella of the same organisation and are subject to the same rules. They are all bound by a duty of confidentiality and a duty of good faith and fidelity to their employer and subject in most cases to detailed additional legal obligations in their employment contracts. There is therefore greater scope for legal controls within an internal intranet.

When to Encode [4.52]

Businesses may need advice on when they may send documents by E-mail without any encryption and where they should encrypt or not entrust the document to this means of communication at all. The American Bar Association's Opinion in **Appendix 9** states that it does not believe that E-mail communications, including those sent unencrypted over the internet, pose any greater risk of interception or disclosure than other modes of communication commonly relied on as having a reasonable expectation of privacy.

Readers will all have their own experiences of faxes sent to the wrong number or couriers losing packages off the back of a motor bike. There are risks with all methods. Anyone intercepting the E-mail is breaking the law in any event. It would be wise to:

- consider how sensitive the communication is;
- determine how much would be lost in financial terms if a disclosure took place; and
- examine how secure the means of communication is.

Different Types of E-mail [4.53]

The US ABA Opinion (at **Appendix 9**) examines four different types of E-mail.

Direct E-mail [4.54]

This is achieved by programming a modem to communicate with the other person's modem. This is much the same as sending a fax.

Private E-mail System [4.55]

This will include internal corporate E-mail systems and extranet networks where one internal system dials another system. This is only slightly more risky than direct E-mail in **4.54** above though there is a chance it may be misdirected within the firm which receives it.

On-line Service Providers [4.56]

E-mail is sometimes provided by third party on-line service providers or OSPs. Users receive a mailbox protected by a password. The mailbox is in a public forum of which other fee paying users are a part. There is a greater risk of misdirection, however, the risks are no greater than with faxes. It is normally regarded, by lawyers at least, as a sufficiently secure means of communication.

Internet E-mail [4.57]

Internet E-mail uses landbased telephone lines and intermediate computers usually from various internet service providers or 'routers'. The risks are with hackers and also with internet service providers exercising their right to monitor E-mail passing through their network. The fact that these people could intercept the E-mail, does not mean the system should not be regarded as reasonably secure.

E-commerce Fraud [4.58]

Risks of using E-mail for commercial transactions include fraud and hacking. The first annual report of the Fraud Advisory Panel has estimated that fraud could be costing £5 billion a year. Internet fraud had increased from 1,280 incidents to 7,750 in the US, according to the National Consumers' League. The Advisory Panel is chaired by George Staple QC who used to be head of the Serious Fraud Office.

Publication and Patents [4.59]

In determining whether to permit employees to use E-mail at all, one factor is the legal consequences of disclosure of the information concerned. A scientist working for a business may wish to publicise to his colleagues his new invention that is of significant benefit not only to the business but also to the world. He needs to be restrained from doing so until patent protection has been applied for under the *Patents Act 1977*. Publication will remove the ability to patent as the invention must not have entered the public domain. Sending E-mails with details of the research concerned can amount to putting such information into the public domain and making it part of the 'state of the art'.

An E-mail policy for employees may therefore warn them in terms such as:

> 'Where you work in our research and development department you need to be particularly careful about using E-mail and making postings/sending messages to newsgroups or bulletin boards. Your work for us is strictly confidential and you are subject to the legal requirements in this respect set out in your contract of employment. You should only engage in such discussions of research and development matters after obtaining the

> consent in writing of your section head. In particular disclosure of confidential information will jeopardise valuable intellectual property protection available to the company.'

Sending an E-mail to someone who has signed a confidentiality agreement or is subject to obligations of confidence because they work for the same employer or are in a confidential relationship, such as between solicitor and client, will not jeopardise the confidentiality of that information. Even where patent protection is not sought or cannot be obtained for the information concerned, that information can still be protected by the laws of confidence and, therefore, it should be kept secret by the employees concerned.

Further Information [4.60]

Building Confidence in Electronic Commerce – A Consultation Document (URN 99/642) (5 March 1999). The DTI Electronic Commerce Bill Team can be contacted on tel: 0171 215 1435, fax: 0171 931 7194. The paper is available at http://www.dti.gov.uk/CII/elec/ elec_com.html.

The EU draft Directives on *Electronic Commerce, Electronic Signatures* and various papers in the E-commerce field can all be accessed from http://www.ispo.cec.be which is one of the best E-commerce sites for EU legislative material.

The Financial Services Authority: http://www.fsa.gov.uk.

The Government's White Paper *Our Competitive Future: Building the Knowledge-Driven Economy* is at: http://www.dti.gov.uk/comp/ competitive.

The Government's Electronic Communications Bill July 1999 is at: http://www.dti.gov.uk/cii/elec.

The Government's *Net Benefit: the electronic commerce agenda for the UK* is at: http:// www.dti.gov.uk/cii/ecom.htm.

OECD Guidelines on Cryptography Policy available at http:// www.oecd.org.

The United Nations Commission on International Trade Law (UNCI-TRAL) and its model law on electronic commerce is at: http://www.un.or.at/uncitral and in **Appendix 7**.

International Chamber of Commerce : General Usage for International Digitally Ensured Commerce (GUIDEC) at http://www.iccwbo.org/home/guidec/guidec.asp and in **Appendix 8**.

5 – Transacting for the Scheme

'An increasing number of transactions in international trade are carried out by means of electronic data interchange and other means of communication, commonly referred to as 'electronic commerce', which involve the use of alternatives to paper-based methods of communication and storage of information'

(Resolution of the General Assembly of the United Nations, 16th December 1996 in adopting the UNCITRAL Model Law of Electronic Commerce)

Executive Summary [5.1]

- Before a website can be set up or internet shopping site activated, contracts with providers of relevant services must be arranged.
- Design and software services will be commissioned – see **3.67** above and **5.6** below.
- Contract and intellectual property law should be carefully considered – see **Chapter 2: THE DOMAIN NAME AND TRADE MARKS** and **Chapter 3: COPYRIGHT AND DATABASE RIGHT**.
- In certain cases public procurement rules will apply.
- Contracts with Internet Service Providers need to be agreed.
- Protection for the buyer can be improved by source code deposit under an escrow agreement.
- Millennium and other dating issues should be considered.

This Chapter looks at transacting for the system – putting in place a website and arrangements for E-commerce, principally by entering into contracts with third party providers of various kinds. Contracts with those placing orders for goods or services advertised over the website are addressed in **Chapter 6: INTERNET SHOPPING. Chapter**

8: PAYMENT FOR GOODS AND SERVICES considers the special requirements relating to payment for goods and services.

Supply of Services – Implied Terms [5.2]

Most supplies in the internet field are of services rather than goods leaving aside the goods shipped using E-commerce covered in **Chapter 6: INTERNET SHOPPING**. The only goods will be computer hardware but in many cases the equipment necessary for E-commerce will already be in place. This section principally examines the purchase of services. The *Supply of Goods and Services Act 1982* applies to people who agree to carry out services. *Section 13* provides:

> 'In a contract for the supply of a service where the supplier is acting in the course of a business, there is an implied term that the supplier will carry out the service with reasonable care and skill'.

Section 14 provides that where the time for the services to be carried out is not fixed there is an implied term that the supplier will carry out the service within a reasonable time. What constitutes a reasonable time is a question of fact.

If the consideration or payment is not fixed in the contract or left to be determined in a manner agreed by the contract, (e.g. on a time and materials basis) then, under *section 15*, where there is no course of dealing between the parties which determines the matter, there is an implied term that the buyer will pay a reasonable charge. What is reasonable is a question of fact.

These implied terms are not particularly helpful in practice. Many suppliers regard the implied term to exercise due skill and care as so legally innocuous that they happily incorporate it expressly in their standard contract terms in a way they would never do with the terms implied into contracts for the sale of goods under the *Sale of Goods Act 1979*. This Act implies terms that goods will be of satisfactory quality and fit for their purpose and most IT contracts routinely exclude such terms.

The implied terms for services will apply when:

● the contract is not in writing, such as where services are performed without any written agreement;

- they are not excluded by any exclusion clause in the contract, in which case they will apply along side and supplement any express warranties which have been obtained; and

- an attempt has been made to exclude the implied terms in circumstances where the *Unfair Contract Terms Act 1977* holds the exclusion to be unreasonable and thus void – note that this will only apply when there is a contract on the supplier's standard terms, not where the exclusion clause has been individually negotiated. Even then many clauses are enforceable and it is risky for a buyer to accept a one-sided clause in the hope it could be proved void later.

The *Unfair Terms in Consumer Contracts Regulations 1999* apply in addition to the the *Unfair Contract Terms Act 1977*, where the supply is to a consumer. This is dealt with in **Chapter 6: INTERNET SHOPPING**.

Example

A consultant designs a web page for a gullible buyer. The buyer knows nothing about the internet and the web page is badly designed and does not work properly. There was no written contract. The buyer sues for breach of the implied term to use due skill and care. He is entitled to damages and can treat the contract as repudiated.

Remedies for Breach of the Implied Terms   [5.3]

Damages can be awarded and the buyer can also refuse to continue with the contract because the breached implied term is a 'condition'. This means it is a fundamental term which goes to the root of the contract.

Contracts in Practice   [5.4]

A surprising number of internet contracts are entered into without proper terms and conditions. This is partly caused by the nature of the people who work within the industry, many of whom do not operate in a conventional way. It should not be assumed that a tight contract which protects the buyer is always desirable. Some clients will want a contract that is balanced and protects both sides, rather than one which is partisan and biased.

The most effective practical advice, whether acting as buyer or seller, is to have a good strong set of standard conditions of contract which are applied to all services contracts and which the contracting party insists should be used. Most contracts are on standard terms and those with IT/internet suppliers need be no exception. Indeed, the astute buyer will be able to take advantage of the slightly anarchic/relaxed web designer who has never thought of contracts, and incorporates the buyer's terms without a qualm.

Express Terms [5.5]

In practice it is the express terms of the agreement which are more relevant than terms implied by law in services contracts, since in most cases there will be written terms which exclude those implied terms and more detailed express terms or warranties, detailing, for example:

- when services will be provided – deadlines and whether they are legally binding, in particular whether 'time is of the essence';
- what services will be supplied;
- to what standard the services will be performed as there may be different rates for different types of support (e.g. for emergency work), service level agreements often define the standards of services in the IT industry but these should be treated with caution and their precise contractual effect ascertained; and
- who will perform the services – whether they can be sub-contracted or whether they must be personally performed.

Software Development Agreements [5.6]

Below is a checklist which can be used for software supply agreements. It can be used with modifications for supplies of other services too. **Appendix 1** contains an example of a software development agreement drafted from the point of view of the supplier. However, such contracts do differ widely and no contract precedent should be used without proper thought. In many cases no special software will need to be written for the setting up of a simple website in any event. Form the buyer's or customer's point of view, the list below can be used as a checklist for examination of the contract and its terms. There are a number of legal books available on the subject of software contracts to which reference can be made including the software contracts in Butterworth's Encyclopedia of Forms and Precedents which is also available on CD Rom to which reference should be made for a detailed examination of software contracts and the wide variety of types of contracts which can be used.

Checklist of Software Contracts for Buyers   [5.7]

This checklist highlights the principal points to consider when examining a contract as both buyer/licensee and seller/supplier. It does not include every possible clause. It applies to the sale of hardware, licensing of software and support but not long-term development contracts.

- **Price**
  - ✓ Check if fixed price or time and materials and any cap on total time and material cost.
  - ✓ For ongoing contracts, check price rise provisions – any cap on rises to the Retail Prices Index.
  - ✓ What currency is payment to be made in and who bears fluctuation risk?
  - ✓ Are there price reductions for delay or liquidated damages provisions?
  - ✓ Rights to charge interest where money is overdue?
  - ✓ Can money owed be set-off against money due?
  - ✓ What is included in the price? Are user manuals in hard copy form provided? Is the user allowed to make further copies?
- **Delivery**
  - ✓ Who delivers? Who insures in transit? Who will install the software? Is there an extra installation charge?
  - ✓ Are the goods/software properly described/are the deliverables clear?
  - ✓ Is the time for delivery of the essence or are delivery dates indicative only?
  - ✓ Are there liquidated damages for delay?
  - ✓ Does title to hardware pass on delivery or on payment? Is any clause reserving liability valid in law? Some such clauses are classed as charges and are void for not being registered.
- **Acceptance**
  - ✓ Are acceptance tests defined? Who signs off on them? What happens if they are not passed can the supplier

---

keep re-testing for as long and on as many occasions as it wants or is there a cut off point?

- Warranties
  - ✓ Check length of any warranty as to its time period. Should it be longer or shorter?
  - ✓ Check what the warranty says – such as compliance with specifications/user requirements document.
  - ✓ Are warranties implied by law (such as goods will be of satisfactory quality and fit for their purpose) excluded or included.
  - ✓ What are the principal expectations of the buyer for the product both as to functionality and quality? The buyer should ensure that these are incorporated as express warranties into the contract.
  - ✓ Year 2000/EMU or other precise warranties?
  - ✓ Are there any statements or representations in letters or made in meetings which the buyer should incorporate into the contract?
  - ✓ Is the buyer paying for maintenance when the warranty period is still operating and is this fair?
  - ✓ Are there manufacturers' warranties offered with goods as well as those of the supplier? If so, how are they passed on?
- Limits on liability
  - ✓ Does the buyer limit its liability for direct losses to the price or by any other formula?
  - ✓ Is there an exclusion of consequential loss? Suppliers should ensure it also excludes loss of profit.
  - ✓ Buyer should increase limit to realistic level.
  - ✓ Does the clause exclude liability for death or personal injury or say all loss is excluded without specifying this is covered? If so, this is void and the entire clause could be in jeopardy. Revise.
- Force majeure
  - ✓ What events excuse the supplier's delay or non-performance? Buyers should ensure force majeure clauses do not include events such as strikes or failures by sub-contractors. Also check whether the contract can ultimately be terminated if the delay is too long.
- Restrictions
  - ✓ Are there any anti-competitive restrictions in the contract which may breach UK or EU competition law?

✓ Is the buyer obliged to take maintenance from the supplier? If not, could the buyer go elsewhere for support without the source code?

● Software

✓ What restrictions are there on use – such as site, machine on which it can be used, user number restrictions (simultaneous or some other formula), licensee? Can these be changed such as where there is a corporate reconstruction. Do other companies in the group or contractors or facilities management companies acting for or with the user, need rights to use the software too?

✓ Who owns the copyright in any modifications made by the supplier or user? May a user make modifications? Is the source code available for this purpose?

✓ In what form is the software supplied? Who installs it?

● Indemnity

✓ Is the licensor of software the owner of it? Is there a warranty to this effect? Does the licensor indemnify the user for breaches of copyright – in the UK, whenever the user is sued or even threatened with such legal action? Check that the indemnity is not limited as to amount.

● Escrow

✓ Will the licensor place the source code in escrow? With which agent? Is it under a bi-partite or tri-partite contract. Tri-partite is better as a user can enforce it against the escrow agent. Who pays the escrow fees? What are the circumstances of release? Liquidation, breach of contract, failure to maintain, Y2K events etc. Is that which is deposited verified (bodies like the National Computing Centre Limited will verify) and are updates to be lodged?

● Support

✓ Does the supplier support the software? Must the buyer take support from the supplier? Is the warranty invalidated if support is obtained from a third party? How can support charges increase? What are the hours of support cover? Consider as buyer extending the working day. Check both response time and how long the supplier will take to fix the fault. If these are not met is the supplier in breach of contract or does the contract just provide that the supplier will use 'reasonable endeavours'.

> ✓ Does the user or the supplier decide if a site visit is necessary?
>
> ✓ What does the support cover? Are updates included?
>
> ✓ Must the user always use the latest version of the product or will older releases continue to be supported?
>
> ● Notice and termination
>
> ✓ In the sale of hardware and the licensing of software, there is normally no fixed term contract. Check whether renewal fees for software licensing have to be paid.
>
> ✓ For long-term contracts such as support, how long does the agreement last? Is that sufficient a commitment to support? Would the user want a shorter or longer period?
>
> ✓ What rights are there to terminate on notice, for breach of contract and on liquidation of one of the parties?
>
> ✓ What happens on termination? Are there different consequences depending on whether one party is in breach or not?
>
> ● Other clauses
>
> ✓ Check that the agreement covers issues such as confidentiality, choice of law (where one party is abroad), poaching of staff, notices, what publicity one party can give about the other and waiver.

Web Design Arrangements [5.8]

Reference should be made to **Chapter 3: COPYRIGHT AND DATABASE RIGHT** which examines a typical web design agreement and hosting contract in detail and gives examples of words to be used for particular clauses. **Appendix 2** contains an example of notes concerning various internet contracts. In addition at **Appendix 2** there are examples of short contracts drafted from the supplier's point of view for web page design, for software to be used on a website, a contract between the designer and sub-contractor, contract for ongoing software services for a buyer's web page and a more general commissioned software contract.

One practical difficulty is that often web designers, whilst good at making designs, are not competent at marketing. The website will principally be used as a marketing tool. The following issues should therefore be born in mind.

✓ How frequently will the website be updated and by whom? Once a month is probably a minimum otherwise people will not regularly visit the site. It is wise to include a notice on the site about how frequently it will be updated.

✓ Will there be photographs and detailed designs which take time to download but look better or will the site be relatively plain? Some businesses have two alternatives so that those in a hurry can simply access the plain version.

✓ How will links to other sites be organised? Can the designer offer any services in this respect?

✓ Will the web designers be able to liaise with the business' normal marketing business so that marketing material will give the website address? It is only if the reference is given that people will be aware of its existence and be able to access it. It should therefore ideally appear on all brochures, business literature and advertisements.

✓ Will the site log those who visit it and note where visitors are located?

✓ Is there any reason a potential customer would visit the website? Would it for example provide free information not easily available elsewhere so that the site could be regularly visited. Who will be responsible for this aspect?

✓ Who will arrange any reciprocal links with other sites which are not competitive?

✓ Has the web designer good graphic design skills? Check other examples of their work. The website should have a logical flow which takes those viewing it to the pages they want without always having to return to the first (home) page.

Before proceeding with a website design agreement, often a separate contract will be negotiated for the exercise of designing a specification for the site. Even if the specification will be provided to a customer free of charge prior to the award of a contract for the design work, it is wise to have a written contract in place so that if the matter does not proceed to a contract it is clear who owns copyright and other rights in the work to be produced.

Once it is clear what is to be produced, the website design agreement will be drawn up. An important issue in any such contracts will be ownership of the copyright in the works produced. In some cases the designer will wish to retain copyright and thus be able to use the designs for other clients. If there is no agreement on this issue then, under the *Copyright, Designs and Patents Act 1988*, ownership will remain with the designer. It is only with design right and registered designs, which are unlikely to be relevant to websites, that the rights automatically go to the business commissioning or paying for the work.

Outsourced or In-house? [5.9]

The buyer needs to decide whether to have the website designed in-house or to buy services to have it made by outsourcing. In most cases it is better to buy the services because, although it is likely that most IT departments have the skills needed to keep the site up-to-date, most are not familiar with the design of a website and it is better to obtain the skills of a business which does this on a regular basis.

However, if the work is done other than by employees, then the contract should clearly state who owns the intellectual property rights. In addition, where the work is outsourced, the contract should include quality control provisions and some delay in payment until the work has been checked and acceptance tests run.

Public Contracting and Procurement [5.10]

Where the body commissioning the website design is a contracting authority under EU *Public Procurement Directives* then, where the contract exceeds the relevant threshold, it may be necessary to follows the public procurement regime and advertise the contract in an open, restricted or negotiated procedure tender. Reference should be made to public procurement textbooks in this respect.

Where the services of a designer are commissioned, then it is likely to be the *Services Directive (92/50/EEC OJL 209*, 24 July 1992) which will apply. This is implemented in the UK by the *Public Services Contracts Regulations 1993 (SI 1993/3228)*. It applies where the contract is worth 200,000 Euros or more. Most web design contracts will be under this threshold. However, even where they are and even where the buyer is not in the public sector, it is wise to put the contract out to tender if it is of relatively large value, to ensure the best price is obtained. That also gives the buyer the opportunity of insisting that its conditions of purchase are used rather than conditions of supply of the web designer.

Contracts with Internet Service Providers   [5.11]

All businesses getting on the internet will enter into a contract with an Internet Service Provider (ISP). In most cases there will be little opportunity to negotiate and/or amend the contract with such providers. **Chapter 3: COPYRIGHT AND DATABASE RIGHT** examines clauses from a contract with a business agreeing to host a website to which reference should be made. An example of such a contract is in **Appendix 2**.

Source Code Deposit   [5.12]

Where design work is to be carried out which involves the production of software the user will require access to the secret source code of the software in order to support and maintain the software. Most software is licensed in object code only and the supplier retains its source code and other confidential materials. However, the buyer may be concerned that this leaves it at the mercy of the supplier in the event that the supplier goes out of business or otherwise fails to maintain the software. In such cases the buyer can request that its licence includes source code. This may be possible with bespoke work in which the intellectual property rights under a contract term will vest in the buyer.

In other cases though the supplier is likely to object to handing over source code. Specifying in the contract that the source code will be handed over if the supplier goes into liquidation or analogous events occur will not work. The *Insolvency Act 1986* gives the liquidator the rights to disclaim onerous contracts such as this. Therefore, the practice of lodging the software's source code with an independent body such as the National Computing Centre Ltd (NCC) has grown. This removes or reduces the risk that the liquidator of the supplier could prevent the source code being handed over on a liquidation because the code is with a third party and therefore there is much less a liquidator could do to prevent the handover.

Details of the NCC can be found at http://www.ncc.co.uk and copies of their various escrow contracts can be downloaded in PDF format.

They will also send copies of their contracts on disk on request (tel: 0161 242 2430). Some banks offer similar services.

Rights to Repair – the Software Directive   [5.13]

An alternative is to give the user a right to maintain the software itself. Indeed, the EU *Software Directive 91/250 (OJ 1991 L122 (17 May 1991))* gives a right to repair to all licensees unless the contract prohibits it. Most contracts do prohibit it but if, for example, there were no written contract, then the user would be entitled to effect the repair without requiring any consent. The right to repair does not bring with it a right to a license of the source code of the software which may be needed to effect the repair. Nor does the limited decompilation right in the Directive help because it does not apply to allow users to repair software.

Forced Licences of Intellectual Property Rights and Competition Law   [5.14]

There is no right to demand source code to repair the software unless, in very limited circumstances at general law, a refusal to repair amounts to an abuse of a dominant position contrary to *Article 82* of the *EC Treaty* or the Chapter II prohibition in the UK of the *Competition Act 1998* (in force from 1 March 2000). A refusal to license copyright will only breach UK or EU competition law where a business is in a dominant position (normally having at least 40% of a market) and where the refusal prevents a new product emerging for which there is consumer demand (as in the *RTE* case [*1995*] *IECR 743*) or in the example given in the *Volvo v Veng* [*1988*] *ECR 6211* decision a car manufacturer refuses to produce spare parts for its vehicles, refuses to license third party repairers and there are still consumers driving the cars who need spares. There is no general obligation to license intellectual property rights to third parties. Some statutes such as legislation on patents will provide that if the invention is not worked on over an extensive period, then a compulsory licence may be available but these are exceptional cases.

In most cases a supplier can control the repair of its own software and cannot be forced to license others.

Year 2000 – Millennium Problems [5.15]

Where software has malfunctioned because of a dating problem such as 1 January 2000, 29 February 2000 or 9 September 1999 then this may affect the operation of a website as much as any other product run by software or chips in which a date is used. There may be a breach of contract in such cases, depending on the contract terms, or the software may not have been of satisfactory quality or fit for its purpose contrary to the implied terms for contracts for the sale of goods under the *Sale of Goods Act 1979*, (though it is by no means decided law that software is goods at all for these purposes). Often the contract will exclude those implied terms but some such exclusions are void in standard form business contracts under the *Unfair Contract Terms Act 1977* if they are unreasonable. This is not always the case so individual legal advice should be sought. Sometimes statutory limitation periods will have run out in any event under the *Limitation Act 1980* before the date change occurs.

Further Information [5.16]

Examples of software contracts can be found in Butterworth's Encyclopedia of Forms and Precedents which is also available on CD Rom.

Most computer lawyers are able to provide customised contracts in this field or provide advice on web design and other contracts such as the author's firm (essingleton@link.org, tel: 020 8866 1934). Details of expert computer lawyers can be found in Chambers & Partners' Annual Directory of the Legal Profession – further details at http://www.chambersandpartners.com. At the site a search of individual solicitors' names and firm names can also be done.

The Sprecher Grier Halberstam web contracts referred to in **Appendix 2** can be purchased by calling 020 7544 5555, or E-mail: law@weblaw.co.uk.

Source code escrow arrangements – see the National Computing Centre's website at: http://www.ncc.co.uk where the various NCC contracts can be viewed and downloaded in PDF format. Tel: 0161 242 2430. Fax: 0161 242 2275.

The Government's Action 2000 body provides basic information on Y2K issues – see http://www.bug2000.gov.uk.

A web page with links to many others on legal Y2K matters is at:
http://www.cix.co.uk/~parkside/y2kweb/y2klegal.htm.

A very full summary of US legal cases to date is at: http://
www.2000law.com.

6 – Internet Shopping

'The Government's intention is to ensure that, as far as possible, the law is technology neutral in its application, providing the same legal environment on-line as off'.

(Building Confidence in Electronic Commerce – March 1999
Consultation)

Executive Summary   [6.1]

- Contracts can easily be formed via the internet under English law.
- Significant savings in intermediary/distributor costs can be made.
- Basic contract law precautions should be taken.
- Contract terms and conditions for internet shopping should be set up.
- Contracts with consumers will be subject to special legal rules.
- Written terms of business are essential and should state which country's laws apply to the contract.

The internet is uniquely placed to sell goods direct to consumers. Internet shopping is changing the face of retail in the UK. Demand for storage depots from which goods are shipped is altering demand for commercial property and margins are being squeezed for many traditional retailers. Consumers are given the power to shop for goods internationally with easy methods of price comparison without necessitating a trip round the shops. Environmental benefits may also flow ultimately from a decline in road transport.

This Chapter looks at the legal issues relating to the formation of contracts over the internet and, in particular, arising from internet shopping. Technical and marketing advice should be sought from professionals expert in those fields. Contracts concerning design of the web page were considered in **Chapters 3: COPYRIGHT AND DATABASE RIGHT** and **5: TRANSACTING FOR THE SCHEME** and **Appendix 2**. Advertising laws are dealt with in **Chapter 7:**

149

INTERNET ADVERTISING. Payment issues which are central to internet shopping are covered in **Chapter 8: PAYMENT FOR GOODS AND SERVICES.**

Tangible Goods – Examples [6.2]

A good source of examples of how businesses have used the internet for retail of tangible goods is at http://www.doc.gov, from the Emergency Digital Economy II, June 1999, (US governmental document on the internet and E-commerce implications). This explains how such services are organised.

Intangible Goods – Examples [6.3]

The internet is ideally placed for the shipment of intangible goods electronically. These can include software, CDs, magazine articles, news broadcasts, stock, airline tickets and insurance policies. Pornography and stocks and shares are the two biggest uses made of the internet and both in their own ways are capable of delivery digitally. 90% of those using the internet use it to gather information. Examples are given in the US June 1999 report at http://www.doc.gov. The April 1998 similar such report gives a case study example of McGraw-Hill (publishers). The benefits that company has found through E-commerce have been:

● creating a unified brand;
● additional revenues; and
● lower distribution costs.

Other examples given include:

● The New York Times;
● Reuters;
● Dun & Bradstreet;
● the travel industry generally;
● American Airlines;
● The Sabre Group (electronic airlines reservations);
● retail banking (in the UK in 1999 the Prudential's 'Egg' branded savings products became available via the internet only to save costs and maintain high interest rates); and
● Wells Fargo (banking); and
● Quicken Insuremarket (insurance).

Whether the goods marketed are tangible or intangible, the law does not differ. However, the intangible goods are delivered electronically rather than shipped by mail as with the tangible goods and, therefore, fewer contracts are required. There will be no requirement to contract with a separate carrier, to lease commercial property or to pay warehouse storage costs. In addition, the contract with the buyer will be different where the intangible goods are purchased. In many cases it will comprise a licence of intellectual property rights in the software or information provided to the customer rather than the sale of any goods. Reference should be made to **Chapter 2: THE DOMAIN NAME AND TRADE MARKS** in relation to copyright issues which are examined there in detail.

Shareware and Freeware [6.4]

Some software is made available on the internet virtually, or entirely, free of charge. Where a nominal payment is suggested this is known as 'shareware'. Where it is entirely free it is called 'freeware'. Software is often marketed in this way as a means of ensuring wide acceptance of it and publicity for it. It has to be assumed that not all 'licensees' of the software will be honest and pay for shareware. Even where the software is supplied free of charge, it is sensible to have terms and conditions because licensors may still be legally liable if it malfunctions and they will want to protect their copyright and prevent further commercial exploitation of their material. Conditions such as those in **Appendix 4** can be adapted accordingly.

Importing Intellectual Property Protected

Products [6.5]

As copyright is a right which is generally recognised by most States and normally does not require registration (see **Chapter 3: COPYRIGHT AND DATABASE RIGHT** for exceptions to this), there are usually no jurisdictional problems with copyright being owned by different people in different countries. However, the position is not the same in regard to goods carrying registered trade marks as these can cause problems where the trade mark is owned by a different proprietor in a different State.

Consideration was given in **Chapter 2: THE DOMAIN NAME AND TRADE MARKS** to international exhaustion of rights and trade marks.

In the EU, trade mark owners can stop their own trade marked products being imported from outside the EEA under current law, although this may well change.

Those involved with selling goods on the internet may want to include a standard clause in their contract with customers, absolving them from liability for a breach of intellectual property rights.

Contract Law [6.6]

Everyone making an internet purchase is party to a contract, whether there are written terms of business or not. Internet transactions are better from a legal point of view than telephone ordering because it is easier to prove that a customer has been shown terms and conditions of business and the details of the order are better recorded. However, it becomes harder for a manufacturer to maintain price differences between distributors and end user customers.

Reference should be made to the 1999 UK Electronic Communications Bill and the EU draft *Electronic Commerce* and *Electronic Signatures Directives* of the European Commission. In particular the EU measures propose acceptance of electronic signatures and formation of contracts by E-mail via the internet.

Appendix 7 reproduces the UNCITRAL Model Law on Electronic Commerce which similarly allows for contracts formed electronically. Singapore was the first country to enact this as part of its national law.

Also of interest are US initiatives. In the United States, every state government has adopted the Uniform Commercial Code (UCC), a codification of substantial portions of commercial law. The National Conference of Commissioners of Uniform State Law (NCCUSL) and the American Law Institute, domestic sponsors of the UCC, already are working to adapt the UCC to cover E-commerce issues. Private sector organisations, including the American Bar Association (ABA) along with other interest groups, are participants in this process. Work is also ongoing on a proposed electronic contracting and records act for transactions not covered by the UCC. The ABA's ethics Opinion concerning E-mail is in **Appendix 9**.

All these measures will not be summarised here and reference can be made instead to the appropriate Appendices. The important points for those involved forming electronic contracts are to ensure that:

> ✓   there are written terms of business;
> ✓   the terms are drawn to the attention of the customer;
> ✓   any terms proffered by the customer are rejected; and
> ✓   the terms specify which country's laws apply (e.g. the 'Excite' terms in **Appendix 3** apply the laws of the State of California).

Terms of Business Provided on Websites   [6.7]

At the 1999 Global Electronic Marketplace Conference in Washington, William Daley, the US Commerce Secretary struck out against lack of consumer protection on the internet. He said that recent studies had found that on sites selling goods on-line, only:

- 9% provide for cancellation terms;
- 26% have refund policies;
- 38% disclose the applicable currency;
- 29% of US websites showed the country of origin explicitly compared with 79% of other States; and
- 21% of US websites had geographic restriction on sales.

This shows that even the most basic of legal issues are being omitted.

Although **Appendix 3** contains some examples of a variety of different terms and conditions for the sale of goods or services over the internet or for use on a website, readers are advised to visit many websites to draw ideas from businesses closest to theirs. All such documents are protected by copyright and must not be copied without consent of the rights owner, which in many cases will not be the business concerned but the law firm which provided them. A particularly good example is that of the computer company Dell at http://www.dell.com.

English Laws Summary   [6.8]

Goods sold on-line are as much protected by English legislation as any other. The *Sale of Goods Act 1979* will imply conditions into contracts for the sale of goods such as that the goods will be of satisfactory quality and fit for their purpose. However, the supplier is free to include in written terms of business which a buyer should click to accept on screen, that these terms are excluded.

It should be noted that such exclusions are sometimes held to be invalid. This will be the case where the terms exclude liability for death or personal injury and also where the term is unreasonable (for standard form business contracts) or unfair for contracts with consumers. The legislation is contained in the *Unfair Contract Terms Act 1977* and the *Unfair Terms in Consumer Contracts Regulations 1999* respectively.

There are many contract law textbooks which address the terms implied by law and exclusion of liability in detail. Those selling on-line require legal advice on their written terms and conditions of business as much as any other trader. Those selling to consumers need to ensure that any additional guarantee offered with the goods does not affect the consumer's statutory rights, for example sometimes a so-called guarantee is so limited as to amount to a restriction of liability.

Traders will also need to ensure they comply with all mail order legislation and should take specialist advice on which statutes apply to their particular industry. Many industry sectors have large quantities of sectorally specific legislation which applies to them, e.g. the toy, food and pharmaceutical industries.

The terms and conditions for shopping on-line will not be very different from those for any other sale by mail order. This will include terms about the returns policy, how payment is made and when goods are shipped to the customer. Rights to cancel may also be given.

When is a Contract Made [6.9]

English law provides that a contract is made when an offer has been accepted, for which there is consideration (normally payment) and there must also be an intention to create legal relations. This simple common law formula means that contracts are often formed verbally. This is not the case in all Member States, nor other countries of the world, where the internet shopper may be located.

The EU's draft *Electronic Commerce Directive* states that:

> 'Article 11 – Moment at which the contract is concluded
>
> 1.   Member States shall lay down in their legislation that, save as otherwise agreed by professional parties and in the case where the recipient is required to express his

consent to accept a service provider's offer by using technological means, such as clicking on an icon, the following principles apply:

○   the contract is concluded when the recipient of the service:

○   receives from the service provider, by electronic means, an acknowledgement of receipt of the recipient's acceptance; and

○   confirms receipt of the acknowledgement of receipt;

○   the acknowledgement of receipt is deemed to be received and the confirmation is deemed to have been given when the parties for whom they are destined are able to access them;

○   the acknowledgement of receipt by the service provider and the confirmation of the service recipient must be sent as quickly as possible.

2.   Member States shall lay down in their legislation that, save as otherwise agreed by professional parties, the service provider must make available to the recipient of the service appropriate means allowing him to identify and correct handling errors'.

These provisions may be altered before enactment. The Commission wants to ensure that all Member States have the same rules so that no customer within the EU is subject to different regimes.

Minors [6.10]

Problems can be caused by the anonymous customer. A child of 10 could place an order for alcohol. Whereas with a telephone order most businesses can detect a child trying to use a parent's credit card, they cannot do so by E-mail. However, there are other circumstances when age cannot be detected (e.g. where an order is placed by typed fax).

The minors can avoid all contracts under English law except those for necessities such as food or certain contracts for apprenticeships – *Minors Contracts Act 1987*. If the child is paying with a credit card, effectively paying in advance, then the seller may not mind what age the individual is and whether the contract can be avoided or not because it has received payment. However, if the goods may not lawfully be sold to persons under a particular age (such as tobacco products and alcohol) then the website should at least impose a requirement that the individual be over a particular age. Whereas in a shop, workers can be trained to check for age where a child tries to buy such a product, this cannot be done by E-mail.

Section 3 of the *Minors Contracts Act 1987* provides that a court can, where it is just and equitable to do so, require a minor to transfer to the other contracting party any property which the minor acquired under the contract which is voidable because of the minor's age.

Liability of Parents [6.11]

A parent is not liable to pay the debts incurred by a child, even for necessities, any more than a stranger would be. However, where the parent has given the child access to his/her credit card, then the position may be different in that the parent may have authorised the child to make the purchase and therefore be liable.

Undesired Purchases [6.12]

Some businesses are unhappy about selling their goods to their competitors. Others may wish to refuse orders from particular customers or dealers (distributors are discussed below at **6.13**). The general legal position is that any seller is entitled to sell to whomsoever it wishes. Only where there is a contract for long-term supply which obliges one party to sell to another, or where the seller is in a dominant position and it abuses that position under *Article 82* of the *EC Treaty* in certain cases of refusal to supply (or Chapter II of the *Competition Act 1998* in the UK from 1 March 2000 when it comes into force) will the law be broken.

It is therefore sensible for all internet sellers to include in their standard conditions a right to refuse any order. It should be made clear that their terms or the advertisements on the site are a mere invitation to treat and any order is an offer by the customer which can either be accepted or rejected by the supplier. By those means the supplier can, to a limited extent, control those to whom it supplies goods.

If a check on the potential customer will be made after the customer has placed the order, then it should be made clear at what point the contract is made and the offer accepted. If this is to be later than the customer sending their card details then the contract should say so, using words such as:

'Once we have your order we shall check it is acceptable and then ship the goods. No contract is made between us until we have undertaken such checks and we reserve the right to reject any order entirely at our discretion'.

Exclusive Distribution Agreements [6.13]

Some suppliers will have an exclusive distributor in particular countries of the world. Such exclusive distribution agreements are permitted in the EU under *Regulation 1983/83* and will also be under the proposed replacement regulation on vertical restraints under *Article 81* of the *EC Treaty*, provided certain conditions are met. Under EU competition law, any exclusive distribution agreement must not restrict the distributor from responding to passive sales requests. A restriction on the distributor advertising outside its territory or setting up a distribution depot there, is allowed in the EU. Such a restriction would prevent the distributor advertising over the internet. A compromise may be to allow the distributor to engage in internet advertising but to specify on the website that orders are not accepted from particular territories.

The problem with doing this is that it may compartmentalise the EU market and indeed other markets around the world, and infringe competition law. The 1999 unpublished draft vertical restraints guidelines of the European Commission treat internet advertising as 'passive selling', rather than active marketing so a dealer with a website is not treated as soliciting sales outside its territory.

The internet is likely to break down national boundaries and make it increasingly hard for suppliers to divide markets and protect geographical areas for distributors. Often customers decide they want to purchase centrally or even internationally. This leaves suppliers with vestiges of exclusive distribution or agency networks and a customer base which is not prepared to pay the costs of the margin of all the distributors and sub-distributors down the distribution chain. However, the manufacturer is limited by contract from removing such a network, at least until such contracts come up for renewal.

Agency Agreements and Central Buying [6.14]

The position is even worse in the EU where agents are used rather than distributors. An agent finds customers for the supplier but never owns the goods concerned, whereas a distributor buys goods and then resells them. Where a supplier wishes to terminate the contracts of exclusive distributors because internet and centralised purchasing has made them an anachronism, the supplier for distributors simply has to give whatever notice period is provided for termination of the agreement in the contract. In some countries (e.g. Belgium) compensation must also be paid.

However, the position for agents is more expensive and complicated. The EU *Agency Directive (86/653)* provides that exclusive agents are entitled to compensation (or an indemnity) where the contract is terminated in such cases, except where the agent is in substantial breach of contract sufficient to justify immediate termination. Information on such compensation can be found in *Commercial Agency Agreements* (Butterworths 1998). The *Agency Directive* can be accessed from the European Commission's website at http://europa.eu.int.

Article 7.2 of the *Agency Directive* provides that an agent is entitled to commission on all orders from his territory. Member States can determine whether this is only from areas where the agent has exclusive rights or not. In the UK it only applies under the *Commercial Agents (Council Directive) Regulations 1993 (SI 1993/3053)* where the agent has an exclusive territory – *Regulation 7(2)*. The Regulations apply in Great Britain and there is a similar set for Northern Ireland. They were amended in 1998 to cover agents appointed under the law in Great Britain under contracts to carry out duties in other Member States. The obligation to pay commission applies both where the agent is appointed to an exclusive geographical territory and to an exclusive group of customers.

Changing Existing Arrangements [6.15]

Anyone proposing to alter or terminate their agency or distribution agreements to allow for internet shopping and centralised buying direct by consumers or large retailers, will need to examine the legal position carefully. The cost of any statutory compensation payable, particularly to agents, will need to be factored into any accounts prepared.

It may not be necessary to alter existing agreements. They may allow for supplies by the principal or manufacturer directly to customers in the territory – i.e. a sole agency or distribution arrangement, rather than an exclusive one or the agent or distributor may be non-exclusive in any event. Many such agreements provide for less or no commission for agents where the customer deals direct or allow the contract to be altered in such circumstances.

In other cases, the distributor or agent may agree a variation in return for some compensation payment or additional territory. There may be a role for a local distributor in undertaking warranty work for defective products and increased sales through internet selling to those in the territory that may infact increase the distributor's profits.

Clauses for New Contracts   [6.16]

Where new agency and distribution agreements are entered into, businesses should anticipate possible future internet shopping by adding a clause such as:

> 'We [the supplier] reserve the right to make direct sales into your territory in response to an express request from a customer in the territory, where the sales are to groups engaged in Centralised Buying [define elsewhere] and where customers from our website place orders direct with us.'

For agency contracts also add:

> 'In such cases you shall not be entitled to commission on such orders.'

Agents or dealers however may want a clause such as:

> 'Where you or another of your distributors/agents make a direct sale in our territory you shall notify us in writing and shall pay commission at the rate of [%] on such sale. Nothing in this Agreement shall prevent our making sales outside our territory and from operating an internet website to solicit sales as we see fit.'

E-mails and Websites – Information to be Provided [6.17]

What information should go on an E-mail sent by a business? This is one of the most basic questions and yet so many businesses differ in their practices. The words for disclaimers and copyright notices on websites were considered in **Chapter 2: THE DOMAIN NAME AND TRADE MARKS** and examples are given in **Appendix 4**.

Companies Act 1985 [6.18]

Section 349 of the *Companies Act 1985* requires that a company must give its name in legible characters in:

> 'all business letters of the company . . . in all its notices and other official publications . . . orders for money or goods purporting to be signed on behalf of the company . . . all its . . . invoices, receipts and letters of credit'.

If a company fails to do this, it can be liable to a fine. Individual officers can also be fined if they authorise documents without this information on them.

Section 351 provides that all 'business letters and order forms' of the company must state:

(a) place of registration and registered number – e.g. registered in England Company No. 123456;
(b) address of its registered office – e.g. 'registered office 123 New Town St, Smith Town';
(c) if it is an investment company, the fact that this is the case; and
(d) if it is exempt from having to use the word 'limited', the fact that this is the case.

Business Names Act 1985 [6.19]

The *Business Names Act 1985* applies not just to companies but also to any other business. There is no longer any register of businesses or business names in the UK which are not limited companies and to ensure the public know with whom they are dealing, a business is not entitled just to use its trading name. *Section 4(1)* of the *Business Names*

Act 1985 provides that businesses must state in legible characters on all 'business letters, written orders for goods or services to be supplied to the business, invoices and receipts issued in the course of the business and written demands for payment of debts arising in the course of the business':

(i)   names of all partners (if it is a partnership) – there are exceptions for partnerships with more than 20 partners (like many solicitors and accountancy firms);

(ii)   name of individual trader – thus 'ABC Drains' cannot just appear. The notepaper has to show 'ABC Drains' and somewhere on the paper 'Mrs JH Smith' if she trades under that name;

(iii)   in the case of a company its corporate name; and

(iv)   an address for service in Great Britain for any document to be served on them (such as a court claim).

Type of Document [6.20]

The first practical point is that it looks more professional if a business shows its full name and contact details on an E-mail. How many readers have been frustrated by being unable to find a telephone number for someone with whom they regularly correspond by E-mail? Therefore, it can make good commercial sense to give customers and suppliers as many means of contacting the other party as possible. So it is wise, whatever the law says, to provide a name, address, telephone and fax number of the business and the full name including surname and job description of the person sending the E-mail. For internet shopping and most countries' consumer protection and other sales laws, it is essential to give the name of the seller and a postal address so whether or not an individual E-mail is a 'business letter' becomes academic.

Perhaps the sender of the communication does not want to give any address other than the E-mail address. The English courts may in such cases permit service of documents at the E-mail address in such cases, at the discretion of the judge.

There is no definition of a business letter, order or receipt in the *Business Names Act 1985*. However, in most cases an 'order' and 'receipt' are easily ascertainable. Customers completing an order form on a web site are placing their order and that order form should give the details at **6.19** above.

Suppliers who usually send a confirmatory email once an order has been placed will be issuing a form of receipt and should assume the *Business Names Act 1985* applies to that too and comply with its terms. 'Invoices' are not defined either but again it is clear what they are. Some web sites allow customers to send a cheque rather than give their card details on-line. They then wait for the cheque to clear before sending the goods or supplying the services. When a 'receipt' is issued, whether in paper form or electronically again the 1985 Act applies and the full corporate or business information must appear.

UK shoppers on US websites, however, may find their contract is governed by the laws of a US State (see **Chapter 11: JURISDICTION**). In that case the requirements of the legislation described above do not have to be followed by the supplier.

Business Letters [6.21]

The more difficult area is the standard business E-mail which is sent out many times a day. It is not an order, a receipt or an invoice. Both the *Companies Act 1985* and the *Business Names Act 1985* apply their rules to business letters. If E-mail is a business letter then the full details must be given. If it is not then they do not. That is subject to one important caveat. Some industries have special rules about notepaper. For example there may be a symbol which a business is authorised to use on notepaper like a Queen's Award for export or indicating membership of a professional body. Always check the rules for when and how such things may or may not be used and remember that using them on a website will mean they can be seen all over the world so other foreign rules may also apply.

The important issue then is whether an E-mail is a business letter. Lawyers cannot agree on this issue. On balance they are probably not. Most businesses appear to have taken this view. The writer's view is that until proven otherwise it is not, but for commercial reasons the more information given the better. It looks more professional to sign oneself J Smith, IT Manger, XYZ Plc than 'John'.

Tortious Liability [6.22]

Some companies operate Internet 'Portals' – gateways giving customers access to shopping services. One example is Excite which in 1999 combined with Intel to offer a new internet shopping service to provide consumers with information (http://www.excite.com). Products are listed according to independent assessment of the quality of the retailer, rather than any link up with Excite. Independent assessments are supplemented by user feedback. The legal position of those providing such portals should be considered carefully.

Even if customers do not have a contract with the business concerned, they may be relying on advice or information given to their detriment and thus may be able to sue in tort where there has been negligence or misrepresentation.

An example of a disclaimer used by Excite (June 1999) is given in **Appendix 4** along with other examples.

In addition, the provisions of the *Contracts (Rights of Third Parties) Act 1999* in England and Wales (when in force) will enable someone who is named in a contract as being able to enforce it, even though they are not a party to the contract or for whose benefit the contract is expressed will be able to enforce it.

Marketing Image and E-mails' Appearance [6.23]

All businesses should ensure they have a consistent policy in this area. From a marketing and corporate image standpoint it does not look professional if E-mails from different departments of a business look different from each other and contain different notices or information about the business' name and other corporate details. Some companies spend lots of money on their brochures, marketing and notepaper materials to ensure a consistent style and then most communications are by poorly presented E-mails.

In addition, many employees do not read E-mails properly and send them with spelling errors or grammatical mistakes which would never be permitted to appear on a letter. They must be exhorted to check E-mails carefully before despatch. Sometimes it can be wise to require E-mails to be checked by certain senior colleagues before despatch though this would remove an advantage for employees of using E-mail.

In other areas the nature of the communication will be such that sending ordinary unencrypted E-mails will not be acceptable and the sender has no right to assume it would be acceptable nor to use the 'default format' above which proceeds on the basis that if they do not hear from the other party they will assume what is proposed is acceptable.

Referring to Websites in E-mails [6.24]

It is also good marketing to refer in a general E-mail notice to the business' website with words such as:

> 'visit our website at www.abcd.com'.

This encourages use. Marketing literature should make a similar reference.

Best Practice – Internet Shopping [6.25]

The following is a checklist of items to include on an internet shopping website. Advice should also be sought from experts on technical requirements. Note that no list can be entirely comprehensive, particularly given the rapidly changing nature of internet shopping.

✓ Full corporate name of seller, registered office address, office address for correspondence, fax number, E-mail address and telephone number, in each case with countries' and international dialling codes.

✓ Copyright and trade mark notices.

✓ Privacy policy – personal data will be processed so it is good practice to include this.

✓ Terms and conditions of sale – the buyer should be able to read these easily and be obliged to click to indicate acceptance. This is better than having them available as an alternative and downloaded on request.

✓ Terms to cover rights to cancel (remembering that in many countries there are automatic rights to cancel and cooling off periods for contracts formed in this way).

✓ Details of a refund policy – e.g. some retailers of clothes allow refunds or replacements even where the goods are not defective. Some countries' mail order laws allow automatic refunds if goods are not shipped within 30 days etc.

✓ Payment details – which currency applies and whether prices can fluctuate.

✓ Full details of shipping charges which can of course make goods which appear cheap to purchase in the UK very expensive when shipping costs from, for example, the US are added.

✓ Details of any customs duties or sales taxes which must be paid.

✓ Where the goods originate from – this is a major area of law in itself. The UK origin marking laws at one stage were held in breach of EU law and had to be changed. Trade marks law and passing off can prevent goods being described as from one place when they are not. Where goods are packaged is also relevant.

✓ Any geographic restriction on sales of goods or services. Some suppliers will not sell to countries where they have exclusive distributors or selective distribution networks. However, such geographic restrictions can breach the EU and other national competition laws so caution should be exercised – see **6.13** above.

✓ Which countries' laws will apply to the contract and where disputes will be handled (see further **Chapter 11: JURISDICTION**).

Restricting Who can Buy [6.26]

The beauty, freedom and almost moral good of the internet is the barriers it breaks down even in the frivolous area of shopping. Barriers to entry and anti-competitive practices become much harder to enforce. However, some suppliers may not want to sell to purchasers in particular countries for whatever reason.

● **Trade blockades:** examples have included Iraq, North Korea, Cuba, Serbia – this can change at a moment's notice so the conditions should allow for this.

● **Unacceptable regimes:** the seller is not prepared to deal with that country even if to do so is lawful in the home state – most sellers can sell to whom they wish so there is no problem with this though it can be hard to enforce. A buyer may have a friend abroad purchase the goods and then import them himself.

● **Trade mark disputes:** there is a different owner of the seller's trade mark in the state of purchase which makes it unlawful to import the goods; here they could be imported if the trade mark were not on them. It may be possible to reach some sort of agreement with the other trade mark owner but always subject to competition laws which in the EU at least frown heavily on trade mark delimitation agreements which unnecessarily partition markets on geographical lines.

- **Different local standards:** the goods do not comply with local standards – in the EU standards are increasingly being harmonised but in some countries of the world a product may be permitted for sale but not in others. The contraceptive pill cannot largely be sold in Japan for example, or some countries may even prohibit import of goods from abroad when they are trying to encourage those in their nation to buy nationally made goods instead – sometimes Buy America or Buy British etc. arrangements can breach international trade laws

- **Differential pricing and dumping issues:** check prices charged carefully – charging different prices in different EU Member States for example may breach competition laws unless the differences can be accounted for by extra transport costs or different formulations or presentations of the products concerned; also the EU anti-dumping regulations will restrict the placing of goods at below their normal value on EU markets where imported from outside the EU – such dumping can result in anti-dumping duties being imposed.

Most businesses will say they cannot check whether their product can be sold in all countries of the world under all local laws and they are right. They can try to foist responsibility for importation on to the buyer by terms in the contract which may mitigate risks. Where it is clear a product cannot lawfully be sold in a particular State, such as the sale of alcohol to certain Middle East destinations, then the website should make that clear. Similarly, where information comes to the attention of the seller, such as special legislation which might exist for the sale of valves in Malaysia, then relevant notices can be placed on the website.

In these ways the risks arising from having to comply with many different laws can be minimised and the massive benefits of internet shopping can be realised.

Further Information [6.27]

US April 1998 Emerging Digital Economy I & II documents are at: http://www.doc.gov.

Secretariat for Electronic Commerce, US Department of Commerce, Washington DC 20230, tel: 00 1 202 482 8369.

The EU *Agency Directive* can be accessed via the European Commission's website at: http://europa.eu.int.

Further information on EU agency law is in *Commercial Agency Agreements* (Butterworths 1998) (ISBN 0 406 90503 7).

An example of comprehensive set of sale conditions is on the Dell website at: http://www.dell.com.

7 – Internet Advertising

'Advertising will allow the new interactive media to offer more affordable products and services to a wider, global audience. Some countries stringently restrict the language, amount, frequency, duration and type of tele-shopping and advertising spots used by advertisers. In principle, the United States does not favor such regulations. While recognizing legitimate cultural and social concerns, these concerns should not be invoked to justify unnecessarily burdensome regulation of the Internet.'

(Framework for Global Electronic Commerce, President Clinton and Vice President Al Gore, 1 July 1997.)

Executive Summary [7.1]

- Advertisements and direct marketing are subject to many different sets of regulations in the UK alone.
- Following certain basic principles in ensuring advertising is accurate and non-controversial can avoid most legal problems.
- The website advertising will be seen all round the world so allowance for national sensibilities and cultural differences should be made.
- Consider national and international legislation and advertising codes as well as laws relating to direct selling and mail order.
- Distance selling legislation is well developed at EU level.
- Ensure contracts with advertising agents address legal responsibility and indemnities for non-compliance with advertising laws.
- Ensure web pages are kept up-to-date.

Advertising over the internet enables many more customers to be reached than any other means of advertising. However, this also means the web page advertising material can be read in all countries of the world, except for those where there is no access to the internet or its access is blocked to citizens for political reasons. Compliance with local advertising laws can be impossible to achieve on a worldwide basis.

This Chapter looks at the principal advertising legal issues which arise.

Web Marketing Checklist [7.2]

A business must first ensure that its website is accessible and that potential customers are aware of its existence. The following checklist will help to achieve this.

✓ Is the website address the domain name a potential client might search for if they did not have the business' accurate address or have rather obscure initials been chosen which bear little relationship to the corporate name or the products of the business concerned? See further **Chapter 2: THE DOMAIN NAME AND TRADE MARKS**.

✓ Does the website address appear on all marketing materials of the business such as brochures, leaflets, advertising in newspapers and magazines, flyers, at the bottom of E-mails and the like?

✓ Does the website offer something to those visiting it other than boring marketing information about the business? If there are details of latest product developments etc. it is more likely to attract visitors.

✓ Is the website regularly updated? If so it is more likely to be visited. Does it say when the last update was?

✓ How is the site promoted? Information on promotion is at http://www.searchenginewatch.com. Registering with search engines can be very time consuming but can lead to results.

✓ Consider registering a different spelling of key words – one example might be a UK business with 'defence' in its name which would register as 'defense' so as to pick up US customers who would be likely to type in the US spelling of the word. A UK solicitor might go for attorney or lawyer as the word 'solicitor' is not connected with law in the US.

✓ How is the performance of the site monitored? It can be automatically monitored by software such as that at http://www.webposition.com or http://www.didit.com. This will help to check how successful it has been.

✓ Has any research been done on internet buying in the sector concerned before significant sums are spent on a website? Research on internet buying is at http://www.nua.ie and http://www.useit.com.

Statutory Provisions [7.3]

There are a number of statutory provisions which businesses advertising over the internet should consider.

Trade Mark Law [7.4]

Marketing goods under a trade mark in any State normally requires permission from the owner of the trade mark in that State. Therefore, if there are different trade mark owners in different States then, ideally, agreement should be reached over which owners can use the mark and in what manner on the internet.

Secondly, importing the goods, whether sold over an internet website or not, requires a licence from the trade mark owner in the State of import.

Thirdly, using a competitor's trade mark on a web page, such as one which compares electricity prices between providers or any other of the number of websites which have proliferated providing price comparisons, is allowed under the EU *Trade Marks Directive* and the *Trade Marks Act 1996* which implemented it in the UK, as long as the use of the competitor's or other business' trade mark does not take unfair advantage of the mark and is in accordance with honest practices in commercial matters. Misrepresenting one business' products on the website so that an unfair comparison is in fact made would breach trade mark law. Comparative advertising is addressed in **Chapter 2: THE DOMAIN NAME AND TRADE MARKS**.

Where there is no registered trade mark then there may still be a risk of passing off (see **2.15** above).

The law relating to hypertext links is considered at **3.52** above.

Trade Descriptions Act 1968 [7.5]

In the UK, the *Trade Descriptions Act 1968* makes it an offence to apply a false trade description to goods. For example, advertising a nylon jumper on a website as 'wool' would breach this statute and be a criminal matter.

Control of Misleading Advertisements Regulations
1998 [7.6]

The *Control of Misleading Advertisements Regulations 1998 (SI 1988/915)* applies to advertisements. These are any form of representation which is made in connection with a trade, business, craft or profession in order to promote the supply or transfer of goods or services, immovable property, rights or obligations.

This clearly covers internet advertising. An advertisement will be misleading if it in any way (including its presentation) deceives or is likely to deceive the persons to whom it is addressed or whom it reaches and if, by reason of its deceptive nature, it is likely to affect their economic behaviour or for those reasons injures a competitor of the person whose interest the advertisement seeks to protect. The rules apply in Scotland too. The Director General of Fair Trading is given powers under *Regulation 9* to investigate misleading advertisements.

Special Regime for Financial Services Advertising [7.7]

The regulations on misleading advertisements described above do not, however, apply to financial services advertising. After pornography, sale of securities is the biggest use made of the internet so this is a crucial exclusion. However, this does not mean that such advertisements are excluded in the financial services sector. Instead, special rules apply in all manner of areas from requirements to notify buyers that 'the value of shares can go down as well as up' to the means of representing the Annual Percentage Rate (APR) on advertisements, from statements about regulation to the whole of the law on consumer credit. Those areas are not addressed in this book. Finally mention must be made in that context of the proposed 1999 *Distance Selling of Financial Services Directive* details of which are on the EU website at: http://www.europa.eu.int. This is still in draft form.

Section 3 of the *Financial Services Act 1986* prohibits anyone from engaging in the provision of investment business in the UK unless authorised or exempt.

Copyright [7.8]

Any material used on an internet website must be cleared for copyright purposes and should not infringe the rights of a third person. Often individuals will license copyright for a paper publication but not for future use. Therefore, when it is proposed that written materials such as articles or drawings for which a business has a general licence will be included on a website, the original licence agreements must be checked carefully to ascertain whether sufficient clearance was obtained in the first place. If not, then fresh licences must be obtained from the licensors or indeed they may refuse at any price to license their rights for this purpose. Going ahead and using the material without a licence would be a breach of the *Copyright, Designs and Patents Act 1988*. (See further **Chapter 3: COPYRIGHT AND DATABASE RIGHT**.)

Contempt [7.9]

Occasionally, publication of material on the internet will be contempt of court for which the English courts have powers to fine offenders or even jail them. This tends to be where ex-spies propose to put secrets on the internet where the Government has already obtained an injunction against disclosure. Where a trial is going on, there are strict rules about what may be reported on the internet, particularly in case jurors in a criminal case are influenced by the material before they reach their verdict.

Sale of Goods Act 1979 [7.10]

Where goods are sold by description (as are all goods sold over the internet), there is an implied term that the goods will correspond with that description. Normally standard terms of business will exclude this implied condition though not all such attempts at excluding it are regarded as reasonable under *the Unfair Contract Terms Act 1977* or, for consumer contracts only, the *Unfair Terms in Consumer Contracts Regulations 1999*. If they are unreasonable (or in a consumer contract unfair) they are void. Many internet shopping conditions contain additional rights to return goods in any event, some of which go further than the *Sale of Goods Act 1979* requires.

Pricing [7.11]

Pricing can be a tricky area with internet advertising. Sometimes prices vary and most websites where orders can be placed make it clear that prices can be altered. The *Unfair Terms in Consumer Contracts Regulations 1999* restricts some of the clauses which can be included about prices and deposits received for contracts with consumers.

The *Consumer Protection Act 1987*, which also implements the EU *Product Liability Directive* in the UK, contains provisions which prohibit misleading prices being applied to goods. On 30 May 1999 the *Product Liability Directive* was amended to cover agricultural products too (*OJ 1999 4 June 1999 L141/20, Directive 1999/34*). The 1987 Act prohibits any attempt to exclude or limit liability for death and personal injury as does unfair terms law. This is why exclusion clauses should be drafted carefully by a lawyer to ensure a special exception for that liability is included. If not, the entire clause can be void. Advertisements on the internet should make all transport costs clear so that a consumer can compare 'like with like'. VAT should also be clearly stated, as well as other additional costs which the consumer will be required to pay.

Finally, a manufacturer whose dealers sell products in different States at different prices should be careful for commercial reasons about setting out details of prices on websites as this can confuse customers. Reference should be made to **Chapter 6: INTERNET SHOPPING** which examines alterations to existing agency and distribution agreements to reflect internet selling.

Checklist for Pricing [7.12]

✓ Is the price stated for the item?
✓ Is the packaging cost (if any) stated?
✓ Is any VAT stated?
✓ Are any customs duties stated?
✓ Are the prices liable to change and if so when?
✓ Is it clear to what goods the price relates?
✓ Are the prices the same to everyone buying in all countries?
✓ Can prices rise if VAT or other taxes rise before an order is placed and/or after an order is placed?
✓ Are servicing, insurance or guarantee costs included?

Codes of Advertising Practice, ITC and

OFTEL [7.13]

Various regulatory bodies have laid claim to the internet. If it were a radio broadcast then the Radio Authority has charge. Television broadcasts are handled by the Independent Television Commission under the *Broadcasting Act 1990*. The Office of Telecommunications (OFTEL) regulates telecommunications but does not currently regulate the internet as such. There have been a few public 'spats' between OFTEL and the ITC on which should exercise control over the medium of the internet and the legal position is not entirely clear.

The British Codes of Advertising and Sales Promotion are a voluntary system which covers most magazine and newspaper advertising in the UK. Their website is at http://www.asa.org.uk. The codes require that advertising be decent honest and truthful. Those who breach the codes face being banned from advertising in many publications. The ASA regularly asks those producing offensive advertisements to remove them.

The ASA takes the view that its codes will apply to internet advertising even though they do not say so explicitly. New versions of the codes are due later in 1999 so the latest position should always be checked.

In 1999 progress was made on the development of internet selling codes of practice. 'Which?' magazine and the Consumers' Association launched a kitemark scheme 'web trader' for web sites which comply with a strict code of practice. In a survey they had found that of 150 items ordered on line 11% did not arrive at all even though payment was charged by credit card. Many sites contained no details of shipping costs or terms of business.

In addition the consultation paper issued with the Electronic Communications Bill proposes a similar voluntary scheme.

Special Products [7.14]

Always check carefully whether any special legislation for particular industry sectors applies for the marketing of the products concerned. For example, in 1999 advertising laws for tobacco products in the UK were strengthened.

Example: BMJ and Medical Websites [7.15]

In June 1999, the UK Medicines Control Agency agreed to reverse its ruling that allowed medical journals to carry advertising for prescription drugs on open websites. Such advertising is allowed in journals such as the British Medical Journal (BMJ) (which is published on the internet at http://www.bmj.com) which are normally only read by doctors. The Consumers' Association lobbied against such advertising being permitted. However, the BMJ maintained that US journals can carry such advertising in any event and patients would just be left with access to lower quality US journals which could advertise the products without restriction and not have any access to advertising in one of the world's top four general medical journals.

This is a good example of special advertising regimes being in place for particular products, in this case drugs only obtainable on prescription.

Foreign laws [7.16]

Compliance must also be achieved with foreign legislation in similar legal areas. In France, for example, it is not lawful to resell goods at less than the price paid for them. Local legal advice should be taken. Some Scandinavian countries do not permit certain advertising of children's toys. In some countries alcohol advertising is banned. Adverts for pork sausages may be offensive in some States. Lingerie advertisements could cause problems abroad. Even broadcast of fundamentalist Christian views of homosexuality in 1999 caused massive public outcry in the UK and apparently led to the cancellation of a contract involving Royal Bank of Scotland.

Checklist for Ad Vetting [7.17]

The list below highlights some key areas.

> ✓ Has an advertising agency been used which purports to check legal matters? Does the contract with them deal with this?
>
> ✓ Are all statements on the website accurate – keep this under review
>
> ✓ Who will be responsible for keeping the website up-to-date?

✓ How regularly will the website be updated?

✓ Is a disclaimer required?

✓ Is a privacy policy recommended?

✓ Have copyright and trade mark notices been given?

✓ Have full corporate details and addresses been provided?

✓ Will terms and conditions for use of the site be required if materials will be downloaded, etc?

✓ Are descriptions of goods on the site accurate, such that any implied conditions under the *Sale of Goods Act 1979* are satisfied?

✓ Are all prices accurate?

✓ Are there any special laws for the products concerned in relation to their marketing?

✓ Are some countries where the goods or services will be sold known for particularly tight restrictions on advertising?

✓ Might the website be offensive because it is pornographic, politically or religiously offensive, controversial, not environmentally sound or does not complying otherwise with the cultural and political norms of the day in any State?

✓ If any of the points above are unclear, err on the side of caution.

Advertising by Spamming [7.18]

Spamming is junk E-mail. The examples below from 1999 show how the law is being used in an attempt to prevent the practice.

BiblioTech [7.19]

A UK based E-mail service, BiblioTech, rejected attempts by US 'spammers' to settle a suit filed in the US. A settlement offer had been put to it which included compensation but one company in the US refused to be bound not to repeat the spamming and Bibliotech wanted those it sued to undertake not to engage in this activity again. The case therefore continued.

Virgin [7.20]

Virgin issued a writ against Adrian Paris, a Surrey businessman for damages for breach of contract and trespass, after he allegedly sent out 250,000 junk E-mails on behalf of Pro-Photo UK using a Virgin Net account. The case settled.

AOL [7.21]

In *America Online Inc v LCDM Inc (10 November 1998) (US District Court for the Eastern District of Virginia)* (see *Electronic Business Law April 1999 p15* which can be ordered through www.irseclipse.co.uk) the US internet service provider, America Online sued the defendants for sending a huge number of unsolicited E-mails advertising their pornographic website to AOL members. As many as 92 million messages at a rate of 300,000 per day may have been sent.

AOL won an injunction. AOL argued that there was dilution of its trade mark under US law – the E-mail messages contained AOL.COM in the heading – and also argued that there was trespass to chattels as its property was used without prior consent. Many members of AOL had assumed AOL had authorised the messages and the pornographic websites.

Statutes and Spamming [7.22]

The sending of E-mails is much more intrusive than advertising on the world wide web. The WWW allows the individual to access the site if they are interested in it. The E-mail is sent without their consent. The data protection implications of the internet are considered at **10.2** below. Unsolicited E-mails are not banned in the UK under either the *Telecommunications (Data Protection and Privacy) (Direct Marketing) Regulations 1998 (SI 1998/3170)* (nor the 1999 Regulations which will replace them) nor EU *Directive 97/66* on which they are based. The EU *Distance Selling Directive (97/7)* requires that Member States must make provision to allow individuals to register so as not to receive unsolicited E-mails.

The UK's Direct Marketing Association has proposals for an email preference scheme though this is not yet up and running – see http://www.dma.org.uk

Legal Compliance – Who is Responsible?   [7.23]

The laws described in this Chapter and those which apply in other States, normally impose liability on the business advertising in the State concerned. Where a breach occurs some of the statutes may result in fines levied on the businesses concerned. Some of these liabilities could be passed to another person by a contract term. For example, it has been common for years for a distribution contract to specify that the local distributor will be responsible for ensuring compliance with local laws and regulations.

> 'The Distributor undertakes at its own expense to comply with all local legal and regulatory requirements at the date of this Agreement and thereafter and inform the Supplier of these rules. The Distributor shall notify the Supplier, keep the Supplier fully informed of and comply with any changes in such requirements.'

The clause may go even further and provide:

> 'The distributor shall indemnify and hold the supplier harmless against all losses costs and liabilities arising from the Distributor's breach of this clause'.

The local distributor is often appointed because of its knowledge of local requirements. However where a business moves to centralised international selling from a website then so the local knowledge of laws and regulations can be lost. This expertise will need to be replaced.

In some cases the advertising agency can, by contract, be obliged to check the relevant legislative provisions and indemnify the seller. However, most agencies are not prepared to take on such responsibilities. As local laws differ so substantially legal advice in all major States should be sought and ideally in every State. Some lawyers are part of international networks which can provide assistance.

Different Websites in Different

States/Languages   [7.24]

Many businesses have websites available in different language versions. Other businesses have entirely different websites in different States, perhaps developed by their local subsidiaries. Others have one English (or other) language website only. Where there are locally different websites then difference in local laws can more easily be accommodated.

Where there is only one website then, in certain cases, it will be necessary to specify that the website is not intended for viewers in certain States if the material on the website breaches local laws. Even then such a disclaimer may not be sufficient to avoid prosecution in the State concerned. Conflict of law issues are addressed in **Chapter 11: JURISDICTION**.

Minimising Liability [7.25]

Words such as those below may help to reduce the risk of legal action.

> 1. The goods and services advertised on this website are supplied solely on our standard terms and conditions of sale and English law and jurisdiction apply.
> 2. The material on this website is designed to comply with English law. Our goods are primarily marketed to those countries from which we accept orders (see our terms and conditions [click] for further details).
> 3. You may be viewing this in a market in which we do not commonly sell our goods or services. We cannot be held responsible for non-compliance with any local advertising laws in relation to the material on this web page.
> 4. No reliance should be placed on information this website. We exclude all liability to the full extent allowed by English law for tortious or other liability arising from information on this website.

In practice such notices can be off putting for customers and in most cases will not affect the local law position a business should take legal advice before adding any such notice.

Legal Notices and Documents to Include on a Website – Checklist [7.26]

The following list is of the types of notices and contracts which a large business might have on its website.

General [7.27]

✓ Copyright notice.
✓ Site terms of use.
✓ Terms and conditions of sale.
✓ Warranties (or these can be part of the terms and conditions).

Privacy [7.28]

✓ Privacy statement.
✓ Store security statement.
✓ Encryption protection.
✓ Cookies (document telling the viewer what a cookie is – a piece of text asking permission to be placed on the user's computer's hard drive, whereupon if agreement is given the user's browser adds the text in a small file).

Further Information [7.29]

Extensive information on website promotion through search engines is at: http://www.searchenginewatch.com.

Software for monitoring performance of a website is at: http://www.webposition.com or http://www.didit.com.

Information on internet buying trends is at: http://www.nua.ie and http://www.useit.com.

Committee of Advertising Practice, 2 Torrington Place, London WC1E 7HW. Tel: 020 7580 555. http:/www.asa.org.uk.

The Office of Telecommunications (Oftel), tel: 020 7634 8700; http://www.oftel.gov.uk

8 – Payment for Goods and Services

'Market research has shown that many payers do not wish
their spending to be traceable – as it is, for example, when a
payment is made by credit card or through a bank account.
However, the question of whether complete anonymity is a
desirable feature of a payment mechanism is a vexed
political issue'

(Internet Law and Regulation, ed Graham JH Smith,
Bird & Bird)

Executive Summary [8.1]

- Orders placed electronically often require customers to place orders by credit card.
- Security measures must be in place to protect customer's information
- Most internet orders are settled by credit card or debit card.
- Contracts with credit card and other providers will need to be arranged before these means of payment can be accepted by sellers over the internet.
- The *Consumer Credit Act 1974* will provide some protection to consumers.

Where orders are placed electronically by customers they can be
permitted to pay by any means. Most suppliers however will want
payment to be by means of credit or debit card. Some are happy to
accept a cheque but obviously then wait for it to clear before shipping
the goods or services/software. As buyer and seller are more likely to be
geographically apart with internet sales, sellers need to be particularly
careful not to extend credit except to established trade customers, as
recovery of sums due is much harder where different jurisdictions are
concerned.

For the purchase of consumer goods or services over the internet, a
credit or debit card arrangement is generally preferable. The contract

183

should state what currency the payment is to be made in and which party, (supplier or buyer) takes the risk of currency fluctuations. Where cheques are permitted it should be stated in what currency and who pays for banking charges. Some businesses would require an international bankers' draft or money order in their local currency. However, in practice, it is credit and debit cards which predominantly are used.

The Euro [8.2]

The Euro can be a useful tool for doing business over the internet in that those countries within the system will all recognise and accept the Euro, enabling prices to be quoted for all those relevant States in one currency. The US company seeking to set up an internet selling site based in Europe might, for example, operate in Euros.

Consumer Credit Act 1974 [8.3]

Some protection for those using credit (and probably debit cards) is offered in the UK under the provisions of the *Consumer Credit Act 1974*. The Act provides that where the card is issued in the UK individual buyers, but not businesses, have protection against misrepresentations and breaches of contract. Claims can be made against the credit card company. This is very useful indeed if the supplier has gone out of business or cannot be tracked down.

A regulated agreement under the *Consumer Credit Act 1974* previously used to be one up to £15,000 in value but is now any credit agreement up to £25,000. *Section 75* provides the relevant protection. It provides for the card issuer to be jointly liable with the supplier for breaches of contract and tort. Therefore, if the customer finds that the supplier has gone out of business for example and the goods are not shipped to the buyer, then the customer has recourse against the credit card company. The UK Office of Fair Trading (OFT) is in charge of this area and believes that *section 75* covers orders of goods both abroad and in the UK by UK credit card holders. Information on *section 75* is at http://www.oft.gov.uk. However, many in the credit card industry take the view that *section 75* only applies to orders in the UK. At one time a voluntary agreement was in existence but this has lapsed. Now many of the businesses who were previously party to this agreement voluntarily do reimburse customers in such cases of purchases abroad but the legal position is unclear as to whether they are obliged to do so.

Anyone setting up a business on the internet and offering credit for the first time to customers is likely to need a licence from the OFT. Details of who will require a licence are on the OFT website at http://www.oft.gov.uk/html/about/credit.htm. About 18,000 licences are issued each year.

Many internet purchases will be under £50 and therefore *section 75* will not apply in any event. However, many providers under their website terms and conditions provide coverage for the first £50 – therefore the user is almost completely covered against loss. Those selling over the internet should be careful not to represent to UK customers that *section 75* will apply to purchases abroad, as the legal position is far from clear and the seller may be sued for misrepresenting the position to such customers who may have entered into transactions lulled into a false sense of security on such basis.

Security and Card Payments [8.4]

The principal issue for customers when paying for good/services on the internet is whether their card details will be kept confidential. Many of those selling goods or services on-line will therefore provide comfort to customers by telling them what policies are offered. An ordering guarantee or other document may be available for customers to read on the website to offer them an assurance and tell them what steps are taken to keep their details confidential. It might typically state that a secure server is used and what encryption methods are employed by the business with whom the buyer operates.

Customers can also rightfully be told that these means are more secure than the giving of a credit card number over the telephone. Indeed the seller need never hold the credit card number details if a third party does so. A provider such as NetBanx (http://www.netbanx/com) may be used by the seller. NetBanx has arrangements with all the major banks who will authorise card details within less than a minute or so. A provider such as this would accept payment in 116 currencies and settlement in 16 currencies (including the Euro) and provide 24 hour a day 365 days a year support. A merchant set up cost is paid as well as a transaction commission charge.

A system would operate by a link to the provider at the point of payment so the customer is directed to the secure payment system. The provider checks the details and confirms to the customer that they are accepted. The supplier then deals with the shipment of the goods.

Extra Guarantees [8.5]

Some sellers will offer their customers additional guarantees for using their credit cards on-line. For example, one business says:

> 'In the unlikely event that your bank or card issuer holds you liable for an unauthorised transaction on your credit or debit we will cover your liability up to a maximum of £50'.

Typically the guarantee would require the user to notify its card provider in the normal way if the card were used for an unauthorised purpose.

Children [8.6]

Parents will normally be liable where their children under the age of 18 take their credit card and use it for internet purchases. Therefore, parents should ensure cards are locked away or children can be trusted. Children are some of the fastest growing new users of the internet and increasingly purchases are directed at them and yet they do not in most cases have a legal means of paying for the goods/services concerned. By analogy, when children's television programmes or advertisements give details of premium rate telephone line numbers a warning is also issued telling the child to obtain permission first from the person who pays the bill, websites should ideally include warnings, particularly on sites appealing to children, about costs and who can place orders.

As was seen at **6.9** above, under English law contracts made by children other than for necessary goods such as food under the *Minors Contracts Act 1987* cannot be legally enforced against the child.

Words such as the following can usefully be added.

> 'We welcome younger customers and encourage them to have their parents or guardians buy products on their behalf. Unfortunately for legal reasons orders are not accepted from people under the age of 18 or, where older, who are 'minors' under their local law. By placing an order you make a representation that you are over such age. Where you place an order and are under that age you are in breach of contract and may otherwise breach the law.

> The holder of the credit or debit card which you use will be fully
> liable for all sums so charged.'

User Security Measures – Checklist [8.7]

Users of websites should take basic precautions before placing an
order.

✓   A secure site will often be called 'https' rather than 'http'.

✓   Check the site is a secure site. Does it display a key or
padlock symbol?

✓   Set browsers to maximum security.

✓   Do not use sites which do not show contact details.

✓   Check what the refund and returns policy is before ordering.

✓   Do not reveal any PIN numbers or passwords.

✓   Are there any rights to cancel after the contract is made? For
financial services the draft EU *Financial Services Distance
Contracts Directive* will include a 14 day cooling off period.

Many suppliers include on their website details of their security policy
or how transactions are encrypted. A good example is on the Dell site
at http://www.dell.com.

Standards [8.8]

Visa and Mastercard with Netscape have developed a Secure Electronic
Transaction Standard (SET) which provides for identification of the
parties and ensures that both parties can be sure they are communicating with each other. This can be used in conjunction with a Secure
Socket Layer Protocol (SSL). This is used to make a safe link between
the buyer and the seller. VISA's website, for example, includes details
on its secure shopping and electronic commerce at: http://www-
s2.visa.com/nt/ecomm/security/main.html.

SET uses digital certificates to verify users. VISA describes it as 'the
electronic equivalent of a consumer looking for a Visa decal in a
merchant's store window and the merchant checking the consumer's
signature on the back of a Visa card.' An animated demonstration of
how SET works is available via the VISA website.

Electronic Cash [8.9]

Several different alternatives to credit and debit card payments have been devised. The EFTPOS (electronic funds transfer at point of sale) system involves immediate on-line debiting of sums from consumers' accounts. Switch and other debit cards do not operate in that way. A company called Digicash has developed an E-cash system. The customer transfers real money into a bank account and it is then stored on a computer in an 'electronic wallet'. The seller has to check the customer has the funds before allowing the goods to be shipped. This may be a better method than using a credit card because all that is risked if security is breached is the money in the account and not the credit card number. Access to the credit card number may enable the fraudster to charge many other purchases to the card. Digicash has since filed for bankruptcy and other E-cash systems have not been particularly successful.

Other alternatives have included electronic bartering of services systems and the cybercoin system of Cybercash.

EU Draft Electronic Signatures Directive [8.10]

The EU proposal for an *Electronic Signatures Directive* (*OJ 1998 C325/5* and amendments at *OJ 1999 C104/49*) would provide for Member States to introduce, where they wish, voluntary accreditation schemes to enhance levels of certification service provision (*Article 3*). The draft Directive is on the internet at the website http://www.ispo.cec.be. It does not address payment systems as such. In particular it provides that Member States should ensure that electronic signatures have legal effect (*Article 5*). See further **4.38** above.

Offer Credit [8.11]

Some suppliers will be prepared to sell now and trust customers to send money or cheques later. Of course this is not normal practice, with most mail order suppliers. However, for certain products may be appropriate, perhaps where the trade is done between large businesses who can perform prior credit checks.

Those who do offer credit in this way, and they are very few, will need to ensure they employ credit control methods, charge interest on over due debts and otherwise ensure payment is received.

Further Information [8.12]

The US papers in this field include useful information at http://www.doc.gov.

Information on the *Consumer Credit Act 1974* is on the Office of Fair Trading website at: http://www.oft.gov.uk.

Details of the netBanx secure on line payment system are at http://www.netbanx/com.

An example of how a company has comprehensively described its payment security policy is on the Dell website at http://www.dell.com.

Details of VISA's secure electronic commerce is at: http://www-s2.visa.com/nt/ecomm/security/main.html and on SET at http://www-s2.visa.com/nt/ecomm/security/set.html.

The draft *Electronic Signatures Directive* is published in the EU's official journal at *OJ 1998 C325/5* and amendments at *OJ 1999 C104/49* and is on the internet at: http://www.ispo.cec.be.

9 – Employer Liability and Defamation

'The employer is vicariously liable for a wrongful act committed by an employee in the course of his employment. The employer is liable even if the act is done in an unauthorised way. But if the act is not one of a type which the employee was employed to carry out, then the employer is not liable. The distinction between these can be extremely fine. However, some parts of the boundary are clear. For instance if an employee is permitted to send E-mail on the employer's business, but is prohibited from sending any unlawful or defamatory matter, the employer will be vicariously liable for any copyright infringement or defamation.'

(Internet Law and Regulation, ed Graham Smith, p59)

Executive Summary [9.1]

- Employers should reduce the risks of employees breaching the law by use of the internet by education and employment policies.
- However the employer will be liable for copyright infringement and defamation in the employee's E-mails sent for work purposes.
- Policies for employees should also address illegal content such as child pornography and content which some employees may find objectionable such as adult pornography.
- **Appendix 6** contains examples of employment guidelines.

Employers are vicariously liable for the activities of their employees at work. This is as much the case with the internet and E-mail as in any other area of business life. The question in each case is whether the employee has been acting in the course of his employment. An employee can be so acting even if working at home or away on business, so the time of day or place at which the activity is done is not a deciding factor.

Acting in the Course of Employment [9.2]

The law on vicarious liability has developed over time through case law and is not contained in any statute. One test has been whether the employee was acting on a 'frolic of his own'. The test was examined in relation to competition law in a case from which analogies to the E-mail area can be drawn. Employees had been told not to breach the company's compliance policy which prohibited anti-competitive agreements in breach of the *Restrictive Trade Practices Act 1976*. The employees disobeyed the company's express instructions in this respect and the court proposed to fine the companies concerned.

The fines were to be for contempt of court because orders of the Restrictive Practices Court had been levied against the companies under the legislation before, breach of which was contempt. In *DGFT v Pioneer Concrete (UK) Ltd* ([*1995*] *Tr LR 355*, (HL)) the court held that the employers were liable. The employees attending secret meetings to fix prices for ready mixed concrete were wearing their company 'hats'. The agreements they made were to be agreements between their employer and the other companies involved. Therefore, the companies were liable even though the senior directors were unaware of what was happening and had prohibited such activity.

Checklist [9.3]

The following checklist will help establish whether an employee was acting in the course of his/her employment.

✓ Were employer computers or other equipment used?

✓ Was the employee sending a work-related E-mail such as to a business contact?

✓ Was the message or activity something to do with the employee's work?

✓ Was the employee acting in breach of business instructions?

✓ Could the employer have been said to have condoned or approved the activity?

✓ Was the employee acting on a 'frolic of his own' or doing the employer's business?

Areas of Liability [9.4]

In his/her use of the internet, the employee may engage in activities which can breach:

● copyright law;
● trade mark law;
● confidentiality;
● defamation;
● criminal laws (particularly relating to hacking and arising from spreading viruses); and
● many other laws (e.g. health and safety and competition law).

Strict Liability Offences [9.5]

Some offences are called offences of 'strict liability'. Limited companies can only act through their employees in any event, so clearly the activities of their employees can put the employer in breach of the law. Strict liability offences are offences without fault or intent. All the injured party has to show is that the goods, services concerned caused the loss. For example under the *Consumer Protection Act 1987* if a product is defective and causes personal injury, physical damage or death, then the manufacturer, supplier, importer into the EEA or person whose trade mark is on the product can all be sued and will be strictly liable for the loss.

Service Providers [9.6]

The Internet Service Provider (ISP) over whose network a defamatory message is sent, for example, may also in certain cases be liable. Liability of ISPs is considered in **9.13** below.

Employment Policies [9.7]

If there is a risk that an employer could be held liable for the activities of its employees (e.g. strict liability – see **9.5** above) then the employer should do all it can to ensure that employees do not breach the law in the first place. Education of employees is crucial. Many employers now set up internet policies (an example appears at **Appendix 6**) and ensure they are part of the employment contract of the employees concerned.

Infringement [9.8]

If an employee copies a document or software in breach of copyright at work for work purposes in most cases the employer will be in breach of the *Copyright, Designs and Patents Act 1988*. The position will be the same with trade marks under the *Trade Marks Act 1994*.

For example, an employer may be liable for breach of copyright where an employee:

● copies a contract for use at work without permission, even if the employee has breached internal guidelines in doing so; or

● uses pirated software at work which he has illegally copied at home where the employee is using the software for work purposes, but not if the employee is playing a pirated computer game in their lunch hour.

Steps to take Where Infringement Allegation is Made [9.9]

If an allegation of infringement is made against the employer the following steps should be taken.

✓ Take a full statement from all relevant employees before antagonising them with threats that they will lose their job.

✓ Take legal advice before replying.

✓ Make no admissions and reserve all legal rights.

✓ Find out as much about the other party and their agenda and financial status as possible early on, do company, internet and credit searches.

✓ If settlement discussions take place ensure they are stated to be 'without prejudice' and remember different legal rules will apply in different countries.

✓ Consider whether a threat is an offence – making threats of infringement of some intellectual property rights can be an offence in itself – the rules on this in relation to trade marks are examined in **Chapter 3: COPYRIGHT AND DATABASE RIGHT**.

✓ If there is any substance in the allegation stop use immediately to minimise losses for which the claimant could claim damages later.

✓ Keep all software and documents as they may be vital evidence later. Do not let employees destroy any evidence, including E-mails.

✓ Take the matter very seriously indeed. Copyright proceedings in the UK High Court will often cost over £50,000 in legal fees. Aim to settle quickly and well, in order to minimise the legal costs.

✓ Call insurers early on as they may take control of any claim. If this is not done insurance policies may be invalidated.

✓ For English court actions consider making a defendant's part 36 offer/payment under the *Civil Procedure Rules 1998* before the action commences, if some liability is clear.

✓ Open up channels of communication and offer mediation through bodies such as the Centre for Dispute Resolution (CEDR) in London rather than going to court. (CEDR E-mail: mediate@cedr.co.uk, tel: 020 7600 0500, fax: 020 7600 0501).

Pirated Software [9.10]

It is not unknown for a departing employee with a grudge against their employer to place pirated software on the employer's system and then call a body such as the Federation Against Software Theft (FAST) to report the matter, leaving the employer to sort the matter out. Often the employer will be liable in such cases.

The employer has a responsibility to check on a regular basis that pirated software is not used at work. Software to check for unlicensed software is available from bodies such as FAST for this purpose.

Contracts [9.11]

Employees bind their employer to contracts under the general provisions of employment and contract law and this is just as much the case with electronically formed contracts as any others. Indeed it will be easier for an employee to be held out as having necessary authority to make the contract by the employer if the employee is using E-mail. The recipient of the acceptance of the offer which forms the contract will have no way of telling from the dress or appearance of the sender that the sender would not have the authority which he/she purports to have, whereas if an office cleaner in work overalls armed with mop and bucket attempts to negotiate the next million pound computer deal, the buyer may in such an extreme case be held to have had effective notice that the employee did not have the necessary authority to bind the employer.

Employers with particular concerns in this area can state in their terms and conditions or in their notices sent to new or potential suppliers, who within their organisation has power to sign contracts so that the other person is put expressly on notice. Words such as the following could be used.

> 'Only directors have authority to bind the company to contracts and to sign contracts. All managers know this and you must not accept any variation of this policy. If you do it is at your own risk and you will have notice that the employee does not have authority for such contract. The contract will not be binding on us.'

Certain industries are more notorious than others for the inaccurate statements made by their employees. In some such as the photocopier industry stringent action has had to be taken to bring salesmen into line and ensure that inaccurate statements are not made which induce customers into contracting with the supplier.

Misrepresentations and Other Torts [9.12]

No matter what words are used to notify others of authority in relation to contractual matters, the business may find itself liable for fraudulent misrepresentations made by employees even though the business cannot be said to have sanctioned such statements. Such liability is in tort and cannot be excluded or limited by any contract term.

It is, however, possible to limit or exclude liability for negligent or innocent misrepresentations and most suppliers' standard computer and internet contracts will purport to do so. Sometimes such exclusions in standard form contracts or contracts with consumers are held to be unreasonable or unfair and therefore void under the *Unfair Contract Terms Act 1977* and *Unfair Terms in Consumer Contracts Regulations 1999*.

The contract will also state that prior representations are not part of the agreement and that the written terms are the entire agreement between the parties. Not all standard terms do these things so the checklist below should be used.

Checklist for Supplier for Checking Standard

Contracts [9.13]

> ✓ Does the contract exclude or limit liability in tort as well as for breach of contract?
>
> ✓ Does the contract in its exclusion clause name the torts of misrepresentation and negligence by name? It is better if it does as it will then be an express exclusions of liability which are more likely to be valid under unfair terms law.
>
> ✓ Does the contract state it is the entire agreement between the parties and supersedes earlier agreements?
>
> ✓ Does the contract state that in the event of a conflict between it and any documents referred to in it or in any appendices to it, the main terms will prevail?
>
> ✓ Does the contract state that liability for both contract and tort claims is limited in any event to a certain figure? This is useful if the general exclusions of liability are held void and the supplier is left with a limit on liability which applies in any event.
>
> ✓ Have the contract terms been recently checked by a solicitor familiar with recent case law in this field and in particular is the clause too broad to be enforceable or limit liability to such a derisory level that the clause may as well not be present such is the risk of its invalidity?
>
> ✓ Has the clause been checked to ensure it clearly defines consequential losses and direct losses following recent case law? Name expressly the liabilities to be excluded and limited.
>
> ✓ Does the contract need a clause stating which types of employees have authority to (a) sign the agreement and (b) amend its term?
>
> ✓ Does the contract exclude liability for fraudulent misrepresentation? This will be void.
>
> ✓ Does the contract clearly state those items which are the responsibility of the buyer such as ensuring compatibility with other systems, keeping the website up to date, checking copyright clearances, viruses etc
>
> ✓ Do not take any action in relation to the employee without taking legal advice from an employment lawyer first to minimise the risk of unfair dismissal claims later.

Pornography and Other Illegal Content [9.14]

Employees may breach many other statutes through their use of computers at work such as laws against hacking. An employee sending lots of unsolicited E-mail relating to the employer's products to potential customers (spamming – see further **10.48**) will be acting in the course of his employment and as such any liability attaching to this will fall on the head of the employer. Employees should be given guidance on the legal issues relating to this too.

The biggest use of the internet is in relation to pornography. Laws on this differ around the world. In the UK pornography is not illegal although some pornography may breach the criminal law and child pornography is illegal. Employers also need to watch out for sex discrimination actions. A female employee who has to work in a room with a group of men whose screensavers are pictures of naked women may bring a claim for sex discrimination or harassment. Again the employer should establish standards and ensure that the rules are enforced. A good written policy is only part of the solution. If everyone ignores the policy and breach of it is condoned then the law is still broken. Having such a policy does not remove the legal responsibilities of the employer as was shown in the *Pioneer* decision (see **9.2** above).

Relevant legislation in the UK includes the:

● *Obscene Publications Act 1959*;
● *Protection of Children Act 1978*;
● *Public Order Act 1994* (which amended both the above statutes); and
● *Telecommunications Act 1984*.

In the US the *Communications Decency Act 1996* makes it an offence to transmit over a communications network obscene material.

Defamation and the Internet [9.15]

(Paras **9.15** to **9.22** were written by Simon Halberstam)

Given its background as a forum for free speech and the dissemination of ideas, it is not surprising that, now E-mail is in the commercial mainstream, its transfer to that forum has produced certain problems. The problem centres on the fact that when sending E-mails, many users feel free to express opinions they would not commit to paper when writing a business letter or talking to a group of colleagues. As a result of this, users often make imprudent statements. The problem with the internet is that once the button is pressed to send a message, or the information or view in question is uploaded onto a website, it is 'published.' In defamation it is at this stage that an offence occurs.

The accepted legal definition of defamation is 'the publication of a statement which tends to lower a person in the estimation of right-thinking members of society generally'. The 'statement' can be words, visual images or some other method of signifying meaning. Defamation takes two forms, libel and slander. Libel involves (amongst other things) writing or printing a defamatory statement. Slander is speech or gestures of a defamatory nature.

A person who is defamed may feel understandably aggrieved and may decide to take action to prevent circulation of the statement. Normally, the person would approach the publisher or the author. The problem with the WWW is that the identity of this entity is often far from obvious. So who does the aggrieved person approach and ultimately sue, particularly if the person who made the statement is untraceable or financially, not worth suing? In a number of notable recent cases, Internet Service Providers have been sued for defamatory newsgroup content on the basis that they as hosts of the newsgroup, are the 'publishers' of the defamation.

US: Cubby v Compuserve [9.16]

In *Cubby v CompuServe 776 F Supp 135 (SDN9 1991)* CompuServe were sued in respect of a message appearing in a local newsgroup. CompuServe had employed another company to edit and post information to the site and CompuServe argued that, as it employed a third party to edit information in the newsgroup, it was akin to a newspaper vendor who has no control over the content of the newspapers it sells. The New York court accepted this argument.

US: Stratton Oakmont Inc v Prodigy [9.17]

In *Stratton Oakmont Inc v Prodigy Serus Co 1995 NY Misc Lexis 229, 23 Media L Rep 1794 (1995)*, another American case concerning a defamatory statement made in a local news forum, despite the fact that Prodigy had employed 'board leaders' to remove material after it was posted, Prodigy were found to be publishers of a defamatory statement.

The reasoning for this was that Prodigy advertised itself as a 'family orientated computer network' which could control site content and prevent publication of inappropriate messages. As such, it had assumed responsibility for the site and was obliged to prevent publication of defamatory statements.

Laurence Godfrey v Demon Internet Limited [9.18]

On 4 April 1999 the High Court handed down a judgement on a similar case in England. In *Laurence Godfrey v Demon Internet Limited* (unreported). In 1997 an unknown person made a posting in the USA in the Demon newsgroup soc.culture.thai. The posting was 'squalid and obscene'. It purported to come from an academic whose name is Laurence Godfrey and invited replies to his E-mail address. Mr Godfrey does exist but was not the author of the statement. The effect of the statement was to defame Mr Godfrey. When Mr Godfrey became aware of the posting he sent a letter to the managing director of Demon informing him that the statement was a forgery and requesting that it be removed. The statement was removed by Demon approximately ten days later in the course of ordinary news 'filleting' (a process of regular removal of material).

Mr Godfrey claimed that this had been too slow. Demon claimed that under the *Defamation Act 1996* they had a defence in that they were not the publishers of the statement. The court agreed that Demon was not the publishers. However, Demon's defence failed as it could not show that it did not 'know or have reason to believe that what [it] did contributed to the publication of a defamatory statement'.

Whilst in the above case, Demon conceded that it had the ability to delete one message from a newsgroup, this is not always possible and in some cases, to prevent publication of one defamatory statement, a whole newsgroup would have to be deleted. It seems obvious that problems will arise in cases where a person claims a statement defames them and the Internet Service Provider (ISP) either has no way of knowing whether the statement is defamatory or whether the complainant is in fact the person defamed. Another concern for ISPs must be whether, by deleting statements or whole newsgroups, they are breaching their contracts with the users who expect to participate in and receive news from newsgroups.

Advice to ISPs **[9.19]**

In light of the *Demon* case, ISPs should consider monitoring sites they host and removing 'offensive' text, as well as implementing a procedure whereby complaints made can be investigated. It would also be advisable for an ISP to review its terms of business so that it can remove or suspend postings without being in breach of its contract with users.

Hosting [9.20]

A slightly different variant of the problem comes with those who host client websites where a third party alleges that the website contains defamatory information. Who does the host believe and should it risk breach of contract with its client by removing the material or 'pulling' the website?

For employers the problem is particularly acute as they are responsible for E-mails sent by their employees.

Norwich Union [9.21]

A defamatory E-mail cost Norwich Union £450,000 in 1998. It is therefore vital for businesses to have proper E-mail policies in place and to make appropriate changes to contracts of employment in order to give the E-mail policy teeth.

British Gas [9.22]

British Gas agreed to pay more than £200,000 in libel damages in 1999 in one of the first email damages cases settled in the UK. An internal memorandum was sent to staff by British Gas stating that they should have no dealings with a competitor, Exoteric Gas Solutions. It had been set up by an ex-British Gas employee, Andrew Duffield, former head of engineering. This led to his suffering loss and damage and there was no justification for the alleged boycott. Damages were paid.

Further Information [9.23]

For mediation of disputes with third parties contact Centre for Dispute Resolution, (CEDR) Princes House, 95 Gresham Street, London EC2V 7NA. E-mail: mediate@cedr.co.uk. Tel: 020 7600 0500. Fax: 020 7600 0501.

See also 'ISPs on the Hook' – (1999) *Communications Law*, p140.

See also **11.4** and the draft *Electronic Commerce Directive*.

10 – Data Protection, Hacking, Security and ISP Liability

'Where an information society service is provided that consists of the transmission in a communication network of information provided by the recipient of the service or the provision of access to a communication network, Member States shall provide in their legislation that the provider of such a service shall not be liable, other than for injunctive relief, for the information transmitted on condition that the provider does not initiate the transmission, does not select the receiver of the transmission and does not select and does not modify the information contained in the transmission.'

(Article 12, EU draft *Electronic Commerce Directive*, 18 November 1998)

Executive Summary [10.1]

- Business internet transactions involve handling of large quantities of personal data
- Data protection legislation applies – in the EU national enactment of the *Data Protection Directive* and in particular in the UK the *Data Protection Act 1998* (due to come into force on 1 March 2000).
- Other security issues arise too and businesses should seek to reduce risks of hacking.
- Hacking is a criminal offence under the *Computer Misuse Act 1990*.
- Spamming (see **10.48** below) can also lead to legal liability.
- Sometimes Internet Service Providers may be liable for activities of those using their services

Huge quantities of personal data are moved around the internet every day. Businesses working over the internet and particularly those selling goods direct to consumers, will receive a large amount of personal data. This is very valuable indeed. This Chapter looks at data protection laws, hacking and other criminal legislation, spamming and liability of Internet Service Providers.

Data Protection Laws [10.2]

In the UK, the *Data Protection Act 1984* requires those who hold personal data about living individuals to register with the Data Protection Office. Under the *1984 Act* it has only been certain data held on computer or in other electronic forms which has been caught. However, that is set to change when the *Data Protection Act 1998* is brought into force on 1 March 2000.

Advice on data protection law in the UK can be obtained from the Commissioner's office. Tel: 01625 545700; http://www.open.gov.uk/dpr/dprhome.htm. A copy of the *1998 Act* is on that website. The *1998 Act* is considered below.

Data [10.3]

The *Data Protection Act 1998* applies to 'data'. Data is defined as information which:

'(*a*) is being processed by means of equipment operating automatically in response to instructions given for that purpose,

(*b*) is recorded with the intention that it should be processed by means of such equipment,

(*c*) is recorded as part of a relevant filing system or with the intention that it should form part of a relevant filing system, or

(*d*) does not fall within paragraph (*a*), (*b*) or (*c*) but forms part of an accessible record as defined in *section 68*'.

The *1998 Act* applies where data are 'processed'. Data are referred to in their correct plural form in the Act. Paragraph (*d*) was added later during the Act's passage through Parliament. *Section 68* defines an 'accessible record' as a health record, and educational record or an accessible public record all of which are defined elsewhere. Such records may not fall within (*a*)–(*c*) hence the addition of paragraph (*d*). The section was added to ensure that certain rights of access to information held in manual records were covered by the *1998 Act*.

These are rights under the *Personal Files Act 1987*, the *Access to Health Records Act 1990* and the *Education (School Records) Regulations 1989* and corresponding legislation in Scotland and Northern Ireland. These are local authority housing and social services records and records held by schools on pupils and former pupils.

Accessible records are health records, defined in *section 68(2)*, educational records defined in *Schedule 11* and accessible public records defined in *Schedule 12*. The full definitions in *Schedules 11* and *12* are not repeated here but for those involved in the areas affected by those provisions careful note should be taken of those Schedules.

What is Personal Data? [10.4]

The *1998 Act* defines personal data as data which relate to a living individual who can be identified from the data or from data and other information which is in the possession of, or is likely to come into the possession of the data controller. It also includes any expression of opinion about the individual and any indication of the intentions of the data controller or any other person in respect of the individual. The *1998 Act* does not apply to data about those who are dead. The *1998 Act* will not apply where the individual cannot be identified from the data or other information, nor to information about limited companies. The *1998 Act* applies to expressions of opinion about a person. Certain maps which identify individual houses, for example, may amount to personal data, whether on the internet or not.

Manual Data [10.5]

Section 1(1) defines a relevant filing system as:

> 'any set of information relating to individuals to the extent that, although the information is not processed by means of equipment operating automatically in response to instructions given for that purpose, the set is structured, either by reference to individuals or by reference to criteria relating to individuals, in such a way that specific information relating to a particular individual is readily accessible'.

Manual data did not come within the *1984 Act* and no registration was necessary by those processing such data. However, as far as the internet is concerned, the personal data would never have been able to benefit from this exemption in any event. Manual records are only caught under the *1998 Act* where:

● they form part of a structured set;

● the structuring is by reference to individuals – such as unique personal identification numbers; or

● structuring is done so that specific information about individuals is readily available.

'Specific information' on a file is to mean information which is distinguished from other information in the file and accessible separately.

Manual Records [10.6]

'Eligible manual data' other than that part of an accessible record are exempt from the data protection principles and Parts II and III of the *1998 Act* for a 'first transitional period'. This runs to 23 October 2001. Eligible manual data is data which is not within (*a*) and (*b*) of *section 1* of the Act – see **10.3** above (which effectively refers to computer data etc). Until 23 October 2001, old manual data is outside the scope of the *1998 Act* (and was always outside the scope of the *1984 Act*). The definition of eligible data contained in *Schedule 8, para 1* refers to data subject 'to processing which was already under way before 24 October 1998'. The significance of 24 October 1998 is that it is the date when the *Data Protection Directive* of the EU should have been brought into force by the Government.

There is a second transitional period too which runs to 24 October 2007. This provides that eligible manual data held immediately before 24 October 1998 is exempt largely from the first Data Protection Principle (see **10.12** below) and the second, third, fourth and fifth data protection principles and *section14(1)–(3)*. It is not, however, exempt in that period from *section 7* – which is an individual's right of subject access. This is contained in *Schedule 8, Part III*.

Processing [10.7]

Section 1(1) of the *1998 Act* states that processing:

'in relation to personal data, means obtaining, recording or holding the information or data or carrying out any operation or set of operations on the information or data, including:

(*a*)   organisation, adaptation or alteration of the information or data,

(*b*)   retrieval, consultation or use of the information or data,

(*c*)   disclosure of the information or data by transmission, dissemination or otherwise making available, or

(*d*)   alignment, combination, blocking, erasure or destruction of the information or data.'.

'Obtaining' or 'recording' of personal data is defined in *section 1(2)* in relation to personal data as including obtaining or recording the information to be contained in the data. 'Using' or 'disclosing' in relation to personal data includes using or disclosing the information contained in the data.

If the information was to be processed or form part of a filing system only after being transferred to a country outside the European Economic Area, the *1998 Act* still applies. *Section 1(3)* states that such an intention is immaterial to whether or not the Act applies.

Most moving and using of personal data over the internet will amount to processing. Under the *1998 Act* such processing no longer needs to be by reference to the data subject to be caught. The *Data Protection Act 1998* is therefore much wider than the *Data Protection Act 1984* which it replaces.

Businesses which make databases available over the internet will have to register if individuals can be identified from the data which is given or from that data in addition to other data which is available to the data controller.

Who must Register? [10.8]

The person who has to register and comply with the act is the person defined as the 'data controller' under the *1998 Act*. Fees must be paid (currently £75 every three years). There will be few businesses in the UK which can escape the need to register, only those that hold no personal data.

Data Subjects [10.9]

The person whose data is used or held by the data controller is known as the 'data subject'.

Registration [10.10]

The principal procedural point is to register under the *1998 Act* though existing registrations under the *1984 Act* will continue in an interim period. Particulars a data controller provides on registration under the *Data Protection Act 1998* are:

● name and address – where the data controller is a limited company this is the address of the registered office and for others the principal place of business in the UK;
● whether the data controller has a nominated representative for the purposes of the *1998 Act* and the name and address of that representative – this might be a data protection director or manager and their address may well differ from that of the company's registered office address;
● a description of the personal data being processed or to be processed by or on behalf of the data controller and the category or categories of data subject to which they relate;
● a description of the purpose or purposes for which the data are being or are to be processed;
● a description of recipients to whom the data will be disclosed;
● names of countries outside the European Economic Area to which the data controller will directly or indirectly transfer the data; and
● whether the data falls under *section 17* and whether the notification does not extend to those data

Under *section 21* it is an offence for a data controller to process data contrary to *section 17* without registering and to fail to comply with the duty imposed in the notification regulations. There is a defence to the second offence above, under *section 21(3)* to show that all due diligence was used to comply with the duty.

The Data Protection Principles [10.11]

In most cases it can be assumed that registration is necessary. Much more important for those involved with the internet is to ensure they do not breach the Act's requirements in their handling, obtaining or using of the data as described below. The *1998 Act* requires that those who hold personal data must ensure they follow the eight data protection principles which are described briefly below.

Fair and Lawful Processing [10.12]

Personal data shall be processed fairly and lawfully and, in particular, shall not be processed unless:

(*a*)   at least one of the conditions in *Schedule 2* is met, and
(*b*)   in the case of sensitive personal data, at least one of the conditions in *Schedule 3* is also met.

The *Schedule 2* conditions are very important indeed. They are that the individual has given their consent to the processing. It is likely this will be taken as requiring an active giving of consent but ticking a box consenting, not a passive consent by way of failing to tick a box objecting but at the date of writing guidance is expected on this shortly from the Commissioner. On the internet such consent could be by clicking on a particular box. Most internet websites have privacy policies or guidelines in any event which set out what principles are followed. If consent is not given then processing is still allowed under *Schedule 2* where necessary to perform a contract or to take steps at the data subject's request to enter into a contract or for other reasons such as to protect the vital interests of the data subject or to administer justice.

Data subjects must be notified of:

- the identity of data controller;
- the identity of any representative appointed for the purposes of the *1998 Act*, if any, by that data controller;
- the purpose or purposes for which the data are intended to be processed; and
- any further information which is necessary, having regard to the specific circumstances in which the data are to be processed to enable the processing in respect of the data subject to be fair.

These items can be given on the website.

Purpose [10.13]

Personal data shall be obtained only for use for one or more specified and lawful purposes, and shall not be further processed in any manner incompatible with that purpose or those purposes. Individuals for example should be told if their data may be passed on or used for other purposes. They also have a right to object to direct mail under another provision of the *1998 Act* (see **10.21** below).

Data to be Adequate, Relevant and not Excessive [10.14]

Personal data must be adequate, relevant and not excessive in relation to the purpose or purposes for which they are processed.

Data to be Accurate and Up-to-date [10.15]

Personal data should be accurate and, where necessary, kept up-to-date. It is a matter of fact whether data is incorrect or misleading in each case.

Data not to be Kept Longer than Purposes Require [10.16]

Personal data processed for any purpose or purposes shall not be kept for longer than is necessary for that purpose or those purposes.

Data Processed in Accordance with Data Subjects' Rights [10.17]

Personal data shall be processed in accordance with the rights of data subjects under this *1998 Act*. This provision is contravened if, but only if, a person contravenes:

- *section* 7 of the *1998 Act*, by failing to supply information which has been duly requested in accordance with that section;
- contravening *sections 10* or *11* by failing to comply with a notice duly given under that section; or
- contravening *section 12* by failing to give a notice under that section.

Security Measures [10.18]

Appropriate technical and organisational measures shall be taken against unauthorised or unlawful processing of personal data and against accidental loss or destruction of, or damage to, personal data. This principle means that those holding data must take steps to stop it being unlawfully processed. They should try to stop hackers getting into their system or other breaches of their security measures. *Part II* of *Schedule 1* provides that regard is had to the state of technological development and the cost of implementing measures.

Transfers Abroad [10.19]

Personal data shall not be transferred to a country or territory outside the European Economic Area unless that country or territory ensures an adequate level of protection for the rights and freedoms of data subjects in relation to the processing of personal data. This is considered in detail below.

Section 7: Right of Access [10.20]

Individuals are given the right by *section 7* of the *1998 Act*:

- to be informed by any data controller as to whether personal data of which the individual is the data subject, are being processed by or on behalf of that data controller;
- where the above applies, to be given by the data controller a description of the personal data concerned, the purposes for which they are being processed and the recipients or classes of recipients to whom they are disclosed or may be disclosed;
- to have communicated to him in an intelligible form the information constituting the personal data and any information available to the controller as to the source of the data; and
- where the processing by automatic means has constituted, or is likely to constitute,the sole basis for a decision significantly relating the data subject, then the data subject has a right to be informed by the data controller of the 'logic involved in that decision-taking' (this includes his performance at work, his creditworthiness, his reliability or his conduct).

There are certain exceptions in *sections 7* and *8*. The data controller should not alter the data by making any amendment or deletion which would not otherwise have been made. No tampering must be made to make the data suitable to the data subject, though it must be supplied in intelligible form. If it is held in code, for example, the data subject is entitled to have it translated. *Section 8(2)* provides that the copy of the information must be supplied in permanent form.

The request will only be complied with where:

- the individual makes the request in writing;
- pays a fee not exceeding the prescribed maximum; and
- the data controller is given the information he may reasonably require in order to satisfy himself as to the identity of the person making the request and to locate the information which that person seeks.

The current fee for access requests is a maximum of £10. There are 40 days in which to respond to requests.

Damage or Distress: Rights to Prevent Processing [10.21]

Section 10 gives data subjects a right to prevent processing of their data which may cause them distress or damage, where the processing is unwarranted and is causing or likely to cause substantial damage or substantial distress to that person or another person. By *Schedule 2* there is no right to object under *section 10* of the *1998 Act* where the data subject has given his consent to the processing or it is necessary to perform a contract or so the data subject can enter into a contract. Nor can the data subject stop the processing when it is necessary to comply with a legal obligation or it is necessary to protect the vital interests of the data subject.

Direct Marketing: Right to Prevent Processing [10.22]

Section 11 provides that data subjects may serve a notice on data controllers requiring them within a reasonable time to cease, or not to begin, processing personal data 'for the purposes of direct marketing'. If the notice does not result in the data controller ceasing the use then a court order can be obtained requiring the data controller to comply. 'Direct marketing' is defined as a means of communication of any advertising or marketing material which is directed to particular individuals (*section 11(3)*). It would include junk mail, junk faxes, junk E-mail and telephone calls.

Distance Selling Directive and ISDN Telecoms Data Protection Directives [10.23]

There is some overlap with other legislation such as the EU *Distance Selling Directive*, draft *Financial Services Distance Selling Directive* and *ISDN Telecommunications Directive* (see **4.41** above).

Automated Decision Taking [10.24]

Section 12 of the *1998 Act* relates to 'automated decision taking'. Decisions which significantly affect data subjects must not be solely based on the processing by automatic means of personal data for the purpose of evaluating that person where an individual has given a notice in writing to the data controller to this effect. *Section 12* does not apply where the decision is taken for the purpose of considering whether to enter into a contract with a data subject. Nor does it apply in the course of performing a contract with the data subject it is not clear what this covers.

Compensation [10.25]

Section 13 of the *1998 Act* gives an individual who suffers damage by reason of any contravention by a data controller of any of the requirements of the Act is entitled to compensation from the data controller for that damage. This applies to contravention of any provision – it might be processing without consent or failure to abide by the 8 Data Protection Principles etc. (see **10.12–10.19**) There is a defence where the person can prove that they have taken such care as in all the circumstances was reasonably required to comply with the requirement concerned (*section 13(3)*). This illustrates the importance of businesses having proper and effective data protection procedures in place which make it more likely they can use the defence.

Rectification and Blocking, Erasure and Destruction [10.26]

Data subjects are given the right, by *section 14*, to obtain a court order where the data about them are inaccurate. In such cases, the court can order that the data controller rectifies, blocks, erases or destroys those data and any other personal data in relation to which a person is the data controller and which contain inaccurate expressions of opinion.

Exemptions [10.27]

There are many exemptions from the *1998 Act* and space does not allow them all to be set out here. However, some are set out at **10.28–10.37** below.

National Security [10.28]

Personal data are exempt from the Data Protection Principles, the provisions of *Parts II, III* and *V* (rights of data subjects, notification by data controllers and enforcement) and *section 55* (the offence of unlawful obtaining for personal data) of the *1998 Act*, if the exemption is required for the purposes of safeguarding national security.

Crime and Taxation [10.29]

There is an exemption for:

● the prevention or detection of crime;
● the apprehension or prosecution of offenders; and
● the assessment or collection of any tax or duty or of any imposition of a similar nature.

This exemption for crime and taxation is an exemption from the first Data Protection Principle (see **10.12** above) – that data shall be processed fairly and lawfully and from *section 7* (see **10.20** above) – right of access but only:

'in any case to the extent in which the application of those provisions to the data would be likely to prejudice any of the matters mentioned in this subsection'.

Statutory Functions [10.30]

Data processed for the purpose of discharging a statutory function and consisting of information obtained for such purpose from a person who had in his possession the information for the purposes of detection of crime or taxation is also exempt but only from the subject information provisions.

Regulations may exempt certain health and social work records.

Regulatory Activity [10.31]

Section 31 contains an exemption for certain regulatory activities.

Journalism, Literature and Art [10.32]

'Special purposes' by *section 3* of the *1998 Act* means the purposes of journalism, artistic purposes and literary purposes. *Section 32* applies to processing of personal data for these special purposes. Such data will be exempt from all the Data Protection Principles except the seventh one (taking security measures to keep it secret etc) and also from *sections 7, 10, 12* and *14(1)–(3)* (right of access, right to stop processing likely to cause damage or distress, rectification and automated decision taking). So journalists can ignore all those provisions of the Act but only where:

● the processing is undertaken with a view to the publication by any person of any journalistic, literary or artistic material;
● the data controller reasonably believes that, having regard in particular to the special importance of freedom of expression, publication would be in the public interest; and
● the data controller reasonably believes that, in all the circumstances, compliance with the provision in question if incompatible with the special purposes.

Research, History and Statistics [10.33]

There are exemptions for data used for 'research purposes' – including statistical or historical purposes. Under *section 33* when applying the second principle (see **10.13** above) – that data should just be obtained and used for the specified purposes – further processing only for research purposes provided this is 'in compliance with the relevant conditions' are not treated as incompatible with the purposes for which they were obtained. The relevant conditions in relation to processing of personal data are:

- that the data are not processed to support measures or decisions with respect to particular individuals; and
- that the data are not processed in such a way that substantial damage or substantial distress is, or is likely to be, caused to any data subject.

Information Available to the Public under the Law [10.34]

There is an exemption from the subject information provisions, the fourth Data Protection Principle (see **10.15** above) and *section 14(1)–(3)* and the non-disclosure provisions if the data consists of information which the data controller is obliged by an enactment to make available to the public – whether by publishing it, making it available for inspection or otherwise and whether gratuitously or on payment of a fee (*section 34*).

Legal Disclosures and Legal Proceedings [10.35]

A further exemption exists for legal disclosures and proceedings.

Domestic purposes [10.36]

Individuals may process data for the purposes of their own personal, family or household affairs, including recreational purposes (*section 36*). That personal data is exempt from the data protection principles and the provisions of *Parts II* and *III* of the *1998 Act*.

Other Exemptions [10.37]

Other exemptions can be made by Order and *Schedule 7* of the *1998 Act* contains miscellaneous other exemptions, including:

- confidential references (employment but not credit references);
- armed forces;
- judicial appointment and honours;

- crown employment;
- management forecasts;
- corporate finance;
- negotiations;
- examination marks;
- examination scripts;
- legal professional privilege; and
- self-incrimination.

Under the *Data Protection Act 1984*, there were exemptions also for payroll, pensions, accounts purposes, processing of simple mailing lists and unincorporated members' clubs and word processing and for back up data. Some regulations may reinstate these in due course and in any event there are complex transitional provisions in relation to many of the exemptions so they are not lost immediately.

Transmitting Data Abroad – Data Protection Act 1998 and EU Data Protection Directive [10.38]

(Paras **10.38** to **10.43** were written by Simon Halberstam)

Under the *Data Protection Act 1984*, there is no automatic prohibition on the transfer of data from the UK to other countries. The Data Protection Registrar can serve a notice prohibiting transfer, but in practice this power has been used very rarely.

However, the position will change significantly when the *1998 Act* comes into force. There are 'grandfather provisions' allowing existing activities to continue over a three-year transitional period (*Sch 8*). However these only apply to the extent that processing was 'under way' before 24 October 1998 (*Sch 8, Part 1, para 1*). It would seem that transfer of data to another country could be regarded in itself as a new processing which was not under way before that date, and that it would therefore be unsafe to rely on this transitional relief.

The principles of data protection which must be observed under the new regime include (*Sch 1, Part 1, para 8*):

'Personal data shall not be transferred to a country or territory outside the European Economic Area unless that country or territory ensures an adequate level of protection for the rights and freedoms of data subjects in relation to the processing of personal data.'

Whether the foreign country 'ensures an adequate level of protection ¼' is clearly a critical question. The Act contains a list of principles to be used in assessing this issue (*Sch 1, Part 2, para 13*). However, if there is a ruling of the EU Commission on the point, this will be binding in accordance with *Article 25* of the Directive (*Sch 1, Part 2, para 15*), and it is contemplated that the general question will be resolved in due course by the EU and through negotiations between the EU and other countries, rather than by the individual member states of the EU.

The EU Commission contemplated at one stage establishing a 'White List' of countries considered to provide an adequate level of protection, but it is now thought that this is politically too controversial. A major difficulty is that it would be difficult to regard many of the states of the US as meeting the requirement without bending the rules, but a negative decision of the EU commission in relation to the US would be highly contentious and disruptive of trade. There have been discussions between the EU and the US Department of Trade, but it appears that these have not produced any resolution.

A possible solution to the general problem of reconciling the Directive with the requirements of international trade with countries which do not have data protection legislation is to allow data transfer in cases where the data is protected by contractual terms. An EU Working Party reported in April 1998 (DG XV D/5005/98 final) that this would be particularly suitable in the case of intra-company transfers, provided that the contract obliged the transferee to comply with the requirements of the Directive.

Against this background, it is thought that the UK authorities will be cautious about making any general findings as to the adequacy of protection in other countries, and will try to decide cases on the basis of the adequacy of the protection of the data in the particular case. This approach can be justified in that the principles for assessing adequacy of protection state that an adequate level 'is one which is adequate in all the circumstances of the case' and go on to refer to any relevant codes of conduct or other rules which are enforceable in that country or territory (whether generally or by arrangement in particular cases), and any security measures taken in respect of the data in that country or territory.' (*Sch 1, Part 2, para 13*).

Contractual Requirements [10.39]

Having regard to the guidance given by the EU Working Party (DG XV D/5005/98 final), the contract should:

- require the other company to comply with the 1st to 7th Principles of Data Protection as set out in the 1998 Act (*Sch 1 part 1*), namely (in summary) that personal data shall:
  - be processed lawfully and fairly (note that what is considered 'fair' is very limited in relation to 'sensitive personal data' such as racial or ethnic origin, political or religious opinions, trade union membership, physical or mental health, sexual life, or criminal offences (*Sch 3*);
  - be obtained only for one or more specified and lawful purposes and not be processed in any manner incompatible with such purpose(s);
  - be adequate, relevant and not excessive in relation to the purpose or purposes for which it is processed;
  - be accurate and kept up-to-date;
  - not be kept for longer than is necessary;
  - be processed in accordance with the rights of the individuals concerned under the Act;
  - be protected by appropriate technical and organisational measures against unauthorised or unlawful processing or accidental loss or damage;
- set out in detail the purposes, methods and circumstances of the data-processing and the way in which the above Principles are to be implemented;
- require compliance with the rights of data subjects under the *Data Protection Act 1998* as regards access, rectification and objections to processing;
- if possible, ensure that the business whose data it is ('Data Controller') retains decision-making control over the processing of the data;
- specify that the Data Controller remains liable to data subjects for any failure to comply with the above Principles;
- prohibit onward transfers of the data to third parties without the consent of the Data Controller (which should only given if the third party enters into a satisfactory contract with the Data Controller).

Other Exemptions [10.40]

The transfer of data is also exempted from the 8th Principle where the:

- data subject has given consent to the transfer;
- transfer is necessary for the performance of a contract between the data subject and the Data Controller or for steps taken at the

request of the data subject with a view to his entering into a
contract with the Data Controller;

● transfer is necessary for the conclusion or performance of a
contract between the data subject and a third party entered into at
the request of or in the interest of the data subject; or

● transfer is authorised or made on terms of a kind approved by the
Data Protection Commissioner on the basis that adequate safeguards for the rights and freedom of data subjects are ensured.

It will therefore be desirable for the Data Owner to obtain consent for
the transfer of the data to other group companies from all employees,
contract staff and other individuals who are the subjects of the data. If
this is done, the transfer will be exempt from the 8th Principle of Data
Protection. Obtaining consents should be straightforward in relation to
all new staff, but may possibly present difficulties in relation to existing
staff. Obtaining consent would also help in ensuring compliance with
the First Principle of Data Protection (fair use).

Registration of Data Owner [10.41]

The Data Owner should be registered already as a Data User and this
registration should be reviewed and, if necessary, amended to cover the
proposed transfer of data. At the same time, the Registrar/
Commissioner can be asked to approve the contract. If it is approved,
the transfers will be exempt. If, as is likely, approval is delayed because
of the workload of the Registry, the Data Owner is unlikely to be
penalised for proceeding with it having made full disclosure to the
Registry.

Confidentiality [10.42]

The Data Owner could be liable for misuse of confidential information
contrary to the general law if it used or disclosed confidential data for
purposes other than those for which the data was confided to it.

Copyright and Database Rights [10.43]

Licences of third party software and databases used by the Data Owner
may be limited to use by the Data Owner alone, or only in the UK, or
on a limited number of computers, or even on particular computers or

at particular premises. The Data Owner should check its contracts in relation to each third party product which may be transferred to other countries.

What to do in Practice – Checklist [10.44]

The list below shows some of the issues which those in business should consider.

> ✓ Have we registered under the Data Protection Act? If not, the position should be rectified immediately.
>
> ✓ Do we have a privacy policy on our website and if not should we have? It is not a legal requirement in the UK but from a commercial point of view it makes the business look more professional and it is a good means of obtaining necessary consents to various forms of processing.
>
> ✓ Do we comply with all the data protection principles including ensuring data is held securely, obtained fairly and not retained from longer than is necessary?
>
> ✓ Will we have problems with export of data when the ban under the *Data Protection Act 1998* comes into force?
>
> ✓ Have we considered asking those visiting our website whether they object to their being subsequently E-mailed and whether we should give them the chance to state that they do and the right to come off the mailing list later if they wish.

Privacy Policies [10.45]

Those selling over the internet may choose to publish a privacy policy to reassure customers who may place orders over the internet. It might state that the business is committed to privacy and confidentiality of all confidential information filed.

For example the books on line (bol.com) part of the Freeserve site states in its Privacy Policy that it is committed to protecting customers' privacy and that it will never sell personal information or share it with third parties. It then provides that it uses customer information in particular ways.

Another good example of a privacy policy for US company is on the Dell site at http://www.dell.com

Emerging Digital Economy [10.46]

Two thirds of websites disclose their privacy policy and information practices, a US 1999 study showed. The annual US report on the Emerging Digital Economy looks at these issues in detail and provides a huge amount of information on E-commerce – see http://www.doc.gov.

International Data Protection [10.47]

Many UK businesses using personal data will also use data of individuals from all over the world. They will have to ensure, so far as is practically possible, compliance with other data protection laws too. However the Western model and a well drawn privacy policy should usually ensure that most legal eventualities are met.

Spamming [10.48]

Unsolicited E-mails may involve the use of personal data under data protection laws described above. *Article 7* of the draft EU *Electronic Commerce Directive* provides that 'member states shall lay down in their legislation that unsolicited commercial communication by electronic mail must be clearly and unequivocally identifiable as such as soon as it is received by the recipient'.

Spamming is sending unsolicited E-mail for commercial advertising. It can either be sent to individuals or to newsgroups. It can cause substantial problems by flooding systems with messages which slow down service provision and is a major problem for many individuals who have many junk E-mails through which to plough. The following measures are in place to prevent it through many Internet Service Providers in the UK:

● Most ISPs have systems installed aimed at combating unsolicited mails, and the London Internet Exchange (LINX: http://www.linx.net) aims to finalise its best practice guidelines for ISPs on dealing with spam late in 1999.

- The Direct Marketing Association (DMA) is working with the US DMA to develop a worldwide E-mail preference scheme similar to those operated in the UK for mail, telephone and fax. The DMA hopes to be the UK part of a global scheme which would operate throughout the world. The DMA website is at http://www.dma.org.uk
- Some ISPs off individual opt out scheme to gain commercial advantage.

The EU *Distance Selling Directive* (*97/7*) has provisions which will enable individuals to register their objections to receipt of unsolicited E-mail. The directive should be implemented by 4 June 2000.

Telecommunications Data Protection Directive [10.49]

The *Telecommunications Data Protection Directive 97/66* does not cover unsolicited E-mails. It does prevent unsolicited faxes to individuals and allow businesses to register so as not to receive them. It was implemented in the UK by the *Telecommunications (Data Protection and Privacy) (Direct Marketing) Regulations 1998 (SI 1998/3170)* on 1 May 1999 but will be replaced by regulations of the same name dated 1999 when the rest of *Directive 97/66* is implemented when the *Data Protection Act 1998* is brought into force – see regulations at http://www.dti.gov.uk/cii/tdpd/regs2/index.htm.

Future Spamming Legislation [10.50]

The EU draft electronic commerce directive would in its current form in 1999 simply require that spam be clearly identified as such. The distance selling directive will permit individuals to opt out of receiving unsolicited E-mail. Those involved in financial services should also consider the provisions of the 1999 draft financial services distance selling directive.

The White Paper on electronic commerce says that the Government believes that until industry self-regulatory initiatives have been given time to work, new legislation is not recommended. It does however mention certain alternatives including adding E-mail to the *Telecoms Data Protection Directive*, legislation to force ISPs to take measures to prevent the sending of unsolicited bulk E-mail, prohibition of 'spoofing'; and establishing of labelling to support anti-spoofing measures and customers registration lists such as by attaching the word 'advertising' to commercial E-mail. Spoofing is misrepresentation of the origin of an E-mail. See also the Electronic Communications Bill, http://www.dti.gov.uk/cii/elec and accompanying notes.

Liability of Internet Service Providers [10.51]

An internet service provider provides the internet access enjoyed by its customers. As such it will have varying degrees of control over the traffic on its networks. There have been few UK court cases in this area. Case law in the US is more developed. (See also **9.15** above and **11.4** below.)

Cubby v Compuserve [10.52]

In US case *Cubby v Compuserve* (*776 F Supp 135 (SDNY 1991)*) the court said CompuServe did not have the change to review the content of the publication in dispute before it was uploaded to computer banks. Its liability in defamation was at the lower standard relating to those selling books in book stores or magazines on newsstands and the test was whether it had knowledge that the material was defamatory, which it did not. The court said:

'Technology is rapidly transforming the information industry. A computerized database is the functional equivalent of a more traditional news vendor and the inconsistent application of a lower standard of liability to an electronic news distributor such as Compuserve than that which is applied to a public library, bookstore or newsstand would impose an undue burden on the free flow of information'.

In *Stratton Oakmont Inc v Prodigy Services Co* (*1995 NY Misc. Lexis 229*) (quoted in Cyberlaw by J Rosenoer) the court held that the ISP's family orientation and control exercised over content did make it liable. It used automatic scanning, guidelines and board leaders to chill freedom of communication in cyberspace 'and it appears that this chilling effect is exactly what Prodigy wants, but for the legal liability that attaches to such censorship.'

UK Case Law: The Demon Internet Court

Decision [10.53]

Godfrey v Demon Internet Ltd (26 March 1999, TLR 20 April 1999) concerned defamatory statements made about Mr Godfrey on a US newserver by an unknown person which eventually found their way on the Demon's news server. Mr Godfrey told the defendants about this and asked them to remove it. They took no action. The judge said that at common law whenever an internet service provider such as Demon published a posting it was acting like a bookseller which sells a libellous book.

The court did not accept that the ISP (Demon) just has a passive role as owners of the electronic device through which postings were transmitted. The defendants had chosen to receive and store the news group which contained the offensive material. They had power to remove it and in fact in the end they did remove it though not for 10 days after being notified of it.

They were not however commercial publishers under *sections 1(2)* and *1(3)* of the *Defamation Act 1996*. However at common law, the law in cases, they were publishers and from the date when they became aware of the defamatory nature of the material they should have removed it.

Mr Godfrey had applied to the court to strike out part of Demon's defence to his legal action. Mr Godfrey said that part of the defence disclosed no sustainable defence to the action.

Under *section 1* of the Act a person has a defence to defamation proceedings if he shows that:

> '(a) he was not the author, editor or publisher of the statement complained of (b) he took reasonable care in relation to its publication and (c) he did not know and had no reason to believe, that what he did caused or contributed to the publication of a defamatory statement.'

Publisher is defined in *s1(2)* as a commercial publisher:

> 'that is a person whose business is issuing material to the public, or a section of the public, who issues material containing the statement in the course of that business.'

Demon was not within this provision and was not a commercial publisher.

Businesses which suffer defamation electronically and individuals like the plaintiff in this case will find it easier now to persuade ISPs to remove libellous postings or obliterate them from news groups. ISPs may be advised to require those sending messages to acknowledge they are not libellous or otherwise in breach of the law and to indemnify the ISP from any loss arising from any posting.

A very detailed summary of case law relating to ISPs' liability throughout the world is in *Special Report on the Internet* ISBN 0 421 63420 0, EIPR December 1997.

Crime and the Internet [10.54]

The Internet is a wonderful medium for the criminal, whether he is attempting to extort money or defraud a bank.

Computer Misuse Act 1990 [10.55]

In the UK, the *Computer Misuse Act 1990*, prohibits unauthorised access to a computer and altering material once such access is obtained though there have been few cases under the legislation. The Metropolitan Police have a computer crime unit which assist forces around the country in this area.

Draft Convention on Cyber Crime [10.56]

The European Council has adopted a draft convention on cyber crime This is published *at OJ 1999 5.6.99 L142/1* and is accessible for a limited period from the EU website http://www.europa.eu.int in the eur-lex section. It says that member states will support the drawing up of the Council of Europe's draft Convention on Cyber Crime. There will be crimes against confidentiality, integrity and availability of computer data, computer related offences such as computer fraud and forgery and content related offences such as child pornography.

Proposals for Change: Law Commission and

Internet Fraud [10.57]

The Law Commission in 1999 decided to propose changes to the law to curb credit card and internet theft. The credit card providers have welcomed the changes though the Serious Fraud Office was reported to be disappointed that the proposals did not include a general new offence of fraud.

The proposals could result in its becoming an offence for the first time to steal services. At present it is simply an offence to steal goods. There would also be a strengthening of legal constraints on fraudulent transfers of financial services such as eurobonds.

Further Information [10.58]

The US Emerging Digital Economy documents which describe companies' privacy and other related policies in this area is at: http://www.doc.gov/E-commerce/emerging.htm.

Data Protection Commissioner, Wycliffe House, Water Lane, Wilmslow, Cheshire SK9 5AF. Tel: 01625 545700; Fax: 01625 524510; http://www.open.gov.uk/dpr/dprhome.htm.

The Direct Marketing Association (DMA) website is at http://www.dma.org.uk.

The London Internet Exchange site is at: http://www.linx.net.

The *Telecommunications (Data Protection and Privacy) Regulations 1999* are at http://dti.gov.uk/cii/tdpd/regs2/index.htm.

Digital Crime: Policing the Cybernation by Neil Barrett, Kogan Page 1997 ISBN 0 7494 2097 9 by an ex computer hacker covers criminal issues in more detail.

Special Report on the Internet ISBN 0 421 63420 0, EIPR December 1997.

Websites on Privacy Issues [10.59]

- http://europa.eu.int/comm/dg15/en/media/dataprot/studies/adequat.htm.
- http://www.ita.doc.gov/ecom/menu.htm.
- International safe harbor privacy principles in draft from US Department of Commerce: http://www.ita.doc.gov/ecom/shprin.html

Website on Security Issues [10.60]

- Clinton Administration Policy on Critical Infrastructure protection http://www.ciao.gov.
- Internet security policy http://www.hcfa.gov (US Healthcare Financing Administration).
- Common criteria – http://csrc.nist.gob/cc.

11 – Jurisdiction

'[The] uncertainty as to "who supervises what" is prejudicial to the free movement of information society service and the control of such services. It is therefore necessary to improve the level of mutual confidence between national authorities by clarifying the application of the principle of free movement of services. This principle . . . tends towards control in the country where the provider is established.'

(EU 1998 Draft Electronic Commerce White Paper, para 6)

Executive Summary [11.1]

- One of the most difficult internet issues is which laws apply.
- Often compliance is required with many different laws as web pages can be read in different States.
- For E-mail contracts the agreement should state which laws apply.
- Many countries have agreed to the Rome Convention including the UK and the rest of the EEA, so a choice of law expressed in a contract will be respected.
- The Brussels Convention similarly respects choice of jurisdiction.

When activities took place in one country it was relatively easy to determine which country's laws applied to any legal dispute. Advertising on the internet allows people in many different states to view the page. If in the territory of receipt a law is broken the advertiser could be held liable. Virgin in the UK was held to have breached US legislation when air fares on its web page had not been kept up-to-date, for example. In that case the company did have flights between the UK and US so some territorial connection could be found. However some countries are even broader in their attempt to improve the jurisdiction and extent of their laws.

Rome Convention [11.2]

Many nations have signed the Rome Convention. All the EEA countries have done so. In the UK it was implemented by the *Contracts Applicable Law Act 1990*. This provides that:

- if a choice of law is made by the parties, such as by a term in internet shopping contracts on the web or in an individual contract made by E-mail by two businesses in different States, then their choice of laws will be respected; or
- if they have not, then the law with the closest connection to the contract will apply.

Jurisdiction [11.3]

A separate issue is where disputes will be handled though it makes sense for the same courts and laws to apply to a transaction. The Brussels and Lugano conventions apply to those countries including the EEA states who have acceded to them. In the UK the *Civil Jurisdiction and Judgments Act 1982* contains the relevant law.

As with the Rome Convention, the basic rule is that if the parties to a contract have chosen which courts will handle a dispute then that will prevail. If they have not then it is the courts normally in place where the contract would be performed.

On 14 July 1999 the European Commission announced that it had adopted a new draft regulation on *Jurisdictions and Recognition and Enforcement of Judgements in Civil and Commercial Matters*. When it is adopted by the Council of Ministers it will replace and update the 1968 Brussels Convention which is the current law. It will reflect new forms of commerce which did not exist in 1968. Further details are in Commission Press Release IP/99/10, 14 July 1999 available on the Commission's web site at http://www.europa.eu.int.

Also once a judgment is obtained from the relevant court signatory countries' local courts should effectively just 'rubber stamp' the foreign judgment and allow it to be enforced whether by seizure of goods or whatever method in the state where the loser is based. This does not always in practice happen but it is much more likely to be the case where the countries have acceded to the relevant convention.

There are many detailed lawyers' text books on conflicts of laws and jurisdiction to which reference should be made.

Proposed EU Law [11.4]

The European Parliament approved in May 1999 amendments to the draft *Electronic Commerce Directive*. Businesses which sell goods to foreign nationals over the internet will be subject to the consumer laws of their home country. Amendments were also adopted to expand responsibility of Internet Service Providers (ISPs) to cover copyright theft and libel. Proposals were rejected that would have required ISPs to 'keep all information necessary for the purpose of tracing and identifying providers of illegal content'.

It seems likely that the home country of the person placing the advertisement will normally be the country the laws of which will apply. However, if the advertiser chooses different laws in contract terms then normally they will be respected. The place of establishment is likely to be the place where the operator pursued its activity through a fixed establishment even if there are websites or servers elsewhere or a mail box in another State.

Exceptions [11.5]

In some cases national courts will not respect a choice of law. The country concerned may not have signed the Rome Convention or the laws to be avoided by an external choice of law may be in the public interest. For example, competition laws or laws protecting against unfair dismissal cannot normally be avoided by those operating or employing people in a particular state by a foreign law choice. Some legislation specifies rules in this field. The EU *Commercial Agents Directive* for example provides that where laws are to apply of a State outside the EU where an agent operates in the EU the agent still has full protection under the directive notwithstanding the choice of a non EU/EEA law. The UK had to amend its implementing regulations 1998 to make it clear that agents operating within the EEA but not in Great Britain, under English law contracts, were protected by the GB regulations.

Cases [11.6]

Prince v Prince (unreported 30 July 1997) [11.7]

Prince Sports Group Inc sells sports equipment under that name in the US. Prince plc is a UK IT service provider which registered 'prince-

.com' in 1995. On 16 January 1997 Prince Sports' US lawyers wrote to Prince plc alleging infringement of UK registered trade marks of the US company through Prince plc's domain name. Prince plc sued for unjustified threats of trade mark infringement (dealt with in **2.30** above).

The English judge, Neuberger J held that threats in a US lawyer's letter did amount to breach of the *Trade Marks Act 1994*. Therefore a threat coming from abroad to a UK company can breach these provisions of this Act.

Mecklermedia v DC Congress (High Court, 6 March 1997) [11.8]

Mecklermedia under licence from VNU published 'Internet World' in the Uk and abroad. It also ran trade shows under that name in the UK and had a website at http://www.iworld.com.

DC Congress organised German trade shows and one of its 1996 shows in Germany was called 'Internet World'. Mecklermedia sued DC Congress. DC had carried out a mailshot in the UK. It had registered the name as a trade mark in Germany. DC applied to strike out Mecklermedia's case in the UK. The judge said:

> 'When an enterprise wants to use a mark or word through-out the world (and that may include an Internet address or domain name) it must take into account that in some places, if not others, there may be confusion. Here it is clear DC Congress knew that Mecklermedia used the name 'Internet World' and I do not think it is surprising that [DC Congress] is met with [legal] actions in places where confusion is considered likely'.

The decision does mean that even those operating abroad need to ensure they do not breach UK trade marks in this way through their internet activities. (See also **2.31** above.)

Breach of Injunctions [11.9]

Another area of concern is if an injunction has been obtained, for example, restraining use of a trade mark in say the UK because of a UK trade mark owner's rights here. Is that breached where a French company restrained by the injunction selling in France launches a website? Yes, if it solicits orders from the UK. It would need to say on the website 'We do not take orders from the UK for legal reasons' though it should ensure first that detailed legal advice is taken on the precise wording of the injunction and on the competition law implications of dividing the EU market which may be contrary to *Article 81* (formerly *Article 85*) of the *EC Treaty*.

Contracts Jurisdictional Checklist [11.10]

> ✓ Do our internet contracts/terms state which country's laws apply to contracts?
>
> ✓ Do we say how disputes are handled? This may be, for example, English or Scottish courts or it may provide for UK arbitration under the *Arbitration Act 1996* or international arbitration. It may also provide for an intermediate stage of mediation or reference to some internet dispute resolution scheme to which the business may be a party depending on the area of business concerned.
>
> ✓ Are there legal reasons why we should not take orders from particular States such as a different trade mark owner of our name there or the goods not meeting local standards? If so do we make this clear on the website and have we checked we do not breach competition law through any market division?
>
> ✓ Have we checked whether any of our existing contracts such as for distribution of the goods concerned restrain us from soliciting sales outside our territory which a website might cause?
>
> ✓ Should we have different language versions of our web page so that our terms and conditions of business can be read and understood by foreign buyers or should we have an entirely different set of conditions compliant with local law where we expect a lot of business from a particular territory where it is unlikely we would succeed in imposing our own legal rules?

Examples of Wording for Internet Site

Conditions [11.11]

Below is typical wording used to cover both choice of law and jurisdiction.

> 'This Agreement is subject to the laws of England and the parties agree to submit to the exclusive jurisdiction of the English courts in connection with any dispute'.

If payment is made in advance by credit or debit card before goods are sent, then it may not matter if the buyer is in a country which does not respect the choice of law and jurisdiction chosen. It will be a different matter if legal disputes are likely to arise later and/or payment is to be recovered after despatch of the goods. In those cases the seller may not be prepared to sell the goods at all.

Another example is where the country of purchase does not properly protect intellectual property rights so the seller may not want to sell its goods to that country at all. When it does so the goods or software may be copied in their thousands and then find their way back on to the seller's other lucrative markets. The seller could in such cases specify that goods are not to be sold to buyers in certain States. The difficulty with the internet is not always knowing the country from which the buyer originates. There is little which can be done about this, other than careful sifting and looking for obvious clues such as language. Sellers will also have to be careful in refusing to supply, not to breach competition laws or race discrimination laws.

12 – Taxation

'For over 50 years, nations have negotiated tariff reductions because they have recognized that the economies and citizens of all nations benefit from freer trade. Given this recognition, and because the Internet is truly a global medium, it makes little sense to introduce tariffs on goods and services delivered over the internet. Further the Internet lacks the clear and fixed geographic lines of transit that historically have characterized the physical trade of goods. Thus, while it remains possible to administer tariffs for products ordered over the Internet but ultimately delivered via surface or air transport, the structure of the Internet makes it difficult to do so when the product or service is delivered electronically.'

(Framework for Global Electronic Commerce, President Clinton, 1 July 1997)

Executive Summary   [12.1]

- Current tax rules are nationally based.
- Even value added tax rates are not harmonised within the EU.
- Those supplying goods over the internet may find themselves subject to a number of different tax regimes.
- Advice from accountants or tax lawyers should be sought before the business even decides where to base its activities.
- The Organisation for Economic Cooperation and Development aim to assist international agreement in certain tax areas.

President Clinton's words (quoted above) hide a mass of complex national tax rules which apply. This Chapter does no more than point out some of the major areas to consider. It is not a substitute for obtaining detailed tax advice.

Value Added Tax [12.2]

Those supplying goods over the internet from the UK will, in most cases, have to register for value added tax purposes and charge the tax to their customers. This is the case where their turnover is over £51,000 from 1 April 1999. The rate is 17.5% for most purposes. Some goods are exempt from VAT (e.g. books and children's clothes), both of which are available over the internet.

UK customers buying from other non-EU suppliers can purchase at their home rates of VAT under certain distance selling rules. Rates of VAT throughout the EU are not harmonised.

Places of Supply [12.3]

VAT is chargeable under English law only where the supply is made in the UK. Where goods are sold then the place where the goods are supplied is considered. For service a test based on where the supplier 'belongs' is taken. This very different treatment of goods and services means that legal advice should always be sought particularly in relation to computer software where it is not always clear whether a supply of goods for VAT purposes has taken place.

Goods exported to other EU and non-EU States are zero-rated for VAT purposes. Certain supplies such as news or licensing of intellectual property are not chargeable to VAT.

Customs Duties [12.4]

Customs duties under the Common Customs Tariff (CCT) are charged on goods imported into the EU. They are not applied to the import of services. Software may fall into either category dependent on its nature.

Software Downloads [12.5]

Where software is downloaded electronically from outside the EU it is difficult to see how customs duties and VAT can be charged because of the difficulties of policing and the lack of clarity in defining software as goods or services.

Stamp Duty [12.6]

Stamp duty is a tax on documents. Many transactions for the transfer of property are able lawfully to avoid the duty by the relevant documents never being taken into the UK. Where the consideration for the assignment of property including rights in copyright, patents, designs and trade marks (but not knowhow) exceeds £60,000 stamp duty is payable on the whole of the consideration. It begins at 1% and increases as set out below.

0 – £60,000	0%
£60,001 – £250,000	1%
£250,001 – £500,000	2.5%
£501,000 and over	3.5%

Transfers by way of gift do not attract stamp duty and transfers of shares and marketable securities attract duty at 0.5%.

It is only likely to be where copyright is assigned for a large lump sum, rather than the standard licences (or rights to use) common in the internet law field, that stamp duty will be relevant and advice should then be sought to ensure the most efficient transfer is made. Where an assignment is made of intellectual property rights it is normal where the consideration is under £60,000 to include a certificate of value certifying as much for stamp duty purposes.

Reform of UK Tax and Intellectual Property Rights [12.7]

Software, audio visual and film transmitted over the internet is protected by copyright. The various intellectual property rights are all taxed in different ways which often seem inconsistent with each other. In 1999 the UK Government issued a consultation paper seeking views on how the system could be improved. Readers should therefore watch this area with particular care, to ensure that resultant changes are noted.

Taxation Framework for Electronic Commerce [12.8]

The Organisation for Economic Cooperation and Development (OECD) has developed Taxation Framework for Electronic Commerce. Information on this is on at http://www.oecd.org and concerning the Ottawa conference at http://www.oecd.org//daf/fa/e_com/Ottawa.htm.

OECD recommends the principles detailed at **12.9** *et seq.* below.

Broad Taxation Principles which Should Apply to Electronic Commerce [12.9]

Neutrality [12.10]

Taxation should seek to be neutral and equitable between forms of electronic commerce and between conventional and electronic forms of commerce. Business decisions should be motivated by economic rather than tax considerations. Taxpayers in similar situations carrying out similar transactions should be subject to similar levels of taxation.

Efficiency [12.11]

Compliance costs for taxpayers and administrative costs for the tax authorities should be minimised as far as possible.

Certainty and Simplicity [12.12]

The tax rules should be clear and simple to understand so that taxpayers can anticipate the tax consequences in advance of a transaction, including knowing when, where and how the tax is to be accounted.

Effectiveness and Fairness [12.13]

Taxation should produce the right amount of tax at the right time. The potential for tax evasion and avoidance should be minimised while keeping counter-acting measures proportionate to the risks involved.

Flexibility **[12.14]**

The systems for the taxation should be flexible and dynamic to ensure that they keep pace with technological and commercial developments.

Consumption Taxes [12.15]

OECD suggests that rules for consumption taxation of cross border trade should result in tax in the country where the consumption takes place and an international consensus should be obtained on this. Consumption taxes in this case in the UK would be VAT.

Digitised products should not be treated as a supply of goods for consumption tax purposes.

Where a business obtains services and intangible property from suppliers outside the country then countries should examine the use of a reverse charge, self assessment or other means to give immediate protection of their revenue base.

Countries should also ensure that proper systems are developed to ensure taxation on the importation of physical goods.

OECD is made up of 29 member countries including the 15 EU member states. It has five working groups on the Taxation Framework. Their current work (1999) is detailed below.

● Consumption Tax – aims to reach agreement on how to define 'place of consumption'.
● Technology – co-operates on product development and use of security systems and procedures for identifying matters.
● Professional Data Assessment – authenticity, reliability and completeness of electronic data co-operation.
● Income Characterisation – examines how to define various kinds of electronic payments such as the different between a royalty and a business profit and whether income from digital software products which are sold online should be sales or licence income.
● Business Profits – looks at how current taxation treaties and OECD's transfer pricing rules apply to E-commerce.

These five tax Advisory Groups (TAGs) are expected to report by the end of 1999.

The Net Effect [12.16]

The Fabian Society's *Net Effect* Policy Report 47 (1999) (www.fabian-society.org.uk) concludes that the traditional tax model is unworkable and easily avoided when applied to electronically enabled commerce. It believes VAT in particular could become particularly difficult to collect and network service providers are unlikely to want to become unpaid tax collectors. It recommends that to make up for lost taxes higher taxes could be imposed on the means of access to interactive networks such as on modems and network PCs or a state licence fee could be paid.

It also focuses on the cost savings where individuals and businesses can file their tax returns electronically and arrange direct payments.

Institute of Directors [12.17]

In August 1999 the UK Institute of Directors published a report on the tax implications of e-trade. The author of the report said:

> 'They cannot collect VAT on music and software delivered electronically from abroad and will not have the time to collect it on the many extra packages which will come in the post.'

They also warned that the Government should begin planning now on this issue. A suggestion is to rely on the countries where the goods and services originate in order to collect the VAT. However, this may not work well outside the EU.

Another alternative is to apply VAT at the point of import. This would not be possible for goods or services downloaded over the internet.

Taxing consumers would be difficult. One suggestion, therefore, would be to leave the providers such as VISA and American Express to deduct tax.

Further Information [12.18]

Further information on the Organisation for Economic Cooperation and Development's recent initiatives in the taxation area of E-commerce are at: http://www.oecd.org//daf/fa/e_com/Ottawa.htm.

Taxation of Intellectual Property Anthony Pickford and David Harris, Butterworths.

The Fabian Society's *Net Effect* Policy Report 47 (www.fabian-society.org.uk), The Fabian Society, 11 Dartmouth Street, London SW1H 9BN, tel: 020 7222 8877; fax: 020 7976 7153.

Appendix 1: Web Contracts

Web Contract 1: Terms and Conditions for the Provision of Web Site and Other Design Services and/or Software

[COMPANY NAME]

[DRAFTED FROM POINT OF VIEW OF THE SUPPLIER]

Date 2000

This document sets out the terms and conditions between us in relation to the provision of web site and/or other design services and/or software. It applies in place of any earlier agreement or understanding between us and supersedes prior correspondence. You signify your agreement to these terms by signing this document on the last page.

This agreement is between [*company name and address*] and the customer named on the Schedule].

1. Services

1.1   The services we shall provide to you and the prices to be paid for such work are set out on the Schedule. Where alterations to the services to be provided are proposed by you or us during the course of the work these shall be agreed by us both in writing before the work proceeds.

1.2   Unless otherwise agreed in writing payment to us for the work to be undertaken under this agreement is due on delivery of the work on receipt by you of an invoice from us and all fees are payable plus value added tax at prevailing rates.

1.3   In addition to the prices/fees set out on the Schedule you will also pay our reasonable out of pocket expenses, including, without limitation, our travel expenses to your premises, where visits are necessary, purchase of consumables, such as diskettes and [telephone charges? [*and add any other expenses to be paid*].

1.4 We will use our reasonable endeavours to abide by dates agreed for delivery of material to you. You agree to supply material you are to provide to us in order for us to perform our work under this agreement (where relevant) at least a month in advance of the delivery date and we will not be liable where failure to deliver is caused by your delay.

1.5 We will not be responsible for any delay or failure to deliver material under this Agreement caused by circumstances beyond our control, such as Acts of God, fire, strikes, failure of subcontractors or suppliers to supply material required. Where such delay occurs our obligations under this Agreement shall be suspended for the period of such delay.

1.6 Where you do not confirm in writing acceptance of the Supplies within [14 days] of delivery to you the Supplies is deemed accepted by you at the earlier of the expiry of such 14 day period or your first live use. Where the Supplies is rejected by you, whether in whole or in part, we shall endeavour to correct the Supplies to ensure compliance with this agreement.

2. Intellectual Property Rights

2.1 'Supplies' means all data, information, programs and other materials and software which we provide to you, but does not include material which we obtained from you.

2.2 We warrant that to the best of our knowledge and belief the Supplies are original to us, however we cannot be, and are not, responsible for compliance of the Supplies with laws of all jurisdictions of the world to which users of any relevant web site have access. It is your responsibility to satisfy yourself of such compliance.

2.3 We grant you a [non-exclusive] licence of the intellectual property rights, including, without limitation, copyright and related rights anywhere in the world, in the Supplies for the duration of this Agreement for the purposes of use on your Web site or otherwise as agreed in writing from the date of your acceptance of the Supplies. For the avoidance of doubt, where you wish to use the Supplies in any other form (such as on a CD) than that set out in this agreement you must agree terms with us in advance and make payments to be agreed between us. We reserve the right to veto any use outside the scope of this licence.

2.4   We assert our moral rights in the Supplies and you confirm that you shall not alter, reuse or otherwise exploit or jeopardise the artistic integrity of the Supplies without our prior written consent.

2.5   You shall ensure that any copyright notice of ours shall not be removed or obscured on the Supplies.

2.6   Where you are licensed with computer software under this Agreement such licence shall be of object code version of the software only and you shall not reverse engineer or decompile such software save as permitted under EU directive 91/250.

2.7   Intellectual property rights in any authorised improvements to the Supplies made by you shall be licensed to us on an exclusive basis, where such improvements are non-severable from the Supplies and on a non-exclusive basis for severable improvements. You will keep us informed of such improvements.

2.8   Where we supply Supplies to you on disk we retain ownership of the disk and no hire of the disk shall occur.

2.9   The termination of this Agreement shall not affect the provisions of this Clause which shall continue thereafter.

3. Warranties

3.1   We confirm that to the best of our knowledge and belief at the date of supply to us that the Supplies is not obscene, blasphemous or defamatory and does not infringe any English law or regulation and does not adversely reflect on your public perception or image.

3.2   You agree that to the best of your knowledge and belief any material provided by you for the Web site or other work to be undertaken by us under this agreement is not obscene, blasphemous or defamatory and does not infringe any English law or regulation and does not adversely reflect on our public perception or image.

4. Indemnity and Limitation of Liability

4.1   We agree that until such time as the Supplies is delivered to you and approved by you, we will indemnify you against all damages awarded by a court in England and Wales incurred by you as a result of breach of clauses 4 and 5 by us.

4.2   You agree that you shall indemnify us against all claims, demands, losses, damage, costs or expenses incurred by us as a result of breach by you of any provision of this Agreement, law or regulation and as a result of any third party legal action or threatened action in relation to material which you have supplied to us or incorporated with the Supplies or through our involvement with you under this agreement. You shall be responsible for ensuring all registrations and formalities are complied with in relation to any web site we prepare for you, including without limitation, registration of trade marks and under data protection laws.

4.3 Save as provided above, you agree our liability for breach of this Agreement or any other liability of us to you shall be limited to the annual total value of the contract and that all implied terms, conditions or other legal provisions are hereby excluded; save that neither party shall exclude or limit its liability to the other for death or personal injury caused by negligence. We agree that the exclusion and limitation of liability in this clause is reasonable, reflects the respective financial positions of the parties and that the price agreed reflects the position on liability. In no event shall we be liable to you for indirect, financial, consequential loss, loss of profit, revenue or goodwill.

4.4 The termination of this Agreement shall not affect the provisions of this clause which shall continue thereafter.

5. Confidential Information

5.1 Any information about us or you or about our products or your products or financial or business information shall be treated as confidential, used only for the purpose of performance of obligations under this Agreement and not disclosed save as permitted under this Agreement, without limit as to time. Provided that information in the public domain otherwise than through the default of the other party shall not be deemed confidential under this clause.

5.2 The termination of this agreement will not affect this clause.

5.3 We shall be entitled to make reference to our relationship with you in our publicity material.

5.4 Where you have signed a confidentiality agreement with us this shall continue without limit as to time in addition to the provisions in this clause.

6. Your Obligations

6.1 You undertake to supply material and other resources to us promptly as agreed between us. [*any others?*]

7. Termination

7.1 This Agreement shall continue until either performance of the work contracted for set out in the schedule, or where an on-going work commitment is signed may be terminated on three months' notice from one of us to the other given at any time to expire on the anniversary of signature of this Agreement or any subsequent anniversary of such date save as provided below.

7.2 Where one party is in breach of this agreement the other may serve written notice to terminate the agreement forthwith, save that where the breach can be remedied 30 days notice to remedy shall first be given and where remedied such termination will not take effect.

7.3 Either party may terminate this agreement forthwith by written notice where the other goes into liquidation or is declared bankrupt or otherwise is unable to pay its debts as they fall due.

7.4 On termination by you for breach or bankruptcy we shall send to you in accordance with your reasonable directions any material relating to the Web site (where relevant) then in our possession or control and the licence to use the Supplies shall continue without limit as to time. On termination by us or by you on three months' notice as provided above all your rights to use the Supplies shall cease and you shall retain no copies thereof.

8. General

8.1 No variation of this agreement will be valid unless agreed in writing by us both.

8.2 You may not assign this agreement without our prior written consent. The licences granted under this agreement are personal to you and only for the purposes and/or media set out in this agreement. Further licences, licensees, uses and other matters not licensed under this agreement shall only be granted where we so consent and usually on payment of additional licence fees.

8.3 This agreement sets out the entire agreement between us save for any confidentiality agreement between us or other documents referred to in the Schedule.

8.4 All representations, warranties or other assurances made by or on behalf of us to you other than as set out in this Agreement do not form part of this Agreement nor shall they be legally enforceable or actionable.

8.5 If any provision of this agreement is found to be invalid or unenforceable, such invalidity or unenforceability shall not affect the other provisions of this agreement, all of which shall remain in full force and effect.

8.6 No forbearance or delay by us in enforcing rights under this agreement will prejudice or restrict rights and no waiver of any breach of such rights or waiver of the rights will be deemed to be a waiver of any other right or of any later breach.

8.7 Nothing in this agreement shall constitute or be deemed to constitute a partnership or joint venture or the relationship of partnership and agent or employer and employee.

8.8 All notices shall be in writing and sent to the address of the recipient set out above or such other address as the recipient may designate by notice given in accordance with this provision. Any notice may be delivered personally by first class prepaid letter or facsimile transmission (confirmed by first class post) and shall be deemed to have been served if by personal delivery when delivered, if by first class post 48 hours after posting and if by facsimile transmission when despatched (with successful transmission report).

8.9 This agreement shall be governed by English law and we both submit to the non-exclusive jurisdiction of the English courts in relation to any dispute under this agreement.

Please confirm your acceptance of these terms by signing below.

Signed by

. . . .

[. . . . .]

In the presence of:

. . . .

Witness

We agree to the above terms

Signed by

. . . .

[. . . . .]

In the presence of

. . . .

Witness

Schedule

1. **Name of Customer:**
2. **Business address:**
3. **Description of work to be undertaken:**
    (Attach any detailed descriptions to form part of the contract, if relevant)
4. **Material to be supplied by you:**
5. **Estimated delivery date:**
6. **Price:**
7. **Special conditions (where relevant):**

Web Contract 2: Supply for Software for use on a Web Site – Sample Letter

[DRAFTED FROM POINT OF VIEW OF DESIGNER]

[ON DESIGNER'S NOTEPAPER]

Date [ ] 2000

To [ ]

Dear [ ]

SUPPLY OF SOFTWARE FOR USE ON WEB SITE

This letter sets out the terms between us relating to the [ ] software for use on the '[*Name*] web site – [*add name of web site*] WWW site 'the Web site', we have agreed to produce for [*company name* as further described in [specification?, attached letter? *need some mechanism whereby the software is clearly described to avoid disputes later*] ('the Software').

1. We agree to write the Software and license it to you on payment of the fees set out below on a non-exclusive basis for use on the Web site only for an initial three month period. For the avoidance of doubt, where you wish to use the Software in any other form (such as on a CD) than that set out in this agreement you must agree terms with us in advance and make payments to be agreed between us. We reserve the right to veto any use outside the scope of this licence.

2. The fee for provision of the Software shall be £[ ] plus VAT payable to us on delivery of the Software to you. We shall install the Software for you on your Web site.

3. We shall use our reasonable endeavours to deliver the Software by [ ], but are not responsible for delays.

4. In addition to the prices/fees set out above you will also pay our reasonable out of pocket expenses, including, without limitation, our travel expenses to your premises, where visits are necessary, purchase of consumables, such as diskettes.

5. You agree to supply material you are to provide to us in order for us to perform our work under this agreement (where relevant) at least a month in advance of the delivery date and we will not be liable where failure to deliver is caused by your delay.

6. We will not be responsible for any delay or failure to deliver the Software under this Agreement caused by circumstances beyond our control, such as Acts of God, fire, strikes, failure of subcontractors or suppliers to supply material required. Where such delay occurs our obligations under this Agreement shall be suspended for the period of such delay.

7. Where you do not confirm in writing acceptance of the Software within [14 days] of delivery to you the Software is deemed accepted by you at the earlier of the expiry of such 14 day period or your first live use. Where the Software is rejected by you, whether in whole or in part, we shall endeavour to correct the Software to ensure compliance with this agreement. [*Many software licences contain more complex acceptance tests which could be added here*]

8. We warrant that to the best of our knowledge and belief the Software is original to us/our subcontractor, however we cannot be, and are not, responsible for compliance of the Software with laws of all jurisdictions of the world to which users of the Web site have access. It is your responsibility to satisfy yourself of such compliance.

9. We assert our moral rights in the artistic works in the screen displays of the Software and any written materials accompanying the Software and you confirm that you shall not alter, reuse or otherwise exploit or jeopardise the artistic integrity of the Software without our prior written consent.

10. You shall ensure that any copyright notice of ours shall not be removed or obscured on the Software.

11. The licence under this agreement is of object code version of the Software only and you shall not reverse engineer or decompile the Software save as permitted under EU directive 91/250.

12. [*Provisions for maintenance or improvements to the Software, upgrades etc is required – add here*]

13. We shall supply one user manual with the Software in electronic form.

14. We confirm that to the best of our knowledge and belief at the date of supply to us that the Software is not obscene, blasphemous or defamatory and does not infringe any English law or regulation and does not adversely reflect on your public perception or image.

15. You agree that to the best of your knowledge and belief the Software is not obscene, blasphemous or defamatory and does not infringe any English law or regulation and does not adversely reflect on our public perception or image.

16. You shall be responsible for ensuring all registrations and formalities are complied with in relation to the Web site on which the Software will be used.

17. You agree our liability for breach of this Agreement or any other liability of us to you shall be limited to the annual total value of the contract and that all implied terms, conditions or other legal provisions are hereby excluded; save that neither party shall exclude or limit its liability to the other for death or personal injury caused by negligence. We agree that the exclusion and limitation of liability in this clause is reasonable, reflects the respective financial positions of the parties and that the price agreed reflects the position on liability. In no event shall we be liable to you for indirect, financial, consequential loss, loss of profit, revenue or goodwill.

18. This Agreement shall continue for an initial three month term and may be renewed thereafter for subsequent such periods at our discretion on payment of our renewal fees current at the date of renewal.

19.1 No variation of this agreement will be valid unless agreed in writing by us both.

19.2 You may not assign this agreement without our prior written consent. The licences granted under this agreement are personal to you and only for the purposes and/or media set out in this agreement. Further licences, licensees, uses and other matters not licensed under this agreement shall only be granted where we so consent and usually on payment of additional licence fees.

19.3 This agreement sets out the entire agreement between us save for any confidentiality agreement between us or other documents referred to in the Schedule.

19.4 All representations, warranties or other assurances made by or on behalf of us to you other than as set out in this Agreement do not form part of this Agreement nor shall they be legally enforceable or actionable.

19.5 If any provision of this agreement is found to be invalid or unenforceable, such invalidity or unenforceability shall not affect the other provisions of this agreement, all of which shall remain in full force and effect.

19.6 No forbearance or delay by us in enforcing rights under this agreement will prejudice or restrict rights and no waiver of any breach of such rights or waiver of the rights will be deemed to be a waiver of any other right or of any later breach.

19.7 Nothing in this agreement shall constitute or be deemed to constitute a partnership or joint venture or the relationship of partnership and agent or employer and employee.

19.8 All notices shall be in writing and sent to the address of the recipient set out above or such other address as the recipient may designate by notice given in accordance with this provision. Any notice may be delivered personally by first class prepaid letter or facsimile transmission (confirmed by first class post) and shall be deemed to have been served if by personal delivery when delivered, if by first class post 419 hours after posting and if by facsimile transmission when despatched (with successful transmission report).

19.9 This agreement shall be governed by English law and we both submit to the non-exclusive jurisdiction of the English courts in relation to any dispute under this agreement.

Please confirm your acceptance of these terms by signing below.

Signed by

. . . .

[*name*]

In the presence of:

. . . .

Witness

We agree to the above terms

Signed by

. . . .

for and on behalf of [*name*]

In the presence of

. . . .

Witness

Schedule

Description of Software

(Attach any detailed descriptions to form part of the contract, if relevant)

Material to be supplied by you:

Estimated delivery date:

Price:

Web Contract 3: Contract with

Subcontractors/Designers

DRAFTED FROM POINT OF VIEW OF BUYER OF

THE SERVICES FROM THE SUBCONTRACTOR

[COMPANY NAME]

This document sets out the terms we have agreed for our use of your services for us. It forms a legal agreement between us [*Company name*] and you. Your details are set out on the attached Schedule.

1. You agree to provide the services to us described on the attached Schedule ('the Services').
2. We shall pay you the fees set out on the schedule either by way of a monthly retainer payment or a fixed fee (see Schedule).
3. We will/will not reimburse your reasonable expenses agreed with us in writing in advance in arrears at the end of each month.
4. You may provide the Services either at your home, other premises or our premises at your discretion save where we reasonably require you to perform the Services at our premises. Where you use our offices and wish to do so in addition for work for other clients of yours you shall inform us in advance and you may proceed unless we notify you that we object to this use of our resources.
5. All intellectual property rights, including without limitation copyright, in material produced by you in the course of perform-ing the Services shall vest in us and you agree to sign all documents necessary to ensure our ownership of those rights. You may only use such material in order to perform this Agreement and may not, in particular but without limitation, use such material for other clients of yours. Where you have already supplied material to us you hereby assign all intellectual property rights in such material to us.
6. You shall ensure that all copyright and other notices we require to appear shall appear on the material to be produced by you and you will claim no intellectual property rights in such material.
7. You waive your moral rights in relation to material provided by you under this Agreement.
8. You will provide the Services for which you are contracted by the date/dates set out in the schedule or otherwise agreed in writing with us. Time shall be of the essence under this clause.

9. You warrant that the material provided by you under this agreement is your own original work and does not infringe the intellectual property rights of any third party, is not defamatory, obscene, blasphemous or in breach of any law or regulation. You agree fully to indemnify us and hold us harmless from all costs, losses and expenses including legal fees arising from any breach of this warranty.

10. You shall ensure that work undertaken for us is given priority by you over other projects or work to be undertaken by you and that you inform us in advance of any holiday or other absence plans which may interfere with the schedule agreed by us for performance of the Services.

11. The Services to be performed shall be carried out with due skill and care and in accordance with the highest standards of the industry and as set out in the Schedule.

12. You shall perform the Services personally. Where you are a limited company you shall ensure that named individuals perform the Services, the names of which individuals we agree in advance.

13. Where computer software or tangible work product is supplied by you as part of the Services it shall be of satisfactory quality and fit for the purpose agreed between us and otherwise in accordance with the description set out in the Schedule or other documentation agreed between us.

14. Your agreement with us is solely for the performance of the Services and we do not undertake to offer you work on any future occasion or have an continuing obligation to utilise your services. You have informed us that you are self-employed and therefore you are responsible for your own national insurance and tax payments. Where you are registered for value added tax you set out your registration number in the Schedule. You are required to work the hours necessary to perform the Services at your discretion in accordance with this agreement. No relationship of employer and employee is contained in these terms.

15. We reserve the right to terminate our contract with you on one month's notice in writing sent to our address above notwithstanding that all the work in relation to the Services has not been completed by you.

16. On termination or expiry of this agreement you shall return to us all documents, information, software or other property of ours and cease to use such materials and shall not retain any copies in any format.

17. You will keep our confidential information strictly confidential and only use it for the purposes of performing this agreement.

18. For the duration of this Agreement you shall not become involved in competitive projects. You will notify us in advance of your current projects/work for clients so we can determine whether such projects are competitive and may preclude your performing the Services.

19. No variation of this agreement will be valid unless agreed in writing by us both.

20. You may not assign this agreement without our prior written consent.

21. This agreement sets out the entire agreement between us save for any confidentiality agreement between us or other documents referred to in the Schedule.

22. If any provision of this agreement is found to be invalid or unenforceable, such invalidity or unenforceability shall not affect the other provisions of this agreement, all of which shall remain in full force and effect.

23. If we are slow to enforce our rights or do not do so, we may still do so in future.

24. All notices shall be in writing and sent to the address of the recipient set out above or such other address as the recipient may designate by notice given in accordance with this provision. Any notice may be delivered personally by first class prepaid letter or facsimile transmission (confirmed by first class post) and shall be deemed to have been served if by personal delivery when delivered, if by first class post 48 hours after posting and if by facsimile transmission when despatched (with successful transmission report).

25. This agreement shall be governed by English law and we both submit to the non-exclusive jurisdiction of the English courts in relation to any dispute under this agreement.

Please confirm your acceptance of these terms by signing below.

Signed by

. . . .

[ ]

In the presence of:

. . . .

Witness

We agree to the above terms

Signed by

. . . .

[ ]

In the presence of

. . . .

Witness

Schedule

1. **Your name:**
2. **Your business address and registered company number, where relevant:**
3. **Your VAT registration number where relevant:**
4. **Description of the Services to be provided:**
5. **Date of commencement of contract:**
6. **Fees – Monthly retainer/fixed fee:**
7. **Delivery date(s):**

Web Contract 4: Letter Agreement Setting out Terms for Provision of Further Services Relating to on-going Website where no Contract Signed originally

(DRAFTED FROM POINT OF VIEW OF SUPPLIER)

[ON CLIENT'S NOTEPAPER]

[Date]

To: [ ]

We have very much enjoyed working with you these last few months and we think it now appropriate to record in writing the terms of our relationship.

1. Services

1.1 Specific Projects
As in the past, we will identify from time to time specific projects related to the [ ] WWW site ('the Web site') on which we would like your assistance. We will agree the sum to be paid in advance of any such project and we will pay that sum when agreed by us in relation to each project, which may include stage payments and payments on completion of the work in accordance with the contract. We will agree in writing details of the work to be done. You undertake to use your reasonable endeavours to abide by dates agreed for delivery of material to us. We agree to supply material to you at least a month in advance of your delivery date to us and you will not be liable where failure to deliver is caused by our delay.

You will not be responsible for any delay or failure to deliver material under this Agreement caused by circumstances beyond your control, such as Acts of God, fire, strikes, failure of subcontractors or suppliers to supply material required. Where such delay occurs your obligations under this Agreement shall be suspended for the period of such delay.

Any future projects which you are asked to carry out by other companies in your group will, in the absence of written agreement, be subject to the terms of this letter.

1.2 General Services Retainer

We will pay you £[ ] plus VAT per calendar month for the following on-going services:

(a) monthly updating for the content of the Web site, including design and programming in accordance with our directions and limited to a schedule of work to be agreed in advance between us;

(b) on request you will advise us on on-going issues related to the Web site;

(c) until further notice and subject to our directions, you will monitor the Web site on a daily basis on the current server at [ ] and notify us immediately you notice that for any reason the Web site is not fully accessible 24 hours a day;

(d) you will provide us with monthly reports in a format approved by us giving statistics on use of the Web site;

[*Add full description of work to be done*]

2. Advertising Agency

You will, as agreed between us, work in conjunction with our advertising agency.

3. Industry Practice

You agree to carry out the obligations in this letter in accordance with best industry practice.

4. Intellectual Property Rights

4.1 Definitions

'Supplier Input' means all data, information, programs and other materials (but excluding the Software, as defined below) which you have provided to us and will provide to us for use in the Web site, but does not include material which you obtained from us nor third party material the inclusion of which we have approved in writing nor 'Background Work' as defined in Clause 4.7 below. 'The Software' means the [ ] software to be provided by us to you under the terms of a separate software agreement the terms of which shall be agreed between us.

4.2   You warrant that to the best of your knowledge and belief the Supplier Input is original to you.

4.3   You grant us an exclusive licence of the intellectual property rights, including, without limitation, copyright and related rights anywhere in the world, in the Supplier Input for the duration of this Agreement for the purposes of use on the Web site. You agree that for the duration of this Agreement you shall not license or use the Supplier Input save for the purposes of your performance of your obligations under this Agreement or otherwise as agreed by us. For the avoidance of doubt, where we wish to use the Supplier Input in any other form (such as on a CD) we shall first obtain your written consent and take a licence for payments to be agreed.

4.4   You confirm that you assert your moral rights in the Supplier Input and we confirm that we shall not alter, reuse or otherwise exploit the Supplier Input without your prior written consent.

4.5   We shall ensure that any copyright notice of yours shall not be removed or obscured on the Supplier Input.

4.6   We will permit other persons to work with you on projects related to the Web site and in development of the Supplier Input provided that you ensure that they enter into a written agreement under which you own the intellectual property rights in any work which they produce.

4.7   Nothing in this clause shall prevent you from using background, existing work not produced specifically for us ('Background Work') under this Agreement. Background Work is not 'Supplier Input' hereunder and where provided to us is licensed on a non-exclusive basis for the duration of this Agreement.

4.8   The termination of this Agreement shall not affect the provisions of this Clause which shall continue thereafter.

5. Compliance

5.1   You agree that to the best of your knowledge and belief at the date of supply to us that the Supplier Input is not obscene, blasphemous or defamatory and does not infringe any English law or regulation and does not adversely reflect on our public perception or image.

5.2   We agree that to the best of our knowledge and belief any material provided by us for the Web site is not obscene, blasphemous or defamatory and does not infringe any English law or regulation and does not adversely reflect on your public perception or image.

6. Indemnity

6.1   You agree that until such time as the Supplier Input is delivered and approved by us you will indemnify us against all claims, demands, losses, damage, costs or expenses incurred by us as a result of breach of clauses 4 and 5 by you.

6.2   We agree that we shall indemnify you against all claims, demands, losses, damage, costs or expenses incurred by you as a result of breach by us of any provision of this Agreement, law or regulation and as a result of any third party legal action or threatened action in relation to material which we have supplied to you or incorporated with the Supplier Input or through your involvement with us through this agreement. We shall be responsible for ensuring all registrations and formalities are complied with in relation to the Web site, including without limitation, registration of trade marks and under data protection laws.

6.3   Save as provided above, we agree your liability for breach of this Agreement or any other liability of you to us shall be limited to the annual total value of the contract to you as varied from time to time and that all implied terms, conditions or other legal provisions are hereby excluded; save that neither party shall exclude or limit its liability to the other for death or personal injury caused by negligence. We agree that the exclusion and limitation of liability in this clause is reasonable, reflects the respective financial positions of the parties and that the price agreed reflects the position on liability. In no event shall you be liable to us for indirect, financial, consequential loss, loss of profit, revenue or goodwill.

6.4   The termination of this Agreement shall not affect the provisions of this clause which shall continue thereafter.

7. Confidential Information

7.1   Any information about us or another company in our group or about our products which you know or ought reasonably to know is confidential must not be disclosed to a third party or used other than in connection with the services described in this agreement.

7.2 The termination of this agreement will not affect this clause.

7.3 Information in the public domain or disclosed in accordance with a legal obligation to do so shall not be 'confidential'.

7.4 We will agree separately in writing terms in relation to publicity in connection with your relationship with us.

8. Exclusivity

8.1 For the duration of this agreement you will not provide similar services to a competitor of ours without our prior written consent. For the purposes of this clause a competitor of ours is any other company engaged in the business of [ ].

9. Termination

9.1 This Agreement shall continue until terminated on three months' notice from one of us to the other given at any time to expire on the anniversary of signature of this Agreement or any subsequent anniversary of such date save as provided below.

9.2 Where one party is in breach of this agreement the other may serve written notice to terminate the agreement forthwith, save that where the breach can be remedied 30 days notice to remedy shall first be given and where remedied such termination will not take effect.

9.3 Either party may terminate this agreement forthwith by written notice where the other goes into liquidation or is declared bankrupt or otherwise is unable to pay its debts as they fall due.

9.4 On termination by us for breach or bankruptcy you shall send to us in accordance with our directions any material relating to the Web site then in your possession or control and the licence to use the Supplier Input and Background Work shall continue without limit as to time. On termination by you or by us on three months' notice all our rights to use the Supplier Input and Background Work shall cease.

10. General

10.1 No variation of this agreement will be valid unless agreed in writing by us both.

10.2 Neither of us shall assign this agreement without the prior written consent of the other, save that we may assign the agreement to another group company.

10.3 We agree to your continuing to subcontract your obligations under this agreement.

10.4 This letter sets out the entire agreement between us, save for the document on confidentiality to be agreed referred to in clause 7.4 and the software agreement referred to in clause 4.1.

10.5 Neither of us shall rely on any representation, warranty or other assurance made by or on behalf of us to the other before the date of this agreement. We and you waive all rights or remedies which, but for this provision, might otherwise be available in respect of any such representation, warranty or assurance, provided that nothing in this agreement shall limit or exclude liability for fraud.

10.6 If any provision of this agreement is found to be invalid or unenforceable, such invalidity or unenforceability shall not affect the other provisions of this agreement, all of which shall remain in full force and effect.

10.7 No forbearance or delay by us or you in enforcing rights under this agreement will prejudice or restrict rights and no waiver of any breach of such rights or waiver of the rights will be deemed to be a waiver of any other right or of any later breach.

10.8 Nothing in this letter shall constitute or be deemed to constitute a partnership or joint venture or the relationship of partnership and agent or employer and employee.

10.9 All notices shall be in writing and sent to the address of the recipient set out above or such other address as the recipient may designate by notice given in accordance with this provision. Any notice may be delivered personally by first class prepaid letter or facsimile transmission (confirmed by first class post) and shall be deemed to have been served if by personal delivery when delivered, if by first class post 48 hours after posting and if by facsimile transmission when despatched (with successful transmission report).

10.10 This letter shall be governed by English law and we both submit to the non-exclusive jurisdiction of the English courts in relation to any dispute under this agreement.

We look forward to a continued mutually profitable working relationship in the future. Please confirm your acceptance of these terms by signing below.

Yours sincerely,

. . . .

[ ]

We agree to the above terms

. . . .

[ ]

[*Name*]

[ ] Date

Web Contract 5: Software Development Agreement

(DRAFTED BY SUPPLIER)

[*Date*]

Parties

1. [*Name*] of [*Address*] (Supplier)

2. [*Name*] of [*Address*] (The Customer)

Signed on behalf of Supplier by:

. . . .

Signature . . . .

Signed on behalf of the Customer by:

. . . .

Signature . . . .

Any comments or queries about this document should be addressed to:

Singletons Solicitors

The Ridge

South View Road

Pinner

Middlesex

HA5 3YD

Tel: 020 8866 1934

Fax: 020 8429 9212

E-mail: essingleton@link.org

1   Introduction
The Customer and Supplier have agreed that Supplier shall act on behalf of the Customer in:

1.1   the design, development and supply of a [ ] Specification,

1.2   the design, development and supply of a [ ] Specification,

1.3   the production of coded software modules,

1.4   the performance of unit testing on individual software modules, and

1.5   the performance of system testing
of the software programs and associated documentation described in Schedule 1 (the Project).
[*Delete 1.1 to 1.5 as applicable to the individual contract.*]
The Project shall be carried out by Supplier in accordance with the terms of this Agreement.

2   Duty of Care
Supplier warrants that it will carry out the Project using reasonable care and skill and that all staff assigned to the performance of the Project shall possess such skill and experience as is appropriate for the proper performance of the Project.

3   The Project

3.1   The Customer shall prepare and deliver to Supplier a user requirement specification describing its requirements for the Project (the Specification). In particular, the Specification shall contain quality provisions for each of the following items associated with the Project:

   3.1.1   *Productivity* – the productivity of development staff during the production of the Project;

3.1.2 *Defects* – number of technical defects arising from the development of the Project;

3.1.3 *Requests for enhancements* – the number of requests for enhancements arising during the first four weeks after acceptance of the Project into production, as a measure of the effectiveness of the Project in capturing the Specification;

3.1.4 *Maintainability* – the annual maintenance costs of the Project as a percentage of total development costs;

3.1.5 *Portability* – the capability of the software associated with the Project to be uninstalled and re-installed in other hardware;

3.1.6 *Availability* – the availability of the Project, expressed as a percentage, to be run in production;

3.1.7 *Reliability* – the number of occasions of down time likely to occur when the Project is in production;

3.1.8 *Response* – the response time of the Project software, measured at the end-user terminal;

3.1.9 *Longevity* – the minimum life span during which the Project should maintain full functionality;

3.1.10 *Accuracy* – the acceptable tolerance in the correct processing of numeric values and non-numeric data;

3.1.11 Security – the security systems built into the Project as a resistance to hacking or other security breaches.

If quality provisions for any of the items listed are not specified in the Specification, Supplier shall apply such reasonable such provisions as it, in its absolute discretion, considers to be appropriate to the Project.

3.2 The Project shall be managed in accordance with a proven methodology agreed in writing prior to the commencement of the Project between the Supplier and the Customer and using structured analysis and design techniques.

3.3 Any Cost Benefit Analysis associated with the Project shall be carried out by the Customer who shall keep Supplier and the Project Manager informed of all appropriate principles and items which are relevant to the Customer's requirements at all times during the development of the Project.

3.4 Prior to the date identified in the Programme of Work for the commencement of development work on the Project, the Customer shall carry out a Risk Analysis identifying those areas which could cause the failure of the Project. Before carrying out such Risk Analysis, the Customer shall notify Supplier in writing of the assumptions made in respect of minimum volumes of data to be processed, technical environment in which the Project is to be used and the compatibility of the Project with the hardware on which it is to be run. If such Risk Analysis is not completed by the date identified for the commencement of development work, or the Customer choose not to carry out such Risk Analysis, Supplier will be not be held liable for any delays or failures arising from the Project which could have been avoided had such Risk Analysis been completed or carried out, as the case may be.

4   Programme of Work

4.1   Any work pursuant to the Project shall be carried out in accordance with a Programme of Work prepared by the Supplier based on the Specification and agreed by the Customer and which shall include:

4.1.1   the timing and sequence of events;

4.1.2   acceptance criteria and the provisions and responsibilities for carrying out acceptance tests;

4.1.3   the resources and charges to be used in carrying out the Project;

4.1.4   any other items identified by the Customer as reasonably required by the Customer.

4.2   The Programme of Work shall include a test programme designed and undertaken to ensure that the Project achieves the service levels required by the Specification and meets all aspects of the Specification (including service level aspects).

In particular, the test programme should include provisions to test the following aspects of the Project:

4.2.1   *functionality* – ensuring the Project reasonably complies with the functions for which it was designed;

4.2.2   *reliability* – the robustness of the system and the likelihood of it requiring maintenance and/or repair;

4.2.3   *response* – that the Project reasonably complies with the response provisions stated in the Specification;

4.2.4   *availability* – that the Project reasonably complies with the availability quality provisions stated in the Specification;

4.2.5   *throughput (volume testing)* – the productivity of the Project, with reference to the effect of increased productivity on response and availability;

4.2.6   *defect rate* – the compliance of the Project with the provision for the number and frequency of defects contained in the Specification;

4.2.7   *requirement for enhancements* – whether the requirement requires enhancement in order to comply with the Specification;

4.2.8 *accuracy* – ensuring that the Project correctly processes numeric values and non-numeric data.

4.3 On completion of the preparation of the Programme of Work for the Project, Supplier shall immediately submit it in writing to the Customer, who shall acknowledge its safe receipt in writing to Supplier. The Programme of Work will be deemed to have been received by the Customer on the date specified in a written notice of receipt sent to Supplier.

4.4 On receipt of the Programme of Work the Customer shall either:

4.4.1 signify its approval, in which case it shall form the Programme of Work for the Project; or

4.4.2 reject the programme, giving in writing its reasons for doing so and its requirements for amendments to the programme.

4.5 If within 15 Working Days of the delivery of the Programme of Work to the Customer (in accordance with clause 4.1 above), Supplier has not received a reply from the Customer in accordance with the terms of sub-clause 4.4.1, it shall issue a written reminder to the Customer indicating that a reply has not been received ,and shall not be required to carry out any part of the Project until approval has been given to the Programme of Work.

5 **The Project Manager**

5.1 The Project will be managed by a Project Manager who shall be appointed by Supplier.

5.2 The Project Manager shall have the following responsibilities in respect of the Project:

5.2.1 to ensure that the Project is run in such a manner that it is completed within the timescales and budget specified in the Programme of Work and in accordance with the Specification;

5.2.2 to report to the Customer and Supplier immediately on becoming aware of the same with details of any variations to the costs and timescales specified in the Programme of Work.

5.2.3 to ensure that appropriate change and quality management procedures are applied to the pursuance of the Project;

5.2.4 to ensure that the best practices of project management are followed in the pursuance of the Project, including:

5.2.4.1 the agreement of deliverables with the Customer and Supplier;

5.2.4.2 the agreement of appropriate milestoes in the Project with the Customer and Supplier;

5.2.4.3 the agreement of appropriate project reporting procedures and formats with the Customer and Supplier and the provision of reports in accordance with such procedures and formats;

5.2.4.4 where not already specified in the Specification or Programme of Work, the agreement with the Customer and Supplier of project phases and modules;

5.2.4.5 the appliance of critical path analysis to the Project;

5.2.4.6 the production of appropriate schedules of work and their application in pursuance of the Project;

5.2.4.7 the reporting to the Customer and Supplier on any aspect of the Project that is likely to have an impact on the Project's cost benefit analysis (as informed to the Project Manager by virtue of clause 3.3);

5.2.4.8 seeking the authorisation of the Customer and Supplier before proceeding from phase to phase of the Project;

5.2.4.9 ensuring that the Project is properly signed off with the Customer and Supplier at each phase and at completion.

5.3 If, in the reasonable opinion of the Customer, the appointed Project Manager fails to perform all or any of his duties as described in clause 5.2 above, the Customer may, by written notice served on Supplier, require the removal of the Project Manager and his replacement with another and Supplier shall comply with such request within a reasonable time.

6   Delivery and Installation

Unless otherwise agreed between the parties Supplier shall be responsible for the delivery and installation of the Project at such premises as may be specified in the Specification PROVIDED THAT such delivery and/or installation and any work associated with it shall only be carried out with the prior written consent of the Customer who shall be responsible for ensuring that appropriate access and facilities are made available to facilitate such delivery and installation.

7   Inspection and Examination

7.1 At all times during the carrying out of the Programme of Work, the Customer may, on giving reasonable prior notice to Supplier inspect, examine and test the analysis, design, documentation, programming and project management techniques and workmanship being used on the Project.

7.2 If, after an inspection, examination and/or test has been carried out by the Customer, the Customer is of the reasonable opinion that the Project is not being developed in accordance with the Programme of Work and/or the appropriate duty of care, the Customer may give written notice within 10 Working Days of such an inspection, examination and/or test requiring Supplier to remedy such defects as may be specified.

8 Acceptance Tests

8.1 The Customer shall provide or ensure the provision of such information and facilities as are necessary to enable Supplier to carry out the acceptance tests specified in the Programme of Work by the date specified in such programme.

8.2 Unless otherwise agreed between Supplier and the Customer, the acceptance tests shall be carried out on the dates specified and within the timescales specified in the Programme of Work and in accordance with such programme.

8.3 If the Project or any part of it fails to pass all or any of the acceptance tests specified in the Programme of Work, repeat tests will be carried out within a reasonable time on the same terms and conditions. If the Project fails to pass all or any of the repeat tests, the Customer may require Supplier to supply, free of charge, such additional hardware or telecommunications capability, software or services as may be necessary to rectify such defects and enable the Project to pass the acceptance tests.

9 Acceptance Certificate

9.1 As soon as the Project, or any phase or part of it, has been completed in accordance with the Programme of Works and has passed the appropriate acceptance tests, the Customer shall issue an Acceptance Certificate, signed by a duly authorised person, stating:

9.1.1 the acceptance date of the phase or the total Project, (as the case may be) or

9.1.2 any outstanding defects in the phase or total Project (as the case may be) and any agreed dates and methods for their rectification, and

9.1.3 any revisions to timescales, resources or costs for the completion of the Project.

9.2 In the case of defects being specified in the Acceptance Certificate, Supplier will carry out within a reasonable time such works as specified by the Customer and which are necessary to remedy such defects.

10 Ownership

10.1 Insofar as software produced by virtue of the Project already exists within the ownership of Supplier (whether or not tailored to suit the requirements of the Project), such software (including any source code, copyright and all other intellectual property rights) shall belong to Supplier, who shall grant to the Customer a perpetual, irrevocable licence, free of charge, to load, run and use such software.

10.2 Supplier undertakes to use its reasonable endeavours to procure the grant to the Customer by the relevant licensor of a licence in respect of such software required in the pursuance of the Project as may be owned by such licensor on such terms as the licensor may require.

[**10.3** Those items of software newly developed by Supplier by virtue of the Project (including any source code, copyright and any other intellectual property rights) shall belong to Supplier/the Customer.]

11   Post Implementation Review

11.1 No earlier than 3 months and no later than 6 months from the date of the Acceptance Certificate issued in respect of the Project, the Project Manager shall carry out a review of the post-implementation operation of the Project and its compliance with the Project quality requirements specified in clause 3.1 above. The Project Manager will report in writing to both Supplier and the Customer with the results of the review, indicating the actual operation of the Project against the specified quality provision. Such report shall be delivered no later than 9 months from the date of the Acceptance Certificate.

11.2 If the Post-Implementation Review Report indicates that any of the appropriate quality provisions fail to be met by the Project, the Customer may request in writing, and Supplier shall carry out within a reasonable time, such works as are necessary to remedy such failure.

12   Remedial Work

Where remedial work is carried out within the provisions of clauses 9.2 and 11.2 above and such work requires the provision of additional hardware, telecommunications capability, software or other services in order to facilitate the proper functioning of the Project, Supplier shall ensure the supply of such items.

13   Access and Facilities

13.1 The Customer shall make available, or ensure that there is available, to Supplier' staff, the Project Manager and his staff assigned to the performance of the Project such access to the Customer's premises, hardware systems, data, computer time and programs, as shall be reasonably necessary for the performance of any of the terms of this Agreement, such access not to be unreasonably withheld.

13.2 Where necessary for the proper performance of the Project, the Customer shall ensure the provision to Supplier and/or the Project Manager of a suitable place of work within the Customer's premises with amenities comparable to those provided for the Customer's staff of similar status to Supplier staff and/or Project Manager's staff assigned to the Project.

13.3 In exercising its right of access described in this clause, Supplier shall ensure that it does not unnecessarily interfere with the operations of the Customer.

14   Discrepancies

The Customer shall be responsible for, and pay any additional costs occasioned by any discrepancies, errors or omissions in information supplied to Supplier or the Project Manager by the Customer.

15   Variation

15.1 The Customer may, at any time prior to the issue of an Acceptance Certificate for the Project (in accordance with clause 9), require Supplier to make amendments to the Programme of Work or alterations, additions or omissions from the Project, provided that:

15.1.1 such variations are made with the written consent of Supplier, and

15.1.2 the Customer shall pay such additional costs and charges as arise as a result of such a variation.

15.2 Prior to implementing a variation to the Project or Programme of Work, Supplier shall provide the Customer with written details of the effect of the variation on the Project and/or Programme of Work, including details of any additional costs and charges. Such details shall be provided to the Customer within 15 Working Days of the receipt by Supplier of a request for a variation from the Customer, or within such other period as may be agreed between the the Customer and Supplier. On the receipt of such details, the Customer shall, within 10 Working Days, notify Supplier in writing if it requires Supplier to proceed with the variation. Supplier shall not be required to proceed without such notification.

16   Payment

16.1 *Payment of Charges*

In consideration of the Services provided by Supplier, the Customer shall pay to the Supplier charges in accordance with the rates specified in Schedule 2. Such charges shall not include value added tax which shall be payable by the Customer in the manner and at the rate from time to time prescribed by law.

16.2 *Invoices*

Supplier will invoice the Customer monthly in arrears using the agreed rates indicated in Schedule 2 for such charges as have arisen since the previous invoice.

Unless disputed by the Customer within 15 days of delivery, invoices shall be paid by the Customer by the end of the calendar month following that in which the invoice is delivered by Supplier.

OR

Supplier may raise an invoice for payment for any phase or completion of the Project at any time after the date of the Acceptance Certificate issued for that phase or the complete Project. Such invoices shall be payable by the end of the calendar month following that in which they are delivered by Supplier.

16.3 *Support of Invoices*

All invoices delivered by Supplier will be supported by sufficient details to support the charges made. Such details shall include:

16.3.1 the appropriate Contract Reference;

16.3.2 [appropriate timesheets – *delete for non-T&M Agreement*]; and

16.3.3 such other information as the Customer may from time to time agree with Supplier to be appropriate.

16.4 *Expenses*

Where any member of Supplier' staff is required to attend at premises other than Supplier' in pursuance of the Project, expenses shall be paid in accordance with the rates specified in Schedule 2

16.5 *Timesheets*

Supplier shall ensure that each member of its staff working on the Project completes a timesheet detailing the hours worked during each week.

16.6 *Period of Validity*

The rates and expenses detailed in Schedule 2 are fixed and valid for the period from the date of this Agreement until [. . . . . .20 . . .] inclusive. Such rates may be increased by Supplier at [. . . . . .20 . . .] and each subsequent anniversary by [an amount that is no more than the corresponding increase during the previous year in the Index of Retail Prices published by HM Government].

16.7 If the payment of any sum due under this Agreement is delayed by the Customer (other than under 16.2. above), Supplier may charge interest at a rate of 3% above Base Rate for the time being of National Westminster Bank plc on the amount of the delayed payment for the period of delay.

16.8 If, by reason of the rise in the costs of materials, labour or other related costs, the cost to Supplier of performing its obligations under this Agreement is increased, the amount of the increase shall be added to the payments referred to in the Schedule, provided that such increase is not as a direct result of an act or default on the part of Supplier.

17 Termination

17.1 Either Party shall have the right to terminate this Agreement by written notice served on the other if the other (the Terminating Party):

    17.1.1 is in breach (other than a minor or inconsequential breach) of any of the terms of this Agreement and does not rectify such breach within 10 Working Days (or such longer period as may be reasonable) of being served notice to do so by the other;

    17.1.2 becomes insolvent or bankrupt or has a receiving order or administration order made against it, or commences to be wound up or carries on business under an administrator or an administrative receiver for the benefit of its creditors or any of them.

17.2 Termination of this Agreement shall not prejudice any rights of either party which had arisen prior to termination. In particular, Supplier shall be entitled to be paid for any work carried out prior to termination on a time and materials basis.

17.3 In the event of termination under the terms of clause 17.1.2. above, the Terminating Party shall have the right, on giving prior notice to the other party, to enter the premises of the other party and to remove any items clearly marked as being the property of the Terminating Party or of its agents.

18 Extension of Time

Where Supplier or the Project Manager are delayed or impeded in their pursuance of the Project by:

18.1 any act or omission on the part of the Customer,

18.2 any circumstances beyond the reasonable control of Supplier,

the Programme of Work shall be extended by such period of time as is reasonable to compensate for such delay or impedance and each respective phase of the Programme of Work will be delayed accordingly.

19 Delays

All additional costs reasonably incurred by Supplier as a result of its being prevented from or delayed in proceeding with the Project by the Customer, its agents or employees or by reason of suspension of the Project by the Customer (other than as a result of some default on the part of Supplier) shall be reimbursed to

Supplier by the Customer within one calendar month of the receipt of an invoice from Supplier giving details of such costs.

20   Limitation of Liability

20.1 To the extent permitted by laws and notwithstanding any other provisions of this Agreement, Supplier shall not be liable to the Customer for loss arising from any breach of this Agreement other than for loss directly resulting from such breach and which at the date of this Agreement was reasonably foreseeable as not unlikely to occur in the ordinary course of events from such breach in respect of:-

    20.1.1 physical damage to the property of the Customer or their respective officers, employees or agents; and/or

    20.1.2 the liability of the Customer to any other person for loss in respect of physical damage to the property of any other person.

20.2 Nothing in this Agreement shall exclude or limit the liability of Supplier for death or personal injury resulting from its negligence or that of any of its officers, employees or agents and Supplier shall indemnify and keep indemnified the Customer, its officers, employees or agents from and against all such and any loss or liability which the Customer may suffer or incur by reason of any claim on account of death or personal injury resulting from the negligence of Supplier or any of its officers, employees or agents.

20.3 Neither Supplier nor any of its officers, employees or agents shall in any circumstances whatsoever be liable to the Customer for:

    20.3.1 any loss of profit, loss of revenue, loss of use, loss of contract or loss of goodwill; or

    20.3.2 any indirect or consequential loss; or

    20.3.3 loss resulting from the liability of the Customer to any other person howsoever and whensoever arising save as provided in Clauses 20.1.2 and 20.2.

20.4 Each of Clauses 20.1, 20.2 and 20.3 shall:-

    20.4.1 be construed as a separate and severable contract term, and if one or more of such Clauses is held to be invalid, unlawful or otherwise unenforceable the other or others of such Clauses shall remain in full force and effect and shall continue to bind the Parties; and

    20.4.2 survive termination of this Agreement.

20.5 For the avoidance of doubt, nothing in this Clause 20 shall prevent or restrict any Party enforcing any obligation (including suing for a debt) owed to it under or pursuant to this Agreement.

20.6 Each Party acknowledges and agrees that the foregoing provisions of this Clause 20 have been the subject of discussion and negotiation and are fair and reasonable having regard to the circumstances as at the date of this Agreement.

21 Confidentiality

21.1 Neither party shall disclose to any third party any part of the software produced by the Project or any other information not owned by it that comes into its possession by virtue of the pursuance of the Project.

21.2 The provisions of 21.1 above shall not apply to:

21.2.1 any information in the public domain otherwise than by breach of this Agreement;

21.2.2 any disclosure made with the prior written consent of the owner of the software or other information (as the case may be).

21.3 The Customer and Supplier shall disclose confidential information only to those employees or sub-contractors who are directly involved in the Project and who require such information in order to pursue the Project. In such circumstances, the Customer and Supplier shall ensure that such employees or sub-contractors are aware of, and comply with, the obligations as to confidentiality contained within this Agreement.

21.4 The provisions of this clause will continue in force notwithstanding the termination of this Agreement.

22 Force Majeure

Neither Party shall be liable to the other for failure to perform its obligations under this Agreement if such failure is a direct result of circumstances beyond the control of the Party in default.

23 Waiver

No delay, neglect or forbearance on the part of either Party in enforcing against the other any provision of this Agreement shall be or be deemed to be a waiver or in any way prejudice the rights of that Party under this Agreement.

24 Entire Agreement

This Agreement contains the whole agreement between the Parties and neither Party has relied on any oral or written representations made to it by the other party or its employees or agents.

25 Arbitration

Subject to any contrary provision of any Act, Licence, Regulation or otherwise, any dispute or difference arising out of or in connection with this Agreement may be referred to arbitration by either of the Parties. In such circumstances such dispute or difference will be referred to a single arbitrator to be agreed between the parties, or failing such agreement within 15 Working Days, to be nominated by the President for the time being of the British Computer Society.

26 Law

The parties agree that this Agreement shall be governed by and construed in all respects in accordance with the laws of England and Wales.

Schedule 1 – The Project

[Insert details of the Software being produced]

A. Production of [ ] Specification

A.1 In accordance with the terms of the Specification, Supplier shall produce a [ ] specification detailing the design of the system.

B. Production of [ ] Specification

B.1 In accordance with the terms of the Specification, Supplier shall produce a [ ] Specification which shall be consistent with the terms of the [ ] Specification relating to the Project. In particular, it shall detail:

B.1.1 the hardware on which the software and programs produced by the Project (the Programs) are to operate;

B.1.2 the software platform required for the operation of the Programs;

B.1.3 the language to be used in the implementation of the Programs;

B.1.4 such other details as may be agreed in writing prior to the commencement of the production of the Specification.

C. Production of Code

In accordance with the terms of the [ ] Specifications Supplier shall write the software modules comprising the Programs and such supporting documentation detailed in the project plan as being necessary for the proper use and operation of the Programs.

D. Performance of Unit Testing

D.1 Supplier shall perform tests on the individual software modules to ensure that such module performs in accordance with the contents of the Physical System Specification.

D.2 The Customer shall provide such information and facilities as are reasonably necessary to enable Supplier to carry out the unit tests specified in the Programme of Work by the date specified in such programme.

D.3 Unless otherwise agreed between Supplier and the Customer, the acceptance tests shall be carried out on the dates specified and within the timescales specified in the Programme of Work and in accordance with such programme.

D.4 If any module fails to pass all or any of the acceptance tests specified in the Programme of Work, repeat tests will be carried out within a reasonable time on the same terms and conditions.

E Performance of System Testing

E.1 Supplier shall perform acceptance tests on the full Project to ensure that the software produced pursuant to the Project conforms with the contents of the [ ] Specification and [ ] Specification relating to the Project.

E.2 The Customer shall provide such information and facilities as are reasonably necessary to enable Supplier to carry out the acceptance tests (whether of an individual module or of the full Program) specified in the Programme of Work by the date specified in such programme.

E.3 Unless otherwise agreed between Supplier and the Customer, the acceptance tests shall be carried out on the dates specified and within the timescales specified in the Programme of Work and in accordance with such programme.

E.4 If the Project or any part of it fail to pass all or any of the acceptance tests specified in the Programme of Work, repeat tests will be carried out within a reasonable time on the same terms and conditions.

Schedule 2: Charges

[ ]

Web Contract 6

SPECIFIC TERMS AND CONDITIONS –

INTERNET ACCESS

These are the terms on which we will provide access to the Internet to you. You will accept these terms by making your first connection to our server.

1. We agree to provide you with access to the Internet. If applicable, we will also provide you with support under the terms set out in a separate document.

2. You agree to pay the installation and set up fees and monthly connection charges from time to time laid down by us.

3. Unless we otherwise agree, your rights to access the Internet through us and any other rights under this Contract are not transferable.

4. Our terms of payment of all charges are 30 days after the date of invoice. If you do not make any payment within that time then Star reserve the right to charge interest on the outstanding balance at a rate of 1½% per month. We also reserve the right to suspend your right to access the Internet or to terminate this Contract.

5. You are responsible for and must provide and pay for all telephone services necessary to access the Internet through us.

6. You agree that you will:

6.1 comply with any reasonable instructions or directions issued by us from time to time concerning access to the Internet;

6.2 only use computer and communications equipment of at least the minimum specification as laid down by us from time to time;

6.3 conform to the protocols and standards published on the Internet from time to time and adopted by the majority of Internet users;

6.4 indemnify us against any liability to third parties resulting from your use of the Internet;

6.5 keep your password secure and confidential, take any steps necessary to ensure that it does not become known to other persons and ensure that it is only used by legitimate members of your organisation.

7 You agree that you will not:

7.1 use the Internet for any unlawful purpose or in breach of English law or any other law applicable to the use of the Internet. These prohibited uses include, but are not limited to:

7.1.1 civil and criminal offences of copyright and trademark infringement; or

7.1.2 transmission or display or posting to a bulletin board of obscene, indecent or pornographic material; or

7.1.3 commission of any criminal offence (including deliberate transmission of computer viruses) under the Computer Misuse Act 1990 or similar legislation in any country; or

7.1.4 any transmission or display or posting to a bulletin board of any material which is of a defamatory, offensive, abusive, or menacing character or which causes annoyance, inconvenience or needless anxiety to any other person; or

7.1.5 transmission or display or posting to a bulletin board of any material in breach of *the Data Protection Act 1984* (or any later statute dealing with data protection or similar legislation in any other country or of any material which is confidential or is a trade secret; or

7.1.6 use of the Internet in any manner which is a violation or infringement of the rights of any individual, firm or company within the United Kingdom and elsewhere.

7.2 use the Internet connection provided by us in any way that makes excessive or profligate use our of network or computing resources or those of other Internet users.

7.3 If we have reasonable grounds for believing that there has been a breach of this Agreement by you, we reserve the right to monitor any and all communications through our service.

8. In addition to our termination rights set out in the General Terms and Conditions, we may, at any time and at our sole option, either suspend your access to the Internet under this Agreement until you give suitable undertakings or terminate this Agreement immediately if:

8.1 you breach any term of this Agreement; or

8.2 any registration fee or connection charge remains unpaid by you for more than 30 days after it is invoiced; or

9. You expressly agree that you use the Internet at your sole risk. We (and our employees and agents) do not warrant that your access to the Internet will be uninterrupted or error-free.

Star Internet

Specific Terms and Conditions – Netstar

These are the additional terms on which we will provide the Netstar service to you.

1. The Netstar service is to some extent a modular service which will be installed in accordance with the options and parameters discussed with you at or before the time of concluding the contract.

2. The Netstar unit itself will be leased to you but if other equipment is required in order to complete the installation, this will be provided on a sale basis, the payment being included in the installation charge referred to below.

3. The installation charge payable covers our charges for installing the Netstar product, including any ancillary equipment required.

4. The monthly charge payable in respect of the Netstar service covers hire payable in respect of the Netstar unit, together with our monthly maintenance and support charges.

5. Prior to agreeing an installation charge with you, we shall carry out a site survey by telephone or written questionnaire. Your answers to this questionnaire will be used by us in calculating the appropriate installation charge. Please note that we reserve the right to charge for any extra work or equipment necessary to effect installation if the information you provide to us is materially inaccurate or incomplete.

6. You agree that you will not tamper with the installation in anyway.

7. Please note that there is a possibility of certain applications which you may add to your network following the Netstar installation interfering with the operation of Netstar. This may result in the Netstar service coming or remaining on line for extended periods thereby incurring line charges with your telecoms provider. Whilst we take every reasonable step to remotely monitor your use of Netstar to prevent this situation we cannot be responsible for the charges which may be made by your telecom provider in these circumstances. We therefore strongly recommend that you seek our advice before adding any software application to your network after the installation of the Netstar service.

8. Without prejudice to any other contractual right you may have, we promise you that any hardware fault in the Netstar service we

provide will, once the problem has been identified, be resolved in the shortest possible time failing which the system will be replaced within 3 working days.

Web Consultancy Services

These are the additional terms on which we will provide Web publishing, Web development and other bespoke Web consultancy services ("the Web Services") to you.

1. In these Specific Terms and Conditions, the following additional definitions will apply:

    1.1 "the Intellectual Property" means patents, trade marks, service marks, design rights, copyright and confidential information;

    1.2 "the Materials" means all original materials developed by us for you in the course of providing the Web Services;

2. We shall:

    2.1 provide the Web Services;

    2.2 perform the Web Services with reasonable care and skill and in a professional manner; and

    2.3 provide you with Materials which will, unless otherwise stated and so far as they do not comprise (a) material originating from you, your employees, agents or contractors, or (b) software code sourced from software libraries, be original works of authorship.

3. You shall:

    3.1 ensure that your employees co-operate fully with us in relation to the provision of the Web Services; and

    3.2 promptly give us such information and documents as we may reasonably request for the proper and efficient provision of the Web Services

4. Subject to the prompt payment by you of all contractual charges due from you to us, you shall be entitled to all rights in the Intellectual Property in the Materials (the "Property Rights") and we assign to you all Property Rights created during the provision of the Web Services except such Property Rights that arise in relation to Excluded Property. The expression "Excluded Property "shall mean:–

    (1) all Intellectual Property owned by us or licensed to us by third parties before the start of this contract; and

    (2) any toolbox methods, code templates or routines used by us in our business.

5.   You shall indemnify us against all claims and liabilities in respect of the infringement of any intellectual property rights, or any breach of confidence relating to material provided by you to us for the purposes of our provision to you of the Web Services.

6.   We are independent contractors and noting in this contract shall be construed as forming any arrangement of agency or partnership between us and you.

Web Hosting Services

These are the additional terms on which we agree to provide Web Hosting services to you. They cover the situation both where we agree to host your website on one of our servers and where we agree to host your server at our premises.

1.   We agree to provide suitable connections to an electricity supply and to an appropriate telecoms link and to pay for all connection and ongoing charges involved. Please note, however, that we can neither guarantee nor be responsible for any breaks in the continuity of the electricity supply or of the telecoms link, which in each case is the responsibility of the third party provider concerned.

2.   We agree to give you or your duly authorised agents all reasonable access to your server or, as the case may be, the server on which your website is hosted, for any reasonable purpose at any reasonable time.

3.   We reserve the right to shut down your website (or server) if we at any time have reasonable grounds for believing that it is being used for any unlawful or unlicensed purpose or has any unlawful or unlicensed content. Such unlawful or unlicensed purpose or content shall include, but not be limited to, the matters listed in clause 7.1.1 of our Specific Terms and Conditions relating to Internet Access above and you agree to indemnify us against all claims and liabilities which may result from any such unlawful or unlicensed use.

4.   Where we are hosting your server, you agree to indemnify us against any loss or damage we may sustain (including claims from other customers to whom we provide Web Hosting services) as a result of any act or omission on your part or any fault which arises in your equipment, unless such fault arises because of work we have carried out under any maintenance agreement.

5.   Please note that our obligation extends only to hosting your website or your server. You will remain responsible at all times for

data security, data backup, data loss and disaster recovery, unless we shall assume responsibility for any of these matters in a separate agreement.

© **Clark Holt**

These terms and conditions were drafted for Star Internet Limited by Clark Holt, Commercial Solicitors. Star Internet Limited is one of the most innovative business-only internet service providers in the UK (www.star.co.uk). Clark Holt are English Lawyers who specialise exclusively in commercial law, with a particular emphasis on the internet.

Clark Holt, 1 Sanford Street, Swindon, Wiltshire SN1 1QQ, Tel: 01793 617444; fax: 01793 617436; http://www.clarkholt.co.uk.

Appendix 2: Web Page Design Guidelines

The guidance notes below refer to three web site agreements which are available to purchase from Sprecher Grier Halberstam.

WEB SITE AGREEMENTS

GUIDANCE NOTES

These notes are intended to be for your guidance. It is important that you do not show or release them to clients.

This package comprises the three agreements, general guidance notes together with guidance notes on each of the agreements. The three agreements are:

1. Web site Specification Agreement (WSA);
2. Web site Design Agreement (WDA);
3. Web site Maintenance and Operation Agreement (WMA).

This sequence reflects the typical commercial order of events. Having concluded a WSA, it is anticipated that the parties will then enter a WDA. After acceptance under a WDA, the parties will normally enter into a WMA.

Because you will not necessarily always use all three agreements, certain terms appear more than once in the different agreements.

If advice on amendments is needed, you should obtain legal advice either from us or from other lawyers with the relevant expertise.

It is important to note that terms are defined in the definitions section of each agreement with upper case first letters and that where the terms are used in the body of the relevant agreement, they will have the defined meaning where the same use of upper case first letters is made.

If it is absolutely necessary to modify or eliminate definitions in any agreement, you must ensure that you make consequential modifications or eliminations throughout the relevant agreement.

You must remember that any changes which you make to any clause numbers in any of the agreements must be followed up by consequential amendments in other clause numbers and clause cross-references must be amended throughout.

NB You may be obliged to amend various clauses in the web agreements in the course of negotiations. However, we would suggest that unless you are sure that such amendments will not be severely detrimental to you, you take legal advice from us or other lawyers before agreeing to such amendments. In any event, you should be particularly cautious before agreeing any amendments to clauses under any of the following headings:
The Agreement, Client's Obligations, Price and Payment, Charges, Additional Charges, Intellectual Property Rights and Indemnities, Limitation of Liability, Warranties and Confidentiality, Warranties and Governing Law.

1. Web site Specification Agreement

This covers the scoping exercise carried out by you after preliminary discussions with a potential client. The specification developed as a result of this agreement may or may not lead to a WDA for the design of a Web site based on that specification. You may choose whether to charge for the specification or not. In any event, it is worth having a signed contract to cover this exercise. This may give some protection from potential liability should relations between the parties deteriorate.

2. Web site Design Agreement

This covers the creation of the Web site on the basis of the agreed specification and encompasses acceptance testing of the Web site by the client. By linking the design to an agreed specification, WDA seeks to define the agreed work and to prevent profit erosion caused by 'shifting goalposts' when clients change their minds and expect you to alter the design without extra charge for the extra work. WDA enables you to charge extra for additional work, falling outside the agreed specification. Intellectual property rights are a major focal point. Once the Web site is completed, WDA provides for relevant copyright to be transferred to the client on receipt of full payment. WDA provides for copyright in the underlying computer code and scripts to be retained by you. This enables you legally to re-use the same code and scripts in other Web site design projects.

3. Web site Maintenance and Operation Agreement

WMA gives you a separate recurring revenue stream for hosting, maintaining and updating the Web site. It enables you to separate out those tasks which are covered by the annual fee from those for which extra charges can be made. This clear separation may well help avoid the financial embarrassment arising from confusion as to which tasks are covered by the maintenance fees and which are not. WMA also provides a mechanism for extra charges to be made for extra work. WMA anticipates the situation where a client wishes to move its Web site to a different host. It enables this transfer to occur but entitles you to charge a fee for licensing the appropriate codes and scripts.

4. The Schedules

Each of the agreements endeavours to cover the most frequently encountered circumstances and problems. As regards those matters where there is much diversity, for example, pricing and payment, you are left to complete the agreement yourself by entering the relevant details in the schedules.

You will have to ensure that every reference in the body of the relevant agreement is covered comprehensively in the appropriate schedule.

5. General

You should read these notes fully before using these Web agreements. Should any dispute arise with the client, you will have to rely on the relevant agreement and will be unable to assert ignorance of the terms. As these will be considered as your own terms, a court or other adjudicator will be particularly unsympathetic to any assertion of ignorance.

These notes provide explanations of certain legal issues in order to facilitate your understanding of the Web agreements. Your understanding of the effect of each term will be crucial to knowing on what issues and to what extent you are willing and able to concede in the course of negotiations.

These notes assume a certain level of understanding by you of basic contractual and legal issues. If, having read these guidance notes, any terms are not fully understood, you should seek legal advice from us or elsewhere before using the Web agreements.

It is most important that the client is given the opportunity to consider the terms of an agreement and signs that agreement before you carry out any work. It is suggested that you institute a standard procedure whereby any enquiry from a prospective client is responded to by despatch of a copy of the relevant agreement, possibly incorporated into your order documentation. In any event, the client should sign a copy of the relevant agreement before you begin work.

Where you are requested by a client to delete or alter a term in an agreement, you should consult the guidance notes for information as to the importance and role of the clause in question. If further guidance is necessary, you should take appropriate advice.

No limitation/exclusion of liability clause is bound to be upheld by a court. It is always a question of reasonableness in the eyes of the court. The court will look at many factors in determining reasonableness. Hence, please give very careful consideration to the maximum liability issue. In general, the lower you set your maximum liability, the less likely it is to be considered reasonable. If the figure set has an obvious rationale, such as being tied into your level of insurance cover this is also likely to be taken into account.

Another issue to consider is whether instead of arbitration, you wish to provide for alternative dispute resolution. This is said by its supporters to be more time and cost effective than arbitration or litigation. Furthermore, because of its less confrontational approach, it is likely to enable a more amicable outcome, providing for an ongoing business relationship. Further information is available from us or the Centre for Dispute Resolution. This may be provided for in the agreements or simply opted for by the parties should a dispute arise.

© **Sprecher Grier Halberstam**

WEB SITE SPECIFICATION AGREEMENT (WSA)

GUIDANCE NOTES

Clause 2.2 if there are to be any additional services, it would be best to set out clearly in a written document what they are to be and what they will cost and to have this document signed by the client to acknowledge acceptance before you provide the additional services.

Clause 2.3 this is optional and may be deleted if this does not reflect how you wish to do business.

Clause 3.1 this is particularly important to ensure that you do not unwittingly infringe third party intellectual property rights. It is quite possible that despite appearances, and maybe reassurances to the contrary, the rights may be owned by a different company in the same group as the client or by an entity completely unrelated to the client.

This would cover, for example, the following situation:-the client gives you a copy of a publicity brochure which includes a photograph which you decide to incorporate in the specification. It then transpires that copyright for electronic transmission of the photograph over WWW has been retained by the photographer. The photographer sues you for breach of his copyright.

Clause 3.2 to benefit from this clause, you should give clear written directions to the client regarding required format for supply of information and the timescale for delivery.

Clauses 3.1 and 3.2 these clauses can be deleted from the agreement if you do not envisage obtaining any material from your client to be incorporated into the specification.

Clause 4.1 it is suggested that you do not actually create the specification in the presence of the client as to do so might create an inference of joint ownership of copyright in the specification.

The further effect of this clause is that if the client does not want you to proceed from the specification to design of the Web site, the client cannot legally take away the specification for use by another Web site designer. If the client does want to do just that, then you would be at liberty to charge a supplemental fee for assignment of the intellectual property rights in the specification. This clause is particularly useful if you have made little or no profit from this agreement having based the

'Fees' on the expectation that the profit would come from the design and maintenance phases of the Web site. The copyright in the specification would generally vest in you, the designer, as a matter of law. However, it is suggested that for the sake of integrity and certainty this clause be included. If the client balks at this clause and wishes it removed or altered, you may ask yourself why as it may well indicate an intention not to enter into a WDA with you. You should price WSA accordingly.

Clause 4.2 this clause protects you against losses sustained on account of the client's actions or omissions, including failure by the client to comply with clause 3.1. It should be mentioned that any indemnity is only as good as the financial standing of the entity giving it.

Clause 4.3 this clause is the reciprocal of clause 4.2 and protects the client if you include any material in the specification which you were not entitled to include.

This indemnity need not be given by you but may well be sought by the client in view of clause 4.2. You can try to limit your liability under the indemnity to the maximum amount stated in clause 6.4. This may reduce the effectiveness of the indemnity. If you do not wish to attempt to cap the indemnity, remove the words: 'Subject always to Clause 6.4 below'.

Clause 4.4 this covers your use of the client's trade marks or logos which you may incorporate into the specification.

Clause 5.1 it is suggested that you issue the invoice for the Fees at the same time that you provide the specification to the client. You are entitled to payment under the terms of this agreement for provision of the specification to the client. Payment is not conditional on you delivering a document which meets with your client's absolute approval. It is suggested that you should not allow yourself to become involved in protracted discussions with the client regarding the suitability of the specification if payment does not seem to be forthcoming.

You may, of course, vary the 14 day period suggested if this does not fit in with your normal terms of business.

Clause 6 there is little if anything of more importance to a contracting party than attempting to limit potential liability. For this reason, very careful consideration should be given to any situation before agreeing to delete any provisions from clause 6. It is also thought best not to merge the provisions together into a single sub-clause but to leave them as separate sub-clauses. the rationale for this is that a court may hold certain elements of clause 6 to be unreasonable. If so, it may delete them. If all the provisions are merged into a single clause and the court objects to one element of that clause, the whole clause may become ineffective.

It is suggested that you consider taking out specific insurance, if available, to cover Web site specification, design and maintenance work and adopt the level of cover as your maximum liability level under clause 6.4 instead of 'Fees', which is used as a maximum in default of knowledge as to whether you have appropriate insurance cover. If you do decide to do this, you should delete the words 'the Fees paid pursuant hereto' and replace them with the £ sign followed by your insurance cover figure.

Clause 6.2 see note on clause 4.1 above. It is suggested most strongly that you do not amend this clause and that you are suspicious of pressure from the client on you to do so.

Clause 6.3 by law, you cannot exclude such liability.

Clause 6.4 the use of the word 'aggregate' seeks to ensure that if the client successfully makes separate claims against you in relation to different problems arising out of this agreement, it cannot in total recover more than the maximum figure.

It must be stressed that no limitation or exclusion of liability clauses are 'watertight' and that therefore you cannot place absolute reliance on any clause being effective.

Clause 7.3 seeks to protect you against claims by the client that you had orally promised to provide certain services or guarantee certain results as a term of this agreement although these promises had not been actually incorporated into this agreement.

Schedule if the specification is to be provided at no charge, simply insert NIL after the £ signs in the schedule.

© **Sprecher Grier Halberstam**

WEB SITE DESIGN AGREEMENT (WDA)
GUIDANCE NOTES

Clause 2 the agreed terms for payment, including times for payment must be clearly set out in Schedule 1. Obviously, it will be in your interest to secure as much payment as possible early on and the client will desire to pay as late as possible. You should consider requesting a sizeable percentage on signature of WDA, with the remainder payable on acceptance. Acceptance will, in accordance with clause 7.2, be deemed to occur 14 days after you have sent written notification of the completion of the Web site to the client. At the same time as giving the notification, you must give the client the opportunity of testing the Web site in accordance with clause 7.2. To some extent, the payment terms will be dictated by prevailing market norms as they develop.

You should avoid committing yourself to fixed delivery dates if possible. However, if the client insists on tying you down to fixed dates for delivery of webpages or completion of the Web site, you should insert the appropriate deadlines in Schedule 3. If you fail to meet those deadlines, clause 11.1 should give you some protection.

Clause 3.2 if there are to be any additional services, it would be best to set out clearly in a written document what they are to be and what they will cost and to have this document signed by the client to acknowledge acceptance before you provide the additional services.

Clause 3.7 if any potential client objects, it should be pointed out that this clause gives you a right not an obligation to suspend performance and that you will use your discretion as to whether to enforce this right.

Clause 3.8 the right to repudiate is the right to treat the agreement as at an end with no further obligations on either side. It is useful to have this right contractually enshrined even if you do not enforce it. The mere existence of such right tends to focus the mind of the client and, to the extent that such matters are within the client's control, tends to reduce the probability of any such occurrence.

Clause 3.9 if you do not wish for the client to have a right to cancel, delete this clause and the definition of Cancellation Fee in the Definitions section. However if the client insists, it is suggested that you fix the Cancellation Fee percentage in Schedule 1 at a very high level to minimise your loss.

Clause 4.1 this is particularly important to ensure that you do not unwittingly infringe third party intellectual property rights. It is quite possible that despite appearances, and maybe reassurances to the contrary, the rights may be owned by a different company in the same group as the client or by an entity completely unrelated to the client.

This would cover, for example, the following situation:-the client gives you a copy of a publicity brochure which includes a photograph which you decide to incorporate in the Web site. It then transpires that copyright for electronic transmission of the photograph over WWW has been retained by the photographer. The photographer sues you for breach of his copyright.

Clause 4.2 addresses the problem frequently encountered by Web site designers whereby the client or its agent provides the information in the incorrect format, necessitating unanticipated extra work for you. The clause also covers the chance of the information being provided later than it is required by you. To take advantage of this clause, you must agree formats and timescales with the Client and set these out clearly in the specification as attached to WDA as Schedule 2.

Clause 4.4 seeks to maintain security where restricted password access to the Web site is given to the client to inspect the Web site during development.

Clause 5.1 seeks to prevent the client rejecting or at least not paying for the Web site but walking off with it to another Web site designer. An appropriate transfer of intellectual property rights is foreseen on payment under clause 7.4.

Clause 5.2 it will generally be the client's employees or agents or other entities connected with the client who are most likely to have knowledge of the code, scripts and workings involved in the Web site and therefore those same entities who are most likely to commit or facilitate an infringement of your copyright or other intellectual property rights by supplying details to third parties or using the information for their own purposes. Such infringement may be quite unwitting, as, for example, the client's employees may be clueless about the law of copyright. This clause seeks to put the client on the alert for such activities. This may in turn enable you to minimise any loss you may suffer through such infringement, which may be unwittingly perpetrated by the client's employees.

Clause 5.3 protects you against losses sustained on account of the client's actions or omissions, including failure to comply with clause

4.1. It should be mentioned that any indemnity is only as good as the financial standing of the entity giving it.

Clause 5.4 is the reciprocal indemnity to clause 5.3. It would cover, for example, a case where you had previously developed a Web site for client A and assigned all copyright in that earlier Web site to client A. If you were then to re-use elements of client A's Web site in the Web site for client B and client A were to sue client B for breach of its copyright, client B would then be able to recover its loss from you under this clause.

Clause 5.5 covers your use of the client's trade marks or logos which you may incorporate into the Web site.

Clause 6 see equivalent guidance note on clause 6 of WSA.

Clause 6.1 seeks to put the onus for fixing the 'goalposts' of the Project firmly on the client's shoulders. The need for this clause is commercial as often the profit element of a Web site design project is lost by the client 'changing the goalposts' during a project and the designer having little choice but to complete extra unforeseen work for the client.

Clause 7.2 the anticipated acceptance testing procedure should be set out as clearly as possible in Schedule 4 so as to endeavour to avoid any arguments later about what are reasonable acceptance tests and, consequentially, what are reasonable grounds for rejection of the Web site. See also note to clause 2 above.

Clause 7.3 the importance of drawing up an accurate and detailed specification is again highlighted by this clause. Any changes requested by client which do not arise from lack of conformity between the specification and the completed Web site should be carried out under the change control mechanism provided in Clause 10 and be chargeable as such.

Clause 7.4 this copyright assignment will only occur on full payment and will enable the client to transfer the Web site to a different service provider for maintenance. However, as you will retain copyright in the codes and script, you should be able to charge a substantial licence fee if the client wants to be entitled to use them independently of you. Such a licence fee would normally be a one-off payment for a perpetual licence. This would avoid the need to have regular contact with a previous client. The terms of such a licence would have to be as restrictive as possible limiting use of the Retained Copyright as far as possible to use connected with the Web site itself. Appropriate legal advice should be taken as to the wording of such a licence should this scenario occur.

Clause 8.2 delete this warranty if you are not going to virus-check the Web site and make consequential amendments to wording of clause 8.4 by deleting reference to clause 8.2.

Clause 8.5 this seeks to negate any later assertion by the client that things were promised by you to the client as part of the 'deal' although the parties did not bother to reduce the precise terms of those promises to writing.

Clause 9.1 this may give the client the comfort it may need in relation to sensitive financial or other business information which it will supply to you during the Project.

Clause 9.2 this seeks to enable you to make use of the existence of the Project for your publicity.

Clause 10 this provides the mechanism for you to cover the 'changing goalposts' syndrome without the profitability of the Project being lost. This procedure should be closely adhered to.

The Specification Addenda should include details of pricing and terms of payment for the modification. It is vital that this Addendum must be totally clear in its definition of the task to be completed.

Clause 10.3 To avoid later disagreement, both parties should sign the Specification Addendum.

Clause 11.1 and 11.2 these seek to protect you against pressure from the client on failure to meet dates agreed for completion of the Project. See note on clause 2.1 above.

Clause 11.3 seeks to enable you to charge for delays in the Project caused by the client.

Clause 19 this is optional but may prove useful.

Schedule 3 this should include a domain name application and registration service if applicable.

© **Sprecher Grier Halberstam**

WEB SITE MAINTENANCE AND OPERATION AGREEMENT (WMA) GUIDANCE NOTES

General

You must ensure that you are registered as appropriate under the Data Protection Act. If you wish for further guidance contact us or the office of the Data Protection Registrar.

Definitions

'Problems' these have been divided into three levels of gravity with corresponding levels of urgency. Your response and reaction obligations will depend on the gravity ie level of the Problem. You must therefore tailor the contents of Schedule 3 to the extent necessary to reflect the levels of service and maintenance you will be offering in respect of each level.

'Specification' you must attach the specification to the Design Agreement together with any Specification Addenda created pursuant to the Design Agreement as Schedule 2.

'Server Performance' this is the proportion of time during which your server is functioning. You must specify this proportion in percentage terms in Schedule 4. This is distinct from the proportion of time during which your ISP link to WWW is functioning.

'Updates' this term is intended to cover revisions to existing Web site data but not any design or other changes to the Web site.

'Working Hours' be sure to enter in Schedule 3 the hours during which you will provide the Services if not as set out in this definition.

Clauses

Clause 2 the reference to 'failure or interruption of services provided by third parties' reflects the fact that the your service to the client will be dependent on the service provided to you by your access provider.

Clause 3 the services set out in this clause are by way of example only and will probably require modification here and, if appropriate, also in Schedule 3. If, for example, you are providing a dedicated telephone support line, clause 3 viii. should be amended accordingly. You must ensure that Schedule 3 is completed fully with the additional information referred to in clause 3 as amended by you.

Clause 3 iv this is an important sub-clause which limits the frequency and extent to which the client can require you to update the contents of the Web site without incurring additional charges. It is important that you realise that you cannot charge extra for work covered by this sub-clause and therefore you should ensure that you strictly and clearly cap in Schedule 3 the frequency and extent of the updates you are offering.

It is also important to make clear to the client before entering this agreement that changes to the layout and format of the contents and changes to the links to the contents of the Web site fall outside the ambit of the Maintenance Fee and will be dealt with as chargeable Enhancements under clause 6.

Clause 3 xv delete this if inapplicable.

Clause 4.2 you must remember to issue invoices towards the end of each quarter. If quarterly billing does not fit in with your normal business practice, amend the wording accordingly. Similarly, if 30 days is too generous, amend the time for payment of invoices accordingly.

Clause 5.2 allows you to charge the client if it decides to remove the Web site from your control and take it to another operator. See also guidance note on clause 10.6 below.

Clause 6 provides the mechanism for effecting Enhancements to the Web site. In this context, you should also read the notes to clause 3 above. The mechanism mirrors the procedure set out in WDA relating to specification, design and acceptance by the client of enhancements made to the Web site. See the equivalent guidance notes on clause 10 of WDA.

Clause 6.3 to avoid later disagreement, both parties should sign the Enhancement Specification. It is vital that this specification must be totally clear in its definition of the task to be completed.

Clause 7.7 this should not be open to negotiation.

Clause 8 see the equivalent guidance notes on clause 5 of WDA.

Clause 9 see the equivalent guidance notes on clause 6 of WSA.

Clause 9.7 seeks to protect you from failure of any services, goods or software provided to you by a third party. This would include interruption in your ISP connection or datastream information services. Your client has a contract with you and not the ISP and therefore any performance warranties given to you by your ISP will not be of any direct benefit to the client. If you wish to pass on to the client the benefit of any warranties you are given by your ISP, it is suggested that you do so by inserting the appropriate wording as clause 11.2.1 and amending clause 11.4 by replacing the words 'and 11.2' with the words ', 11.2 and 11.2.1'.

Clause 9.11 it is hoped that this sub-clause will provide you with a defence to a defamation suit under the forthcoming defamation legislation. At the time of drafting, the legislation has not been finalised and the effectiveness of this clause will have to be reviewed in a future edition of these contracts.

Clause 10.1 The agreement is structured to continue for a year subject to the events set out in clause 10.2. If your client suggests a shorter period e.g. 3 months notice, you must amend this clause and also clause 10.3 accordingly. A suitable notice period would be before the commencement of each quarter starting with the date the agreement was entered into.

Clause 10.6 in the event that the client decides to terminate your services under this agreement but wishes to continue using the Web site designed by you, this clause entitles you to charge the client a one-off licence fee for use of any scripts or coding you have incorporated into the Web site. Advice on the terms of an appropriate licence should be sought from us or other lawyers. Your right to make this charge arises from the fact that you will have retained copyright under clause 7.4 of WDA. This is in addition to your right to charge under clause 5.2 of WDA.

Clause 11.4 see note on clause 9.7 above.

Clause 11.5 see the equivalent guidance notes on clause 8.5 of WDA.

Clause 12 this seeks to give the client the comfort it may need in relation to sensitive financial or other business information which it will supply to you during the period of the agreement.

Schedules

Schedule 2 If you institute a profit sharing scheme with your client, the Maintenance Fee in Schedule 2 should be expressed to include a percentage commission in respect of business transacted over the Internet as a result of the Web site. You may wish to have a separate contract to cover this activity.

Reference to charges per hit i.e. individual visits to the site may also be built in if appropriate.

Schedule 3 Clear indication must be given in Schedule 3 as to whether the support services are to be available and response times to be calculated in terms of Working Hours or on a 24 hour per day basis.

You may be obliged to insert a minimum percentage uptime of your server.

© **Sprecher Grier Halberstam**

Fixed Price Template Contracts for Website Specification, Design, Maintenance and Operation

Sprecher Grier Halberstam specialise in computer law and Internet law. A significant proportion of our clients are either software houses or web site designers. We are located close to Fleet Street in the heart of legal London.

From our work with some of the leading web site designers, we have identified problems which designers frequently encounter when dealing with their clients. These often arise through the failure of the parties properly to define their respective rights and obligations in suitably worded contracts.

We appreciate that as a web site designer, you need to protect your position and profitability. From working with designers we have identified three principal potential revenue streams and have tailored agreements specifically to enable you to maximise your revenue and minimise your liability. These agreements have been designed to help you to avoid the erosion of project profitability due to your client changing the 'goal posts' in the middle of the project, or failing to provide you with the appropriate material in the appropriate format and timescale. We have dealt in detail with the potential difficult issues arising from web design and operation; including ownership of copyright and other intellectual property rights as well as liability for viruses and defamation.

The package is designed for repeated use by your with your different clients. With the benefit of the extensive guidance notes and the consultation included, your future need to consult lawyers should be minimised. Although designed to protect your interests, the agreements are balanced and therefore should enable you to avoid wasting time and money negotiating relatively unimportant issues. Any future delays caused by waiting for the 'legals' to be sorted out should be minimised.

The agreements provide you with a strong back bone of core contractual clauses common to all your web site transactions, together with suitable schedules which gives you the flexibility to adapt to the particular transaction you are dealing with. The package, comprising 40 pages, provides you with a 'one off' solution for all your contractual requirements in this core area of your business.

The Agreements Package

- Web site Specification Agreement.
- Web site Design Agreement.
- Web site Maintenance and Operation Agreement.
- General guidance notes.
- Specific guidance notes for each of the three agreements.
- 1 hour of advice to tailor the package to your needs.

Extracts from the Agreements

Who is liable for information put on the site which causes problems?

Clause:

The Operator shall not be liable for ensuring that there is not any material, data or information on the Web site which is illegal or unlawful, obscene, defamatory or otherwise infringes any third party rights whatsoever.

We lose money because neither we nor the client are sure what activities are covered by our maintenance and operation agreement.

Clauses:

The Services shall comprise:

- installation and operation of the Web site on the Operator's server as described in Schedule 3;
- facilitating and maintaining public access to the Web site;
- marketing the Web site as specified in Schedule 3;
- Updates limited to the extent specified in Schedule 3 . . .

The Operator shall be entitled to charge the Client at its Billing Rates for time spent: providing any other services not forming part of the Services.

How can we protect ourselves against the risks associated with clients giving us something to include on the Web, that they are not entitled to use on WWW?

Clause:

The Client undertakes to secure copyright and other appropriate licences or consents where necessary for the inclusion of any material, data and information provided to the Designer pursuant hereto to enable the Designer to incorporate such material, data and information into the Web site.

We are often blamed for delays in completing the Web site because the client does not give us the information on time and in the agreed format.

Clause:

The Client undertakes that it will provide or procure the provision of the information, data and material required for the purposes hereof by the Designer in whatever formats and timescales agreed by the parties and set out in the Specification.

Price

[ ] pounds sterling plus VAT for unlimited use.

Further Information

To purchase the package or to discuss your specific needs, please contact Simon Halberstam by phone, fax or E-mail as below. If you would like to come to our offices to view the agreements, please call to arrange a mutually convenient time and date.

Sprecher Grier Halberstam

Lincoln House

300 High Holborn

London

WC1V 7JH

Tel: 0171–544 5555

Fax: 0171–544 5565

E-mail: law@weblaw.co.uk

Appendix 3: Internet Shopping and Services Terms

Example 1 – Terms of Service

Excite Terms of service

Welcome! When using Excite's services, you agree to the terms and conditions listed on this page (the 'Terms of Service'), which may be updated by us from time to time. You can check out the most current version of these Terms of Service at http://www.excite.com/terms.html.

Excite's search technology automatically produces search results that reference sites and information located worldwide throughout the Internet. Because we have no control over such sites and information, we make no guarantee as to such sites and information, including the accuracy, currency, content or quality of any such sites and information and we assume no responsibility as to whether the search locates unintended or objectionable content. Furthermore, because some content on the Internet consists of material that is adult-oriented or otherwise objectionable to some people, the results of your search on our sites may automatically and intentionally generate links or references to objectionable material. We make no claim that such surprises might not occur.

Under Excite's privacy policy, we may disclose to third parties certain aggregate information contained in our users' registration applications, but we will not disclose your name, address, email address or telephone number without your prior written consent, except as required by law. A complete statement of our privacy policy can be found at http://www.excite.com/privacy_policy.

You are responsible for maintaining the confidentiality of your account number and/or password. You are responsible for all uses of your account, whether or not actually or expressly authorized by you.

Users alone are responsible for the contents of the messages they communicate when using our services and as well as the consequences of any such messages. You agree that you will not use our services for chain letters, junk mail, 'spamming' or commercial solicitations or to engage in illegal activities. You further agree not to use our services to send any message or material that is unlawful, gives rise to civil liability or otherwise violates the community standards described on our sites. The community standards for Excite Chat and Excite Boards may be found at http://www.excite.com/communities/resources/standards and the ones for Excite Communities are located at: http://www.excite.com/communities/resources/standards/communities.

In order to ensure that Excite is able to provide high quality services which are responsive to customer needs, you must consent to Excite employees being able to access your account and records on a case by case basis to investigate complaints or other allegations or abuse. Excite shall not disclose the existence or occurrence of such an investigation unless required by law. Violation of terms of service may result in immediate deletion of a users account.

All chat and bulletin board communications are public and not private communications. Although we reserve the right to remove without notice any bulletin board posting for any reason, we have no obligation to delete content that you may find objectionable or offensive.

We may modify or discontinue our services or your account with us, with or without notice, without liability to you, any other user or any third party. We reserve the right to terminate your account if we learn that you have provided us with false or misleading registration information, interfered with other users or the administration of Excite's services, or violated these Terms of Service.

You understand and agree that Excite's services are provided 'AS-IS'.

Excite assumes no responsibility for the timeliness, deletion, misdelivery or failure to store any user communications or personalization settings. In particular, but not by way of limitation, Excite may delete e-mail accounts or the information therein if the account is inactive for greater than ninety (90) days.

YOU UNDERSTAND AND EXPRESSLY AGREE THAT USE OF EXCITE'S SERVICES ARE AT YOUR SOLE RISK, THAT ANY MATERIAL AND/OR DATA DOWNLOADED OR OTHER-WISE OBTAINED THROUGH THE USE OF EXCITE'S SERV-

ICES IS AT YOUR OWN DISCRETION AND RISK AND THAT YOU WILL BE SOLELY RESPONSIBLE FOR ANY DAMAGE TO YOUR COMPUTER SYSTEM OR LOSS OF DATA THAT RESULTS FROM THE DOWNLOAD OF SUCH MATERIAL AND/OR DATA.

EXCEPT AS EXPRESSLY SET FORTH ON OUR SITES, EXCITE DISCLAIMS ALL WARRANTIES OF ANY KIND, EXPRESS OR IMPLIED, INCLUDING WITHOUT LIMITATION ANY WARRANTY OF MERCHANTABILITY, FITNESS FOR A PARTICULAR PURPOSE OR NON-INFRINGEMENT AND IT MAKES NO WARRANTY OR REPRESENTATION REGARDING THE RESULTS THAT MAY BE OBTAINED FROM THE USE OF EXCITE'S SERVICES, REGARDING THE ACCURACY OR RELIABILITY OF ANY INFORMATION OBTAINED THROUGH EXCITE'S SERVICES, REGARDING ANY GOODS OR SERVICES PURCHASED OR OBTAINED THROUGH EXCITE'S SERVICES, REGARDING ANY TRANSACTIONS ENTERED INTO THROUGH EXCITE'S SERVICES OR THAT EXCITE'S SERVICES WILL MEET ANY USER'S REQUIREMENTS, BE UNINTERRUPTED, TIMELY, SECURE OR ERROR FREE.

EXCITE WILL NOT BE LIABLE FOR ANY DIRECT, INDIRECT, INCIDENTAL, SPECIAL, CONSEQUENTIAL OR PUNITIVE DAMAGES OF ANY KIND RESULTING FROM THE USE OF OR THE INABILITY TO USE EXCITE'S SERVICES, RESULTING FROM ANY GOODS OR SERVICES PURCHASED OR OBTAINED OR MESSAGES RECEIVED OR TRANSACTIONS ENTERED INTO THROUGH EXCITE'S SERVICES, RESULTING FROM LOSS OF, UNAUTHORIZED ACCESS TO OR ALTERATION OF A USER'S TRANSMISSIONS OR DATA OR FOR THE COST OF PROCUREMENT OF SUBSTITUTE GOODS AND SERVICES, INCLUDING BUT NOT LIMITED TO DAMAGES FOR LOSS OF PROFITS, USE, DATA OR OTHER INTANGIBLES, EVEN IF EXCITE HAD BEEN ADVISED OF THE POSSIBILITY OF SUCH DAMAGES.

You agree to indemnify, defend and hold harmless Excite, its affiliates, officers, directors, employees, consultants and agents from any and all third party claims, liability, damages and/or costs (including, but not limited to, attorneys fees) arising from your use of our services, your violation of the Terms of Service or your infringement, or infringement by any other user of your account, of any intellectual property or other right of any person or entity. The Terms of Service will inure to the benefit of Excite's successors, assigns and licensees.

These Terms of Service will be governed by and construed in accordance with the laws of the State of California, without giving effect to its conflict of laws provisions or your actual state or country of residence.

If for any reason a court of competent jurisdiction finds any provision or portion of the Terms of Service to be unenforceable, the remainder of the Terms of Service will continue in full force and effect.

These Terms of Service constitute the entire agreement between the parties with respect to the subject matter hereof and supersedes and replaces all prior or contemporaneous understandings or agreements, written or oral, regarding such subject matter. Any waiver of any provision of the Terms of Service will be effective only if in writing and signed by Excite.

Reproduced with the kind permission of Excite Inc.

Excite is a trade mark and/or service mark of Excite, Inc, a subsidiary of At Home Corporation, and may be registered in various jurisdictions. Excite screen displays copyright 1995–1999 Excite, Inc.

Example 2 – Payment and Security

Desktop Lawyer's Safe Ordering Guarantee

Why it's safe . . .

Using a secure server the Internet is perhaps the most secure method to pay using a credit or debit card. We are working with NetBanx who will take and verify your card securely and immediately for the Desktop Lawyer service.

1. Your credit or debit card details are taken through NetBanx secure server, where they employ encryption and multi-level safeguards to ensure data integrity. This means that your card details are converted into code, which is securely transmitted to NetBanx servers over the Internet. Desktop Lawyer does not have or ever holds your credit card details.

2. All the major banks are now working with NetBanx and will authorise your card – usually within 60 seconds.

3. NetBanx leads in service with 24-hour 365-day support and Cardholder telephone support.

4. In the In the event of unauthorised use of your credit or debit card, most banks will completely cover your liability or limit your liability to £50.00 or less.

Our Guarantee . . .

So sure are we of the security of our ordering system and the quality of our legal service we offer the following guarantee:

1. In the unlikely event that your bank or card issuer holds you liable for an unauthorised transaction on your credit or debit we will cover your liability up to a maximum of fifty pounds (£50.00 GBP).

2. If within 30 days of your order you are not completely satisfied with the Rapidocs legal document(s) purchased we will refund your money.

Important terms of the above Guarantee:

1. The guarantee applies to the on-line purchase of Rapidocs legal documents and not telephone support.
2. The guarantee applies only to purchases made through the NetBanx secure server used through the Freeserve Desktop Lawyer service operated by Desktop Lawyer (Freeserve) Limited.
3. The guarantee relating to unauthorised use of your credit or debit card covers a maximum liability of £50.00 GBP.
4. In the event that your credit or debit card is used for any unauthorised purpose, you must notify your card provider in accordance with its reporting rules and procedures.

Reproduced with the kind permission of Desktop Lawyer (www.desktoplawyer.freeserve.net)

Desktop Lawyer is run by Epoch Software and allows you to tailor make legal documents using intelligent documents prepared by top UK barristers. The same technology contained on the site is also available to law firms. For further information please contact the sales department on 0181 931 3030.

Example 3: Terms and Conditions for the Free use of the Pharmalicensing Site

Terms & Conditions for Subscribers and Users of the Site

Definitions:

Pharmalicensing Limited

Subscriber

The Person, Organisation, Firm or Company which subscribes to the services of PL

User

The Person, Individual, Firm or Company which enters the Web Site.

Web Site

http://www.pharmalicensing.com

User Centre

Administration page to be found at the Web Site.

Contents

Any information, data, text, graphics, links or computer code published on or contained within the Web Site.

Product

Includes any and all company profiles, licensing opportunities, recruitment, event, press release, service provider, custom enquiry forms, company entry, keyword alerting, CV entry, industry newsletter and any other information and data whether offered free or for a fee.

Product Period

The period the Product is supplied by PL from the Commencement Date until PL ceases to provide the Service to the Subscriber.

Commencement Date

The date PL first offers the Subscriber the Service or any other date agreed.

Service

As detailed in PL's then current Product brochure on the Web Site.

Agreement

The contract between PL and the Subscriber incorporating these Terms and Conditions irrespective of the country of issue.

1. Parties

The Agreement is between PL and the Subscriber as identified on the PL's Subscription Letter and which is subject to these Terms and Conditions. The Subscriber accepts these Terms and Conditions by pressing the 'I have read and accept the terms and conditions' button on the Web Site order form or by returning a signed subscription letter.

The User signifies their acceptance of these Terms and Conditions by entering and using the Web Site. Subscribers and Users may print and keep a copy of this Agreement. For Subscribers and Users convenience a current version of this Agreement is available in the User Centre on the Web Site. PL may revise the Terms and Conditions at any time and without notice at its sole discretion. Any change will be deemed to take effect four hours after Web Site posting and will be deemed to be accepted by Subscribers and Users who continue to access the Web Site.

2. Service

PL shall supply the Subscriber with the Service for the Product Period from the Commencement Date.

PL will use its reasonable endeavours to maintain the Service. The Subscriber or User will not be eligible for any compensation because they cannot use the Service or because of the failure suspension or withdrawal of all or part of the Service. PL may change suspend or cancel the Service at its sole discretion at any time.

3. Subscribers

Subscribers shall not assign, or sublicense or otherwise transfer or dispose of their rights or obligations hereunder, without prior written permission from PL.

Any alteration to the Terms and Conditions for the use of the Web Site by PL shall be provided to subscribers in writing or by e-mail and will be deemed to have taken effect the day after posting or four hours after sending by e-mail. Subscribers will keep their passwords and identity name secure and will not disclose them to third parties for any purpose. Subscribers will change any password which they believe may have become compromised and notify PL.

Subscribers are fully responsible for their Contents including its truthfulness and accuracy and non-infringement of any other person's legal or proprietary rights, for any materials or work submitted for publication on the User Centre or the Web Site in general. The Subscriber will not allow the Service or their User Centre to be used for storing sending or receiving any material which is obscene menacing threatening offensive abusive indecent defamatory fraudulent criminal or which infringes the rights of other parties.

It is the Subscriber's responsibility to retain copies of their own data. PL accepts no responsibility for the loss of any data in any form which may result from inclusion on the Web Site or from the use of the Service.

The Subscriber will indemnify PL from and against any and all liabilities, expenses (including any legal fees) and damages arising out of claims based upon submissions made by the Subscriber to PL for inclusion on the Web Site and which are subsequently published by PL.

4. Payment

Subscription for the Service shall be on an annual basis unless specifically agreed otherwise in writing between PL and the Subscriber. The Subscriber will pay PL annually in advance. PL may as a specific concession which may be withdrawn at any time, agree to the payment of the subscription by instalments as indicated on the Subscription Letter. In this case no invoice or receipt will be sent if the Subscriber opts for a concession payment. All Services are made on a single supply.

PL will notify the Subscriber at the end of the current Subscription Period of PL's current fee for renewal which fee will subsequently be confirmed in the invoice.

All fees are exclusive of VAT sales or other taxes which will be in addition to the fee at the prevailing rate at the time.

Invoices not paid within thirty days of the invoice date shall be subject to interest at 5% per annum above the UK base rate for Barclays Bank PLC prevailing from time to time. If the instalment concession has been agreed then payments must be made on the due date for each instalment otherwise interest may be charged as previously stated.

PL reserves the right to suspend or close the use of the Service by the Subscriber in the event of non payment without prior written notice to the Subscriber. In the event of non payment the Subscriber will be responsible for all costs incurred by PL including without limitation any legal fees incurred.

5. Ownership

All the Contents and images on the User Centre or the Web Site are the copyright of PL and will at all times remain the property of PL. All rights are reserved. No portion of the User Centre or Web Site may be reproduced in any form or by any means without the prior written permission from PL.

The pharmalicensing name and logo and all related product and service names, design marks and slogans are the trade names, service marks, or trademarks of PL, and may not be used without the prior written consent of PL.

All product names mentioned are acknowledged as the trade marks or registered trade marks of their respective owners. All trade marks are acknowledged. While every effort is made to ensure that information on this site is accurate PL assumes no responsibility for errors or omissions.

The ownership of information, data, trademarks, corporate logos and graphics remain the property of their owners, which are supplied to PL for restricted use on the Web Site and associated publications.

Nothing in this agreement is intended to or will create any form of partnership or joint venture, agency, franchise, sales representation or employment relationship between PL and/or the Subscriber and/or the User.

No rights to, or property in the Web Site shall pass to the Subscriber or User.

6. User

The User subject to Clause 6.2 hereof shall not copy, duplicate, translate into any language or in any way reproduce the Web Site or any part thereof or any of its Contents or knowingly permit the same without written permission of PL and the respective copyright owner.

The User shall be permitted to reproduce a reasonable number of copies of the Contents, (but not the computer code or any part thereof copy of which is strictly forbidden) for purposes of the User's own research or private study.

All and any copies of extracts from the Contents shall be clearly and conspicuously marked with PL copyright notice as follows: 'Pharmalicensing Ltd (http://www.pharmalicensing.com)'. Ensure that all Users' employees and representatives are made aware of the above conditions and comply with them. Each User assumes full responsibility for all risks arising from use of the Web Site.

Contents published on the Web Site are for information purposes only and it is the responsibility of the User to identify and confirm the accuracy and suitability of the Contents and Subscribers for whatever purpose the User requires or wishes to use the Contents.

Each User will indemnify PL, its servants and agents, and hold PL, its servants and agents, harmless against all claims, liability, losses, damages and expenses, including, without limitation, legal fees and costs arising out of or incurred as the result of any claims made, or litigation brought, against PL, its servants and agents, as a result of the use by User of the Web Site Contents or part thereof for whatever purpose.

7. Warranties and Liabilities

PL warrants that it will use all reasonable care and skill in carrying out obligations under this Agreement. All other conditions warranties and obligations implied by statute common law or otherwise and any liabilities arising therefrom are excluded to the extent permissible by law.

PL accepts no liability for the completeness or accuracy of any Contents supplied to PL by the Subscriber for placing on the Web Site.

Subscriber and User will hold PL free of any and all actions against it as a consequence of data supplied by Subscriber or User which is authorised for display on the Web Site, including all reasonable legal costs that PL suffer or incur by reason of any claim or the defence of any claim relating to the person or company materials they have displayed on the Web Site and it is acknowledged that PL makes no warranties representations or conditions with regard to any of the Contents whether expressed or implied arising by law or otherwise and which have been supplied by the Subscriber and there is no implied warranty of merchantability or fitness for a particular purpose.

PL shall be liable only to the extent of the subscription fee payable by the Subscriber if it fails to deliver performance of the Service or for any other breach of the Agreement or fails to remedy any failure within 30 days of written notice from the Subscriber.

PL does not limit its liability to the Subscriber or the User for death or personal injury caused by any of PL's acts or omissions or those of its employees or agents acting in the course of their employment Limitation to Damages: Under no circumstances shall PL or any of its officers, directors, employees, subsidiaries, agents, parents, or affiliates be held liable for any indirect, incidental, special or consequential damages, even if PL has been advised of the possibility of damages, (including, without limitation, damages for losses whether of a personal, public, institutional or corporate nature, loss of any revenues or profits) arising in contract, tort or otherwise from the use of or inability to use the Web Site, or any of the Contents, or from any action or decision taken as a result of using the Web Site or the Contents. PL's liability for breach of this Agreement is limited to the amount actually paid (if any) by the Subscriber for use of the Services. PL is hereby released from any and all obligations, liabilities and claims in excess of this limitation.

Indemnification: Subscribers agree to indemnify PL from and against any and all liabilities, expenses (including any legal fees) and damages arising out of claims based upon submissions for inclusion in the Web Site that are subsequently published by PL on the Web Site, including any claim of libel, defamation, violation of rights of privacy or publicity, loss of service by other customers and infringement of intellectual property or other rights.

All provisions of this Clause limiting or excluding liability operate separately and shall survive independently of the other provisions.

8. Termination

PL reserves the right to decline, withdraw or terminate access to the Web Site without notice and in particular if PL suspect that any material stored or disseminated by the Subscriber may be in contravention of clause 3.4 above PL reserve the right at all times to inspect the material and if it is found to be in contravention of Clause 3.4 above to remove the material from the Subscriber's User Centre and/or suspend part or all of the Service and/or terminate this Agreement immediately without any further obligation to the Subscriber.

In the event that:

(a) the Subscriber is in breach of these Terms and Conditions and if capable of remedy fails to remedy them within thirty days of receipt of notice in writing or by e-mail from PL requiring them to do so, or

(b) the Subscriber becomes insolvent and unable to pay its debts bankrupt or placed in the hands of a receiver or administrator or wound up (other than for a solvent reconstruction) then PL may immediately terminate the Service.

Effects of termination. The Subscriber:

(a) will remain liable to pay PL all sums accrued due on or prior to the date of termination;

(b) will continue to respect and uphold all confidentiality and copyright obligations

(c) will if requested by PL, return all materials belonging to PL and will specifically certify that they have done so

9. Force Majeure

No party shall be held to be in breach of its obligations hereunder (except in relation to the obligation to make payments) nor liable to the other for any loss or damage which may be suffered by another party due to any cause beyond its reasonable control including without limitation any act of God, failure, flood, lightning, fire, strike, lock out, trade dispute act or omission of government regulatory authorities other total communications operators or other competent authority.

10. Notices

Any notice required to be given under this Agreement shall be sent by first class post or fax or electronic mail and shall be deemed to be given two days after posting if sent by post to the other party's address as notified by the party, at the time the fax is sent if sent by fax before 4.00 pm in the afternoon otherwise 9.00 am the next working day and at the time the e-mail is received at either party's e-mail address if sent by electronic mail.

11. General

Any failure by any party to exercise or enforce any of its rights under this Agreement shall not be deemed to be a waiver of any such rights or operate so as to bar the subsequent exercise or enforcement of any such right.

This Agreement represents the entire understanding between us in relation to its subject matter and supersedes all other agreements or representations made by either of us whether oral or written. If any provision of this Agreement is held to be invalid or unenforceable the validity or enforceability of the remaining provisions shall not be affected thereby.

Notices and communication to:

PL:

should be sent for the attention of:

Sales Administrator
Pharmalicensing Limited
Innovation Centre
York Science Park
Heslington
YORK YO1 5DG
United Kingdom

By hand, by first class mail, by fax to: +44 870 0547781 or by electronic mail: admin@pharmalicensing.com

Subscriber:

should be sent for the attention of:

Current name at the address fax or electronic mail supplied by Subscriber in Web Site registration form, or as subsequently notified in writing by the Subscriber to PL for such purposes.

12. Law

This Agreement shall be governed by and construed in accordance with the Laws of England and the parties hereto submit to the exclusive jurisdiction of the English Courts.

Reproduced with the kind permission of Pharmalicensing Ltd (www.pharmalicensing.com).

Appendix 4: Notices for Web Sites and E-mails, Copyright Permission Notices, Disclaimers and Privacy Policies

E-mails

1. Confidentiality Notice for E-mails

'This message may be confidential information and will be protected by copyright. If you receive it in error, notify us, delete it and do not make use of or copy it.'

2. Confidentiality Notice for E-mails

'This E-mail is intended only for the addressee named above. As this e-mail may contain confidential or privileged information, if you are not the named addressee, or the person responsible for delivering the message to the named addressee, please notify us immediately. The contents must not be disclosed to any other person nor copies taken.'

3. Confidentiality Notice for E-mails (lawyer as sender)

'This email is confidential. It may also be privileged or otherwise protected by work product immunity or other legal rules. If you are not the intended recipient please notify the sender by telephone on +44 20 8866 1934 and delete the message from all places in your computer where it is stored. You should not copy the email or use it for any purpose or disclose its contents to any other person. To do so may be unlawful.

'E-mail is an informal means of communicating and may be subject to data corruption accidentally or deliberately. For this reason it is inappropriate to rely on advice contained in an email without obtaining written confirmation of it first.

'A list of the partners of our firm is available for inspection at [*address*]. The partners are solicitors.

'Visit our web site at www.abcd.com'.

4. Confidential notice for E-mails (lawyer as sender)

'*Confidentiality*

This electronic transmission is strictly confidential and intended solely for the addressee. It may contain information which is covered by legal, professional or other privilege. If you are not the intended addressee, you must not disclose, copy or take any action in reliance of this transmission. If you have received this transmission in error, please notify us as soon as possible.

Regulated by the Law Society in the conduct of investment business.

A list of partners' names is available for inspection at [*address*]'

5. Confidentiality notice for E-mails with encryption notice

'This E-mail may contain confidential and privileged material for the sole use of the intended recipient. Any review or distribution by others is strictly prohibited. If you are not the intended recipient please contact the sender and delete all copies. This email is not encrypted. See www.xyzcom and select 'About our firm' for instructions on how to receive encrypted email from us.'

Web Sites

Trade Mark Notices

Registered marks: ABC HGY ®

Use: ABC SDD ™ to indicate an unregistered mark.

Trade Mark Notices where the mark cannot be used in certain countries

NB even with use of this wording national trade mark rights may be breached. Take local law advice.

'We do not accept orders from [Canada]'

Or a company could say:

'The trade mark [ ] is owned by VVV Corporation in Canada and we do not market our goods under that trade mark in Canada. Contact our local dealer by clicking here for further information'.

Copyright Notices

An example of a notice is: © E S Singleton 2000

Some countries' laws require the wording: All Rights Reserved

LawNet Copyright Notice

Copyright Notice

The Copyright in this Internet site and in all of the documents, files, graphics, devices, code and links contained in it or linked to it is owned by LawNet Ltd or by the publishers of those sites to which these pages link.

Anyone is entitled to view any non-passworded parts of the site and to use for their own purposes the information contained therein provided:

It is used for information purposes only and not for reproduction on any other web site or for direct commercial gain.

Any links created to the site are made to the homepage and not to parts only of the site and that any such links are notified to and approved by LawNet Limited before they are created.

© LawNet Ltd, Ince House, 60 Kenilworth Road, Leamington Spa, Warwickshire CV32 6JY

Tel: 01926-886990 Fax: 01926 886553'

Reproduced with the kind permission of LawNet

Database Rights Notice

Where the work on the web site attracts database right rather than copyright protection, in the EU.

'Database Right: XYZ plc 1999'

Contact Details

It is also sensible to give people a set of contact details too in case they want to seek copyright permission.

> 'For copyright and other rights permissions and questions contact The Copyright Officer, Singletons, The Ridge, South View Road, Pinner, Middlesex HA5 3YD, UK, tel +44 20 886 1934; fax +44 20 8429 9212, email essingleton@link.org.'

General Disclaimer – LawNet Example

DISCLAIMER

Whilst LawNet Limited has taken every precaution in compiling this site, neither it, nor its member firms or any contributors to the site can be held responsible for any action (or the lack thereof) taken by any person or organisation, wherever they shall be based, as a result, direct or otherwise, of information contained in or accessed through this Internet site.

Anyone reading this site is recommended to seek specific advice from a suitably qualified person before dealing with any situation which may be covered by any information contained in any part of this site or before embarking on any course of action.

Unless otherwise indicated the law stated in this site relates to England & Wales. Scotland, Northern Ireland, the Republic of Ireland and the Channel Islands all have legal systems which differ from that of England & Wales to a lesser or greater extent. Please ensure that when seeking legal advice that you do so from a lawyer qualified in the the appropriate legal jurisdiction.

© LawNet Ltd, Ince House, 60 Kenilworth Road, Leamington Spa, Warwickshire CV32 6JY

Tel: 01926-886990 Fax: 01926 886553'

Reproduced with the kind permission of LawNet

Web Site Disclaimers

Law firm

'The works on this web site are given for general information purposes only and do not constitute legal or other professional advice. We do not accept any responsibility for loss which may arise from relying on the information contained on this site.'

Excite – Internet Services

Excite is provided to you free of charge, 'as is.' Excite uses its best efforts to maintain Excite, but is not responsible for the results of any defects that may be found to exist in Excite, or any lost profits or other consequential damages that may result from such defects. You should not assume that Excite is error-free or that it will be suitable for the particular purpose that you have in mind when using it.

The Excite technology automatically produces search results that reference sites and information located worldwide throughout the Internet. Because Excite has no control over such sites and information, Excite makes no guaranties as to such sites and information, including as to: (i) the accuracy, currency, content, or quality of any such sites and information, or (ii) whether an Excite search may locate unintended and objectionable content.

Because some of the content on the Internet consists of material that is adult-oriented or otherwise objectionable to some people, the results of your search using Excite may automatically and unintentionally generate links or references to objectionable material. Excite can make no claim that such surprises will not occur. Computerized search technology does not give you search results limited to only the hits that you were seeking. There may be extraneous hits as well.

Reproduced with the kind permission of Excite Inc.

Excite is a trade mark and/or service mark of Excite, Inc, a subsidiary of At Home Corporation, and may be registered in various jurisdictions. Excite screen displays copyright 1995-1999 Excite, Inc.

Terms of Use of Website Disclaimer: Sprecher Grier Halberstam

Target Audience

This website is intended for use by UK residents only and only in relation to their activities within the UK. It may be very dangerous to apply any of the information on this website to activities outside of the UK.

The information contained on this website is not intended to be used by anyone less than 18 years of age. No one under that age should carry out any activity whatsoever based on the information on this website.

Professional Regulations

On this website, we are only able to give some indicative information regarding the [ ]. The reader must ensure that he/she is aware of and follows the latest regulations set by and guidance available from [ ] in relation to all activities covered by this website including without limitation [ ].

Professional Advice

You must seek professional advice in relation to any area covered by this website in respect of which you have any doubts whatsoever.

Copyright

All website design, text, graphics, the selection and arrangement thereof, and all software Copyright © 1999, Limited (' ') ALL RIGHTS RESERVED.

Disclaimer of Warranty and Liability

[ ] does not represent or warrant that the information accessible via this website is accurate, complete or current. Except in the case of personal injury or death caused by the negligence of [ ]. [ ] has no liability whatsoever in respect of any use which you make of such information.

The information provided on this website has not been written to meet your individual requirements and it is your sole responsibility to satisfy yourself prior to using this information in any way that it is suitable for your purposes. Before making any decisions based on any information contained on this website, you are strongly advised to refer to alternative independent sources of information to substantiate the basis for your decision.

Viruses

Whilst [ ] makes all reasonable attempts to exclude viruses from the website, it cannot ensure such exclusion and no liability is accepted for viruses. Thus, you are recommended to take all appropriate safeguards before downloading information from this website.

Law Governing this Website and this Disclaimer

These terms and this disclaimer and any claim based on use of information from this website shall be governed by the laws of England and the parties submit to the exclusive jurisdiction of the Courts of England and Wales.

In order to access the information on this website, you must signal acceptance of the terms and disclaimer set out above by clicking on the 'I accept' button below.

© Sprecher Grier Halberstam

Appendix 5: Example Contract Terms for Exchanges of Products and Designs Electronically

For Subcontractors Supply to Contractor

1. Supplier's approval to receive and use computerised data shall be in accordance with documents [*add internal reference numbers of documents concerning submission electronically*]

2. Supplier will use a digital data request (DDR) form (as provided by Buyer) to request any data to be provided by Buyer to Supplier in performance of this Contract.

3. Any such data provided by Buyer to Supplier may be used in the performance of this Contract for any Order only if in accordance with Buyer's authority for such use. Any use other than in accordance with such procedures, whether provided by Buyer or otherwise acquired by Supplier, shall be considered unofficial and shall be used in the performance of this Contract only if prior authorisation to do so is given in writing by Buyer.

4. If data such as tapes, plots, printouts partially or completely defines the geometry of any Product, such output will constitute the sole definition of that part of such Product's geometric configuration. The source data shall be on the Product Drawing. Such output shall not be automatically sent to Supplier with any Drawing; however, Supplier may request Buyer to provide output in conformity with the specific manufacturing and inspection requirements of Supplier.

5. All plots, tapes, aperture cards or other representation of any such data which are produced through a Buyer-approved process, may be used in the same way and to the same extent as such other data.

System/Software Compatibility Between Buyer and Supplier

6. After Supplier is qualified to use the data exchange methods identified in [ ] above Supplier shall maintain compatibility with Buyer's systems in accordance with document [ ]. Buyer shall provide timely notification to Supplier of revisions to Buyer's systems.

Electronic Communications and Data Exchange Via Telecommunications

7. In the event that the Parties agree to utilise electronic communications and data exchange via telecommunications, the Parties shall transmit Digital Data, and other communications by Electronic Communication as defined by and in accordance with Exhibit A. Provided, that any amendments to the Contract, change authorisations and any other matter requiring written authorisation shall be communicated in writing and not solely by Electronic Communication.

8. Each Party shall be responsible for its costs associated with such exchange of information, including but not limited to any Third Party Service Provider expenses, equipment and software.

9. Supplier shall provide and maintain the equipment, software and services, and perform all testing necessary to reliably transmit, receive and archive Electronic Communications as set forth in Exhibit A.

EXHIBIT A

Email, EDI and Digital Data Exchange.

Supplier and Buyer shall comply with the following requirements relating to electronic communications between Buyer and Supplier.

A. Definitions

'[ ] Standards' shall mean those standards published by the [ ] Standards Institute identified in Attachment I to this Exhibit A.

'Archive' or 'Archiving' shall mean the procedure by which electronic communications are stored unchanged for defined period of time.

'Digital Data' shall mean digital information used to produce any product either in part or in its entirety, through the use of computer systems for which an associated dataset exists (e.g. CAD/CAM/CAE)

'Electronic Communications' shall mean the electronic communication of text, documents or Computer-Aided Design, Computer-Aided Manufacturing, or Computer-Aided Engineering.

'Electronic Data Interchange' or 'EDI' shall mean the movement between the Parties, in a structured format meeting [ ] Standards, of the transaction sets identified in Attachment II to this Exhibit A.

'Electronic Mail' or 'E-Mail' shall mean the electronic communication of textual information in a non-structured format between the parties.

'Functional Acknowledgement' shall mean an electronic message from the receiving Party's Receipt Computer Software Application, which verifies receipt of the E-Mail message, or digital data, sent automatically at the moment of receipt.

'Garbled Transmission' shall mean an attempted electronic communication which cannot be decoded by the receiving Party's Host Application and is therefore completely unreadable. 'Garbled Transmission' shall be differentiated from errors in transmission which are unreadable in part and/or contain inadvertent error(s).

'Host Application Level' or 'Host Application' shall mean each Party's internal computer application system from which electronic communications are sent and the other Party's electronic communications are received.

'Product Definition Data' shall mean all information reasonably identified as Proprietary Information related to or concerning any Buyer product including, among other data, information related to the marketing, engineering, design or manufacture.

'Software Application' shall mean the software which runs on a computer and translates Documents into and out of a format meeting [ ] Standards.

'Third Party Service Provider(s)' or 'Provider(s)' shall mean an entity, other than Buyer and Supplier, which provides electronic communication services or equipment.

B. Requirements

1. Documents
    (a) EDI – Each Party may electronically transmit to or receive from the other Party by EDI any of the transaction sets listed in Attachment II of Exhibit A, as it may be amended from time to time by mutual agreement of the Parties. (Collectively 'Documents'). Any transmission of data by EDI shall be in a format meeting [ ] Standards.
    (b) E-Mail – Each Party may electronically transmit to or receive textual information ('Messages') from the other Party by E-Mail. For E-Mail, each Party shall include in each Message it transmits: its name, the date and time of the transmissions, the purchase order (if any) to which it relates, and the name and telephone number of the individual authorised to transmit the Message.
    (c) Digital Data Exchange – Each Party may electronically transmit to or receive from the other Party any form of Digital Data listed in Attachment II to this Exhibit A. Supplier shall request Digital Data from Buyer on Buyer form [ ] (DDR).
2. Third Party Service Providers
    (a) Documents and Messages shall be transmitted electronically to each Party either directly or through any Third Party Service Provider with which either Party may contract. Either Party may modify its election to use, not use or change a Provider upon 30 days prior written notice to the other Party. The Providers are listed in Attachment III to this Exhibit A.
3. System Operations
    Each Party shall provide and maintain the equipment, software and services, and perform the testing necessary reliably to transmit, receive and archive Electronic Communications in accordance with the requirements of this Exhibit A.

4. Security Procedures

(a) Each Party shall implement and adhere to security procedures, and utilise those security products and tools which ensure all transmissions of Electronic Communications are authorised by the transmitting Party. Each Party shall protect and secure business records and data from loss, alteration, destruction or access by unauthorised individuals or entities.

(b) Each Party shall monitor the performance of its security products, tools and procedures ('Security System') and shall perform tests necessary to confirm the Security System ensures the integrity of all transmissions at all times.

(c) Each Party's Security System shall further:

1. Establish an organisational responsibility to initiate, expedite and sustain implementation and tracking of requirements.

2. Authorise use of computing systems and specifying the limits of such use (Least Privilege Principle).

3. Have the capability to terminate access privileges.

4. Monitor system activities.

5. Grant or withdraw access privileges on a current, timely basis.

6. Control access on the basis of authenticated individual user identification and specific current authorisation sponsorship.

7. Not authorise anonymous, shares, or guest accounts.

8. Ensure identification authentication passwords and access control passwords are:
    – Limited
    – Not obvious
    – Not less than six characters
    – Used by a single individual
    – Cancelled/reassigned upon termination of need
    – Changed immediately if inadvertently disclosed
    – Not changed in the event of misuse until Security directs
    – Changed every ninety days or less

9. Encrypt passwords.

10. Provide for continuing education of employees.

11. Encrypt sensitive data/information.

12. Maintain physical and personnel security.

13. Maintain backup and disaster recovery preparedness.

14. Detect and report loss or misuse.

15. Provide visibility to the user of last account usage.

16. Not take actions which could affect investigative options.
17. Maintain audit records.
18. Provide appropriate reports in response to Security investigations.
19. Prevent unauthorised access to action/residual data/ information.
    – Overwriting before releasing to surplus or vendor exchange.
    – Erasing sensitive data before releasing disk space.
    – Using automatic system features.

5. *Signatures*

(a) EDI Transmissions – For EDI transmissions each Party shall adopt as its signature an electronic identification consisting of symbol(s) or code(s) which are affixed to or contained in each Document transmitted by such Party ('EDI Signature').

(b) E–Mail Transmissions – For E–Mail transmissions, the name of the Party, together with the name and electronic address of the authorised individual transmitting the Message shall constitute the signature of the sending Party on the Message ('E–Mail Signature').

Each Party agrees that any EDI Signature of such Party affixed to or contained in any transmitted Document and any E–Mail Signature affixed to or contained in any such Message shall be sufficient to confirm such Party originated such Document or Message.

(c) Digital Data Exchange Transmissions – for digital data exchange transmissions each Party shall adopt as its signature an electronic identification consisting of symbol(s) or code(s) which are affixed to or contained in each digital data exchange transmitted by such Party ('Digital Data Exchange Signature').

(d) Exchange and Protection – Each Party shall furnish to the other its EDI Signature, a list of the individuals authorised by it to send Messages by E–Mail and the appropriate Digital Data Exchange Signature. These signatures shall be handled as Proprietary Information.

C. Transmissions

1. Proper Delivery and Receipt – Electronic Communications shall not be deemed properly received, and no Electronic

Communications shall give rise to any obligation, until accessible to the receiving Party at such Party's receipt computer designated in Attachment I to this Exhibit ('Receipt Computer'). All time periods for performing any obligations arising out of the receipt of Electronic Communications shall run from the time of receipt at the Receipt Computer, regardless of whether or not the receiving Party is actually aware of the receipt of the Electronic Communications by its Receipt Computer.

2. Verification – Immediately upon receipt of any Electronic Communications, at its Receipt Computer, the receiving Party's Receipt Computer shall automatically transmit a Functional Acknowledgement in return.

3. Acceptance – In addition, Supplier's commencement of performance, or acceptance in any manner of any Electronic Communication received by it pursuant to this Exhibit shall conclusively evidence the Supplier's acceptance of such Electronic Communication order as transmitted by Buyer.

4. Garbled Transmissions – If any Electronic Communication transmitted in accordance with the provisions of this Document is received as a Garbled Transmission, the receiving Party shall notify the originating Party (if identifiable) in a prompt and reasonable manner.

5. Errors in Transmission – If any Electronic Communication transmitted in accordance with this Document is received in a form which is unreadable in part or contains inadvertent errors, the receiving Party shall promptly notify the originating Party and seek clarification if such error in transmission is reasonably apparent to the receiving Party.

6. Inability to Send Transmissions – Buyer and Supplier acknowledge each may be unable to transmit Electronic Communications from time to time. At such times, communication shall be by other appropriate alternative methods of communication, including, telecopy, telefacsimile, or telephone.

7. Archiving of Transmissions – All Electronic Communications or other communications transmitted in accordance with this Document shall be Archived at the Host Application Level or in the case of alternative methods of communication, in some other appropriate retention system, and must be maintained unchanged for seven (7) years from the time of completion of the Contract.

D. Transaction Terms

1. Encryption – All data or information disclosed, transmitted or otherwise revealed in accordance with this Exhibit which is

marked or otherwise designated as Buyer Proprietary Information shall only be transmitted from source computer to destination computer in end-to-end encrypted form.

2. Completion of Test Plans – Completion of Electronic Mail, Electronic Data Interchange, and/or Digital Data Exchange Test Plan(s) referenced in Attachment I and/or Attachment II, as evidenced by execution and dating, constitutes agreement to use such formats for electronic communications format(s). Accordingly, the paragraphs of this Exhibit A applicable to the selected electronic communications format(s) shall become effective as of the date contained on such Test Plan(s) with respect to electronic communications thereafter.

Exhibit A: Attachment I

Applicable [ ] Standard

All data transmitted by EDI shall conform to version [ ] of [*name of standard*] Standards.

Designation of Receipt Computer

The following computer will constitute the Receipt Computer at Buyer:

[*name of computer*]

The following computer will constitute the Receipt Computer of Supplier:

[*name of computer*]

Minimum Performance Standards

Supplier's E-Mail, EDI and Digital Data Exchange operational systems shall, at a minimum, continue to be able to perform successfully the tests identified as 'passed' on the Index of Tests listed below:

[*add index here*]

Exhibit A: Attachment II

A. Transaction Sets

The parties may transmit by EDI the following transaction sets in accordance with the procedures agreed upon by the parties in that test plan signed by the parties on [*date*]

Transaction Set

[*Add name, transaction set and number*]

B. Digital Data Formats

The parties may transmit by Digital Data Exchange the following formats in accordance with the procedures agreed upon by the parties in that test plan signed by the parties on [*date]*

Digital Data Formats

[*Complete*]

Exhibit A: Attachment III

A. Designation of Provider:

Buyer has selected the following Third Party Service Provider(s):

[*Add name*]

Supplier has selected the following Third Party Service Provider(s):

[*Add name*]

Appendix 6

E-mail, the Internet and the Workplace – Legal Issues

Whilst this document aims to provide general information and practical guidance to companies, it is no substitute for expert legal advice based on knowledge of the exact circumstances faced by an individual company.

If you have any queries, do not hesitate to contact Simon Halberstam, Head of the Internet & E-commerce law group at Sprecher Grier Halberstam, Solicitors.

Tel: 0171 544 5555. Fax: 0171 544 5565.

Email: law@weblaw.co.uk. or simonh@sprgr.co.uk

Website: http://www.weblaw.co.uk

This document is written for employers and seeks to advise them:

- on the legal implications of the use of email and the internet in the workplace
- on employment law issues and what to include in contracts of employment
- on an email policy which can be issued to employees (this is an appendix to this document)
- on copyright and other intellectual property issues
- contract law issues
- other legal areas such as defamation and confidentiality

1. Introduction

E-mail and the internet are useful business tools but must be used correctly. Never assume employees will know what the law is. Common misconceptions are that any document 'in the public domain' on the internet is not protected by copyright or that no legal liability can arise from an E-mail message. Many send email messages without proper forethought. Staff need to be constantly reminded of the legal issues in this field. A once only education exercise is not enough. Senior management must be seen to follow whatever rules are put in place and the rules must be consistently enforced. New staff must be educated as to what the rules are and the rules should be made part of the contract of employment either by inclusion in the contract or by incorporation in any relevant staff handbook.

2. Websites and Intellectual Property Rights

2.1 Copyright

Internet websites are a valuable advertising tool for companies on the internet. Caution needs to be exercised when commissioning art or design work for such sites. If third parties, design companies or freelance staff are used, it is essential that the company obtains a written assignment of the intellectual property rights from the designer in advance before work is done. If not, then under the Copyright Designs and Patents Act 1988 the designer will own all copyright in the work for which the company has paid and all the company will receive is a limited licence to use the work. This does not allow the company to prevent the designer using the designs for other people's websites. However if an agreement is drawn up in advance then it can be made very clear and legally water tight as to who will own copyright and any other intellectual property rights in the work.

2.2 Moral rights

In addition, designers may have moral rights in certain copyright works even if they do not own the works. These rights for example allow the designer to prevent the works being altered in certain cases. Contracts can provide that moral rights are 'waived'.

2.3 Sprecher Grier Halberstam Terms

For information on website agreements reference should be made to one of the Sprecher Grier Halberstam websites – at **weblaw-.co.uk**. Sprecher Grier Halberstam has a standard set of terms and conditions for website agreements which can be used to ensure that all legal issues are covered. It is preferable to have one's own set of terms rather than be governed by almost invariably one-sided terms provided by and favouring the designer.

2.4 Copyright Notices and Restrictions

If copyright works appear on a web page, it is sensible, though not essential, for protection, to include a notice such as '(c) XYZ 1998.' It is also important to make clear what people accessing the page may do – may they print it and the information on it? May they download it? May they send it to other people? May they do what they like with it including commercialise or re-use it? If there are no restrictions that does not mean that third parties can use others' copyright works as they please. Employees must be told that information on the internet is not necessarily free of copyright restrictions. A company may allow readers, for example, to read its journal on-screen but not take that material and use it in a brochure or competitive magazine.

2.5 Trade Marks

The web page may well use registered or unregistered trade marks of the company. Ensure that those trade marks where registered appear with an 'R' in a circle to indicate the mark is registered or the letters 'TM' to indicate an unregistered mark. It is an offence under the Trade Marks Act 1994 to claim a mark is registered when it is not. If an application for registration has been made at the Trade Marks Registry or, for EU-wide marks, the Community Trade Mark Office in Alicante, then the letters 'TM' must be used until the mark has been granted. Although rights in a mark are not lost if a notice such as this is not used, such a notice is a valuable warning to third parties that the names or devices are protected and should not be copied.

2.6 National and International Trade Mark Issues

Note that marks obtain protection only in the countries where they are registered. If a company through the use of the internet will begin to make sales abroad then the company should seriously consider protecting itself in those markets by registration of local trade marks. Indeed, before supplying and advertising abroad, it is advisable to do a trade mark search to check whether a third party already has the mark there. If they have, then an import whether through an email order or otherwise may amount to a breach of trade mark rights of that third party and expensive trade mark infringement proceedings may follow. Cautious companies may avoid problems by including a notice on their web page saying orders are accepted only from certain countries (such as those where they know they own the trade marks); or use a different name for sales of products to countries where a third party owns the same trade mark.

Sprecher Grier Halberstam can provide full international trade mark search and registration services either directly or through its Trade Mark Services network.

2.7 Domain Names

Choose domain names with care because they may be third parties' trade marks. In the UK at the end of 1997 BT, M&S and other companies were successful in an action in the English High Court against a company One-in-a-Million which had registered as domain names their famous and proprietary trading names. The court ordered that the names be transferred to the true owners. However the position is not as straightforward when two businesses trade under the same or similar names and in any event such litigation is very expensive. Take legal advice in cases of doubt and do not give in to demands from third party registration companies offering 'your' name for a fee. A solicitor's letter back requiring them to assign the name for nothing may result in a much cheaper acquisition of the name in question.

3. Forming Contracts

3.1 Offer and acceptance

The question here centres on whether businesses should permit staff to form contracts by email. Under English law, provided an offer has been accepted and there is consideration (usually payment) then most types of contract can be made regardless of whether there is a signed document. This may be formed over the telephone, in a meeting, by letter, fax or email. In other countries complicated formalities are required such as the presence of witnesses, signature of a written agreement signed on every page and signatures which are notarised.

3.2 Choice of law

The first contract formation issue is therefore which country's law applies to a particular transaction. Those supplying goods over the internet or forming contracts in that way need to have written terms of trading. Those terms of sale must be sent to customers before a contract is made. If the terms are on the back of an invoice which is not sent out until after the goods are shipped the terms are not part of the contract. They are sent too late to be effective under most countries' laws.

3.3 Accepting terms

Ensure that web pages which advertise goods or services also include the terms and conditions of supply and that buyers must accept those conditions by reading and clicking on an 'okay' box before an order is placed. Staff should be told that if the buyer rejects the supplier's conditions and offers their own then further advice should be sought from the legal department or sales department senior staff before the order is accepted.

3.4 Compliance with foreign laws

This note does not summarise the necessary content of terms and conditions of supply. These can be drafted on request and will vary from business to business. If the goods or services in question may breach laws in certain countries then the web page should make clear that orders from those countries are not accepted. For example, there may be approval for a pharmaceutical product only in certain states or in some countries it may be forbidden to supply alcoholic products or to sell magazines which show parts of female anatomy. In some countries third parties may own patent or other intellectual property rights in the goods to be supplied so that if orders from those countries are accepted, intellectual property right infringement proceedings are likely to follow.

3.5 Avoid misrepresentations

Ensure that no inaccurate statements are given on the website as this is likely to breach trade descriptions or other laws and those browsing may be induced by a misrepresentation to enter into a contract. Legal proceedings for misrepresentation may follow. One difficulty which has put some companies off use of the internet altogether is that web pages must comply with laws in all states. Even if the page clearly states that English or Scottish law applies, it is common for some countries to override such choice of law on public policy grounds to protect local businesses. In practice it is impossible to check compliance of a page with laws in over 100 countries. A compromise is to mention certain major markets from which orders are accepted or make sure the web page is so anodyne as to be incapable of offending the laws of any state.

Areas to watch include:

- use of offensive material
- use of religious symbols or images or words
- use of obscene material or pictures
- use of swear words
- use of well known trade marks of other people
- use of other people's copyright works without their consent
- telling lies or exaggerating about products
- criticising competitors – in some states comparative advertising is allowed but not everywhere.

3.6 The conditions of sale should state which country's laws apply to transactions and which courts have jurisdiction to hear disputes

3.7 Not too risky

Do not be put off by the international law issues mentioned here. In some ways there is less risk with internet sales than others. It may be harder for a third party to track the supplier down. For example, in the case of a trader who breaches Saudi decency laws, it may be impossible to bring him/her to justice in that jurisdiction if he/she has no assets there and no future trading plans for that state.

3.8 Reliability

A contract made electronically is just as likely to be valid as one made by telephone or by fax. In fact, it is more likely that conditions can be effectively incorporated into an agreement made electronically than when a fax is used in which case staff may forget to fax the back of the order form which includes the all important contractual conditions. Although there remains a risk that emails will go astray, this is becoming less of a problem as systems become more sophisticated. If an order is not received then it will never be accepted (or rejected). This will damage business reputation of the supplier but is not a breach of contract. Normally the buyer will receive a message back saying its message did not get through in any event.

3.9 Credit card orders

If orders are accepted on the basis of the supply of a credit card number, one must ensure that appropriate security procedures are in place. In one case, a boy from South America ordered thousands of pounds worth of chocolate bars in this way by using an 'invented' credit card number which happened to be someone else's. The third party received a large bill but the chocolate company, happy with the free world-wide publicity it received, appears to have written off the debt.

3.10 Keep records

Keep a record of emails, preferably electronically so that in the event of a dispute later about whether a buyer rejected terms of sale or was offered better terms than the supplier normally offers. the information is available. Indeed, email may provide a better record than when the telephone is used for orders. For those trading in the EU, note the provisions of the 1997 EU distance selling directive which affect all sales negotiated at a distance such as internet and tele-sales. Standard information must be provided to purchasers. The directive will be implemented throughout the EU in the year 2000 and procedures should be altered now to ensure compliance in time. Sprecher Grier Halberstam can advise you on the best method of dealing with the legal implications.

4. Data Protection

4.1 Be cautious about the supply of personal data about individuals as the Data Protection Act 1984 will apply. We can provide guidance on the use of the internet and personal data.

4.2 The EU data protection directive 95/46 harmonises the law on data protection throughout the 15 member states of the EU. Under the directive, which is published in the EU's official journal 1995 L281/31, member states had until 24 October 1998 to implement the directive. In the UK we have now implemented the Data Protection Act 1998. Unfortunately this Act has deferred the issues rather than dealt with them.

4.3 Under the new Act, each member state must have the equivalent of a data protection registrar. Those holding personal data must register and follow strict privacy principles in relation to the obtaining, storing and holding and use of such data. Whereas the 1984 Act only applied to electronic records, the new Act also applies to data held manually and will therefore increase the burden on businesses.

5. Other legal areas

5.1 Checking identities

It may be hard to verify from whom an email has been received. It is relatively easy to set up a false identity over the internet. For important matters check up on the other party through other means such as by telephone, companies house searches, and by post. Legislation is afoot to govern electronic signatures and independent verification bodies called trusted third parties.

5.2 Competition/Anti-trust law

Watch out for breach of competition law. Artificially partitioning the EU market may breach Article 85 of the Treaty of Rome and lead to fines of up to 10% of world-wide turnover. The EU regulation on exclusive distribution agreements 1983/93 does, though, allow a restriction in a contract with an exclusive distributor preventing the distributor from advertising outside his area. Make sure that the contract makes clear whether internet advertising is allowed by the distributor or not. Dominant companies refusing to supply companies for anti-competitive reasons may also breach EU competition law or local competition law whether the sale is over the internet or not.

5.3 Defamation

Employees should be warned that they may breach libel laws if they defame third parties. Damages for defamation may be awarded against both the employee and the employer. It is therefore imperative to ensure that all staff are aware of the need to be careful as to what they say. The guidance notes attached highlight the importance of checking emails carefully before despatch and not unnecessarily copying too many people in on the message. Libel can be committed both over the internet with emails to third parties or internally over an intranet. Norwich Union recently discovered this to its cost.

5.4 Having a policy – security

Each company must decide what it is prepared to have sent by email. Sending an email can be akin to sending a post card unless encryption is used. Set clear rules for employees about what may be sent by email and what may not. Some companies are happy for lengthy commercial contracts to be sent in this way whereas others are not. Remember that documents can go astray just as easily when sent by courier or fax to the wrong recipient as when sent by email.

6. Terms of Employment

6.1 The first legal employment issue is effecting any change to existing employment conditions. In theory a change to an employment contract must be agreed by the employee. If the employee does not agree then, in some cases, the employee forced to accept the change may, instead, leave and claim he or she was constructively dismissed because of the unilateral imposition of the new terms. He or she can then claim damages for unfair and/or wrongful dismissal. It is doubtful whether an industrial tribunal would regard a change in employment conditions as they relate to the use of the internet at work as being a material change sufficient to justify an employee walking out.

6.2 There should therefore be no difficulty in imposing a new policy. However it is important to ensure that it is explained to employees and any questions answered promptly. This will facilitate acceptance by a workforce who understand why changes are being made to their working practices.

6.3 The personnel department should also be familiar with the rules and ensure that all new staff or staff returning from maternity or other leave are informed about the new policy. If these rules will replace an existing Email policy then this should be made clear too so that employees know what policy they are expected to follow. Similarly companies within the same corporate group should consider co-ordinating any rules that there are within the group to ensure that everyone is working to the same standards and requirements.

6.4 Taking disciplinary action

If an employee breaks the rules then action must be taken otherwise the policy is undermined and other staff will realise that the rules are not enforced. If a member of staff were to use the internet to access material that another employee of the opposite sex found offensive, the latter might sue the company for sexual discrimination. There is no limit on damages for unfair dismissal on the grounds of sex discrimination following recent EU case law and if such conduct continues staff may walk out and claim constructive dismissal and large sums in damages.

6.5 However, never rush to sack someone. It always best practice to give them an opportunity to put their side of the story. Sometimes employees lie about each other. The facts presented to management by one employee may be completely untrue. Seek advice from an employment law solicitor specialist before sacking anyone.

6.6 Wording for employment contracts

Wording for employment contracts depends on the rules of the company and these will vary from business to business. Words such as the following may be used:

> 'The Employee must comply with the Company's Email and Internet Policy a copy of which has been supplied to the Employee. Breach of the Policy may be serious misconduct depending on the nature of the offence. The downloading or transmission of pornography or other illegal material will result in summary dismissal.

7. Summary

7.1 Every business and its email needs are different so this set of notes simply provides an overview of some of the more major areas. Similarly, the attached email policy should be used more as an aide memoire than a comprehensive document relevant to every company.

7.2 Technology changes quickly and users of this document need to ensure they regularly update their contracts, their email policies and their knowledge of the law in this field. New EU directives on copyright and the information society are in the process of being agreed. International agreement on internet issues is likely to be achieved in the next few years. This is a fast moving area but the changes in technology and the law should not put off companies using the internet and email to keep themselves ahead of their rivals.

E-mail and Internet Policy

This document sets out our new email policy which is being introduced throughout the Company. It seeks to provide advice and assistance to you in your use of email at work and also lists rules about email and the internet which you must follow. These rules are now incorporated into our staff handbook/conditions of employment and all employees are subject to them. Depending on the seriousness of the breach, a failure to comply with the rules may amount to misconduct or serious misconduct. You are required to sign the bottom of this page to indicate you have had a copy of the rules and will follow them. They have been designed to ensure that the company and you gain the most from email and the internet without imposing an unnecessary cost and risk burden on the company. If you have any questions on this document contact your line manager or [*Mr XYZ in our legal department*].

I acknowledge receipt of a copy of the company's email and internet policy and agree to be bound by the rules contained in this document.

. . . .

Signed

Date . . . .

Rules

1. Use of the Internet at Work

1.1 Those employees provided with a computer with access to the internet or who have access through use of colleagues' or communal computers are permitted to use the internet during working hours for business use with the prior permission of their line manager.

1.2 Some employees because of the special nature of their job are given wider access to the internet and will be notified of this in writing. If you believe you should have such wider access please put your business case in writing to your line manager and it will be considered

1.3 Employees are not allowed to use the internet for any purpose unconnected with their work during or out of working hours. Employees wanting to email a personal message or surf the internet may make a written request to their line manager but use will be at his or her discretion and may be refused. In particular, extensive or expensive searches will be prohibited.

2. Illegal Activities

2.1 You will be aware of our equal opportunities policy. We therefore take it as misconduct if the internet is used at work for the use, viewing, down or uploading of pornographic material. Anyone found engaging in criminal activities such as those relating to child pornography will be summarily dismissed.

2.2 Staff must not send obscene or defamatory emails and must not place obscene or offensive screen savers on their PCs.

3. Defamation

3.1 The UK has strict laws of defamation – libel for emails and the written word and slander for verbal statements. An email sent to another person which denigrates a third person is potentially libellous and might expose the company to being sued for damages.

3.2 Beware that an email sent to one person may, for various reasons, be read by others and that this exacerbates the risk of libel.

3.3 Do not issue defamatory material over the internet or an intranet. Untrue statements may lead to expensive court action. Check all emails carefully before despatch and if you are not sure about their accuracy, do not send them!

4. Websites

4.1 We have a website on the internet and you may become involved in updating it or using it. If you commission designers or self-employed people to work on it, you must ensure that they sign a written contract in advance which the company will provide for you. If you do not do this, then the company will not obtain ownership of the relevant copyright and other rights it will require.

4.2 We need to check carefully that information on our website is accurate and complies with certain laws. Make sure that all information placed on the website goes through our internal approval process.

4.3 If you come across anything on our website which is wrong or not up to date, tell your line manager immediately and we will correct it.

4.4 Our trade marks and some copyright works are used on the website and we reserve our rights in these.

5. Copyright and the Internet

Information on the internet may be protected by copyright law. This means that you may break the law if you copy it. Sometimes information is made available on other people's websites and they say you may freely copy it. Even this may not be sufficient to protect you and our company because occasionally information is posted on the web by someone other than the owner of the copyright or other rights in the work. Check carefully before using information in this way.

6. Viruses

Do not download information except to a standalone PC which we have for this purpose. All information downloaded must be virus checked. Contact the IT department for further information.

7. Contracts

7.1 We take orders for our goods and services via email. You must make sure that buyers accept our terms and conditions of sale which are posted on our website. All enquiries by email to our sales department must be replied to promptly and with our conditions attached.

7.2 If a potential customer rejects our conditions and prepares its own, then you should immediately discuses the matter with your line manager and unless the line manager instructs you otherwise, send an email straight back saying that its offer is not accepted and that you will revert to them as soon as possible. If, instead, you take no action and the goods are shipped to the customer, then the supply will be on its terms and conditions of purchase which may be unacceptable to us. Every sale which we conclude via email is exclusively subject to English law and jurisdiction. We make this clear in our conditions.

7.3 Be careful in email as in any other correspondence not to form a contract by mistake. Do not reach any agreement and do mark any preliminary correspondence 'Subject to Contract'. Be careful about making representations about our goods or services by email otherwise you may expose the company to liability for a misrepresentation even if a contract is not made.

8. Other Email Guidelines

8.1 Think before writing. Grammar and spelling mistakes look just as unprofessional on screen as they do on paper.

8.2 Check you are sending it to the right destination before you send it – once it has gone, you cannot get it back.

8.3 Print out copies of all email, which you are intending to send and ensure that you obtain the written approval of your line manager before despatching such email.

8.4 Ensure that all emails contain our standard header and footer as will be notified to you from time to time.

8.5 After despatch of an email, ensure that you file a copy as you would a letter or fax.

8.6 Insert terms such as 'Without Prejudice' where this would be appropriate on other written correspondence.

8.7 Top and tail emails in a business like manner. For example, Dear Sir and Yours faithfully.

Appendix 6

For further information on any of the areas covered in this document contact [ ] on [telephone/email]

....

Director

© **Sprecher Grier Halberstam**

EMAIL, INTERNET AND EXTERNAL DISK

INTRODUCTION POLICY

This document sets out the E-mail and Internet policy which the Firm is adopting. It seeks to provide advice and assistance to you in your use of email at work and also lists rules about email and the internet which you must follow. These rules are now incorporated into the Firm's conditions of employment and all members of staff are subject to them. Depending on the seriousness of the breach, a failure to comply with the rules may amount to misconduct or serious misconduct. Please sign at the bottom of this page to indicate you have had a copy of the rules and will follow them. They have been designed to ensure that the Firm and you gain the most from email and the Internet without imposing an unnecessary cost and risk burden on the Firm. If you have any questions regarding this document contact a partner.

I acknowledge receipt of a copy of the Firm's email and internet policy and agree to be bound by the rules contained in this document.

. . . .

Signed

Date 199

Rules

1.   Use of the Internet at work

1.1   No Personal Use

Those members of staff provided with a computer with access to the internet or who have access through use of colleagues' or communal computers are permitted to use the internet solely for purposes strictly connected with the business of the firm, including without limitation, downloading research materials from websites authorised by one or more partners of the Firm. This restriction also applies to computers which are used outside of the Firm's offices.

1.2   Members of staff wanting to email a personal message or surf the Internet may make a written request on each occasion to a partner but use will be at his or her discretion and may be refused. In particular, extensive or expensive searches will be prohibited and no incoming personal email is permitted.

2.   **Illegal Activities**

2.1   The Firm considers as serious misconduct use of the Internet at work for the viewing, down or uploading of pornographic or other obscene or offensive material and such conduct will lead to summary dismissal.

2.2   Staff must not send obscene or defamatory emails and must not place obscene or offensive screen savers on their PCs.

3.   **Defamation**

The UK has strict laws of defamation – libel for emails and the written word and slander for verbal statements. An email sent to another person which denigrates a third person is potentially libellous and might expose the Firm to a suit for damages. Beware that an email sent to one person may for various reasons be read by others and that by increasing the number of persons to whom the libellous statement is published, increases the likelihood of libel proceedings.

4.   **Guidelines**

4.1   Set out below is a list of rules to follow which should help you to use email in the most effective way and ensure that you do not issue defamatory material. Even if you believe that only one person will receive a message which may be derogatory of someone else, it is possible a secretary of the recipient has been delegated to read messages in the recipient's absence or that there is independent checking of emails, so many people may read a message. Untrue statements may lead to expensive court action. Check all emails carefully before despatch and if you are unsure about their accuracy do not send them.

4.2.1   Think before writing! Grammar and spelling mistakes look just as unprofessional on screen as they do on paper.

4.2.2   Check you are sending it to the right destination before you send it! – once it has gone you cannot get it back.

4.2.3   Ensure that all email contain the Firm's standard header and footer as will be notified to you from time to time!

4.2.4   After despatch of an email, ensure that you file a hard copy as you would a letter or fax!

4.2.5   Be careful in email as in any other correspondence not to form a contract by mistake. Do not reach any agreement and mark any preliminary correspondence 'Subject to contract'!

4.2.6   Insert terms such as 'Without Prejudice' where this would be appropriate on other forms of written correspondence.

4.2.7   Top and tail emails in a business like manner!

4.2.8   Be careful about making representations about the Firm's goods or services by email otherwise you may expose the Firm to liability for a misrepresentation even if a contract is not made.

5.   Partner Approval
Print out copies of all emails, which you are intending to send and ensure that you obtain the written approval of a partner before despatching such email.

6.   Websites

6.1   The Firm has websites on the Internet and you may become involved in updating or usage. Do not commission anyone to work on the website(s) without ensuring that they have sign a written contract in advance which has been approved by a partner of the Firm. If you do not do this then the Firm will not obtain ownership of the relevant copyright and other rights it will require.

6.2   The Firm needs to check carefully that information on the Firm's website(s) is accurate and complies with certain laws. Make sure that all information placed on the website(s) goes through the Firm's internal approval process.

6.3   If you come across anything on the Firm's website(s) which is wrong or not up to date, tell a partner immediately and the Firm will correct it.

7.   Copyright and the Internet
Information on the Internet may be protected by copyright law. This means that you may break the law if you copy it. Sometimes information is made available on other people's websites and they say you may freely copy it. Even this may not be sufficient to protect you and the Firm because occasionally information is posted on the world wide web internet by someone other than

the owner of the copyright or other rights in the work. Check carefully before using information in this way.

8. Viruses

8.1 Do not download information from the Internet except otherwise than strictly for the purposes of the Firm's business. Such information may only be downloaded on a PC which has been loaded with appropriate virus-checking software.

8   2 Do not load any files or other material onto any of the Firm's computers if the files or material come from a disk or other medium which has been brought into the Firm from external sources. Such disks must be given to Anita Burrage for checking and loading.

8.3 Do not download materials from the Internet or access email attachments without the prior permission of a partner.

9. New Clients

If the Firm's initial contact with a client is via email, you must ensure that the Firm's procedures which would apply to any new client are followed.

For further information on any of the areas covered in this document, please contact Simon Halberstam. Tel: 0171 544 5555

© **Simon Halberstam**

Appendix 7 – Uncitral Model Law on Electronic Commerce with Guide to Enactment 1996

with additional article 5 bis as adopted in 1998

UNITED NATIONS

CONTENTS

GENERAL ASSEMBLY RESOLUTION 51/162 OF 16 DECEMBER 1996

UNCITRAL MODEL LAW ON ELECTRONIC COMMERCE

Part one. Electronic commerce in general

Article 4. Variation by agreement

Chapter II. Application of legal requirements to data messages
Article 5. Legal recognition of data messages
Article 5 bis. Incorporation by reference
Article 6. Writing
Article 7. Signature
Article 8. Original
Article 9. Admissibility and evidential weight of data messages
Article 10. Retention of data messages

Chapter III. Communication of data messages
Article 11. Formation and validity of contracts
Article 12. Recognition by parties of data messages
Article 13. Attribution of data messages
Article 14. Acknowledgement of receipt
Article 15. Time and place of dispatch and receipt of data messages

Part two. Electronic commerce in specific areas

Chapter I. Carriage of goods

Article 16. Actions related to contracts of carriage of goods

Article 17. Transport documents

	Paragraphs
Guide to Enactment of the UNCITRAL Model Law on Electronic Commerce	1-150
Purpose of this Guide	1
I. Introduction to the Model Law	2–23
A. Objectives	2-6
B. Scope	7-10
C. Structure	11-12
D. A "framework" law to be supplemented by technical regulations	13-14

Resolution adopted by the General Assembly

[on the report of the Sixth Committee (A/51/628)]

51/162 Model Law on Electronic Commerce adopted by the
United Nations Commission on International Trade Law

The General Assembly,

Recalling its resolution 2205 (XXI) of 17 December 1966, by which it
created the United Nations Commission on International Trade Law,
with a mandate to further the progressive harmonization and unification of the law of international trade and in that respect to bear in
mind the interests of all peoples, in particular those of developing
countries, in the extensive development of international trade,

Noting that an increasing number of transactions in international trade
are carried out by means of electronic data interchange and other
means of communication, commonly referred to as "electronic commerce", which involve the use of alternatives to paper-based methods
of communication and storage of information,

Recalling the recommendation on the legal value of computer records
adopted by the Commission at its eighteenth session, in 1985,(1) and
paragraph 5(b) of General Assembly resolution 40/71 of 11 December
1985, in which the Assembly called upon Governments and international organizations to take action, where appropriate, in conformity
with the recommendation of the Commission,(1) so as to ensure legal
security in the context of the widest possible use of automated data
processing in international trade,

Convinced that the establishment of a model law facilitating the use of
electronic commerce that is acceptable to States with different legal,
social and economic systems, could contribute significantly to the
development of harmonious international economic relations,

Noting that the Model Law on Electronic Commerce was adopted by the Commission at its twenty-ninth session after consideration of the observations of Governments and interested organizations,

Believing that the adoption of the Model Law on Electronic Commerce by the Commission will assist all States significantly in enhancing their legislation governing the use of alternatives to paper-based methods of communication and storage of information and in formulating such legislation where none currently exists,

1. *Expresses* its appreciation to the United Nations Commission on International Trade Law for completing and adopting the Model Law on Electronic Commerce contained in the annex to the present resolution and for preparing the Guide to Enactment of the Model Law;

2. *Recommends* that all States give favourable consideration to the Model Law when they enact or revise their laws, in view of the need for uniformity of the law applicable to alternatives to paper-based methods of communication and storage of information;

3. *Recommends* also that all efforts be made to ensure that the Model Law, together with the Guide, become generally known and available.

85th plenary meeting

16 December 1996

UNCITRAL Model Law on Electronic Commerce

[Original: Arabic, Chinese, English, French, Russian, Spanish]

Part one. Electronic commerce in general

Chapter I. General provisions

Article 1. Sphere of application*

This Law** applies to any kind of information in the form of a data message used in the context*** of commercial**** activities.

* The Commission suggests the following text for States that might wish to limit the applicability of this Law to international data messages:

"This Law applies to a data message as defined in paragraph (1) of article 2 where the data message relates to international commerce."

** This Law does not override any rule of law intended for the protection of consumers.

*** The Commission suggests the following text for States that might wish to extend the applicability of this Law: "This Law applies to any kind of information in the form of a data message, except in the following situations: [. . .]."

**** The term "commercial" should be given a wide interpretation so as to cover matters arising from all relationships of a commercial nature, whether contractual or not. Relationships of a commercial nature include, but are not limited to, the following transactions: any trade transaction for the supply or exchange of goods or services; distribution agreement; commercial representation or agency; factoring; leasing; construction of works; consulting; engineering; licensing; investment; financing; banking; insurance; exploitation agreement or concession; joint venture and other forms of industrial or business cooperation; carriage of goods or passengers by air, sea, rail or road

Article 2. Definitions

For the purposes of this Law:

(a)   "Data message" means information generated, sent, received or stored by electronic, optical or similar means including, but not limited to, electronic data interchange (EDI), electronic mail, telegram, telex or telecopy;

(b)   "Electronic data interchange (EDI)" means the electronic transfer from computer to computer of information using an agreed standard to structure the information;

(c)   "Originator" of a data message means a person by whom, or on whose behalf, the data message purports to have been sent or generated prior to storage, if any, but it does not include a person acting as an intermediary with respect to that data message;

(d)   "Addressee" of a data message means a person who is intended by the originator to receive the data message, but does not include a person acting as an intermediary with respect to that data message;

(e)   "Intermediary", with respect to a particular data message, means a person who, on behalf of another person, sends, receives or stores that data message or provides other services with respect to that data message;

(f)   "Information system" means a system for generating, sending, receiving, storing or otherwise processing data messages.

Article 3. Interpretation

(1)   In the interpretation of this Law, regard is to be had to its international origin and to the need to promote uniformity in its application and the observance of good faith.

(2)   Questions concerning matters governed by this Law which are not expressly settled in it are to be settled in conformity with the general principles on which this Law is based.

Article 4. Variation by agreement

(1) As between parties involved in generating, sending, receiv-ing, storing or otherwise processing data messages, and except as otherwise provided, the provisions of chapter III may be varied by agreement.
(2) Paragraph (1) does not affect any right that may exist to modify by agreement any rule of law referred to in chapter II.

Chapter II. Application of legal requirements to data messages

Article 5. Legal recognition of data messages

Information shall not be denied legal effect, validity or enforce-ability solely on the grounds that it is in the form of a data message.

Article 5 bis. Incorporation by reference

(as adopted by the Commission at its thirty-first session, in June 1998)

Information shall not be denied legal effect, validity or enforceability solely on the grounds that it is not contained in the data message purporting to give rise to such legal effect, but is merely referred to in that data message.

Article 6. Writing

(1) Where the law requires information to be in writing, that requirement is met by a data message if the information con-tained therein is accessible so as to be usable for subsequent reference.
(2) Paragraph (1) applies whether the requirement therein is in the form of an obligation or whether the law simply provides consequences for the information not being in writing.
(3) The provisions of this article do not apply to the following: [. . .].

Article 7. Signature

(1)   Where the law requires a signature of a person, that requirement is met in relation to a data message if:

  (a)   a method is used to identify that person and to indicate that person's approval of the information contained in the data message; and

  (b)   that method is as reliable as was appropriate for the purpose for which the data message was generated or communicated, in the light of all the circumstances, including any relevant agreement.

(2)   Paragraph (1) applies whether the requirement therein is in the form of an obligation or whether the law simply provides consequences for the absence of a signature.

(3)   The provisions of this article do not apply to the following: [. . .].

Article 8. Original

(1)   Where the law requires information to be presented or retained in its original form, that requirement is met by a data message if:

  (a)   there exists a reliable assurance as to the integrity of the information from the time when it was first generated in its final form, as a data message or otherwise; and

  (b)   where it is required that information be presented, that information is capable of being displayed to the person to whom it is to be presented.

(2)   Paragraph (1) applies whether the requirement therein is in the form of an obligation or whether the law simply provides consequences for the information not being presented or retained in its original form.

(3)   For the purposes of subparagraph (a) of paragraph (1):

  (a)   the criteria for assessing integrity shall be whether the information has remained complete and unaltered, apart from the addition of any endorsement and any change which arises in the normal course of communication, storage and display; and

  (b)   the standard of reliability required shall be assessed in the light of the purpose for which the information was generated and in the light of all the relevant circumstances.

(4)   The provisions of this article do not apply to the following: [. . .].

Article 9. *Admissibility and evidential weight of data messages*

(1)   In any legal proceedings, nothing in the application of the rules of evidence shall apply so as to deny the admissibility of a data message in evidence:

(a)   on the sole ground that it is a data message; or,

(b)   if it is the best evidence that the person adducing it could reasonably be expected to obtain, on the grounds that it is not in its original form.

(2)   Information in the form of a data message shall be given due evidential weight. In assessing the evidential weight of a data message, regard shall be had to the reliability of the manner in which the data message was generated, stored or communicated, to the reliability of the manner in which the integrity of the information was maintained, to the manner in which its originator was identified, and to any other relevant factor.

Article 10. *Retention of data messages*

(1)   Where the law requires that certain documents, records or information be retained, that requirement is met by retaining data messages, provided that the following conditions are satisfied:

(a)   the information contained therein is accessible so as to be usable for subsequent reference; and

(b)   the data message is retained in the format in which it was generated, sent or received, or in a format which can be demonstrated to represent accurately the information generated, sent or received; and

(c)   such information, if any, is retained as enables the identification of the origin and destination of a data message and the date and time when it was sent or received.

(2)   An obligation to retain documents, records or information in accordance with paragraph (1) does not extend to any information the sole purpose of which is to enable the message to be sent or received.

(3)   A person may satisfy the requirement referred to in paragraph (1) by using the services of any other person, provided that the conditions set forth in subparagraphs (a), (b) and (c) of paragraph (1) are met.

Chapter III. Communication of data messages

Article 11. Formation and validity of contracts

(1)   In the context of contract formation, unless otherwise agreed by the parties, an offer and the acceptance of an offer may be expressed by means of data messages. Where a data message is used in the formation of a contract, that contract shall not be denied validity or enforceability on the sole ground that a data message was used for that purpose.

(2)   The provisions of this article do not apply to the following: [. . .].

Article 12. Recognition by parties of data messages

(1)   As between the originator and the addressee of a data message, a declaration of will or other statement shall not be denied legal effect, validity or enforceability solely on the grounds that it is in the form of a data message.

(2)   The provisions of this article do not apply to the following: [. . .].

Article 13. Attribution of data messages

(1)   A data message is that of the originator if it was sent by the originator itself.

(2)   As between the originator and the addressee, a data message is deemed to be that of the originator if it was sent:

   (a)   by a person who had the authority to act on behalf of the originator in respect of that data message; or

   (b)   by an information system programmed by, or on behalf of, the originator to operate automatically.

(3)   As between the originator and the addressee, an addressee is entitled to regard a data message as being that of the originator, and to act on that assumption, if:

   (a)   in order to ascertain whether the data message was that of the originator, the addressee properly applied a procedure previously agreed to by the originator for that purpose; or

   (b)   the data message as received by the addressee resulted from the actions of a person whose relationship with the originator or with any agent of the originator enabled that person to gain access to a method used by the originator to identify data messages as its own.

(4) Paragraph (3) does not apply:

    (a) as of the time when the addressee has both received notice from the originator that the data message is not that of the originator, and had reasonable time to act accordingly; or

    (b) in a case within paragraph (3)(b), at any time when the addressee knew or should have known, had it exercised reasonable care or used any agreed procedure, that the data message was not that of the originator.

(5) Where a data message is that of the originator or is deemed to be that of the originator, or the addressee is entitled to act on that assumption, then, as between the originator and the addressee, the addressee is entitled to regard the data message as received as being what the originator intended to send, and to act on that assumption. The addressee is not so entitled when it knew or should have known, had it exercised reasonable care or used any agreed procedure, that the transmission resulted in any error in the data message as received.

(6) The addressee is entitled to regard each data message received as a separate data message and to act on that assumption, except to the extent that it duplicates another data message and the addressee knew or should have known, had it exercised reasonable care or used any agreed procedure, that the data message was a duplicate.

Article 14. Acknowledgement of receipt

(1) Paragraphs (2) to (4) of this article apply where, on or before sending a data message, or by means of that data message, the originator has requested or has agreed with the addressee that receipt of the data message be acknowledged.

(2) Where the originator has not agreed with the addressee that the acknowledgement be given in a particular form or by a particular method, an acknowledgement may be given by

    (a) any communication by the addressee, automated or otherwise, or

    (b) any conduct of the addressee,

sufficient to indicate to the originator that the data message has been received.

(3) Where the originator has stated that the data message is conditional on receipt of the acknowledgement, the data message is treated as though it has never been sent, until the acknowledgement is received.

(4) Where the originator has not stated that the data message is conditional on receipt of the acknowledgement, and the acknowledgement has not been received by the originator within the time specified or agreed or, if no time has been specified or agreed, within a reasonable time, the originator:

    (a) may give notice to the addressee stating that no acknowledgement has been received and specifying a reasonable time by which the acknowledgement must be received; and

    (b) if the acknowledgement is not received within the time specified in subparagraph (a), may, upon notice to the addressee, treat the data message as though it had never been sent, or exercise any other rights it may have.

(5) Where the originator receives the addressee's acknowledgement of receipt, it is presumed that the related data message was received by the addressee. That presumption does not imply that the data message corresponds to the message received.

(6) Where the received acknowledgement states that the related data message met technical requirements, either agreed upon or set forth in applicable standards, it is presumed that those requirements have been met.

(7) Except in so far as it relates to the sending or receipt of the data message, this article is not intended to deal with the legal consequences that may flow either from that data message or from the acknowledgement of its receipt.

Article 15. Time and place of dispatch and receipt of data messages

(1) Unless otherwise agreed between the originator and the addressee, the dispatch of a data message occurs when it enters an information system outside the control of the originator or of the person who sent the data message on behalf of the originator.

(2) Unless otherwise agreed between the originator and the addressee, the time of receipt of a data message is determined as follows:

    (a) if the addressee has designated an information system for the purpose of receiving data messages, receipt occurs:

        (i) at the time when the data message enters the designated information system; or

    (ii) if the data message is sent to an information system of the addressee that is not the designated information system, at the time when the data message is retrieved by the addressee;

  (b) if the addressee has not designated an information system, receipt occurs when the data message enters an information system of the addressee.

(3) Paragraph (2) applies notwithstanding that the place where the information system is located may be different from the place where the data message is deemed to be received under paragraph (4).

(4) Unless otherwise agreed between the originator and the addressee, a data message is deemed to be dispatched at the place where the originator has its place of business, and is deemed to be received at the place where the addressee has its place of business. For the purposes of this paragraph:

  (a) if the originator or the addressee has more than one place of business, the place of business is that which has the closest relationship to the underlying transaction or, where there is no underlying transaction, the principal place of business;

  (b) if the originator or the addressee does not have a place of business, reference is to be made to its habitual residence.

(5) The provisions of this article do not apply to the following: [. . .].

Part two. Electronic commerce in specific areas

Chapter I. Carriage of goods

Article 16. Actions related to contracts of carriage of goods

Without derogating from the provisions of part one of this Law, this chapter applies to any action in connection with, or in pursuance of, a contract of carriage of goods, including but not limited to:

  (a)(i) furnishing the marks, number, quantity or weight of goods;

  (ii) stating or declaring the nature or value of goods;

(iii)   issuing a receipt for goods;

(iv)   confirming that goods have been loaded;

(b)(i) notifying a person of terms and conditions of the contract;

(ii)   giving instructions to a carrier;

(c)(i) claiming delivery of goods;

(ii)   authorizing release of goods;

(iii) giving notice of loss of, or damage to, goods;

(d)   giving any other notice or statement in connection with the performance of the contract;

(e)   undertaking to deliver goods to a named person or a person authorized to claim delivery;

(f)   granting, acquiring, renouncing, surrendering, transferring or negotiating rights in goods;

(g)   acquiring or transferring rights and obligations under the contract.

Article 17. Transport documents

(1)   Subject to paragraph (3), where the law requires that any action referred to in article 16 be carried out in writing or by using a paper document, that requirement is met if the action is carried out by using one or more data messages.

(2)   Paragraph (1) applies whether the requirement therein is in the form of an obligation or whether the law simply provides consequences for failing either to carry out the action in writing or to use a paper document.

(3)   If a right is to be granted to, or an obligation is to be acquired by, one person and no other person, and if the law requires that, in order to effect this, the right or obligation must be conveyed to that person by the transfer, or use of, a paper document, that requirement is met if the right or obligation is conveyed by using one or more data messages, provided that a reliable method is used to render such data message or messages unique.

(4)   For the purposes of paragraph (3), the standard of reliability required shall be assessed in the light of the purpose for which the right or obligation was conveyed and in the light of all the circumstances, including any relevant agreement.

(5)   Where one or more data messages are used to effect any action in subparagraphs (f) and (g) of article 16, no paper document used to effect any such action is valid unless the use of data messages has been terminated and replaced by the use of paper documents. A paper document issued in these circumstances shall contain a

statement of such termination. The replacement of data messages by paper documents shall not affect the rights or obligations of the parties involved.

(6) If a rule of law is compulsorily applicable to a contract of carriage of goods which is in, or is evidenced by, a paper document, that rule shall not be inapplicable to such a contract of carriage of goods which is evidenced by one or more data messages by reason of the fact that the contract is evidenced by such data message or messages instead of by a paper document.

(7) The provisions of this article do not apply to the following: [. . .].

Guide to Enactment of the UNCITRAL Model Law on Electronic Commerce (1996)

Purpose of this guide

1. In preparing and adopting the UNCITRAL Model Law on Electronic Commerce (hereinafter referred to as "the Model Law"), the United Nations Commission on International Trade Law (UNCITRAL) was mindful that the Model Law would be a more effective tool for States modernizing their legislation if background and explanatory information would be provided to executive branches of Governments and legislators to assist them in using the Model Law. The Commission was also aware of the likelihood that the Model Law would be used in a number of States with limited familiarity with the type of communication techniques considered in the Model Law. This Guide, much of which is drawn from the travaux préparatoires of the Model Law, is also intended to be helpful to users of electronic means of communication as well as to scholars in that area. In the preparation of the Model Law, it was assumed that the draft Model Law would be accompanied by such a guide. For example, it was decided in respect of a number of issues not to settle them in the draft Model Law but to address them in the Guide so as to provide guidance to States enacting the draft Model Law. The information presented in this Guide is intended to explain why the provisions in the Model Law have been included as essential basic features of a statutory device designed to achieve the objectives of the Model Law. Such information might assist

States also in considering which, if any, of the provisions of the Model Law might have to be varied to take into account particular national circumstances.

I. INTRODUCTION TO THE MODEL LAW

A. Objectives

2. The use of modern means of communication such as electronic mail and electronic data interchange (EDI) for the conduct of international trade transactions has been increasing rapidly and is expected to develop further as technical supports such as information highways and the INTERNET become more widely accessible. However, the communication of legally significant information in the form of paperless messages may be hindered by legal obstacles to the use of such messages, or by uncertainty as to their legal effect or validity. The purpose of the Model Law is to offer national legislators a set of internationally acceptable rules as to how a number of such legal obstacles may be removed, and how a more secure legal environment may be created for what has become known as "electronic commerce". The principles expressed in the Model Law are also intended to be of use to individual users of electronic commerce in the drafting of some of the contractual solutions that might be needed to overcome the legal obstacles to the increased use of electronic commerce.

3. The decision by UNCITRAL to formulate model legislation on electronic commerce was taken in response to the fact that in a number of countries the existing legislation governing communication and storage of information is inadequate or outdated because it does not contemplate the use of electronic commerce. In certain cases, existing legislation imposes or implies restrictions on the use of modern means of communication, for example by prescribing the use of "written", "signed" or "original" documents. While a few countries have adopted specific provisions to deal with certain aspects of electronic commerce, there exists no legislation dealing with electronic commerce as a whole. This may result in uncertainty as to the legal nature and validity of information presented in a form other than a traditional paper document. Moreover, while sound laws and practices are necessary in all countries where the use of EDI and electronic mail is becoming

widespread, this need is also felt in many countries with respect to such communication techniques as telecopy and telex.

4. The Model Law may also help to remedy disadvantages that stem from the fact that inadequate legislation at the national level creates obstacles to international trade, a significant amount of which is linked to the use of modern communication techniques. Disparities among, and uncertainty about, national legal regimes governing the use of such communication techniques may contribute to limiting the extent to which businesses may access international markets.

5. Furthermore, at an international level, the Model Law may be useful in certain cases as a tool for interpreting existing international conventions and other international instruments that create legal obstacles to the use of electronic commerce, for example by prescribing that certain documents or contractual clauses be made in written form. As between those States parties to such international instruments, the adoption of the Model Law as a rule of interpretation might provide the means to recognize the use of electronic commerce and obviate the need to negotiate a protocol to the international instrument involved.

6. The objectives of the Model Law, which include enabling or facilitating the use of electronic commerce and providing equal treatment to users of paper-based documentation and to users of computer-based information, are essential for fostering economy and efficiency in international trade. By incorporating the procedures prescribed in the Model Law in its national legislation for those situations where parties opt to use electronic means of communication, an enacting State would create a media-neutral environment.

B. Scope

7. The title of the Model Law refers to "electronic commerce". While a definition of "electronic data interchange (EDI)" is provided in article 2, the Model Law does not specify the meaning of "electronic commerce". In preparing the Model Law, the Commission decided that, in addressing the subject matter before it, it would have in mind a broad notion of EDI, covering a variety of trade-related uses of EDI that might be referred to broadly under the rubric of "electronic commerce" (see A/CN.9/360, paras. 28-29), although other descriptive terms could also be used. Among the means of communication encompassed in the notion of "electronic commerce" are the following modes of transmission based on the use of electronic techniques:

communication by means of EDI defined narrowly as the computer-to-computer transmission of data in a standardized format; transmission of electronic messages involving the use of either publicly available standards or proprietary standards; transmission of free-formatted text by electronic means, for example through the INTERNET. It was also noted that, in certain circumstances, the notion of "electronic commerce" might cover the use of techniques such as telex and telecopy.

8. It should be noted that, while the Model Law was drafted with constant reference to the more modern communication techniques, e.g., EDI and electronic mail, the principles on which the Model Law is based, as well as its provisions, are intended to apply also in the context of less advanced communication techniques, such as telecopy. There may exist situations where digitalized information initially dispatched in the form of a standardized EDI message might, at some point in the communication chain between the sender and the recipient, be forwarded in the form of a computer-generated telex or in the form of a telecopy of a computer print-out. A data message may be initiated as an oral communication and end up in the form of a telecopy, or it may start as a telecopy and end up as an EDI message. A characteristic of electronic commerce is that it covers programmable messages, the computer programming of which is the essential difference between such messages and traditional paper-based documents. Such situations are intended to be covered by the Model Law, based on a consideration of the users' need for a consistent set of rules to govern a variety of communication techniques that might be used interchangeably. More generally, it may be noted that, as a matter of principle, no communi-cation technique is excluded from the scope of the Model Law since future technical developments need to be accommodated.

9. The objectives of the Model Law are best served by the widest possible application of the Model Law. Thus, although there is provision made in the Model Law for exclusion of certain situations from the scope of articles 6, 7, 8, 11, 12, 15 and 17, an enacting State may well decide not to enact in its legislation substantial restrictions on the scope of application of the Model Law.

10. The Model Law should be regarded as a balanced and discrete set of rules, which are recommended to be enacted as a single statute. Depending on the situation in each enacting State, however, the Model Law could be implemented in various ways, either as a single statute or in several pieces of legislation (see below, para. 143).

C. Structure

11. The Model Law is divided into two parts, one dealing with electronic commerce in general and the other one dealing with electronic commerce in specific areas. It should be noted that part two of the Model Law, which deals with electronic commerce in specific areas, is composed of a chapter I only, dealing with electronic commerce as it applies to the carriage of goods. Other aspects of electronic commerce might need to be dealt with in the future, and the Model Law can be regarded as an open-ended instrument, to be complemented by future work.

12. UNCITRAL intends to continue monitoring the technical, legal and commercial developments that underline the Model Law. It might, should it regard it advisable, decide to add new model provisions to the Model Law or modify the existing ones.

D. A "framework" law to be supplemented by technical regulations

13. The Model Law is intended to provide essential procedures and principles for facilitating the use of modern techniques for recording and communicating information in various types of circumstances. However, it is a "framework" law that does not itself set forth all the rules and regulations that may be necessary to implement those techniques in an enacting State. Moreover, the Model Law is not intended to cover every aspect of the use of electronic commerce. Accordingly, an enacting State may wish to issue regulations to fill in the procedural details for procedures authorized by the Model Law and to take account of the specific, possibly changing, circumstances at play in the enacting State, without compromising the objectives of the Model Law. It is recommended that, should it decide to issue such regulation, an enacting State should give particular attention to the need to maintain the beneficial flexibility of the provisions in the Model Law.

14. It should be noted that the techniques for recording and communicating information considered in the Model Law, beyond raising matters of procedure that may need to be addressed in the implementing technical regulations, may raise certain legal questions the answers to which will not necessarily be found in the Model Law, but rather in other bodies of law. Such other bodies of law may include, for

example, the applicable administrative, contract, criminal and judicial-procedure law, which the Model Law is not intended to deal with.

E. The "functional-equivalent" approach

15. The Model Law is based on the recognition that legal requirements prescribing the use of traditional paper-based documentation constitute the main obstacle to the development of modern means of communication. In the preparation of the Model Law, consideration was given to the possibility of dealing with impediments to the use of electronic commerce posed by such requirements in national laws by way of an extension of the scope of such notions as "writing", "signature" and "original", with a view to encompassing computer-based techniques. Such an approach is used in a number of existing legal instruments, e.g., article 7 of the UNCITRAL Model Law on International Commercial Arbitration and article 13 of the United Nations Convention on Contracts for the International Sale of Goods. It was observed that the Model Law should permit States to adapt their domestic legislation to developments in communications technology applicable to trade law without necessitating the wholesale removal of the paper-based requirements themselves or disturbing the legal concepts and approaches underlying those requirements. At the same time, it was said that the electronic fulfilment of writing requirements might in some cases necessitate the development of new rules. This was due to one of many distinctions between EDI messages and paper-based documents, namely, that the latter were readable by the human eye, while the former were not so readable unless reduced to paper or displayed on a screen.

16. The Model Law thus relies on a new approach, sometimes referred to as the "functional equivalent approach", which is based on an analysis of the purposes and functions of the traditional paper-based requirement with a view to determining how those purposes or functions could be fulfilled through electronic-commerce techniques. For example, among the functions served by a paper document are the following: to provide that a document would be legible by all; to provide that a document would remain unaltered over time; to allow for the reproduction of a document so that each party would hold a copy of the same data; to allow for the authentication of data by means of a signature; and to provide that a document would be in a form acceptable to public authorities and courts. It should be noted that in respect of all of the above-mentioned functions of paper, electronic records can provide the same level of security as paper and, in most

cases, a much higher degree of reliability and speed, especially with respect to the identification of the source and content of the data, provided that a number of technical and legal requirements are met. However, the adoption of the functional-equivalent approach should not result in imposing on users of electronic commerce more stringent standards of security (and the related costs) than in a paper-based environment.

17. A data message, in and of itself, cannot be regarded as an equivalent of a paper document in that it is of a different nature and does not necessarily perform all conceivable functions of a paper document. That is why the Model Law adopted a flexible standard, taking into account the various layers of existing requirements in a paper-based environment: when adopting the "functional-equivalent" approach, attention was given to the existing hierarchy of form requirements, which provides distinct levels of reliability, traceability and unalterability with respect to paper-based documents. For example, the requirement that data be presented in written form (which constitutes a "threshold requirement") is not to be confused with more stringent requirements such as "signed writing", "signed original" or "authenticated legal act".

18. The Model Law does not attempt to define a computer-based equivalent to any kind of paper document. Instead, it singles out basic functions of paper-based form requirements, with a view to providing criteria which, once they are met by data messages, enable such data messages to enjoy the same level of legal recognition as corresponding paper documents performing the same function. It should be noted that the functional-equivalent approach has been taken in articles 6 to 8 of the Model Law with respect to the concepts of "writing", "signature" and "original" but not with respect to other legal concepts dealt with in the Model Law. For example, article 10 does not attempt to create a functional equivalent of existing storage requirements.

F. Default rules and mandatory law

19. The decision to undertake the preparation of the Model Law was based on the recognition that, in practice, solutions to most of the legal difficulties raised by the use of modern means of communication are sought within contracts. The Model Law embodies the principle of party autonomy in article 4 with respect to the provisions contained in chapter III of part one. Chapter III of part one contains a set of rules of the kind that would typically be found in agreements between parties,

e.g., interchange agreements or "system rules". It should be noted that the notion of "system rules" might cover two different categories of rules, namely, general terms provided by communication networks and specific rules that might be included in those general terms to deal with bilateral relationships between originators and addressees of data messages. Article 4 (and the notion of "agreement" therein) is intended to encompass both categories of "system rules".

20. The rules contained in chapter III of part one may be used by parties as a basis for concluding such agreements. They may also be used to supplement the terms of agreements in cases of gaps or omissions in contractual stipulations. In addition, they may be regarded as setting a basic standard for situations where data messages are exchanged without a previous agreement being entered into by the communicating parties, e.g., in the context of open-networks communications.

21. The provisions contained in chapter II of part one are of a different nature. One of the main purposes of the Model Law is to facilitate the use of modern communication techniques and to provide certainty with the use of such techniques where obstacles or uncertainty resulting from statutory provisions could not be avoided by contractual stipulations. The provisions contained in chapter II may, to some extent, be regarded as a collection of exceptions to well-established rules regarding the form of legal transactions. Such well-established rules are normally of a mandatory nature since they generally reflect decisions of public policy. The provisions contained in chapter II should be regarded as stating the minimum acceptable form requirement and are, for that reason, of a mandatory nature, unless expressly stated otherwise in those provisions. The indication that such form requirements are to be regarded as the "minimum acceptable" should not, however, be construed as inviting States to establish requirements stricter than those contained in the Model Law.

G. Assistance from UNCITRAL secretariat

22. In line with its training and assistance activities, the UNCITRAL secretariat may provide technical consultations for Governments preparing legislation based on the UNCITRAL Model Law on Electronic Commerce, as it may for Governments considering legislation based on other UNCITRAL model laws, or considering adhesion to one of the international trade law conventions prepared by UNCITRAL.

23. Further information concerning the Model Law as well as the Guide and other model laws and conventions developed by UNCITRAL, may be obtained from the secretariat at the address below. The secretariat welcomes comments concerning the Model Law and the Guide, as well as information concerning enactment of legislation based on the Model Law.

International Trade Law Branch

Office of Legal Affairs

United Nations Vienna International Centre

P.O. Box 500

A-1400, Vienna, Austria

Telephone: (43-1) 26060-4060 or 4061

Telefax: (43-1) 26060-5813 or (43-1) 2692669

Telex: 135612unoa

E-mail: uncitral@unov.un .or.at

Internet Home Page: http://www.un.or.at/uncitral

II. ARTICLE-BY-ARTICLE REMARKS

Part one. Electronic commerce in general

Chapter I. General provisions

Article 1. Sphere of application

24. The purpose of article 1, which is to be read in conjunction with the definition of "data message" in article 2(a), is to delineate the scope of application of the Model Law. The approach used in the Model Law is to provide in principle for the coverage of all factual situations where

information is generated, stored or communicated, irrespective of the medium on which such information may be affixed. It was felt during the preparation of the Model Law that exclusion of any form or medium by way of a limitation in the scope of the Model Law might result in practical difficulties and would run counter to the purpose of providing truly "media-neutral" rules. However, the focus of the Model Law is on "paperless" means of communication and, except to the extent expressly provided by the Model Law, the Model Law is not intended to alter traditional rules on paper-based communications.

25. Moreover, it was felt that the Model Law should contain an indication that its focus was on the types of situations encountered in the commercial area and that it had been prepared against the background of trade relationships. For that reason, article 1 refers to "commercial activities" and provides, in footnote ★★★★, indications as to what is meant thereby. Such indications, which may be particularly useful for those countries where there does not exist a discrete body of commercial law, are modelled, for reasons of consistency, on the footnote to article 1 of the UNCITRAL Model Law on International Commercial Arbitration. In certain countries, the use of footnotes in a statutory text would not be regarded as acceptable legislative practice. National authorities enacting the Model Law might thus consider the possible inclusion of the text of footnotes in the body of the Law itself.

26. The Model Law applies to all kinds of data messages that might be generated, stored or communicated, and nothing in the Model Law should prevent an enacting State from extending the scope of the Model Law to cover uses of electronic commerce outside the commercial sphere. For example, while the focus of the Model Law is not on the relationships between users of electronic commerce and public authorities, the Model Law is not intended to be inapplicable to such relationships. Footnote ★★★ provides for alternative wordings, for possible use by enacting States that would consider it appropriate to extend the scope of the Model Law beyond the commercial sphere.

27. Some countries have special consumer protection laws that may govern certain aspects of the use of information systems. With respect to such consumer legislation, as was the case with previous UNCITRAL instruments (e.g., the UNCITRAL Model Law on International Credit Transfers), it was felt that an indication should be given that the Model Law had been drafted without special attention being given to issues that might arise in the context of consumer protection. At the same time, it was felt that there was no reason why situations involving consumers should be excluded from the scope of the Model

Law by way of a general provision, particularly since the provisions of the Model Law might be found appropriate for consumer protection, depending on legislation in each enacting State. Foot-note ** thus recognizes that any such consumer protection law may take precedence over the provisions in the Model Law. Legislators may wish to consider whether the piece of legislation enacting the Model Law should apply to consumers. The question of which individuals or corporate bodies would be regarded as "consumers" is left to applicable law outside the Model Law.

28. Another possible limitation of the scope of the Model Law is contained in the first footnote. In principle, the Model Law applies to both international and domestic uses of data messages. Footnote is intended for use by enacting States that might wish to limit the applicability of the Model Law to international cases. It indicates a possible test of internationality for use by those States as a possible criterion for distinguishing international cases from domestic ones. It should be noted, however, that in some jurisdictions, particularly in federal States, considerable difficulties might arise in distinguishing international trade from domestic trade. The Model Law should not be interpreted as encouraging enacting States to limit its applicability to international cases.

29. It is recommended that application of the Model Law be made as wide as possible. Particular caution should be used in excluding the application of the Model Law by way of a limitation of its scope to international uses of data messages, since such a limitation may be seen as not fully achieving the objectives of the Model Law. Furthermore, the variety of procedures available under the Model Law (particularly articles 6 to 8) to limit the use of data messages if necessary (e.g., for purposes of public policy) may make it less necessary to limit the scope of the Model Law. As the Model Law contains a number of articles (articles 6, 7, 8, 11, 12, 15 and 17) that allow a degree of flexibility to enacting States to limit the scope of application of specific aspects of the Model Law, a narrowing of the scope of application of the text to international trade should not be necessary. Moreover, dividing communications in international trade into purely domestic and international parts might be difficult in practice. The legal certainty to be provided by the Model Law is necessary for both domestic and international trade, and a duality of regimes governing the use of electronic means of recording and communication of data might create a serious obstacle to the use of such means.

References(2)

A/50/17, paras. 213-219;

A/CN.9/407, paras. 37-40;

A/CN.9/406, paras. 80-85; A/CN.9/WG.IV/WP.62, article 1;

A/CN.9/390, paras. 21-43; A/CN.9/WG.IV/WP.60, article 1;

A/CN.9/387, paras. 15-28; A/CN.9/WG.IV/WP.57, article 1;

A/CN.9/373, paras. 21-25 and 29-33; A/CN.9/WG.IV/WP.55, paras. 15-20.

Article 2. Definitions

"Data message"

30. The notion of "data message" is not limited to communication but is also intended to encompass computer-generated records that are not intended for communication. Thus, the notion of "message" includes the notion of "record". However, a definition of "record" in line with the characteristic elements of "writing" in article 6 may be added in jurisdictions where that would appear to be necessary.

31. The reference to "similar means" is intended to reflect the fact that the Model Law was not intended only for application in the context of existing communication techniques but also to accommodate foreseeable technical developments. The aim of the definition of "data message" is to encompass all types of messages that are generated, stored, or communicated in essentially paperless form. For that purpose, all means of communication and storage of information that might be used to perform functions parallel to the functions performed by the means listed in the definition are intended to be covered by the reference to "similar means", although, for example, "electronic" and "optical" means of communication might not be, strictly speaking, similar. For the purposes of the Model Law, the word "similar" connotes "functionally equivalent".

32. The definition of "data message" is also intended to cover the case of revocation or amendment. A data message is presumed to have a fixed information content but it may be revoked or amended by another data message.

"Electronic Data Interchange (EDI)"

33. The definition of EDI is drawn from the definition adopted by the Working Party on Facilitation of International Trade Procedures (WP.4) of the Economic Commission for Europe, which is the United Nations body responsible for the development of UN/EDIFACT technical standards.

34. The Model Law does not settle the question whether the definition of EDI necessarily implies that EDI messages are communicated electronically from computer to computer, or whether that definition, while primarily covering situations where data messages are communicated through a telecommunications system, would also cover exceptional or incidental types of situation where data structured in the form of an EDI message would be communicated by means that do not involve telecommunications systems, for example, the case where magnetic disks containing EDI messages would be delivered to the addressee by courier. However, irrespective of whether digital data transferred manually is covered by the definition of "EDI", it should be regarded as covered by the definition of "data message" under the Model Law.

"Originator" and "Addressee"

35. In most legal systems, the notion of "person" is used to designate the subjects of rights and obligations and should be interpreted as covering both natural persons and corporate bodies or other legal entities. Data messages that are generated automatically by computers without direct human intervention are intended to be covered by subparagraph *(c)*. However, the Model Law should not be misinterpreted as allowing for a computer to be made the subject of rights and obligations. Data messages that are generated automatically by computers without direct human intervention should be regarded as "originating" from the legal entity on behalf of which the computer is operated. Questions relevant to agency that might arise in that context are to be settled under rules outside the Model Law.

36. The "addressee" under the Model Law is the person with whom the originator intends to communicate by transmitting the data message, as opposed to any person who might receive, forward or copy the data message in the course of transmission. The "originator" is the person who generated the data message even if that message was transmitted by another person. The definition of "addressee" contrasts with the definition of "originator", which is not focused on intent. It should be noted that, under the definitions of "originator" and "addressee" in the Model Law, the originator and the addressee of a given data message could be the same person, for example in the case where the data message was intended for storage by its author. However, the addressee who stores a message transmitted by an originator is not itself intended to be covered by the definition of "originator".

37. The definition of "originator" should cover not only the situation where information is generated and communicated, but also the situation where such information is generated and stored without being communicated. However, the definition of "originator" is intended to eliminate the possibility that a recipient who merely stores a data message might be regarded as an originator.

"Intermediary

38. The focus of the Model Law is on the relationship between the originator and the addressee, and not on the relationship between either the originator or the addressee and any intermediary. However, the Model Law does not ignore the paramount importance of intermediaries in the field of electronic communications. In addition, the notion of "intermediary" is needed in the Model Law to establish the necessary distinction between originators or addressees and third parties.

39. The definition of "intermediary" is intended to cover both professional and non-professional intermediaries, i.e., any person (other than the originator and the addressee) who performs any of the functions of an intermediary. The main functions of an intermediary are listed in subparagraph *(e),* namely receiving, transmitting or storing data messages on behalf of another person. Additional "value-added services" may be performed by network operators and other intermediaries, such as formatting, translating, recording, authenticating, certifying and preserving data messages and providing security services for electronic transactions. "Intermediary" under the Model Law is

defined not as a generic category but with respect to each data message, thus recognizing that the same person could be the originator or addressee of one data message and an intermediary with respect to another data message. The Model Law, which is focused on the relationships between originators and addressees, does not, in general, deal with the rights and obligations of intermediaries.

"Information system"

40. The definition of "information system" is intended to cover the entire range of technical means used for transmitting, receiving and storing information. For example, depending on the factual situation, the notion of "information system" could be indicating a communications network, and in other instances could include an electronic mailbox or even a telecopier. The Model Law does not address the question of whether the information system is located on the premises of the addressee or on other premises, since location of information systems is not an operative criterion under the Model Law.

References

A/51/17, paras. 116–138;

A/CN.9/407, paras. 41–52;

A/CN.9/406, paras. 132–156; A/CN.9/WG.IV/WP.62, article 2;

A/CN.9/390, paras. 44–65; A/CN.9/WG.IV/WP.60, article 2;

A/CN.9/387, paras. 29–52; A/CN.9/WG.IV/WP.57, article 2;

A/CN.9/373, paras. 11–20, 26–28 and 35–36; A/CN.9/WG.IV/WP.55, paras. 23–26;

A/CN.9/360, paras. 29–31; A/CN.9/WG.IV/WP.53, paras. 25–33.

Article 3. Interpretation

41. Article 3 is inspired by article 7 of the United Nations Convention on Contracts for the International Sale of Goods. It is intended to provide guidance for interpretation of the Model Law by courts and

other national or local authorities. The expected effect of article 3 is to limit the extent to which a uniform text, once incorporated in local legislation, would be interpreted only by reference to the concepts of local law.

42. The purpose of paragraph (1) is to draw the attention of courts and other national authorities to the fact that the provisions of the Model Law (or the provisions of the instrument implementing the Model Law), while enacted as part of domestic legislation and therefore domestic in character, should be interpreted with reference to its international origin in order to ensure uniformity in the interpretation of the Model Law in various countries.

43. As to the general principles on which the Model Law is based, the following non-exhaustive list may be considered: (1) to facilitate electronic commerce among and within nations; (2) to validate transactions entered into by means of new information technologies; (3) to promote and encourage the implementation of new information technologies; (4) to promote the uniformity of law; and *(5)* to support commercial practice. While the general purpose of the Model Law is to facilitate the use of electronic means of communication, it should not be construed in any way as imposing their use.

References

A/50/17, paras. 220-224;

A/CN.9/407, paras. 53-54;

A/CN.9/406, paras. 86-87; A/CN.9/WG.IV/WP.62, article 3;

A/CN.9/390, paras. 66-73; A/CN.9/WG.IV/WP.60, article 3;

A/CN.9/387, paras. 53-58; A/CN.9/WG.IV/WP.57, article 3;

A/CN.9/373, paras. 38-42; A/CN.9/WG.IV/WP.55, paras. 30-31.

Article 4. Variation by agreement

44. The decision to undertake the preparation of the Model Law was based on the recognition that, in practice, solutions to the legal difficulties raised by the use of modern means of communication are

mostly sought within contracts. The Model Law is thus intended to support the principle of party autonomy. However, that principle is embodied only with respect to the provisions of the Model Law contained in chapter III of part one. The reason for such a limitation is that the provisions contained in chapter II of part one may, to some extent, be regarded as a collection of exceptions to well-established rules regarding the form of legal transactions. Such well-established rules are normally of a mandatory nature since they generally reflect decisions of public policy. An unqualified statement regarding the freedom of parties to derogate from the Model Law might thus be misinterpreted as allowing parties, through a derogation to the Model Law, to derogate from mandatory rules adopted for reasons of public policy. The provisions contained in chapter II of part one should be regarded as stating the minimum acceptable form requirement and are, for that reason, to be regarded as mandatory, unless expressly stated otherwise. The indication that such form requirements are to be regarded as the "minimum acceptable" should not, however, be construed as inviting States to establish requirements stricter than those contained in the Model Law.

45. Article 4 is intended to apply not only in the context of relationships between originators and addressees of data messages but also in the context of relationships involving intermediaries. Thus, the provisions of chapter III of part one could be varied either by bilateral or multilateral agreements between the parties, or by system rules agreed to by the parties. However, the text expressly limits party autonomy to rights and obligations arising as between parties so as not to suggest any implication as to the rights and obligations of third parties.

References

A/51/17, paras. 68, 90 to 93, 110, 137, 188 and 207 (article 10);

A/50/17, paras. 271-274 (article 10);

A/CN.9/407, para. 85;

A/CN.9/406, paras. 88-89; A/CN.9/WG.IV/WP.62, article 5;

A/CN.9/390, paras. 74-78; A/CN.9/WG.IV/WP.60, article 5;

A/CN.9/387, paras. 62-65; A/CN.9/WG.IV/WP.57, article 5;

A/CN.9/373, para. 37; A/CN.9/WG.IV/WP.55, paras. 27-29.

Chapter II. Application of legal requirements to data messages

Article 5. Legal recognition of data messages

46. Article 5 embodies the fundamental principle that data messages should not be discriminated against, i.e., that there should be no disparity of treatment between data messages and paper documents. It is intended to apply notwithstanding any statutory requirements for a "writing" or an original. That fundamental principle is intended to find general application and its scope should not be limited to evidence or other matters covered in chapter II. It should be noted, however, that such a principle is not intended to override any of the requirements contained in articles 6 to 10. By stating that "information shall not be denied legal effectiveness, validity or enforceability solely on the grounds that it is in the form of a data message", article 5 merely indicates that the form in which certain information is presented or retained cannot be used as the only reason for which that information would be denied legal effectiveness, validity or enforceability. However, article S should not be misinterpreted as establishing the legal validity of any given data message or of any information contained therein.

References

A/S 1/17, paras. 92 and 97 (article 4);

A/50/17, paras. 225-227 (article 4);

A/CN.9/407, para. 55;

A/CN.9/406, paras. 91-94; A/CN.9/WG.IV/WP. 62, article S *bis;*

A/CN.9/390, paras. 79-87; A/CN.9/WG.IV/WP. 60, article 5 *bis;*

A/CN.9/387, paras. 93-94.

Article 5 bis. Incorporation by reference

46-1. Article *5 bis* was adopted by the Commission at its thirty-first session, in June 1998. It is intended to provide guidance as to how legislation aimed at facilitating the use of electronic commerce might deal with the situation where certain terms and conditions, although not stated in full but merely referred to in a data message, might need to be recognized as having the same degree of legal effectiveness as if they had been fully stated in the text of that data message. Such recognition is acceptable under the laws of many States with respect to conventional paper communications, usually with some rules of law providing safeguards, for example rules on consumer protection. The expression "incorporation by reference" is often used as a concise means of describing situations where a document refers generically to provisions which are detailed elsewhere, rather than reproducing them in full.

46-2. In an electronic environment, incorporation by reference is often regarded as essential to widespread use of electronic data interchange (EDI), electronic mail, digital certificates and other forms of electronic commerce. For example, electronic communications are typically structured in such a way that large numbers of messages are exchanged, with each message containing brief information, and relying much more frequently than paper documents on reference to information accessible elsewhere. In electronic communications, practitioners should not have imposed upon them an obligation to overload their data messages with quantities of free text when they can take advantage of extrinsic sources of information, such as databases, code lists or glossaries, by making use of abbreviations, codes and other references to such information.

46-3. Standards for incorporating data messages by reference into other data messages may also be essential to the use of public key certificates, because these certificates are generally brief records with rigidly prescribed contents that are finite in size. The trusted third party which issues the certificate, however, is likely to require the inclusion of relevant contractual terms limiting its liability. The scope, purpose and effect of a certificate in commercial practice, therefore, would be ambiguous and uncertain without external terms being incorporated by reference. This is the case especially in the context of international communications involving diverse parties who follow varied trade practices and customs.

46-4. The establishment of standards for incorporating data messages by reference into other data messages is critical to the growth of a computerbased trade infrastructure. Without the legal certainty fostered by such standards, there might be a significant risk that the application of traditional tests for determining the enforceability of terms that seek to be incorporated by reference might be ineffective when applied to corresponding electronic commerce terms because of the differences between traditional and electronic commerce mechanisms.

46-5. While electronic commerce relies heavily on the mechanism of incorporation by reference, the accessibility of the full text of the information being referred to may be considerably improved by the use of electronic communications. For example, a message may have embedded in it uniform resource locators (URLs), which direct the reader to the referenced document. Such URLs can provide "hypertext links" allowing the reader to use a pointing device (such as a mouse) to select a key word associated with a URL. The referenced text would then be displayed. In assessing the accessibility of the referenced text, factors to be considered may include: availability (hours of operation of the repository and ease of access); cost of access; integrity (verification of content, authentication of sender, and mechanism for communication error correction); and the extent to which that term is subject to later amendment (notice of updates; notice of policy of amendment).

46-6. One aim of article 5 *bis* is to facilitate incorporation by reference in an electronic context by removing the uncertainty prevailing in many jurisdictions as to whether the provisions dealing with traditional incorporation by reference are applicable to incorporation by reference in an electronic environment. However, in enacting article S *bis,* attention should be given to avoid introducing more restrictive requirements with respect to incorporation by reference in electronic commerce than might already apply in paper-based trade.

46-7. Another aim of the provision is to recognize that consumer-protection or other national or international law of a mandatory nature (e.g., rules protecting weaker parties in the context of contracts of adhesion) should not be interfered with. That result could also be achieved by validating incorporation by reference in an electronic environment "to the extent permitted by law", or by listing the rules of law that remain unaffected by article S *bis.* Article S *bis* is not to be interpreted as creating a specific legal regime for incorporation by reference in an electronic environment. Rather, by establishing a principle of non-discrimination, it is to be construed as making the domestic rules applicable to incorporation by reference in a paper-based environment equally applicable to incorporation by reference for the purposes of electronic commerce. For example, in a number of jurisdictions, existing rules of mandatory law only validate incorporation by reference provided that the following three conditions are met: (a) the reference clause should be inserted in the data message; (b) the document being referred to, e.g., general terms and conditions, should actually be known to the party against whom the reference document might be relied upon; and (c) the reference document should be accepted, in addition to being known, by that party.

References

A/53/17, paras. 212-221;

A/CN.9/450;

A/CN.9/446, paras. 14-24;

A/CN.9/WG.IV!WP.74;

A/52/17, paras. 248-250;

A/CN.9/437, paras. 151-155;

A/CN.9/WG.IV/WP. 71, paras 77-93;

A/51/17, paras. 222-223;

A/CN.9/421, paras. 109 and 114;

A/CN.9/WG.IV/WP.69, paras. 30, 53, 59-60 and 91;

A/CN.9/407, paras. 100-105 and 117;

A/CN.9/WG.IV/WP.66;

A/CN.9/WG.IV/WP.65;

A/CN.9/406, paras. 90 and 178-179;

A/CN.9/WG.IV/WP.55, para. 109-113;

A/CN.9!360, paras. 90-95;

A/CN.9/WG.IV/WP.53, paras. 77-78;

A/CN.9/350, paras. 95-96;

A/CN.9/333, paras. 66-68.

Article 6. Writing

47. Article 6 is intended to define the basic standard to be met by a data message in order to be considered as meeting a requirement (which may result from statute, regulation or judge-made law) that information be retained or presented "in writing" (or that the information be contained in a "document" or other paper-based instrument). It may be noted that article 6 is part of a set of three articles (articles 6, 7 and 8), which share the same structure and should be read together.

48. In the preparation of the Model Law, particular attention was paid to the functions traditionally performed by various kinds of "writings" in a paper-based environment. For example, the following non-exhaustive list indicates reasons why national laws require the use of "writings": (1) to ensure that there would be tangible evidence of the existence and nature of the intent of the parties to bind themselves; (2) to help the parties be aware of the consequences of their entering into a contract; (3) to provide that a document would be legible by all; (4) to provide that a document would remain unaltered over time and provide a permanent record of a transaction; (5) to allow for the reproduction of a document so that each party would hold a copy of the same data; (6) to allow for the authentication of data by means of a signature; (7) to provide that a document would be in a form acceptable to public authorities and courts; (8) to finalize the intent of the author of the "writing" and provide a record of that intent; (9) to allow for the easy storage of data in a tangible form; (10) to facilitate control and sub-sequent audit for accounting, tax or regulatory purposes; and (11) to bring legal rights and obligations into existence in those cases where a "writing" was required for validity purposes.

49. However, in the preparation of the Model Law, it was found that it would be inappropriate to adopt an overly comprehensive notion of the functions performed by writing. Existing requirements that data be presented in written form often combine the requirement of a "writing" with concepts distinct from writing, such as signature and original. Thus, when adopting a functional approach, attention should be given to the fact that the requirement of a "writing" should be considered as the lowest layer in a hierarchy of form requirements, which provide distinct levels of reliability, traceability and unalterability

with respect to paper documents. The requirement that data be presented in written form (which can be described as a "threshold requirement") should thus not be confused with more stringent requirements such as "signed writing", "signed original" or "authenticated legal act". For example, under certain national laws, a written document that is neither dated nor signed, and the author of which either is not identified in the written document or is identified by a mere letterhead, would be regarded as a "writing" although it might be of little evidential weight in the absence of other evidence (e.g., testimony) regarding the authorship of the document. In addition, the notion of unalterability should not be considered as built into the concept of writing as an absolute requirement since a "writing" in pencil might still be considered a "writing" under certain existing legal definitions. Taking into account the way in which such issues as integrity of the data and protection against fraud are dealt with in a paper-based environment, a fraudulent document would nonetheless be regarded as a "writing". In general, notions such as "evidence" and "intent of the parties to bind themselves" are to be tied to the more general issues of reliability and authentication of the data and should not be included in the definition of a "writing".

50. The purpose of article 6 is not to establish a requirement that, in all instances, data messages should fulfil all conceivable functions of a writing. Rather than focusing upon specific functions of a "writing", for example, its evidentiary function in the context of tax law or its warning function in the context of civil law, article 6 focuses upon the basic notion of the information being reproduced and read. That notion is expressed in article 6 in terms that were found to provide an objective criterion, namely that the information in a data message must be accessible so as to be usable for subsequent reference. The use of the word "accessible" is meant to imply that information in the form of computer data should be readable and interpretable, and that the software that might be necessary to render such information readable should be retained. The word "usable" is not intended to cover only human use but also computer processing. As to the notion of "subsequent reference", it was preferred to such notions as "durability" or "non-alterability", which would have established too harsh standards, and to such notions as "readability" or "intelligibility", which might constitute too subjective criteria.

51. The principle embodied in paragraph (3) of articles 6 and 7, and in paragraph (4) of article 8, is that an enacting State may exclude from the application of those articles certain situations to be specified in the legislation enacting the Model Law. An enacting State may wish to

exclude specifically certain types of situations, depending in particular on the purpose of the formal requirement in question. One such type of situation may be the case of writing requirements intended to provide notice or warning of specific factual or legal risks, for example, requirements for warnings to be placed on certain types of products. Another specific exclusion might be considered, for example, in the context of formalities required pursuant to international treaty obligations of the enacting State (e.g., the requirement that a cheque be in writing pursuant to the Convention providing a Uniform Law for Cheques, Geneva, 1931) and other kinds of situations and areas of law that are beyond the power of the enacting State to change by means of a statute.

52. Paragraph (3) was included with a view to enhancing the acceptability of the Model Law. It recognizes that the matter of specifying exclusions should be left to enacting States, an approach that would take better account of differences in national circumstances. However, it should be noted that the objectives of the Model Law would not be achieved if paragraph (3) were used to establish blanket exceptions, and the opportunity provided by paragraph (3) in that respect should be avoided. Numerous exclusions from the scope of articles 6 to 8 would raise needless obstacles to the development of modern communication techniques, since what the Model Law contains are very fundamental principles and approaches that are expected to find general application.

References

A/51/17, paras. 180-181 and 185-187 (article *5);*

A/50/17, paras. 228-241 (article *5);*

A/CN.9/407, paras. 56-63;

A/CN.9/406, paras. 95-101; A/CN.9/WG.IV/WP.62, article 6;

A/CN.9/390, paras. 88-96; A/CN.9/WG.IV/WP.60, article 6;

A/CN.9/387, paras. 66-80; A/CN.9/WG.IV/WP.57, article 6;

A/CN.9/WG.IV/WP.58, annex;

A/CN.9/373, paras. 45-62; A/CN.9/WG.IV/WP.55, paras. 36-49;

A/CN.9/360, paras. 32-43; A/CN.9/WG.IV/WP.53, paras. 37-45;

A/CN.9/350, paras. 68-78;

A/CN.9/333, paras. 20-28;

A/CN.9/265, paras. 59-72.

Article 7. Signature

53. Article 7 is based on the recognition of the functions of a signature in a paper-based environment. In the preparation of the Model Law, the following functions of a signature were considered: to identify a person; to provide certainty as to the personal involvement of that person in the act of signing; to associate that person with the content of a document. It was noted that, in addition, a signature could perform a variety of functions, depending on the nature of the document that was signed. For example, a signature might attest to the intent of a party to be bound by the content of a signed contract; the intent of a person to endorse authorship of a text; the intent of a person to associate itself with the content of a document written by someone else; the fact that, and the time when, a person had been at a given place.

54. It may be noted that, alongside the traditional handwritten signature, there exist various types of procedures (e.g., stamping, perforation), sometimes also referred to as "signatures", which provide various levels of certainty. For example, in some countries, there exists a general requirement that contracts for the sale of goods above a certain amount should be "signed" in order to be enforceable. However, the concept of a signature adopted in that context is such that a stamp, perforation or even a typewritten signature or a printed letterhead might be regarded as sufficient to fulfil the signature requirement. At the other end of the spectrum, there exist require-ments that combine the traditional handwritten signature with addi-tional security procedures such as the confirmation of the signature by witnesses.

55. It might be desirable to develop functional equivalents for the various types and levels of signature requirements in existence. Such an approach would increase the level of certainty as to the degree of legal recognition that could be expected from the use of the various means of authentication used in electronic commerce practice as substitutes

for "signatures". However, the notion of signature is intimately linked to the use of paper. Furthermore, any attempt to develop rules on standards and procedures to be used as substitutes for specific instances of "signatures" might create the risk of tying the legal framework provided by the Model Law to a given state of technical development.

56. With a view to ensuring that a message that was required to be authenticated should not be denied legal value for the sole reason that it was not authenticated in a manner peculiar to paper documents, article 7 adopts a comprehensive approach. It establishes the general conditions under which data messages would be regarded as authenticated with sufficient credibility and would be enforceable in the face of signature requirements which currently present barriers to electronic commerce. Article 7 focuses on the two basic functions of a signature, namely to identify the author of a document and to confirm that the author approved the content of that document. Paragraph (l)(a) establishes the principle that, in an electronic environment, the basic legal functions of a signature are performed by way of a method that identifies the originator of a data message and confirms that the originator approved the content of that data message.

57. Paragraph (1)*(b)* establishes a flexible approach to the level of security to be achieved by the method of identification used under paragraph (1)(a). The method used under paragraph (1)(a) should be as reliable as is appropriate for the purpose for which the data message is generated or communicated, in the light of all the circumstances, including any agreement between the originator and the addressee of the data message.

58. In determining whether the method used under paragraph (1) is appropriate, legal, technical and commercial factors that may be taken into account include the following: (1) the sophistication of the equipment used by each of the parties; (2) the nature of their trade activity; (3) the frequency at which commercial transactions take place between the parties; (4) the kind and size of the transaction; (5) the function of signature requirements in a given statutory and regulatory environment; (6) the capability of communication systems; (7) compliance with authentication procedures set forth by intermediaries; (8) the range of authentication procedures made available by any intermediary; (9) compliance with trade customs and practice; (10) the existence of insurance coverage mechanisms against unauthorized messages; (11) the importance and the value of the information contained in the data message; (12) the availability of alternative methods of identification and the cost of implementation; (13) the degree of acceptance or

non-acceptance of the method of identification in the relevant industry or field both at the time the method was agreed upon and the time when the data message was communicated; and (14) any other relevant factor.

59. Article 7 does not introduce a distinction between the situation in which users of electronic commerce are linked by a communication agreement and the situation in which parties had no prior contractual relationship regarding the use of electronic commerce. Thus, article 7 may be regarded as establishing a basic standard of authentication for data messages that might be exchanged in the absence of a prior contractual relationship and, at the same time, to provide guidance as to what might constitute an appropriate substitute for a signature if the parties used electronic communications in the context of a communication agreement. The Model Law is thus intended to provide useful guidance both in a context where national laws would leave the question of authentication of data messages entirely to the discretion of the parties and in a context where requirements for signature, which were usually set by mandatory provisions of national law, should not be made subject to alteration by agreement of the parties.

60. The notion of an "agreement between the originator and the addressee of a data message" is to be interpreted as covering not only bilateral or multilateral agreements concluded between parties exchanging directly data messages (e.g., "trading partners agreements", "communication agreements" or " interchange agreements") but also agreements involving intermediaries such as networks (e.g., "third-party service agreements"). Agreements concluded between users of electronic commerce and networks may incorporate "system rules", i.e., administrative and technical rules and procedures to be applied when communicating data messages. However, a possible agreement between originators and addressees of data messages as to the use of a method of authentication is not conclusive evidence of whether that method is reliable or not.

61. It should be noted that, under the Model Law, the mere signing of a data message by means of a functional equivalent of a handwritten signature is not intended, in and of itself, to confer legal validity on the data message. Whether a data message that fulfilled the requirement of a signature has legal validity is to be settled under the law applicable outside the Model Law.

References

A/51/17, paras. 180-181 and 185-187 (article 6);

A/50/17, paras. 242-248 (article 6);

A/CN.9/407, paras. 64-70;

A/CN.9/406, paras. 102-105; A/CN.9/WG.IV/WP.62, article 7;

A/CN.9/390, paras. 97-109; A/CN.9/WG.IV/WP.60, article 7;

A/CN.9/387, paras. 81-90; A/CN.9/WG.IV/WP.57, article 7;

A/CN.9/WG.IV/WP.58, annex;

A/CN.9/373, paras. 63-76; A/CN.9/WG.IV/WP.55, paras. 50-63;

A/CN.9/360, paras. 71-75; A/CN.9/WG.IV/WP.53, paras. 61-66;

A/CN.9/350, paras. 86-89;

A/CN.9/333, paras. 50-59; A/CN.9/265, paras. 49-58 and 79-80.

Article 8. Original

62. If "original" were defined as a medium on which information was fixed for the first time, it would be impossible to speak of "original" data messages, since the addressee of a data message would always receive a copy thereof. However, article 8 should be put in a different context. The notion of "original" in article 8 is useful since in practice many disputes relate to the question of originality of documents, and in electronic commerce the requirement for presentation of originals constitutes one of the main obstacles that the Model Law attempts to remove. Although in some jurisdictions the concepts of "writing", "original" and "signature" may overlap, the Model Law approaches them as three separate and distinct concepts. Article 8 is also useful in clarifying the notions of "writing" and "original", in particular in view of their importance for purposes of evidence.

63. Article 8 is pertinent to documents of title and negotiable instruments, in which the notion of uniqueness of an original is particularly relevant. However, attention is drawn to the fact that the

Model Law is not intended only to apply to documents of title and negotiable instruments, or to such areas of law where special requirements exist with respect to registration or notarization of "writings", e.g., family matters or the sale of real estate. Examples of documents that might require an "original" are trade documents such as weight certificates, agricultural certificates, quality or quantity certificates, inspection reports, insurance certificates, etc. While such documents are not negotiable or used to transfer rights or title, it is essential that they be transmitted unchanged, that is in their "original" form, so that other parties in international commerce may have confidence in their contents. In a paper-based environment, these types of document are usually only accepted if they are "original" to lessen the chance that they be altered, which would be difficult to detect in copies. Various technical means are available to certify the contents of a data message to confirm its "originality". Without this functional equivalent of originality, the sale of goods using electronic commerce would be hampered since the issuers of such documents would be required to retransmit their data message each and every time the goods are sold, or the parties would be forced to use paper documents to supplement the electronic commerce transaction.

64. Article 8 should be regarded as stating the minimum acceptable form requirement to be met by a data message for it to be regarded as the functional equivalent of an original. The provisions of article 8 should be regarded as mandatory, to the same extent that existing provisions regarding the use of paper-based original documents would be regarded as mandatory. The indication that the form requirements stated in article 8 are to be regarded as the "minimum acceptable" should not, however, be construed as inviting States to establish requirements stricter than those contained in the Model Law.

65. Article 8 emphasizes the importance of the integrity of the information for its originality and sets out criteria to be taken into account when assessing integrity by reference to systematic recording of the information, assurance that the information was recorded without lacunae and protection of the data against alteration. It links the concept of originality to a method of authentication and puts the focus on the method of authentication to be followed in order to meet the requirement. It is based on the following elements: a simple criterion as to "integrity" of the data; a description of the elements to be taken into account in assessing the integrity; and an element of flexibility, i.e., a reference to circumstances.

66. As regards the words "the time when it was first generated in its final form" in paragraph (1)(a), it should be noted that the provision is

intended to encompass the situation where information was first composed as a paper document and subsequently transferred on to a computer. In such a situation, paragraph (1)(a) is to be interpreted as requiring assurances that the information has remained complete and unaltered from the time when it was composed as a paper document onwards, and not only as from the time when it was translated into electronic form. However, where several drafts were created and stored before the final message was composed, paragraph (1)(a) should not be misinterpreted as requiring assurance as to the integrity of the drafts.

67. Paragraph (3)(a) sets forth the criteria for assessing integrity, taking care to except necessary additions to the first (or "original") data message such as endorsements, certifications, notarizations, etc. from other alterations. As long as the contents of a data message remain complete and unaltered, necessary additions to that data message would not affect its "originality". Thus when an electronic certificate is added to the end of an "original" data message to attest to the "originality" of that data message, or when data is automatically added by computer systems at the start and the finish of a data message in order to transmit it, such additions would be considered as if they were a supplemental piece of paper with an "original" piece of paper, or the envelope and stamp used to send that "original" piece of paper.

68. As in other articles of chapter II of part one, the words "the law" in the opening phrase of article 8 are to be understood as encompassing not regarded as mandatory, to the same extent that existing provisions regarding the use of paper-based original documents would be regarded as mandatory. The indication that the form requirements stated in article 8 are to be regarded as the "minimum acceptable" should not, however, be construed as inviting States to establish requirements stricter than those contained in the Model Law.

69. Paragraph (4), as was the case with similar provisions in articles 6 and 7, was included with a view to enhancing the acceptability of the Model Law. It recognizes that the matter of specifying exclusions should be left to enacting States, an approach that would take better account of differences in national circumstances. However, it should be noted that the objectives of the Model Law would not be achieved if paragraph (4) were used to establish blanket exceptions. Numerous exclusions from the scope of articles 6 to 8 would raise needless obstacles to the development of modern communication techniques, since what the Model Law contains are very fundamental principles and approaches that are expected to find general application.

References

A/51/17, paras. 180-181 and 185-187 (article 7);

A/50/17, paras. 249-255 (article 7);

A/CN.9/407, paras. 71-79;

A/CN.9/406, paras. 106-110; A/CN.9/WG.IV/WP.62, article 8;

A/CN.9/390, paras. 110-133; A/CN.9/WG.IV/WP.60, article 8;

A/CN.9/387, paras. 91-97; A/CN.9/WG.IV/WP.57, article 8;

A/CN.9/WG.IV/WP.58, annex;

A/CN.9/373, paras. 77-96; A/CN.9/WG.IV/WP.55, paras. 64-70;

A/CN.9/360, paras. 60-70; A/CN.9/WG.IV/WP.53, paras. 56-60;

A/CN.9/350, paras. 84-85;

A/CN.9/265, paras. 43-48.

Article 9. Admissibility and evidential weight of data messages

70. The purpose of article 9 is to establish both the admissibility of data messages as evidence in legal proceedings and their evidential value. With respect to admissibility, paragraph (1), establishing that data messages should not be denied admissibility as evidence in legal proceedings on the sole ground that they are in electronic form, puts emphasis on the general principle stated in article 4 and is needed to make it expressly applicable to admissibility of evidence, an area in which particularly complex issues might arise in certain jurisdictions. The term "best evidence" is a term understood in, and necessary for, certain common law jurisdictions. However, the notion of "best evidence" could raise a great deal of uncertainty in legal systems in which such a rule is unknown. States in which the term would be regarded as meaningless and potentially misleading may wish to enact the Model Law without the reference to the "best evidence" rule contained in paragraph (1).

71. As regards the assessment of the evidential weight of a data message, paragraph (2) provides useful guidance as to how the evidential value of data messages should be assessed (e.g., depending on whether they were generated, stored or communicated in a reliable manner).

References

A/50/17, paras. 256-263 (article 8);

A/CN.9/407, paras. 80-81;

A/CN.9/406, paras. 111-113; A/CN.9/WG.IV/WP.62, article 9;

A/CN.9/390, paras. 139-143; A/CN.9/WG.IV/WP.60, article 9;

A/CN.9/387, paras. 98-109; A/CN.9/WG.IV/WP.57, article 9;

A/CN.9/WG.IV/WP.58, annex;

A/CN.9/373, paras. 97-108; A/CN.9/WG.IV/WP.55, paras. 71-81;

A/CN.9/360, paras. 44-59; A/CN.9/WG.IV/WP.53, paras. 46-55;

A/CN.9/350, paras. 79-83 and 90-91;

A/CN.9/333, paras. 29-41;

A/CN.9/265, paras. 27-48.

Article 10. Retention of data messages

72. Article 10 establishes a set of alternative rules for existing requirements regarding the storage of information (e.g., for accounting or tax purposes) that may constitute obstacles to the development of modern trade.

73. Paragraph (1) is intended to set out the conditions under which the obligation to store data messages that might exist under the applicable law would be met. Subparagraph (a) reproduces the conditions established under article 6 for a data message to satisfy a rule which prescribes the presentation of a "writing". Subparagraph *(b)* emphasizes that the message does not need to be retained unaltered as long as the

information stored accurately reflects the data message as it was sent. It would not be appropriate to require that information should be stored unaltered, since usually messages are decoded, compressed or converted in order to be stored.

74. Subparagraph *(c)* is intended to cover all the information that may need to be stored, which includes, apart from the message itself, certain transmittal information that may be necessary for the identification of the message. Subparagraph *(c)*, by imposing the retention of the transmittal information associated with the data message, is creating a standard that is higher than most standards existing under national laws as to the storage of paper-based communications. However, it should not be understood as imposing an obligation to retain transmittal information additional to the information contained in the data message when it was generated, stored or transmitted, or information contained in a separate data message, such as an acknowledgement of receipt. Moreover, while some transmittal information is important and has to be stored, other transmittal information can be exempted without the integrity of the data message being compromised. That is the reason why subparagraph *(c)* establishes a distinction between those elements of transmittal information that are important for the identification of the message and the very few elements of transmittal information covered in paragraph (2) (e.g., communication protocols), which are of no value with regard to the data message and which, typically, would automatically be stripped out of an incoming data message by the receiving computer before the data message actually entered the information system of the addressee.

75. In practice, storage of information, and especially storage of transmittal information, may often be carried out by someone other than the originator or the addressee, such as an intermediary. Nevertheless, it is intended that the person obligated to retain certain transmittal information cannot escape meeting that obligation simply because, for example, the communications system operated by that other person does not retain the required information. This is intended to discourage bad practice or wilful misconduct. Paragraph (3) provides that in meeting its obligations under paragraph (1), an addressee or originator may use the services of any third party, not just an intermediary.

References

A/51/17, paras. 185-187 (article 9);

A/50/17, paras. 264-270 (article 9);

A/CN.9/407, paras. 82-84;

A/CN.9/406, paras. 59-72; A/CN.9/WG.IV/WP.60, article 14;

A/CN.9/387, paras. 164-168; A/CN.9/WG.IV/WP.57, article 14;

A/CN.9/373, paras. 123-125; A/CN.9/WG.IV/WP.55, para. 94.

Chapter III. Communication of data messages

Article 11. Formation and validity of contracts

76. Article 11 is not intended to interfere with the law on formation of contracts but rather to promote international trade by providing increased legal certainty as to the conclusion of contracts by electronic means. It deals not only with the issue of contract formation but also with the form in which an offer and an acceptance may be expressed. In certain countries, a provision along the lines of paragraph (1) might be regarded as merely stating the obvious, namely that an offer and an acceptance, as any other expression of will, can be communicated by any means, including data messages. However, the provision is needed in view of the remaining uncertainties in a considerable number of countries as to whether contracts can validly be concluded by electronic means. Such uncertainties may stem from the fact that, in certain cases, the data messages expressing offer and acceptance are generated by computers without immediate human intervention, thus raising doubts as to the expression of intent by the parties. Another reason for such uncertainties is inherent in the mode of communication and results from the absence of a paper document.

77. It may also be noted that paragraph (1) reinforces, in the context of contract formation, a principle already embodied in other articles of the Model Law, such as articles 5, 9 and 13, all of which establish the legal effectiveness of data messages. However, paragraph (1) is needed since the fact that electronic messages may have legal value as evidence and produce a number of effects, including those provided in articles 9 and 13, does not necessarily mean that they can be used for the purpose of concluding valid contracts.

78. Paragraph (1) covers not merely the cases in which both the offer and the acceptance are communicated by electronic means but also cases in which only the offer or only the acceptance is communicated electronically. As to the time and place of formation of contracts in cases where an offer or the acceptance of an offer is expressed by means of a data message, no specific rule has been included in the Model Law in order not to interfere with national law applicable to contract formation. It was felt that such a provision might exceed the aim of the Model Law, which should be limited to providing that electronic communications would achieve the same degree of legal certainty as paper-based communications. The combination of existing rules on the formation of contracts with the provisions contained in article 15 is designed to dispel uncertainty as to the time and place of formation of contracts in cases where the offer or the acceptance are exchanged electronically.

79. The words "unless otherwise stated by the parties", which merely restate, in the context of contract formation, the recognition of party autonomy expressed in article 4, are intended to make it clear that the purpose of the Model Law is not to impose the use of electronic means of communication on parties who rely on the use of paper-based communication to conclude contracts. Thus, article 11 should not be interpreted as restricting in any way party autonomy with respect to parties not involved in the use of electronic communication.

80. During the preparation of paragraph (1), it was felt that the provision might have the harmful effect of overruling otherwise applicable provisions of national law, which might prescribe specific formalities for the formation of certain contracts. Such forms include notarization and other requirements for "writings", and might respond to considerations of public policy, such as the need to protect certain parties or to warn them against specific risks. For that reason, paragraph (2) provides that an enacting State can exclude the application of paragraph (1) in certain instances to be specified in the legislation enacting the Model Law.

References

A/51/17, paras. 89-94 (article 13);

A/CN.9/407, para. 93;

A/CN.9/406, paras. 34-41; A/CN.9/WG.IV/WP.60, article 12;

A/CN.9/387, paras. 145-151; A/CN.9/WG.IV/WP.57, article 12;

A/CN.9/373, paras. 126-133; A/CN.9/WG.IV/WP.55, paras. 95-102;

A/CN.9/360, paras. 76-86; A/CN.9/WG.IV/WP.53, paras. 67-73;

A/CN.9/350, paras. 93-96;

A/CN.9/333, paras. 60-68.

Article 12. Recognition by parties of data messages

81. Article 12 was added at a late stage in the preparation of the Model Law, in recognition of the fact that article 11 was limited to dealing with data messages that were geared to the conclusion of a contract, but that the draft Model Law did not contain specific provisions on data messages that related not to the conclusion of contracts but to the performance of contractual obligations (e.g., notice of defective goods, an offer to pay, notice of place where a contract would be performed, recognition of debt). Since modern means of communication are used in a context of legal uncertainty, in the absence of specific legislation in most countries, it was felt appropriate for the Model Law not only to establish the general principle that the use of electronic communication should not be discriminated against, as expressed in article 5, but also to include specific illustrations of that principle. Contract formation is but one of the areas where such an illustration is useful and the legal validity of unilateral expressions of will, as well as other notices or statements that may be issued in the form of data messages, also needs to be mentioned.

82. As is the case with article 11, article 12 is not to impose the use of electronic means of communication but to validate such use, subject to contrary agreement by the parties. Thus, article 12 should not be used as a basis to impose on the addressee the legal consequences of a message, if the use of a non-paper-based method for its transmission comes as a surprise to the addressee.

References

A/51/17, paras. 95-99 (new article 13 *bis*).

Article 13. Attribution of data messages

83. Article 13 has its origin in article S of the UNCITRAL Model Law on International Credit Transfers, which defines the obligations of the sender of a payment order. Article 13 is intended to apply where there is a question as to whether a data message was really sent by the person who is indicated as being the originator. In the case of a paper-based communication the problem would arise as the result of an alleged forged signature of the purported originator. In an electronic environment, an unauthorized person may have sent the message but the authentication by code, encryption or the like would be accurate. The purpose of article 13 is not to assign responsibility. It deals rather with attribution of data messages by establishing a presumption that under certain circumstances a data message would be considered as a message of the originator, and goes on to qualify that presumption in case the addressee knew or ought to have known that the data message was not that of the originator.

84. Paragraph (1) recalls the principle that an originator is bound by a data message if it has effectively sent that message. Paragraph (2) refers to the situation where the message was sent by a person other than the originator who had the authority to act on behalf of the originator. Paragraph (2) is not intended to displace the domestic law of agency, and the question as to whether the other person did in fact and in law have the authority to act on behalf of the originator is left to the appropriate legal rules outside the Model Law.

85. Paragraph (3) deals with two kinds of situations, in which the addressee could rely on a data message as being that of the originator: firstly, situations in which the addressee properly applied an authentication procedure previously agreed to by the originator; and secondly, situations in which the data message resulted from the actions of a person who, by virtue of its relationship with the originator, had access to the originator's authentication procedures. By stating that the addressee "is entitled to regard a data as being that of the originator", paragraph (3) read in conjunction with paragraph (4)(a) is intended to indicate that the addressee could act on the assumption that the data message is that of the originator up to the point in time it received notice from the originator that the data message was not that of the originator, or up to the point in time when it knew or should have known that the data message was not that of the originator.

86. Under paragraph (3)(a), if the addressee applies any authentication procedures previously agreed to by the originator and such application

results in the proper verification of the originator as the source of the message, the message is presumed to be that of the originator. That covers not only the situation where an authentication procedure has been agreed upon by the originator and the addressee but also situations where an originator, unilaterally or as a result of an agreement with an intermediary, identified a procedure and agreed to be bound by a data message that met the requirements corresponding to that procedure. Thus, agreements that became effective not through direct agreement between the originator and the addressee but through the participation of third-party service providers are intended to be covered by para-graph (3)(a). However, it should be noted that paragraph (3)(a) applies only when the communication between the originator and the addressee is based on a previous agreement, but that it does not apply in an open environment.

87. The effect of paragraph (3)(b), read in conjunction with paragraph (4)(b), is that the originator or the addressee, as the case may be, is responsible for any unauthorized data message that can be shown to have been sent as a result of negligence of that party.

88. Paragraph (4)(a) should not be misinterpreted as relieving the originator from the consequences of sending a data message, with retroactive effect, irrespective of whether the addressee had acted on the assumption that the data message was that of the originator. Paragraph (4) is not intended to provide that receipt of a notice under subparagraph *(a)* would nullify the original message retroactively. Under subparagraph *(a),* the originator is released from the binding effect of the message after the time notice is received and not before that time. Moreover, paragraph (4) should not be read as allowing the originator to avoid being bound by the data message by sending notice to the addressee under subparagraph *(a),* in a case where the message had, in fact, been sent by the originator and the addressee properly applied agreed or reasonable authentication procedures. If the addressee can prove that the message is that of the originator, paragraph (1) would apply and not paragraph (4)(a). As to the meaning of "reasonable time", the notice should be such as to give the addressee sufficient time to react. For example, in the case of just-in-time supply, the addressee should be given time to adjust its production chain.

89. With respect to paragraph (4)(b), it should be noted that the Model Law could lead to the result that the addressee would be entitled to rely on a data message under paragraph (3)(a) if it had properly applied the agreed authentication procedures, even if it knew that the data message was not that of the originator. It was generally felt when preparing the

Model Law that the risk that such a situation could arise should be accepted, in view of the need for preserving the reliability of agreed authentication procedures.

90. Paragraph *(5)* is intended to preclude the originator from disavowing the message once it was sent, unless the addressee knew, or should have known, that the data message was not that of the originator. In addition, paragraph *(5)* is intended to deal with errors in the content of the message arising from errors in transmission.

91. Paragraph (6) deals with the issue of erroneous duplication of data messages, an issue of considerable practical importance. It establishes the standard of care to be applied by the addressee to distinguish an erroneous duplicate of a data message from a separate data message.

92. arly drafts of article 13 contained an additional paragraph, expressing the principle that the attribution of authorship of a data message to the originator should not interfere with the legal consequences of that message, which should be determined by other applicable rules of national law. It was later felt that it was not necessary to express that principle in the Model Law but that it should be mentioned in this Guide.

References

A/51/17, paras. 189-194 (article 11);

A/50/17, paras. 275-303 (article 11);

A/CN.9/407, paras. 86-89;

A/CN.9/406, paras. 114-131; A/CN.9/WG.IV/WP.62, article 10;

A/CN.9/390, paras. 144-153; A/CN.9/WG.IV/WP.60, article 10;

A/CN.9/387, paras. 110-132; A/CN.9/WG.IV/WP.57, article 10;

A/CN.9/373, paras. 109-115; A/CN.9/WG.IV/WP.55, paras. 82-86.

Article 14. Acknowledgement of receipt

93. The use of functional acknowledgements is a business decision to be made by users of electronic commerce; the Model Law does not intend to impose the use of any such procedure. However, taking into account the commercial value of a system of acknowledgement of receipt and the widespread use of such systems in the context of electronic commerce, it was felt that the Model Law should address a number of legal issues arising from the use of acknowledgement procedures. It should be noted that the notion of "acknowledgement" is sometimes used to cover a variety of procedures, ranging from a mere acknowledgement of receipt of an unspecified message to an expression of agreement with the content of a specific data message. In many instances, the procedure of "acknowledgement" would parallel the system known as "return receipt requested" in postal systems. Acknowledgements of receipt may be required in a variety of instruments, e.g., in the data message itself, in bilateral or multilateral communication agreements, or in "system rules". It should be borne in mind that variety among acknowledgement procedures implies variety of the related costs. The provisions of article 14 are based on the assumption that acknowledgement procedures are to be used at the discretion of the originator. Article 14 is not intended to deal with the legal consequences that may flow from sending an acknowledgement of receipt, apart from establishing receipt of the data message. For example, where an originator sends an offer in a data message and requests acknowledgement of receipt, the acknowledgement of receipt simply evidences that the offer has been received. Whether or not sending that acknowledgement amounted to accepting the offer is not dealt with by the Model Law but by contract law outside the Model Law.

94. The purpose of paragraph (2) is to validate acknowledgement by any communication or conduct of the addressee (e.g., the shipment of the goods as an acknowledgement of receipt of a purchase order) where the originator has not agreed with the addressee that the acknowledgement should be in a particular form. The situation where an acknowledgement has been unilaterally requested by the originator to be given in a specific form is not expressly addressed by article 14, which may entail as a possible consequence that a unilateral requirement by the originator as to the form of acknowledgements would not affect the right of the addressee to acknowledge receipt by any communication or conduct sufficient to indicate to the originator that the message had been received. Such a possible interpretation of paragraph (2) makes it particularly necessary to emphasize in the

Model Law the distinction to be drawn between the effects of an acknowledgement of receipt of a data message and any communication in response to the content of that data message, a reason why paragraph (7) is needed.

95. Paragraph (3), which deals with the situation where the origin-ator has stated that the data message is conditional on receipt of an acknowledgement, applies whether or not the originator has specified that the acknowledgement should be received by a certain time.

96. The purpose of paragraph (4) is to deal with the more common situation where an acknowledgement is requested, without any state-ment being made by the originator that the data message is of no effect until an acknowledgement has been received. Such a provision is needed to establish the point in time when the originator of a data message who has requested an acknowledgement of receipt is relieved from any legal implication of sending that data message if the requested acknowledgement has not been received. An example of a factual situation where a provision along the lines of paragraph (4) would be particularly useful would be that the originator of an offer to contract who has not received the requested acknowledgement from the addressee of the offer may need to know the point in time after which it is free to transfer the offer to another party. It may be noted that the provision does not create any obligation binding on the originator, but merely establishes means by which the originator, if it so wishes, can clarify its status in cases where it has not received the requested acknowledgement. It may also be noted that the provision does not create any obligation binding on the addressee of the data message, who would, in most circumstances, be free to rely or not to rely on any given data message, provided that it would bear the risk of the data message being unreliable for lack of an acknowledgement of receipt. The addressee, however, is protected since the originator who does not receive a requested acknowledgement may not automatically treat the data message as though it had never been transmitted, without giving further notice to the addressee. The procedure described under paragraph (4) is purely at the discretion of the originator. For example, where the originator sent a data message which under the agreement between the parties had to be received by a certain time, and the originator requested an acknowledgement of receipt, the addressee could not deny the legal effectiveness of the message simply by withholding the requested acknowledgement.

97. The rebuttable presumption established in paragraph (5) is needed to create certainty and would be particularly useful in the context of

electronic communication between parties that are not linked by a trading-partners agreement. The second sentence of paragraph (5) should be read in conjunction with paragraph (5) of article 13, which establishes the conditions under which, in case of an inconsistency between the text of the data message as sent and the text as received, the text as received prevails.

98. Paragraph (6) corresponds to a certain type of acknowledgement, for example, an EDIFACT message establishing that the data message received is syntactically correct, i.e., that it can be processed by the receiving computer. The reference to technical requirements, which is to be construed primarily as a reference to "data syntax" in the context of EDI communications, may be less relevant in the context of the use of other means of communication, such as telegram or telex. In addition to mere consistency with the rules of "data syntax", technical requirements set forth in applicable standards may include, for example, the use of procedures verifying the integrity of the contents of data messages.

99. Paragraph (7) is intended to dispel uncertainties that might exist as to the legal effect of an acknowledgement of receipt. For example, paragraph (7) indicates that an acknowledgement of receipt should not be confused with any communication related to the contents of the acknowledged message.

References

A/51/17, paras. 63-88 (article 12);

A/CN.9/407, paras. 90-92;

A/CN.9/406, paras. 15-33; A/CN.9/WG.IV/WP.60, article 11;

A/CN.9/387, paras. 133-144; A/CN.9/WG.IV/WP.57, article 11;

A/CN.9/373, paras. 116-122; A/CN.9/WG.IV/WP.55, paras. 87-93;

A/CN.9/360, para. 125; A/CN.9/WG.IV/WP.53, paras. 80-81;

A/CN.9/350, para. 92;

A/CN.9/333, paras. 48-49.

Article 15. Time and place of dispatch and receipt of data messages

100. Article 15 results from the recognition that, for the operation of many existing rules of law, it is important to ascertain the time and place of receipt of information. The use of electronic communication techniques makes those difficult to ascertain. It is not uncommon for users of electronic commerce to communicate from one State to another without knowing the location of information systems through which communication is operated. In addition, the location of certain communication systems may change without either of the parties being aware of the change. The Model Law is thus intended to reflect the fact that the location of information systems is irrelevant and sets forth a more objective criterion, namely, the place of business of the parties. In that connection, it should be noted that article 15 is not intended to establish a conflict-of-laws rule.

101. Paragraph (1) defines the time of dispatch of a data message as the time when the data message enters an information system outside the control of the originator, which may be the information system of an intermediary or an information system of the addressee. The concept of "dispatch" refers to the commencement of the electronic transmission of the data message. Where "dispatch" already has an established meaning, article 15 is intended to supplement national rules on dispatch and not to displace them. If dispatch occurs when the data message reaches an information system of the addressee, dispatch under paragraph (1) and receipt under paragraph (2) are simultaneous, except where the data message is sent to an information system of the addressee that is not the information system designated by the addressee under paragraph (2)(a).

102. Paragraph (2), the purpose of which is to define the time of receipt of a data message, addresses the situation where the addressee unilaterally designates a specific information system for the receipt of a message (in which case the designated system may or may not be an information system of the addressee), and the data message reaches an information system of the addressee that is not the designated system. In such a situation, receipt is deemed to occur when the data message is retrieved by the addressee. By "designated information system", the Model Law is intended to cover a system that has been specifically designated by a party, for instance in the case where an offer expressly specifies the address to which acceptance should be sent. The mere indication of an electronic mail or telecopy address on a letterhead or other document should not be regarded as express designation of one or more information systems.

103. Attention is drawn to the notion of "entry" into an information system, which is used for both the definition of dispatch and that of receipt of a data message. A data message enters an information system at the time when it becomes available for processing within that information system. Whether a data message which enters an information system is intelligible or usable by the addressee is outside the purview of the Model Law. The Model Law does not intend to overrule provisions of national law under which receipt of a message may occur at the time when the message enters the sphere of the addressee, irrespective of whether the message is intelligible or usable by the addressee. Nor is the Model Law intended to run counter to trade usages, under which certain encoded messages are deemed to be received even before they are usable by, or intelligible for, the addressee. It was felt that the Model Law should not create a more stringent requirement than currently exists in a paper-based environment, where a message can be considered to be received even if it is not intelligible for the addressee or not intended to be intelligible to the addressee (e.g., where encrypted data is transmitted to a depository for the sole purpose of retention in the context of intellectual property rights protection).

104. A data message should not be considered to be dispatched if it merely reached the information system of the addressee but failed to enter it. It may be noted that the Model Law does not expressly address the question of possible malfunctioning of information systems as a basis for liability. In particular, where the information system of the addressee does not function at all or functions improperly or, while functioning properly, cannot be entered into by the data message (e.g., in the case of a telecopier that is constantly occupied), dispatch under the Model Law does not occur. It was felt during the preparation of the Model Law that the addressee should not be placed under the burdensome obligation to maintain its information system functioning at all times by way of a general provision.

105. The purpose of paragraph (4) is to deal with the place of receipt of a data message. The principal reason for including a rule on the place of receipt of a data message is to address a circumstance characteristic of electronic commerce that might not be treated adequately under existing law, namely, that very often the information system of the addressee where the data message is received, or from which the data message is retrieved, is located in a jurisdiction other than that in which the addressee itself is located. Thus, the rationale behind the provision is to ensure that the location of an information system is not the determinant element, and that there is some reasonable connection

between the addressee and what is deemed to be the place of receipt, and that that place can be readily ascertained by the originator. The Model Law does not contain specific provisions as to how the designation of an information system should be made, or whether a change could be made after such a designation by the addressee.

106. Paragraph (4), which contains a reference to the "underlying transaction", is intended to refer to both actual and contemplated underlying transactions. References to "place of business", "principal place of business" and "place of habitual residence" were adopted to bring the text in line with article 10 of the United Nations Convention on Contracts for the International Sale of Goods.

107. The effect of paragraph (4) is to introduce a distinction between the deemed place of receipt and the place actually reached by a data message at the time of its receipt under paragraph (2). That distinction is not to be interpreted as apportioning risks between the originator and the addressee in case of damage or loss of a data message between the time of its receipt under paragraph (2) and the time when it reached its place of receipt under paragraph (4). Paragraph (4) merely establishes an irrebuttable presumption regarding a legal fact, to be used where another body of law (e.g., on formation of contracts or conflict of laws) require determination of the place of receipt of a data message. However, it was felt during the preparation of the Model Law that introducing a deemed place of receipt, as distinct from the place actually reached by that data message at the time of its receipt, would be inappropriate outside the context of computerized transmissions (e.g., in the context of telegram or telex). The provision was thus limited in scope to cover only computerized transmissions of data messages. A further limitation is contained in paragraph *(5)*, which reproduces a provision already included in articles 6, 7, 8, 11 and 12 (see above, para. 69).

References

A/S 1/17, paras. 100-115 (article 14);

A/CN.9/407, paras. 94-99;

A/CN.9/406, paras. 42-58; A/CN.9/WG.IV/WP.60, article 13;

A/CN.9/387, paras. 152-163; A/CN.9/WG.IV/WP.57, article 13;

A/CN.9/373, paras. 134-146; A/CN.9/WG.IV/WP.55, paras. 103-108;

A/CN.9/360, paras. 87-89; A/CN.9/WG.IV/WP.53, paras. 74-76;

A/CN.9/350, paras. 97-100;

A/CN.9/333, paras. 69-75.

Part two. Electronic Commerce in Specific Areas

108. As distinct from the basic rules applicable to electronic commerce in general, which appear as part one of the Model Law, part two contains rules of a more specific nature. In preparing the Model Law, the Commission agreed that such rules dealing with specific uses of electronic commerce should appear in the Model Law in a way that reflected both the specific nature of the provisions and their legal status, which should be the same as that of the general provisions contained in part one of the Model Law. While the Commission, when adopting the Model Law, only considered such specific provisions in the context of transport documents, it was agreed that such provisions should appear as chapter I of part two of the Model Law. It was felt that adopting such an open-ended structure would make it easier to add further specific provisions to the Model Law, as the need might arise, in the form of additional chapters in part two.

109. The adoption of a specific set of rules dealing with specific uses of electronic commerce, such as the use of EDI messages as substitutes for transport documents does not imply that the other provisions of the Model Law are not applicable to such documents. In particular, the provisions of part two, such as articles 16 and 17 concerning transfer of rights in goods, presuppose that the guarantees of reliability and authenticity contained in articles 6 to 8 of the Model Law are also applicable to electronic equivalents to transport documents. Part two of the Model Law does not in any way limit or restrict the field of application of the general provisions of the Model Law.

Chapter I. Carriage of goods

110. In preparing the Model Law, the Commission noted that the carriage of goods was the context in which electronic communications were most likely to be used and in which a legal framework facilitating

the use of such communications was most urgently needed. Articles 16 and 17 contain provisions that apply equally to non-negotiable transport documents and to transfer of rights in goods by way of transferable bills of lading. The principles embodied in articles 16 and 17 are applicable not only to maritime transport but also to transport of goods by other means, such as road, railroad and air transport.

Article 16. Actions related to contracts of carriage of goods

111. Article 16, which establishes the scope of chapter I of part two of the Model Law, is broadly drafted. It would encompass a wide variety of documents used in the context of the carriage of goods, including, for example, charter-parties. In the preparation of the Model Law, the Commission found that, by dealing comprehensively with contracts of carriage of goods, article 16 was consistent with the need to cover all transport documents, whether negotiable or non-negotiable, without excluding any specific document such as charter-parties. It was pointed out that, if an enacting State did not wish chapter I of part two to apply to a particular kind of document or contract, for example if the inclusion of such documents as charter-parties in the scope of that chapter was regarded as inappropriate under the legislation of an enacting State, that State could make use of the exclusion clause contained in paragraph (7) of article 17.

112. Article 16 is of an illustrative nature and, although the actions mentioned therein are more common in maritime trade, they are not exclusive to such type of trade and could be performed in connection with air transport or multimodal carriage of goods.

References

A/51/17, paras. 139-172 and 198-204 (draft article x);

A/CN.9/421, paras. 53-103; A/CN.9/WG.IV/WP.69, paras. 82-95;

A/50/17, paras. 307-309;

A/CN.9/407, paras. 106-118; A/CN.9/WG.IV/WP.67, annex;

A/CN.9/WG.IV/WP.66, annex II;

A/49/17, paras. 198, 199 and 201;

A/CN.9/390, para. 155-158.

Article 17. Transport documents

113. Paragraphs (1) and (2) are derived from article 6. In the context of transport documents, it is necessary to establish not only functional equivalents of written information about the actions referred to in article 16, but also functional equivalents of the performance of such actions through the use of paper documents. Functional equivalents are particularly needed for the transfer of rights and obligations by transfer of written documents. For example, paragraphs (1) and (2) are intended to replace both the requirement for a written contract of carriage and the requirements for endorsement and transfer of possession of a bill of lading. It was felt in the preparation of the Model Law that the focus of the provision on the actions referred to in article 16 should be expressed clearly, particularly in view of the difficulties that might exist, in certain countries, for recognizing the transmission of a data message as functionally equivalent to the physical transfer of goods, or to the transfer of a document of title representing the goods.

114. The reference to "one or more data messages" in paragraphs (1), (3) and (6) is not intended to be interpreted differently from the reference to "a data message" in the other provisions of the Model Law, which should also be understood as covering equally the situation where only one data message is generated and the situation where more than one data message is generated as support of a given piece of information. A more detailed wording was adopted in article 17 merely to reflect the fact that, in the context of transfer of rights through data messages, some of the functions traditionally performed through the single transmission of a paper bill of lading would necessarily imply the transmission of more than one data message and that such a fact, in itself, should entail no negative consequence as to the acceptability of electronic commerce in that area.

115. Paragraph (3), in combination with paragraph (4), is intended to ensure that a right can be conveyed to one person only, and that it would not be possible for more than one person at any point in time to lay claim to it. The effect of the two paragraphs is to introduce a requirement which may be referred to as the "guarantee of singularity". If procedures are made available to enable a right or obligation to be conveyed by electronic methods instead of by using a paper document, it is necessary that the guarantee of singularity be one of the essential features of such procedures. Technical security devices

providing such a guarantee of singularity would almost necessarily be built into any communication system offered to the trading communities and would need to demonstrate their reliability. However, there is also a need to overcome requirements of law that the guarantee of singularity be demonstrated, for example in the case where paper documents such as bills of lading are traditionally used. A provision along the lines of paragraph (3) is thus necessary to permit the use of electronic communication instead of paper documents.

116. The words "one person and no other person" should not be interpreted as excluding situations where more than one person might jointly hold title to the goods. For example, the reference to "one person" is not intended to exclude joint ownership of rights in the goods or other rights embodied in a bill of lading.

117. The notion that a data message should be "unique" may need to be further clarified, since it may lend itself to misinterpretation. On the one hand, all data messages are necessarily unique, even if they duplicate an earlier data message, since each data message is sent at a different time from any earlier data message sent to the same person. If a data message is sent to a different person, it is even more obviously unique, even though it might be transferring the same right or obligation. Yet, all but the first transfer might be fraudulent. On the other hand, if "unique" is interpreted as referring to a data message of a unique kind, or a transfer of a unique kind, then in that sense no data message is unique, and no transfer by means of a data message is unique. Having considered the risk of such misinterpretation, the Commission decided to retain the reference to the concepts of uniqueness of the data message and uniqueness of the transfer for the purposes of article 17, in view of the fact that the notions of "uniqueness" or "singularity" of transport documents were not unknown to practitioners of transport law and users of transport documents. It was decided, however, that this Guide should clarify that the words "a reliable method is used to render such data message or messages unique" should be interpreted as referring to the use of a reliable method to secure that data messages purporting to convey any right or obligation of a person might not be used by, or on behalf of, that person inconsistently with any other data messages by which the right or obligation was conveyed by or on behalf of that person.

118. Paragraph *(5)* is a necessary complement to the guarantee of singularity contained in paragraph (3). The need for security is an overriding consideration and it is essential to ensure not only that a method is used that gives reasonable assurance that the same data

message is not multiplied, but also that no two media can be simultaneously used for the same purpose. Paragraph *(5)* addresses the fundamental need to avoid the risk of duplicate transport documents. The use of multiple forms of communication for different purposes, e.g., paper-based communications for ancillary messages and electronic communications for bills of lading, does not pose a problem. However, it is essential for the operation of any system relying on electronic equivalents of bills of lading to avoid the possibility that the same rights could at any given time be embodied both in data messages and in a paper document. Paragraph (5) also envisages the situation where a party having initially agreed to engage in electronic communications has to switch to paper communications where it later becomes unable to sustain electronic communications.

119. The reference to "terminating" the use of data messages is open to interpretation. In particular, the Model Law does not provide information as to who would effect the termination. Should an enacting State decide to provide additional information in that respect, it might wish to indicate, for example, that, since electronic commerce is usually based on the agreement of the parties, a decision to "drop down" to paper communications should also be subject to the agreement of all interested parties. Otherwise, the originator would be given the power to choose unilaterally the means of communication. Alternatively, an enacting State might wish to provide that, since paragraph *(5)* would have to be applied by the bearer of a bill of lading, it should be up to the bearer to decide whether it preferred to exercise its rights on the basis of a paper bill of lading or on the basis of the electronic equivalent of such a document, and to bear the costs for its decision.

120. Paragraph *(5),* while expressly dealing with the situation where the use of data messages is replaced by the use of a paper document, is not intended to exclude the reverse situation. The switch from data messages to a paper document should not affect any right that might exist to surrender the paper document to the issuer and start again using data messages.

121. The purpose of paragraph (6) is to deal directly with the application of certain laws to contracts for the carriage of goods by sea. For example, under the Hague and Hague-Visby Rules, a contract of carriage means a contract that is covered by a bill of lading. Use of a bill of lading or similar document of title results in the Hague and Hague-Visby Rules applying compulsorily to a contract of carriage. Those rules would not automatically apply to contracts effected by one or more data message. Thus, a provision such as paragraph (6) is needed

to ensure that the application of those rules is not excluded by the mere fact that data messages are used instead of a bill of lading in paper form. While paragraph (1) ensures that data messages are effective means for carrying out any of the actions listed in article 16, that provision does not deal with the substantive rules of law that might apply to a contract contained in, or evidenced by, data messages.

122. As to the meaning of the phrase "that rule shall not be inapplicable" in paragraph (6), a simpler way of expressing the same idea might have been to provide that rules applicable to contracts of carriage evidenced by paper documents should also apply to contracts of carriage evidenced by data messages. However, given the broad scope of application of article 17, which covers not only bills of lading but also a variety of other transport documents, such a simplified provision might have had the undesirable effect of extending the applicability of rules such as the Hamburg Rules and the Hague-Visby Rules to contracts to which such rules were never intended to apply. The Commission felt that the adopted wording was more suited to overcome the obstacle resulting from the fact that the Hague-Visby Rules and other rules compulsorily applicable to bills of lading would not automatically apply to contracts of carriage evidenced by data messages, without inadvertently extending the application of such rules to other types of contracts.

References

A/51/17, paras. 139-172 and 198-204 (draft article x);

A/CN.9/421, paras. 53-103; A/CN.9/WG.IV/WP.69, paras 82-95;

A/50/17, paras. 307-309

A/CN.9/407, paras. 106-118 A/CN.9/WG.IV/WP.67, annex;

A/CN.9/WG.IV/WP.66, annex II;

A/49/17, paras. 198, 199 and 201;

A/CN.9/390, para. 155-158.

III. HISTORY AND BACKGROUND OF THE MODEL LAW

123. The UNCITRAL Model Law on Electronic Commerce was adopted by the United Nations Commission on International Trade Law (UNCITRAL) in 1996 in furtherance of its mandate to promote the harmonization and unification of international trade law, so as to remove unnecessary obstacles to international trade caused by inadequacies and divergences in the law affecting trade. Over the past quarter of a century, UNCITRAL, whose membership consists of States from all regions and of all levels of economic development, has implemented its mandate by formulating international conventions (the United Nations Conventions on Contracts for the International Sale of Goods, on the Limitation Period in the International Sale of Goods, on the Carriage of Goods by Sea, 1978 ("Hamburg Rules"), on the Liability of Operators of Transport Terminals in International Trade, on International Bills of Exchange and International Promissory Notes, and on Independent Guarantees and Stand-by Letters of Credit), model laws (the UNCITRAL Model Laws on International Commercial Arbitration, on International Credit Transfers and on Procurement of Goods, Construction and Services), the UNCITRAL Arbitration Rules, the UNCITRAL Conciliation Rules, and legal guides (on construction contracts, countertrade transactions and electronic funds transfers).

124. The Model Law was prepared in response to a major change in the means by which communications are made between parties using computerized or other modern techniques in doing business (sometimes referred to as "trading partners"). The Model Law is intended to serve as a model to countries for the evaluation and modernization of certain aspects of their laws and practices in the field of commercial relationships involving the use of computerized or other modern communication techniques, and for the establishment of relevant legislation where none presently exists. The text of the Model Law, as reproduced above, is set forth in annex I to the report of UNCITRAL on the work of its twenty-ninth session.(3)

125. The Commission, at its seventeenth session (1984), considered a report of the Secretary-General entitled "Legal aspects of automatic data processing" *(A/CN.9/254)*, which identified several legal issues relating to the legal value of computer records, the requirement of a "writing", authentication, general conditions, liability and bills of lading. The Commission took note of a report of the Working Party on

Facilitation of International Trade Procedures (WP.4), which is jointly sponsored by the Economic Commission for Europe and the United Nations Conference on Trade and Development, and is responsible for the development of UN/EDIFACT standard messages. That report suggested that, since the legal problems arising in this field were essentially those of international trade law, the Commission as the core legal body in the field of international trade law appeared to be the appropriate central forum to undertake and coordinate the necessary action.(4) The Commission decided to place the subject of the legal implications of automatic data processing to the flow of international trade on its programme of work as a priority item.(5)

126. At its eighteenth session *(1985),* the Commission had before it a report by the Secretariat entitled "Legal value of computer records" *(A/CN.9/265).* That report came to the conclusion that, on a global level, there were fewer problems in the use of data stored in computers as evidence in litigation than might have been expected. It noted that a more serious legal obstacle to the use of computers and computer-to-computer telecommunications in international trade arose out of requirements that documents had to be signed or be in paper form. After discussion of the report, the Commission adopted the following recommendation, which expresses some of the principles on which the Model Law is based:

"The United Nations Commission on International Trade Law,

"*Noting* that the use of automatic data processing (ADP) is about to become firmly established throughout the world in many phases of domestic and international trade as well as in administrative services,

"*Noting* also that legal rules based upon pre-ADP paper-based means of documenting international trade may create an obstacle to such use of ADP in that they lead to legal insecurity or impede the efficient use of ADP where its use is otherwise justified,

"*Noting* further with appreciation the efforts of the Council of Europe, the Customs Co-operation Council and the United Nations Economic Commission for Europe to overcome obstacles to the use of ADP in international trade arising out of these legal rules,

"Considering at the same time that there is no need for a unification of the rules of evidence regarding the use of computer records in international trade, in view of the experience showing that substantial differences in the rules of evidence as they apply to the paper-based system of documentation have caused so far no noticeable harm to the development of international trade,

"Considering also that the developments in the use of ADP are creating a desirability in a number of legal systems for an adaptation of existing legal rules to these developments, having due regard, however, to the need to encourage the employment of such ADP means that would provide the same or greater reliability as paper-based documentation,

"1. *Recommends* to Governments:

"(a) to review the legal rules affecting the use of computer records as evidence in litigation in order to eliminate unnecessary obstacles to their admission, to be assured that the rules are consistent with developments in technology, and to provide appropriate means for a court to evaluate the credibility of the data contained in those records;

"(b) to review legal requirements that certain trade transactions or trade related documents be in writing, whether the written form is a condition to the enforceability or to the validity of the transaction or document, with a view to permitting, where appropriate, the transaction or document to be recorded and transmitted in computer-readable form;

"(c) to review legal requirements of a handwritten signature or other paper-based method of authentication on trade related documents with a view to permitting, where appropriate, the use of electronic means of authentication;

"(d) to review legal requirements that documents for submission to governments be in writing and manually signed with a view to permitting, where appropriate, such documents to be submitted in computer-readable form to those administrative services which have acquired the necessary equipment and established the necessary procedures;

"2. *Recommends* to international organizations elaborating legal texts related to trade to take account of the present Recommendation in adopting such texts and, where appropriate, to consider modifying existing legal texts in line with the present Recommendation."(6)

127. That recommendation (hereinafter referred to as the "1985 UNCITRAL Recommendation") was endorsed by the General Assembly in resolution 40/71, paragraph *5(b)*, of 11 December 1985 as follows:

"The General Assembly,

". . . Calls upon Governments and international organizations to take action, where appropriate, in conformity with the Commission 's recommendation so as to ensure legal security in the context of the widest possible use of automated data processing in international trade; . . .".(7)

128. As was pointed out in several documents and meetings involving the international electronic commerce community, e.g. in meetings of WP. 4, there was a general feeling that, in spite of the efforts made through the 1985 UNCITRAL Recommendation, little progress had been made to achieve the removal of the mandatory requirements in national legislation regarding the use of paper and handwritten signatures. It has been suggested by the Norwegian Committee on Trade Procedures (NORPRO) in a letter to the Secretariat that "one reason for this could be that the 1985 UNCITRAL Recommendation advises on the need for legal update, but does not give any indication of how it could be done". In this vein, the Commission considered what follow-up action to the 1985 UNCITRAL Recommendation could usefully be taken so as to enhance the needed modernization of legislation. The decision by UNCITRAL to formulate model legislation on legal issues of electronic data interchange and related means of communication may be regarded as a consequence of the process that led to the adoption by the Commission of the 1985 UNCITRAL Recommendation.

129. At its twenty-first session (1988), the Commission considered a proposal to examine the need to provide for the legal principles that would apply to the formation of international commercial contracts by electronic means. It was noted that there existed no refined legal structure for the important and rapidly growing field of formation of contracts by electronic means and that future work in that area could help to fill a legal vacuum and to reduce uncertainties and difficulties encountered in practice. The Commission requested the Secretariat to prepare a preliminary study on the topic.(8)

130. At its twenty-third session (1990), the Commission had before it a report entitled "Preliminary study of legal issues related to the forma-

tion of contracts by electronic means" (A/CN.9/333). The report summarized work that had been undertaken in the European Communities and in the United States of America on the requirement of a "writing" as well as other issues that had been identified as arising in the formation of contracts by electronic means. The efforts to overcome some of those problems by the use of model communication agreements were also discussed.(9)

131. At its twenty-fourth session (1991), the Commission had before it a report entitled "Electronic Data Interchange" *(A/CN.9/350)*. The report described the current activities in the various organizations involved in the legal issues of electronic data interchange (EDI) and analysed the contents of a number of standard interchange agreements already developed or then being developed. It pointed out that such documents varied considerably according to the various needs of the different categories of users they were intended to serve and that the variety of contractual arrangements had sometimes been described as hindering the development of a satisfactory legal framework for the business use of electronic commerce. It suggested that there was a need for a general framework that would identify the issues and provide a set of legal principles and basic legal rules governing communication through electronic commerce. It concluded that such a basic framework could, to a certain extent, be created by contractual arrangements between parties to an electronic commerce relationship and that the existing contractual frameworks that were proposed to the community of users of electronic commerce were often incomplete, mutually incompatible, and inappropriate for international use since they relied to a large extent upon the structures of local law.

132. With a view to achieving the harmonization of basic rules for the promotion of electronic commerce in international trade, the report suggested that the Commission might wish to consider the desirability of preparing a standard communication agreement for use in international trade. It pointed out that work by the Commission in this field would be of particular importance since it would involve participation of all legal systems, including those of developing countries that were already or would soon be confronted with the issues of electronic commerce.

133. The Commission was agreed that the legal issues of electronic commerce would become increasingly important as the use of electronic commerce developed and that it should undertake work in that field. There was wide support for the suggestion that the Commission should undertake the preparation of a set of legal principles and basic

legal rules governing communication through electronic commerce.(10) The Commission came to the conclusion that it would be premature to engage immediately in the preparation of a standard communication agreement and that it might be preferable to monitor developments in other organizations, particularly the Commission of the European Communities and the Economic Commission for Europe. It was pointed out that high-speed electronic commerce required a new examination of basic contract issues such as offer and acceptance, and that consideration should be given to legal implications of the role of central data managers in international commercial law.

134. After deliberation, the Commission decided that a session of the Working Group on International Payments would be devoted to identifying the legal issues involved and to considering possible statutory provisions, and that the Working Group would report to the Commission on the desirability and feasibility of undertaking further work such as the preparation of a standard communication agreement.(11)

135. The Working Group on International Payments, at its twenty-fourth session, recommended that the Commission should undertake work towards establishing uniform legal rules on electronic commerce. It was agreed that the goals of such work should be to facilitate the increased use of electronic commerce and to meet the need for statutory provisions to be developed in the field of electronic commerce, particularly with respect to such issues as formation of contracts; risk and liability of commercial partners and third-party service providers involved in electronic commerce relationships; extended definitions of "writing" and "original" to be used in an electronic commerce environment; and issues of negotiability and documents of title (A/CN.9/360).

136. While it was generally felt that it was desirable to seek the high degree of legal certainty and harmonization provided by the detailed provisions of a uniform law, it was also felt that care should be taken to preserve a flexible approach to some issues where legislative action might be premature or inappropriate. As an example of such an issue, it was stated that it might be fruitless to attempt to provide legislative unification of the rules on evidence that may apply to electronic commerce massaging (ibid., para. 130). It was agreed that no decision should be taken at that early stage as to the final form or the final content of the legal rules to be prepared. In line with the flexible approach to be taken, it was noted that situations might arise where the preparation of model contractual clauses would be regarded as an appropriate way of addressing specific issues (ibid., para. 132).

137. The Commission, at its twenty-fifth session (1992), endorsed the recommendation contained in the report of the Working Group (ibid., paras. 129-133) and entrusted the preparation of legal rules on electronic commerce (which was then referred to as "electronic data interchange" or "EDI") to the Working Group on International Payments, which it renamed the Working Group on Electronic Data Interchange.(12)

138. The Working Group devoted its twenty-fifth to twenty-eighth sessions to the preparation of legal rules applicable to "electronic data interchange (EDI) and other modern means of communication" (reports of those sessions are found in documents A/CN.9/373, 387, 390 and 406).(13)

139. The Working Group carried out its task on the basis of background working papers prepared by the Secretariat on possible issues to be included in the Model Law. Those background papers included A/CN.9/WG.IV/WP.53 (Possible issues to be included in the programme of future work on the legal aspects of EDI) and A/CN.9/WG.IV/WP.55 (Outline of possible uniform rules on the legal aspects of electronic data interchange). The draft articles of the Model Law were submitted by the Secretariat in documents A/CN.9/WG.IV/WP.57, 60 and 62. The Working Group also had before it a proposal by the United Kingdom of Great Britain and Northern Ireland relating to the possible contents of the draft Model Law (A/CN.9/WG.IV/WP.58).

140. The Working Group noted that, while practical solutions to the legal difficulties raised by the use of electronic commerce were often sought within contracts (A/CN.9/WG.IV/WP.53, paras. 35-36), the contractual approach to electronic commerce was developed not only because of its intrinsic advantages such as its flexibility, but also for lack of specific provisions of statutory or case law. The contractual approach was found to be limited in that it could not overcome any of the legal obstacles to the use of electronic commerce that might result from mandatory provisions of applicable statutory or case law. In that respect, one difficulty inherent in the use of communication agreements resulted from uncertainty as to the weight that would be carried by some contractual stipulations in case of litigation. Another limitation to the contractual approach resulted from the fact that parties to a contract could not effectively regulate the rights and obligations of third parties. At least for those parties not participating in the contractual arrangement, statutory law based on a model law or an international convention seemed to be needed (see *A/CN.9/350,* para. 107).

141. The Working Group considered preparing uniform rules with the aim of eliminating the legal obstacles to, and uncertainties in, the use of modern communication techniques, where effective removal of such obstacles and uncertainties could only be achieved by statutory provisions. One purpose of the uniform rules was to enable potential electronic commerce users to establish a legally secure electronic commerce relationship by way of a communication agreement within a closed network. The second purpose of the uniform rules was to support the use of electronic commerce outside such a closed network, i.e., in an open environment. However, the aim of the uniform rules was to enable, and not to impose, the use of EDI and related means of communication. Moreover, the aim of the uniform rules was not to deal with electronic commerce relationships from a technical perspective but rather to create a legal environment that would be as secure as possible, so as to facilitate the use of electronic commerce between communicating parties.

142. As to the form of the uniform rules, the Working Group was agreed that it should proceed with its work on the assumption that the uniform rules should be prepared in the form of statutory provisions. While it was agreed that the form of the text should be that of a "model law", it was felt, at first, that, owing to the special nature of the legal text being prepared, a more flexible term than "model law" needed to be found. It was observed that the title should reflect that the text contained a variety of provisions relating to existing rules scattered throughout various parts of the national laws in an enacting State. It was thus a possibility that enacting States would not incorporate the text as a whole and that the provisions of such a "model law" might not appear together in any one particular place in the national law. The text could be described, in the parlance of one legal system, as a "miscellaneous statute amendment act". The Working Group agreed that this special nature of the text would be better reflected by the use of the term "model statutory provisions". The view was also expressed that the nature and purpose of the "model statutory provisions" could be explained in an introduction or guidelines accompanying the text.

143. At its twenty-eighth session, however, the Working Group reviewed its earlier decision to formulate a legal text in the form of "model statutory provisions" (A/CN.9/390, para. 16). It was widely felt that the use of the term "model statutory provisions" might raise uncertainties as to the legal nature of the instrument. While some support was expressed for the retention of the term "model statutory provisions the widely prevailing view was that the term "model law" should be preferred. It was widely felt that, as a result of the course

taken by the Working Group as its work progressed towards the completion of the text, the model statutory provisions could be regarded as a balanced and discrete set of rules, which could also be implemented as a whole in a single instrument (A/CN.9/406, para. *75)*. Depending on the situation in each enacting State, however, the Model Law could be implemented in various ways, either as a single statute or in various pieces of legislation.

144. The text of the draft Model Law as approved by the Working Group at its twenty-eighth session was sent to all Governments and to interested international organizations for comment. The comments received were reproduced in document A/CN.9/409 and Add.1-4. The text of the draft articles of the Model Law as presented to the Commission by the Working Group was contained in the annex to document A/CN.9/406.

145. At its twenty-eighth session *(1995),* the Commission adopted the text of articles 1 and 3 to 11 of the draft Model Law and, for lack of sufficient time, did not complete its review of the draft Model Law, which was placed on the agenda of the twenty-ninth session of the Commission.(14)

146. The Commission, at its twenty-eighth session,(15) recalled that, at its twenty-seventh session (1994), general support had been expressed in favour of a recommendation made by the Working Group that preliminary work should be undertaken on the issue of negotiability and transferability of rights in goods in a computer-based environment as soon as the preparation of the Model Law had been completed.(16) It was noted that, on that basis, a preliminary debate with respect to future work to be undertaken in the field of electronic data interchange had been held in the context of the twenty-ninth session of the Working Group (for the report on that debate, see A/CN.9/407, paras. 106-118). At that session, the Working Group also considered proposals by the International Chamber of Commerce *(A/CN.9/WG.IV/ WP.65)* and the United Kingdom of Great Britain and Northern Ireland (A/CN.9/WG.IV/WP.66) relating to the possible inclusion in the draft Model Law of additional provisions to the effect of ensuring that certain terms and conditions that might be incorporated in a data message by means of a mere reference would be recognized as having the same degree of legal effectiveness as if they had been fully stated in the text of the data message (for the report on the discussion, see A/CN.9/407, paras. 100-105). It was agreed that the issue of incorporation by reference might need to be considered in the context of future work on negotiability and transferability of rights in goods

(A/CN.9/407, para. 103). The Commission endorsed the recommendation made by the Working Group that the Secretariat should be
entrusted with the preparation of a background study on negotiability
and transferability of EDI transport documents, with particular emphasis on EDI maritime transport documents, taking into account the
views expressed and the suggestions made at the twenty-ninth session
of the Working Group.(17)

147. On the basis of the study prepared by the Secretariat (A/CN.9/
WG.IV/WP.69), the Working Group, at its thirtieth session, discussed
the issues of transferability of rights in the context of transport
documents and approved the text of draft statutory provisions dealing
with the specific issues of contracts of carriage of goods involving the
use of data messages (for the report on that session, see A/CN.9/421).
The text of those draft provisions as presented to the Commission by
the Working Group for final review and possible addition as part II of
the Model Law was contained in the annex to document A/CN.9/
421.

148. In preparing the Model Law, the Working Group noted that it
would be useful to provide in a commentary additional information
concerning the Model Law. In particular, at the twenty-eighth session
of the Working Group, during which the text of the draft Model Law
was finalized for submission to the Commission, there was general
support for a suggestion that the draft Model Law should be accompanied by a guide to assist States in enacting and applying the draft Model
Law. The guide, much of which could be drawn from the *travaux
prjiaratoires* of the draft Model Law, would also be helpful to users of
electronic means of communication as well as to scholars in that area.
The Working Group noted that, during its deliberations at that session,
it had proceeded on the assumption that the draft Model Law would be
accompanied by a guide. For example, the Working Group had
decided in respect of a number of issues not to settle them in the draft
Model Law but to address them in the guide so as to provide guidance
to States enacting the draft Model Law. The Secretariat was requested
to prepare a draft and submit it to the Working Group for consideration at its twenty-ninth session (A/CN.9/406, para. 177).

149. At its twenty-ninth session, the Working Group discussed the draft
Guide to Enactment of the Model Law (hereinafter referred to as "the
draft Guide") as set forth in a note prepared by the Secretariat
(A/CN.9/WG.IV/WP.64). The Secretariat was requested to prepare a
revised version of the draft Guide reflecting the decisions made by the
Working Group and taking into account the various views, suggestions

and concerns that had been expressed at that session. At its twenty-eighth session, the Commission placed the draft Guide to Enactment of the Model Law on the agenda of its twenty-ninth session.(18)

150. At its twenty-ninth session (1996), the Commission, after consideration of the text of the draft Model Law as revised by the drafting group, adopted the following decision at its 605th meeting, on 12 June 1996:

"The United Nations Commission on International Trade Law,

"*Recalling* its mandate under General Assembly resolution 2205 (XXI) of 17 December 1966 to further the progressive harmonization and unification of the law of international trade, and in that respect to bear in mind the interests of all peoples, and in particular those of developing countries, in the extensive development of international trade,

"Noting that an increasing number of transactions in international trade are carried out by means of electronic data interchange and other means of communication commonly referred to as 'electronic commerce', which involve the use of alternatives to paper-based forms of communication and storage of information,

"*Recalling* the recommendation on the legal value of computer records adopted by the Commission at its eighteenth session, in 1985, and paragraph *5(b)* of General Assembly resolution 40/71 of 11 December 1985 calling upon Governments and international organizations to take action, where appropriate, in conformity with the recommendation of the Commission(19) so as to ensure legal security in the context of the widest possible use of automated data processing in international trade,

"*Being of the opinion* that the establishment of a model law facilitating the use of electronic commerce, and acceptable to States with different legal, social and economic systems, contributes to the development of harmonious international economic relations,

"*Being convinced* that the UNCITRAL Model Law on Electronic Commerce will significantly assist all States in enhancing their legislation governing the use of alternatives to paper-based forms of communication and storage of information, and in formulating such legislation where none currently exists,

"1. *Adopts* the UNCITRAL Model Law on Electronic Commerce as it appears in annex I to the report on the current session;

"2. *Requests* the Secretary-General to transmit the text of the UNCITRAL Model Law on Electronic Commerce, together with the Guide to Enactment of the Model Law prepared by the Secretariat, to Governments and other interested bodies;

"3. *Recommends* that all States give favourable consideration to the UNCITRAL Model Law on Electronic Commerce when they enact or revise their laws, in view of the need for uniformity of the law applicable to alternatives to paper-based forms of communication and storage of information.(20)

Footnotes

1. See Official Records of the Genera lAssembly, Fortieth Session, Supplement No. 17 (A/40/17), chap. VI, sect. B.
2. Reference materials listed by symbols in this Guide belong to the following three categories of documents:
    A/50/17 and A/S 1/17 are the reports of UNCITRAL to the General Assembly on the work of its twenty-eighth and twenty-ninth sessions, held in 1995 and 1996, respectively;
    A/CN.9/ . . . documents are reports and notes discussed by UNCITRAL in the context of its annual session, including reports presented by the Working Group to the Commission;
    A/CN.9/WG.IV/ . . . documents are working papers considered by the UNCITRAL Working Group on Electronic Commerce (formerly known as the UNCITRAL Working Group on Electronic Data Interchange) in the preparation of the Model Law.
3. Official Records of the General Assembly, Fifty-first Session, Supplement No. 17 (A/51/17), Annex I.
4. "Legal aspects of automatic trade data interchange" (TRADE/WP.4/R.185/Rev.1). The report submitted to the Working Party is reproduced in A/CN.9/238, annex.
5. Official_Records of the General Assembly, Thirty-ninth Session, Supplement No. 17 (A/39/17), para. 136.

6. Official Records of the General Assembly, Fortieth Session, Supplement No. 17 (A/40/17), para. 360.
7. Resolution 40/71 was reproduced in United Nations Commission on International Trade Law Yearbook, 1985, vol. XVI, Part One, D. (United Nations publication, Sales No. E.87.V.4).
8. Official Records of the General Assembly, Forty-third Session, Supplement No. 17 (A/43/17), paras. 46 and 47, and ibid., Forty-fourth Session, Supplement No. 17 (A/44/17), para. 289.
9. Ibid., Forty-fifth Session, Supplement No.17 (A/45/17), paras. 38 to 40.
10. It may be noted that the Model Law is not intended to provide a comprehensive set of rules governing all aspects of electronic commerce. The main purpose of the Model Law is to adapt existing statutory requirements so that they would no longer constitute obstacles to the use of paperless means of communication and storage of information.
11. Official Records of the General Assembly, Forty-sixth Session, Supplement No. 17 (A/46/17), paras. 311 to 317.
12. Ibid., Forty-seventh Session Supplement No. 17 (A/47/17), paras. 141 to 148.
13. The notion of "EDI and related means of communication" as used by the Working Group is not to be construed as a reference to narrowly defined EDI under article 2(b) of the Model Law but to a variety of trade-related uses of modern communication techniques that was later referred to broadly under the rubric of "electronic commerce". The Model Law is not intended only for application in the context of existing communication techniques but rather as a set of flexible rules that should accommodate foreseeable technical developments. It should also be emphasized that the purpose of the Model Law is not only to establish rules for the movement of information communicated by means of data messages but equally to deal with the storage of information in data messages that are not intended for communication.
14. Official Records of the General Assembly, Fiftieth Session, Supplement No. 17 (A/50/17), para. 306.
15. Ibid., para. 307.
16. Ibid_ Forty-ninth Session, Supplement No. 17 (A/49/17), para. 201.
17. Ibid., Fiftieth Session, Supplement No. 17 (A/5O/17), para. 309.
18. Ibid., para. 306.
19. Ibid_ Fortieth Session, Supplement No. 17 (A/40/17), paras. 354–360.
20. Ibid., Fifty-first Session, Supplement No. 17 (A/51/17), para. 209.

Appendix 8

GUIDEC: General Usage for International Digitally Ensured Commerce; a Living Document

Restrictions

The GUIDEC is a copyrighted work of the ICC.

Preface

This General Usage for International Digitally Ensured Commerce (GUIDEC) has been drafted by the International Chamber of Commerce (ICC) Information Security Working Party, under the auspices of the ICC Electronic Commerce Project. The ICC Electronic Commerce Project is an international, multidisciplinary effort to study, facilitate and promote the emerging global electronic trading system. Existing ICC Commissions participating in the Electronic Commerce Project include the commissions on Banking, Air Transport, Maritime and Surface Transport, Computing, Telecommunications and Information Policies, Commercial Practices, Financial Services and Insurance to provide a globally comprehensive approach to implementing digital commerce.

The Electronic Commerce project brings together leading corporations, lawyers, information technology specialists, government representatives and industry associations world-wide to focus on pivotal issues in digital commerce. Electronic Commerce working groups have been formed to examine specific critical issues in the context of digital commerce.

The proposal to develop international guidelines was raised at the ICC in November 1995 in the context of ICC work on the legal aspects of electronic commerce and on the establishment of an international chain of registration and certification authorities.

Upon examination, the ICC and its Electronic Commerce Project determined that the issues involved in electronic commerce, including the use of digital signatures, and the role of certification authorities in enabling their use, were sufficiently complex to merit a distinct new group.

The GUIDEC was first drafted and discussed under the name of the Uniform International Authentication and Certification Practices (UIACP). During the consultation period the title was changed to the current GUIDEC to reflect the use of the word 'Ensure' in the title (for a definition and explanation of this concept, see post).

The GUIDEC aims to draw together the key elements involved in electronic commerce, to serve as an indicator of terms and an exposition of the general background to the issue. It also addresses one of the key problems in talking about electronically signed messages, in that they are not signed physically , but require the intervention of an electronic medium.

This in turn alters the function of the signer , and introduces problems which a physical signature does not encounter, most especially the possibility of use of the medium by a third party. The GUIDEC therefore adopts a specific term , 'ensure', to describe what elsewhere is called a 'digital signature' or 'authentication', in an attempt to remove the element of ambiguity inherent to other terms employed.

Contents

General Usage in International Digitally Ensured Commerce

Preface

I. Background

1.   Scope and Objectives

2.   Underlying Policies of the GUIDEC

II. The Advent of Commercial Electronic Transactions

1.   The Emerging Global Electronic Trading System
2.   EDI and Closed Networks
3.   EDI and Efficiencies derived from electronic forms
4.   EDI Trading Agreements
5.   Transition from Closed Systems to Open Systems and the Internet

III. Electronic Transactions and Information Security

1.   Open Networks
2.   Information Security
3.   Public Key Cryptography and Digital Signatures
4.   Ensuring and Certification Authorities
5.   Biometric Technology

IV. Existing Law and Electronic Transactions

1.   General
2.   Form Requirements
3.   Common Law Issues
4.   Civil Law Issues
5.   Consequences

V. International Legal Approaches

1.   UNCITRAL Model Law on Electronic Commerce

The Core Concepts

VI. Glossary of Terms

1.   Ensure
2.   Certificate
3.   Certification Practice Statement
4.   Certifier
5.   Repository
6.   Digital Signature
7.   Hold a private key
8.   Human-readable form
9.   Issue a certificate
10.   Notice
11.   Person
12.   Public key certificate
13.   Revoke a public key certificate
14.   Subscriber

15. Suspend a public key certificate
16. Technologically reliable
17. Trustworthy
18. Valid certificate
19. Verify a digital signature

Best Practices

VII. Ensuring a message

1. Ensuring a message as a Factual Matter
2. Attribution and Legal Significance of Ensuring a Message
3. Ensuring a message by an Agent
4. Appropriate Practices for Ensuring a Message
5. Scope of an Ensured Message
6. Safeguarding an Ensuring Device
7. Representations to a Certifier

VIII. Certification

1. Effect of a Valid Certificate
2. Accuracy of Representations in Certificate
3. Trustworthiness of a Certifier
4. Notice of Practices and Problems
5. Financial Ressources
6. Records
7. Termination of a Certifier's Business
8. Suspension of Public Key Certificate by Request
9. Revocation of Public Key Certificate by Request
10. Suspension or Revocation of Public Key Certificate Without Consent
11. Notice of Revocation or Suspension of a Public Key Certificate

Conclusion

GUIDEC

General Usage in International Digitally Ensured Commerce

I. Background:

1. Scope and Objectives

This document is intended to provide the context and policy under-pinnings of the GUIDEC, with the objective of promoting the world business community's understanding of the issues relating to the use of techniques in electronic commerce. In its effort to balance different legal traditions, the GUIDEC reflects both the civil and common-law treatment of the subject as well as pertinent international principles. In doing so, the GUIDEC presents both business and governments with a comprehensive statement of best practices for the emerging global infrastructure.

The GUIDEC also attempts to address the problem of terminology, in that a digital signature is not really a signature at all. It has therefore employed the term 'Ensure', to denote the act of digitally signing an electronic message. Please refer to the explanation given in the section on 'Core Concepts' for a fuller explanation.

2. Underlying Policies of the GUIDEC

The principle objective of the GUIDEC is to establish a general framework for the ensuring and certification of digital messages, based upon existing law and practice in different legal systems. In so doing the GUIDEC provides a detailed explanation of ensuring and certifi-cation principles, particularly as they relate to information system security issues and public key cryptographic techniques. It also provides succinct standard practices or recommendations relating to ensuring or secure authentication of digital information, and comments upon relevant Civil and Common Law issues.

The GUIDEC framework attempts to allocate risk and liability equitably between transacting parties in accordance with existing business practice, and includes a clear description of the rights and responsibilities of subscribers, certifiers, and relying parties.

The underlying policies articulated and promoted in the GUIDEC are:

1. to enhance the ability of the international business community to execute secure digital transactions;
2. to establish legal principles that promote trustworthy and reliable digital ensuring and certification practices;
3. to encourage the development of trustworthy ensuring and certification systems;
4. to protect users of the digital information infrastructure from fraud and errors;
5. to balance ensuring and certification technologies with existing policies, laws, customs and practices;
6. to define and clarify the duties of participants in the emerging ensuring and certification system, and;
7. to foster global awareness of developments in ensuring and certification technology and its relationship to secure electronic commerce.

The GUIDEC treats the core concepts, best practices and certification issues in the context of international commercial law and practice. In so doing, the document assumes practices in which transacting parties are expert commercial actors, operating under the lex mercatoria. The document does not attempt to define rights and responsibilities for transactions involving consumers. Neither is it intended to outline practices for transactions in which overriding national or other public interests may demand additional transactional security, such as notarial or other public intervention, although many notarial principles are enshrined in the document. In this regard, it is also important to note that the GUIDEC does not attempt to set out rules for certification of information relating to authority, legal competence, etc., which notaries are often called upon to certify.

Although the GUIDEC is organised primarily as an outline for parties involved in public key based systems (i.e., 'digital signatures'), the fact that it draws upon existing law means that it is not technology specific; it may be equally applied to paper-based and other methods for ensuring.

The GUIDEC acknowledges the groundwork laid out in the Digital Signature Guidelines of the Information Security Committee of the

Science and Technology Division of the American Bar Association, and attempts to enhance some of the concepts set out therein from an international and commercial point of view.

The document also draws upon and extends existing international law treatment of digital signatures in particular that articulated in the United Nations Model Law on Electronic Commerce (UNCITRAL Model Law).

II. The Advent of Electronic Commercial Transactions

1. The Emerging Global Electronic Trading System

The movement of commercial and other related information has become a critical part of the international trading infrastructure. Businesses throughout the world are transmitting and exchanging commercial information, software, and services electronically, setting the stage for a revolution in the way commerce is transacted. Fuelling this revolution are the substantial efficiencies to be gained from the transition from paper-based to electronic data exchange in the global economy. The rapid evolution of digital communications technologies and expansion of computer networks form the basis for the emerging global electronic trading system.

Electronic Data exchange technologies, such as electronic data interchange (EDI), have long held the promise for a less burdensome, more highly efficient system for transacting global business, as well as the possibility for creating new channels for distribution, sales, and licensing. Overall, the application of digital technologies to business ommunications have offered a powerful new means for international commercial expansion, permitting businesses to forge new paths toward higher productivity, competitiveness and growth.

2. EDI and Closed Networks

Until recently, businesses engaging in electronic commerce did so solely over closed networks. Closed network communication systems permitted businesses to control physical access to the system, conduct communications according to written and approved procedures, maintain record systems designed to facilitate quality assurance, and created legal obligations between users and the organisation responsible for operating the system. Closed network technologies such as electronic data interchange (EDI) combined the functional capabilities of computers and telecommunications, permitting the computer-to-computer transmission of commercial information. Through EDI technology, two parties could directly exchange information electronically, reducing and in some cases eliminating the use of paper. By decreasing reliance on paper in business-to-business communications, EDI technology has dramatically affected the way commercial relationships are conducted and defined.

Through EDI, business have been able to communicate with greater speed, respond faster to business demand, and significantly reduce repetitive computer input, inventory needs, time needed to market products, and errors in commercial data exchange.

EDI therefore represents an important first step towards overcoming the traditional physical barriers to a seamless and efficient global trading system.

3. EDI and Efficiencies derived from electronic forms

The use of EDI technology requires parties to agree on a broad range of technical issues including those related to message format, standards and implementation guidelines, third party providers, and computer and communications development and maintenance. The process of negotiating and implementing these agreements resulted in the emergence of electronic forms, enabling electronic data communications between distant commercial parties according to pre-arranged standards. Today, electronic forms have evolved into a highly efficient vehicle for the exchange of standardised information, facilitating purchases and sales with minimal human intervention. Electronic forms offer standard message formats enabling automated data handling and eliminating language and interpretation problems between senders and receivers of electronic data. The use of electronic forms permit highly efficient means of storing and reconstituting data, enhance the speed, accuracy and security, and reduce the expenses and delays normally associated with traditional modes of data transmissions between commercial actors. Overall, the development of electronic forms have established economies of scale and permitted the fulfilment of digital communications less expensively than was previously possible.

4. EDI Trading Agreements

EDI trading agreements (or 'interchange agreements') have also served a critical function in facilitating a global electronic trading system. The use of EDI trading agreements has evolved in the absence of standardised rules governing the complete data exchange process. Through these private agreements, parties seeking to use EDI technology have been able to structure their electronic communications relationship and benefit from contractual allocations of responsibilities and liabilities arising in that exchange. The use of private agreements to govern electronic trading arrangements through the use of EDI confers important benefits. Trading partners used contractual agreements to minimise risk and address legal uncertainties for activities that may not yet have been adequately addressed by law. Through such private agreements, parties could analyse and provide for the appropriate allocation of risk, including risk of errors or omissions in the electronic transmission or the apportionment of liability for the acts of third parties. Electronic interchange agreements have also allowed parties to specify procedures and safeguards needed to protect system security and integrity and address critical issues such as the extent of access to and use of data transmitted electronically and the confidentiality of that data. Electronic trading agreements have thereby offered parties a flexible means by which they could establish specific procedures and conditions by which to govern their rights and obligations within the framework established by their technological arrangement.

The earliest international mode interchange agreement was published by the ICC as long ago as 1987 in response to the need for harmonised principles promoting certainty in electronic commercial transactions conducted through EDI, as well as the need to promote parity between trading partners. These Uniform Rules of Conduct for Interchange of Trade Data by Teletransmission (UN-CID) have serves as the basis for many of the model or standard trading agreements issued by national, regional and sectoral organisations.

Despite significant differences, many of these model agreements address common issues, including technical requirements, acknowledgement or verification, third party service providers, record storage and audit trails, digital security, confidentiality, and data protection. In doing so, the development of model trading agreements established the foundation for a contractually-based legal structure for electronic commerce.

5. Transition from Closed Systems to Open Systems and the Internet

The fast pace of technological innovation and the increasing development and adoption of universal standards both as communication protocols and for message development have permitted the proliferation of computer networks that are inter-operable and interconnected. User demands have also evolved, as businesses world-wide seek technological tools to strengthen productivity and minimise costs. Together, these developments are establishing a new information infrastructure of 'open' networks, such as the Internet, enabling a truly global electronic trading infrastructure. The proliferation of business applications for these open, non-proprietary networks holds the promise of a new platform for inexpensive global communication and electronic commerce. Open network systems offer access and communication between multiple parties not contractually obligated to system managers, thereby exposing businesses to trading partners with whom those businesses have no prior relationship.

Unlike closed network systems like EDI, which have traditionally developed along defined lines and been implemented between existing trading partners with ongoing commercial relationships, open network systems offer the possibility for broadening market access to new participants and provide a means for potential trading partners to conduct business through exchanges of information in the absence of a pre-existing relationship.

III. Electronic Transactions and Information Security

1. Open Networks

The current movement from closed network to open network communications systems, such as the Internet, poses significant challenges to implementation of a global electronic trading system. Among the most significant barriers to global electronic commerce over open networks are those pertaining to information security. Conducting commercial transactions over open networks poses the challenge of 'many-to-many' transactions. With the expanding use of publicly available infrastructures such as the Internet to effect corporate communication among geographically dispersed locations, securing transactions that occur over this infrastructure becomes of paramount importance. The importance of security and reducing the risk of fraud and unauthorised access will increase significantly with the growth of the number and volume of international commercial transactions over networked computers.

Information security refers to the level of trust present in the transfer of information between parties. In its simplest form, information security issues arise when information is transferred from one party (a sender) to another party (a recipient). Information security risk is compounded when commercial dealings are transacted over open networks such as the Internet, which is a public infrastructure and for which no single locus of responsibility exists.

Companies engaging in electronic commerce over closed network systems, nowadays called 'Intranets', had assurance of the identity and authority of transacting parties through contractual agreements and closed network security procedures. In open networks, however, these mechanisms for establishing the technical and legal security of transactions are no longer adequate to prevent unauthorised access, fraud or other commercially detrimental risks.

Industry recognises the need for a reliable framework for ensuring and certifying parties to a transaction. New technologies for strengthening the reliability and security for digital commercial transactions are developing every day. However, without an underlying legal framework for information security, these technological innovations cannot deliver their promise of a truly trustworthy electronic commercial environment.

Infrastructure solutions should be industry-driven, with government providing support through legislation and international agreements. An efficient and fully effective information security infrastructure for digital commerce over open networks cannot be realised only by contractual means, particularly with respect to resolving security issues. As electronic transactions become commonplace and involve ever more numerous potential parties, the need for a more generally applicable legal approach increases. This General Usage in International Digitally Ensured Commerce attempts to enhance legal predictability by providing a statement of commercial ensuring and certifying practices, thereby enhancing the overall level of trust in the electronic information infrastructure.

2. Information Security

Security systems for commercial transactions have long been developed and established by businesses seeking to raise the level of trust in commercial transactions. Existing systems include those used for checks, telephone trading, and credit card purchases. Stronger systems are needed for use on open networks, given the challenges posed by the increased number of users, vulnerability to computer hackers, and the risk of unauthorised access.

Ensuring, as defined within this document, presents the opportunity for higher security in electronic commercial transactions, thereby raising the level of trust that will be placed by users in the global communications infrastructure. Through specific cryptographic technologies, including digital signatures, a new infrastructure is emerging that offers the key benefits of higher levels of non-repudiation, message integrity and verification.

3. Public Key Cryptography and Digital Signatures

Public key encryption assures two things for commercial actors:

a)   that their messages are secure, and

b)   that other transacting parties are authenticated.

Using this technology, senders and receivers of electronic messages each possess two keys – -a public key and a private key – one of which is never shared with anybody, and the other of which is shared with everyone.

These two keys correspond to each other, so that whatever is encoded with one key can only be decoded by the other. In the encrypting process, the sender of the message encodes it with the recipient's public key (which has been shared with him and all other parties), making it impossible for any party other than the one holding the private key to decrypt the message. Encryption protects the message from all parties other than the recipient, without the recipient having to divulge his private key to the sender.

By reversing the process described above, public key cryptography also provides a highly dependable mechanism, known in the GUIDEC as 'ensuring a message', or within a Public Key Infrastructure as a 'digital signature'.

This ensuring, or digital signature, is an attachment to a set of data which is composed by taking the output of a hash function, or digest, of the original data that is encrypted with the sender's private key. The hash function puts the original data through an algorithm, resulting in a data sequence unique to a particular message but much shorter than the message itself. The resulting digital signature can only be decrypted if the recipient has the correct public key, thereby permitting a recipient to verify the identity of the sender. In a given transaction, therefore, the sender encrypts the message with the public key of the recipient, and digitally signs or ensures the message with his own private key, and the recipient uses his private key to decrypt the message, and the public key of the sender to verify the message ensured.

Because an ensured message is difficult to forge, its use binds the signatory, precluding a later repudiation of the message. Digital signature technology also forms the basis for forming legally binding contracts in the course of electronic commercial transactions since it can provide electronically the same forensic effect a signed paper message provides.

4. Ensuring and Certification Authorities

The use of public key cryptography for digital signature purposes require that a trusted third party establish that holders of public keys are indeed who they purport to be. Without a trusted third party certifying that a given individual is in fact the holder of a public key, it is impossible for other transacting parties on the network to know for certain that the holder of the public key is not an impostor. This third party, known in the GUIDEC as a Certifier , will form the trust backbone for all types of commercial and non-commercial transactions taking place over open networks. Certifiers will certify the identity of the public key holder, and publish and update public keys, in a process referred to as certificate issuance. The effectiveness of the ensuring process depends upon establishing certifiers to provide parties with a means for reliably associating the public and private key pair with an identified person, and a trustworthy means of ascertaining the public key needed for verification. Given the importance of the accuracy of the information provided by the third party institution (i.e. the public key of the sender), the certifier should be sufficiently trustworthy to assure a high level of trust in electronic commercial transactions. In communications among different organisations, a certification author-ity must be an institution trusted by all parties relying on its information. To provide further assurance of actual trustworthiness, a hierarchy of certification authorities may need to be established to represent that individuals comply with rules, such as those articulated in the GUIDEC. In a hierarchy of multiple certifiers, each certifier has an ensured text certified by the certificate authority above it, forming a certificate chain to assure that sub-certifiers are identifiable.

Because certificates issued by certifiers will essentially be guarantees of the certificate holder's commercial identity, laws are currently being developed which prescribe clear rules and liabilities for certifiers. This document outlines the general set of international rules that govern ensuring and certifying for commercial applications. The GUIDEC is designed to restate and harmonise existing law and practice relating to the particulars of the ensuring, certification, and verification process.

5. Biometric Technology

There are also in existence some technologies which are designed to mirror the current paper based function involved in signing, in that they make use of a template upon which the signer physically reproduces his or her signature. The technology then either relates the template signature to a previously archived and identified signature 'specimen', thereby assuming part of the function of a Certifier, or it makes use of the string produced to attach itself to the file which is being ensured. As much of the technical approach in achieving this varies considerably from Public Key Cryptography, reference is made to this technique here, but it is not felt that the general legal principles behind it, at least as far as the GUIDEC is concerned, differ substantially from those involved within a public key infrastructure.

IV. Existing Law and Electronic Transactions

1. General

Although many of the technological issues pertaining to global digital commerce are being readily addressed, significant legal questions remain unresolved, posing significant barriers to further development of a global electronic trading system. The continued vitality of the emerging global electronic trading system depends on the progressive adaptation of international and domestic laws to the rapidly evolving networked infrastructure. Although analogy to existing rules may be possible in many cases, the application of pre-existing rules that have not been reconsidered in light of progressive technologies may lead to inappropriate results. Applying paper-based rules to electronic transactions without sufficient consideration of the ramifications of such rules increases uncertainty, working to the detriment of the international trading community.

Similarly, conflicting legislative efforts directed at facilitating electronic commerce at the domestic level can effectively deter the development of a coherent global framework. This concern applies both to consistency among individual domestic states and consistency between nations, amplifying the need for convergence and harmonisation in legislative approaches. Substantive and procedural legal incompatibilities between countries threaten to create a complex and unpredictable environment for international electronic commerce.

The increasing importance of open networks such as the Internet, which promotes borderless interactivity between users, compounds the need for a uniform and harmonised approach to developing an international legal infrastructure for ensuring. The increasing importance of raising the level of trust and reliability in these new communications systems stimulates the need for a globally coherent, unified regulatory approach to information security, and in particular ensuring and certifying messages.

2. Form Requirements

The traditional rationale for requiring the formalities of a signed writing for commercial transactions has been to discourage reliance on oral agreements. The requirement of a written record of commercial transactions has also endured for regulatory purposes, such as to discharge administrative tariffs and fees associated with taxation, customs, et cetera. Despite this traditional formality, however, writings have not been required to the exclusion of other evidence of a transaction or agreement. Indeed, in common law countries, where requirements for writing may exist in the context of sales of goods, a writing is loosely defined as anything that contains the essential elements of the contract.

Under civil law regimes, a writing is merely treated as better evidence than the lack of one. Nevertheless, the use of digital signatures for commercial purposes faces a number of existing legal impediments that derive from both common and civil law treatment of form requirements for many types of commercial transactions. In both the common and civil law traditions, existing law imposes specific requirements relating to written, signed, certified, and/or original form which do not contemplate the use of electronic messages. Several areas of the law, such as land law, are rife with requirements relating to form that presuppose the use of a traditional pen and ink signature on a paper message. This is especially true in the civil law, where form requirements for transactions involving notarial intervention impose a rigidly defined legal regime for authenticating commercial and other messages.

3. Common Law Issues

One of the most nettlesome problems arising out of the use of electronic means of communications in common law-based jurisdictions derives from uncertainty as to whether or not electronic transmissions satisfy the writing and signature requirements to be found in the Statute of Frauds, embodied in United States law in U.C.C. Article 2-201, or originally in section 40 of the English Law of Property Act 1925, now to be found in section 2 of the Law of Property (Miscellaneous Provisions) Act 1989.

Because there is virtually no case law regarding these issues involving the use of electronic means for transacting commercially, general thinking on the question of electronic messages as signed writings has focused on common law commercial theory and judicial precedent involving other forms of non-traditional writing used in commerce, such as teletype and facsimile evidence.

The U.C.C. defines 'signature' as 'any symbol executed or adopted by a party with present intention to authenticate a writing." The Official Comment to section 1-201 emphasises that the appropriate focus of the signature requirement is the 'intention to authenticate' rather than the manner of symbol adopted by the parties. This is borne out by the courts, which have found a number of non-written signatures to be the functional equivalent of one, including a typewritten name, a hand printed name, company letterhead, a sales brochure, and a tape recording. Although these interpretations would suggest that ensuring techniques probably satisfy statute of fraud requirements for signatures, this is unclear without specific judicial precedent or statutory provision.

4. Civil Law Issues

Civil law systems typically contain a variety of form requirements. For example, under German Law, contracts may generally be concluded if the parties have given declarations of will to be bound. As a general principle, such a declaration may be given electronically, such as by ensuring the message.

However, there are many cases where statute or the relevant code of laws require that certain declarations of will be made in written form; in such cases, the code defines what it means – generally a written signature made by pen on paper. This is the case in German and French law with respect to real estate, and contracts which do not observe this written form are considered to be void.

5. Consequences

The historical and currently perceived function of formalities has an important effect on their adaptability to electronic commerce. The advent of electronic commerce has challenged, and will continue to challenge, the validity of these formalities. As electronic commerce becomes more and more a reality in the international trade, the function of legal formalities which govern these transactions must evolve to include electronic means. At the present time a number of national and international efforts to treat the use of digital messages, including message ensuring techniques, have begun to address form requirements as a legal barrier to electronic commerce. Many of these efforts, particularly those state-based legislative implementations in the United States treating the use of digital signatures, as well as related efforts in Australia, Austria, Chile, Denmark, France, Germany, Italy, Japan, Malaysia, Singapore, South Korea, Sweden, and the United Kingdom, have been influential in the drafting of this document.

The United Nations Commission on International Trade Law (UNCITRAL) Model Law on Electronic Commerce, certainly the most comprehensive international legal treatment of form requirements as they relate to electronic commercial transactions in existence today, is also extensively drawn upon in the GUIDEC.

V. International Legal Approaches to Digital Signatures

1. UNCITRAL Model Law on Electronic Commerce

The most definitive treatment of the issues for international electronic commercial transactions is that embodied in the United Nations Commission on International Trade Law Model Law on Electronic Commerce (the UNCITRAL Model Law), adopted by UNCITRAL during its 29th Session. Although the Model Law provides for the legal enforceability of electronic ensuring methods for commercial transactions, it does not specifically treat the surrounding issues. In this regard, the GUIDEC is designed to build upon and extend the Model Law's treatment through the concept of ensuring a message, particularly with regard to certification of ensurer identity information.

The Model Law treats electronic signatures as they relate generally to problems deriving from form requirements in existing commercial laws of the major legal systems. Specifically, the Model Law provides that form requirements relating to signatures may be met in relation to data messages where a method is used that identifies the person and indicates that person's approval of the contents of the data message, and where the reliability of the method of signing is appropriate under the circumstances. Recognising that signature requirements derive from fundamental commercial law and public policy issues relating to intent of contracting parties, the Model Law does not specify what method of signing a data message might be appropriate under what circumstances. The Draft Guide to the Model law does indicate, however, that it may be useful in the context of data messages, to 'develop functional equivalents for the various types and levels of signature requirements in existence.' The GUIDEC attempts to build upon the Model Law in this regard, by defining requirements for signatures used in international commerce, in particular digital signatures, in which there is the additional requirement of certification.

The Model Law further treats signature requirements in the context of the evidential weight of data messages based upon the reliability of the manner in which the data message was generated, stored, communicated, and maintained in general. In the context of storage and retention of data messages for evidentiary purposes, the Model Law provides that document retention provisions may be satisfied for data messages if the following conditions are met:

- the information contained in the data message is accessible so as to be subsequently usable;
- the data message is maintained in the same format in which it was generated and communicated, or in another format which demonstrably maintains the accuracy of the message's content, and;
- the information is retained in a fashion that enables the identification of the origin, destination, date, and time it was sent and received.

The Model Law recognises that data message retention will often be undertaken by intermediaries and other third parties which do not fall under the definition of 'intermediary' in the Model Law, and provides that data messages may be retained by third parties as long as the above requirements are met. Although the Draft Guide makes it clear that retention may be carried out by non-'intermediary' third parties, it does not distinguish whether responsibilities of these parties in the context of the Model law would be regarded as the same or similar to those of intermediaries, or whether third party obligations fall outside the ambit of the Model Law.

The GUIDEC treats these issues much more fully than the Model Law with regard to certifiers acting in the capacity of intermediaries or non-intermediary third parties, and outlines specific rules of practice for certifiers relating to the issues enumerated above for the purposes of assuring that digitally authenticated or ensured messages retain their non-repudiable characteristics for evidentiary purposes.

Because the Model Law treats signature issues only generally, and because it indicates that different ensuring mechanisms employed in international electronic commerce need to be more fully articulated, the Information Security Working Party, saw its role in drafting the GUIDEC as expanding upon the Model Law treatment of signatures to more fully define how these issues need to be treated in the context of ensuring digital signatures and digital certification.

The Core Concepts

VI. Glossary of Terms

1. Ensure

To record or adopt a digital seal or symbol associated with a message, with the present intention of identifying oneself with the message.

Clarification

'Ensure': In American usage, the term 'authenticate' is often used to denote the act of identifying oneself with a message, but in European usage 'authenticate' is more associated with the verification of a signature (see post). Furthermore, there is a fundamental difficulty in the concept of 'digitally signing' a message, in that there are significant differences between a physical signature, and one effected through an electronic medium. The most important difference is that most digital signatures rely upon a smartcard or some other storage facility in order to reproduce the algorithm necessary for securing the 'signature' to the message with which it is to be associated. It then follows that if this storage facility is accessed by someone other that the person to whom it belongs, a message can be 'signed' and appear to have originated from the owner, either with or without his consent.

It is for this reason that we have employed the term 'Ensure', which is defined by Webster's Universal College Dictionary as '1. To secure or guarantee. 2. To make sure or certain. 3. To make secure or safe, as from harm'. It is exactly this which is being sought in an electronic message – to make it secure from subsequent alterations. 'message': This means only the message that is ensured. If the message is altered (other than by the ensurer with ratification), then there is no intention of the ensurer to be identified with the message, and the ensuring around the message does not apply to the alteration.

'intention of identifying oneself with the message': The act of ensuring may be founded on additional intentions besides the minimal identification of the ensurer with the message. Often, it further indicates the ensurer's approval of, or intent to be legally bound by, the message. Based on the expression of these various intentions through ensuring, the law and/or commercial usage give the message a certain effect as the formally recognised act of the ensurer; (see post: 'legal significance of ensuring a message'). Certification addresses the need for guaranteeing the effectiveness of ensuring, and some legal systems require it for certain messages, particularly when public filing is required or permitted, or the risks of false identification affect some other interest protected under a legal system's policy.

See UNCITRAL Model Law art. 6 (criteria for satisfaction of signature requirements), art. 11 (attribution of data messages) (1995); United Nations Convention on International Bills of Exchange and Promissory Notes art. 5(k) (1988) ("'Signature' means a hand-written signature, its facsimile or an equivalent authentication . . .').

Commentary

(1) Fundamentally and minimally, ensuring a message provides evidence that a. the ensurer had contact with the message and b. the message has been preserved intact since it was ensured.

Ensuring may also indicate more, depending on the circumstances, or have legal significance deriving from an agreement or law. Further, most means of authentication provide only imperfect evidence of the ensurer's contact and the message's integrity, and are vulnerable to forgery or tampering.

(2) A forged message which had been ensured, altered without the ensurer's authorisation creates no binding obligation on the ensurer. It is void, or subject to being declared void at the instance of the purported ensurer.

In some legal systems, a spoilt message, one materially altered without its ensurer's authorisation, is traditionally considered void, and may not be enforced according to its original tenor. Preferably, and according to many other jurisdictions, tampering with a message is simply ignored, and the message may be enforced as originally ensured.

2. Certificate

A message ensured by a person, which message attests to the accuracy of facts material to the legal efficacy of the act of another person.

Clarification

'message ensured': A certificate is itself a message, and ensuring its authenticity is ordinarily an important fact. In order for the certificate to be clearly reliable in commerce, the certifier creating it should exercise a degree of care exceeding the care for ensured messages generally.

'fact material to the legal efficacy of the act of another person': Examples of facts which may be the subject of certification include the identity of the person performing an act such as ensuring a message, circumstances affecting that person's existence as a valid legal entity, and/or the authority of a person to perform an act in question. A single certificate may attest to one or more such facts.

Commentary

(1) A variety of different types of certificates are recognised. Notaries of various legal systems issue certificates varying in form and effect, such as the public or authentic, and private forms of the civil law tradition, and the less rigorous 'acknowledgement' of North American notaries. Technical computer standards typically envisage a certificate whose validity is measured according to a time period, whereas traditional certificates are valid on a per-transaction basis. Public key certificates as defined below are a specific type of certificate, but nevertheless fit within this general definition. This definition recognises the often profound distinctions in the concept of a 'certificate' but nevertheless seeks to focus on a common gist.

(2) A certificate does not, by definition, include an indication of the scope of its intended effect. A certificate valid for only one message or transaction fits this definition, as well as one valid for multiple transactions over a specified time. If a certificate is valid for only one message or transaction, it should so state and be clearly associated with that message or transaction. If a certificate is limited according to a time period, that time period should ordinarily be specified in the certificate.

(3) The content of a certificate depends on the type and purpose of the certificate, and is often prescribed by law or custom.

3. Certification practice statement

A statement of the practices which a certifier employs in issuing certificates generally, or employed in issuing a particular certificate.

Clarification

'statement': The statement may include a technical standard, rules of professional conduct or practice, laws applicable to the certifier, or a brand or a mark representing other rules with which the certifier complies.

Commentary

(1) If a certification practice statement is not already well-known or agreed upon by the parties to a particular transaction, widely accepted by usage and generally well known in the trade, or a matter of widely

known custom and/or relevant national law, its form should be optimised to provide notice to relying parties and for efficient reference and utilisation. A certification practice statement need not necessarily be documentary in form; however, its expression should provide for a reasonably high degree of readability, accessibility, and efficiency. It should also make advantageous use of electronic means of delivery and presentation, if electronic means are contemplated for the transaction or material to it, in order to reasonably facilitate automated processing and/or computer-assisted look-up of important terms. A certification practice statement functions mainly as notice of a certifier's practices in issuing certificates, and a certifier acts trustworthily and perhaps even in bad faith if an important portion of a certification practice statement is unreasonably obscure.

(2) This document may serve as a guide for the contents and form of a certification practice statement.

4. Certifier

A person who issues a certificate, and thereby attests to the accuracy of a fact material to the legal efficacy of the act of another person.

Clarification

'person': is defined in this publication to include any physical being or legal entity capable of ensuring a message, and would therefore include corporations, partnerships, governmental agencies, and other legal entities. However, these non-physical entities have no human senses and cannot perceive certain facts, except through their human agents.

Ultimately, therefore, the process of certification must be performed by human beings, although incorporeal legal entities may assist in providing facilities, services, and assistance.

Commentary

(1) Examples of certifiers include notaries, public key certification authorities (which may also include notaries and other trusted entities), and governmental officers and other persons.

5. Repository

A computer-based system for storing and retrieving certificates and other messages relevant to ensuring a message.

Commentary

A digital certificate repository may be provided by a firm specialised for such a business, in conjunction with services as a certifier or other person involved in electronic commerce. A digital repository is distinct from a repository of messages on paper.

6. Digital signature

A transformation of a message using an asymmetric cryptosystem such that a person having the ensured message and the ensurer's public key can accurately determine:

(a) whether the transformation was created using the private key that corresponds to the signer's public key, and

(b) whether the signed message has been altered since the transformation was made.

Clarification

'cryptosystem': This term signifies an information system employing cryptographic techniques to provide data security over communication channels that may not be secure. The data security thus provided includes the capability of associating a given message with a particular cryptographic key, and one or more operations for determining whether a given message is precisely the same as when the operation was previously performed.

'asymmetric cryptosystem': An asymmetric cryptosystem, also often termed a 'public key cryptosystem', is an information system utilizing an algorithm or series of algorithms which provide a cryptographic key pair consisting of a private key and a corresponding public key. The keys of the pair have the properties that (1) the public key can verify a digital signature that the private key creates, and (2) it is computationally infeasible to discover or derive the private key from the public key. The public key can therefore be disclosed without significantly risking disclosure of the private key.

'the ensurer's': The ensurer is the person employing the algorithm in order to be associated with the content of the message. This definition assumes that a cryptographic key pair has itself been associated with an identified person, so that the digital signatures created by that person can be reliably attributed to him by others. The association of a person with a key pair can be accomplished by a certificate identifying the person and including the person's public key. Such a certificate is termed a 'public key certificate' in this document.

'correspond': 'Correspond', as used in this definition with regard to cryptographic keys, means to belong to the same key pair.

'private key': In an asymmetric cryptosystem, the cryptographic keys are paired, as mentioned above. The private key is the one of the pair used to create a digital signature. It must therefore be available only to the ensurer, and the ensurer accordingly has a duty to maintain exclusive control over the private key; (see safeguarding an ensuring device).

'public key': In an asymmetric cryptosystem, at least one cryptographic key of a pair may be disclosed without making discovery of the private key possible. The key that may thus be disclosed is generally termed the 'public key'.

Commentary

(1) Some methods of authenticating electronic messages do not employ an asymmetric cryptosystem. The results of such methods do not fall within the above definition of 'digital signature'. Thus, a digitally scanned image of a handwritten signature, a signature by means of a stylus and digitising tablet, a name signed using the keyboard, the use of passwords or other techniques for controlling access, and similar procedures could be used for ensuring a message, but are not 'digital signatures' as the term is used in this document.

(2) A digital signature should be securely and unambiguously linked to its message. As long as such a link is maintained, it is unimportant whether a digital signature is kept within the message, appended or prefixed to it, or retained in a separate electronic file or information system.

7. Hold a private key

To use or be able to use a private key.

Clarification

'to use or be able to use': The principal concept underlying this definition is availability or access as a matter of fact, rather than as a matter of right or legal entitlement. A person who obtains a key by theft, or who has access or use of the key subject to pre-emption by another, nevertheless 'holds the key' as here defined.

Commentary

(1) Since the private key is essentially a device capable of creating a digital signature when used in an information system for the purpose, and since a digital signature can be considered as ensuring a message, the ability to use a private key for digital signature purposes must be limited to the ensurer only. Holding a private key should therefore legally be the exclusive right of ensurer.

(2) Holding a private key may include an employment or other agency relation, or another legally recognised relation in which rights of custody and control (or ownership, if 'property' is involved) are shared or divided in a manner recognised under applicable law. For example, a corporate employer may designate a private key for use by an employee in the name of the corporate employer. Digital signatures by that private key could well be attributable to the corporate employer by application of agency or authorisation principles, although the digital signatures would also be traceable to the employee. See also post 'ensuring a message by an agent'.

(3) Ordinarily, a private key should have but one holder, unless holding is intentionally shared or divided. If an asymmetric cryptosystem is properly designed, implemented, and maintained, duplicate private keys occur rarely or not at all, unless a duplicate is obtained illicitly. If an unauthorised duplicate is discovered, a holder should immediately suspend the certificate pending an investigation, and, depending on the outcome, revoke the certificate.

8. Human-readable form

A presentation of a digital message such that it can be perceived by human beings.

Clarification

'digital message': The information processed by nearly all computer-based information systems is fundamentally variations in voltage, alternating magnetic polarities, pits on plastic, and similar approaches to representing digital bits in physical matter and electrical energy. As a practical matter, bits thus represented are imperceptible and unreadable by human beings, unless the information system presents them as symbols such as letters, numerals, punctuation marks and formatting.

Reference is made to the UNCITRAL Model Law art. 7 (1995) (satisfaction of requirements or preferences for the original).

Commentary

(1) A human-readable representation is not, by definition, rendered by a technologically reliable information system nor ensured; in other words, this definition includes no assurance that the information system has accurately translated the message from its basic digital form into a human-readable form, or that that human-readable form is the same as another form perceived by an ensurer of the message. Whether a message is represented the same as it was for its ensurer generally depends on whether the ensurer included parameters adequately specifying the human-readable representation within the ensured message. See post 'in determining the scope of an ensured message, variations in the form of the message may or may not be significant'.

9. Issue a certificate

The process by which a certifier creates a certificate and gives notice to the subscriber listed in the certificate of its contents.

Clarification

'creates': Creation of a new certificate does not imply formation of a new client relationship with the subscriber. For certificates whose validity is limited according to a time period, the new certificate may substitute for or 'renew' an earlier one, which has expired or been revoked, or is about to expire or be revoked.

'notice' and 'subscriber' see post. Issuance of a certificate does not necessarily guarantee effective delivery.

Commentary

(1) Certain Civil Law legal systems or national customs may prescribe the manner in which a certificate may be issued, particularly for specific transactions. Civil law legal systems generally require that a notary officiate at certain types of transactions in which certificates are issued. Civil law notarial practices often include detailed inquiry into the parties' intent and the transactional context, in order to be certain that the parties are fully informed about the consequences of their transaction.

10. Notice

To communicate information to another person in a manner likely under the circumstances to impart knowledge thereof to the other person.

Clarification

'information': Notice could occasion a claim for intentional or negligent misrepresentation, should the information prove to be inaccurate. Care by the notifier in drawing conclusions may be appropriate. A notifier may inform the recipient of relevant evidence or of an uncertain event, and leave the recipient to determine whether to rely on the notice as accurate. The recipient is often in the best position to weigh the indications and uncertainty in light of its risks.

'likely under the circumstances to impart knowledge' A duty to notify may be satisfied, even though the intended recipient of the notice fails to become aware of its contents, provided that the notifier acts in good faith and takes action which, in the ordinary course of business, should suffice to cause the notice to be delivered to the intended recipient and come to its attention. The UNIDROIT Principles of International Commercial

Contracts note:

Where notice is required it may be given by any means appropriate to the circumstances.

(1) . . .

(2) A notice is effective when it reaches the person to whom it is given.

(3) For the purpose of paragraph (2) a notice 'reaches' a person when given to that person orally or delivered at that person's place of business or mailing address.

(4) For the purpose of this article 'notice' includes a declaration, demand, request or any other communication of intention.

International Institution for the Unification of Private Law (UNID-ROIT), Principles of International Commercial Contracts art. 1.9 (1994). Comment 4 of the same article states in defining 'reach' that notice reaches the addressee as soon as [it is] delivered . . .to [the addressee's] place of business or mailing address. The particular communication in question need not come into the hands of the addressee. It is sufficient that it be . . . received by the addressee's fax, telex or computer.

In an electronic setting, dispatching a reliably ensured message addressed to the intended recipient through a technologically reliable system, without apparent error, should suffice as a means of notification, unless the parties agree otherwise.

Commentary

(1) If the parties have formed a contract, it or a general contractual duty of good faith may well include a notice requirement, and perhaps an agreed upon definition better tailored to the parties. However, the parties may also find themselves in a pre-contractual state, and the ensuring of a message or certification which is the subject of the notice is part of an effort to form a contract or satisfy the form requirements for a contract. In such a pre-contractual setting, a duty to refrain from misrepresentation or to bargain in good faith, or the doctrine of culpa in contrahendo supply and define a basic requirement of notice.

11. Person

A human being or any entity which is either:

(a)   recognised by applicable law as capable of ensuring a message, or
(b)   capable of ensuring a message as a matter of fact.

Clarification

'entity': Information systems and other devices are not 'entities' as the word is used in this definition. Rather, such systems and devices are the instruments of the persons who own and operate them.

12. Public key certificate

A certificate identifying a public key to its subscriber, corresponding to a private key held by that subscriber.

Clarification

'public key': Public keys can be used by a person having a digital signature to determine which private key created the digital signature and whether the signed message was altered since it was signed. See ante

'digital signature' and post 'verify a digital signature'

'identifying': The process whereby the certifier ascertains the veracity of the statements made in the certificate.

13. Revoke a public key certificate

The act of a certifier in declaring a public key certificate permanently invalid from a specified time forward.

Clarification

'declaring': Revocation is a mere declaration, and does not include destruction of the invalidated certificate. The invalidated certificate remains available for verification of digital signatures effected while the certificate was still valid.

'time': This definition presumes that the validity of the public key certificate is limited to a specified period of time, which revocation cuts short. Public key certificates whose validity is limited to a particular transaction or by other criteria could perhaps be invalidated after issuance, but this document would not term such invalidation 'revocation'.

Commentary

(1) Although not an element of this definition, notice (see ante for definition) is required for a revocation.

14. Subscriber

A person who is the subject of a certificate.

Clarification

'subject of a certificate': Not every ensurer is a subscriber, since not every ensured message has an associated certification. 'Subscriber' may well refer to an ensurer, but as the subject of a certificate, rather than as an ensurer per se.

Commentary

(1) For example, if a public key certificate states, either explicitly or by some form of incorporation: I hereby certify on this 4th day of August, 1997, that John William Thompson of 38 Cours Albert 1er, 75008 Paris, France, personally appeared before me and was identified by . . . Further, the same John William Thompson demonstrated to me that he held the private key corresponding to the following public key . . . then John William Thompson is the subscriber of that certificate.

(2) In some instances, a subscriber may consist of a person acting by the authority of another. Thus, the above example could include the following:

The same John William Thompson also produced a resolution of the XYZ Corporation SA, which I authenticated by . . . Said resolution, a copy of which is attached hereto, authorises the said John William Thompson, to act in certain matters on behalf of XYZ Corporation SA as its authorised signatory.

Ensuring a message by the private key corresponding to the public key listed in the certificate would, by application of domestic agency law, be legally recognised as ensuring a message of the principal through an act of the agent.

(3) A subscriber is generally also a client of, or under contract with, a certifier.

15. Suspend a public key certificate

The act of a certifier in declaring a public key certificate temporarily invalid for a specified time period.

Clarification

'invalid': If the certificate is invalid, then it cannot be relied upon by a third party, though this does not preclude the legal concept that if the relying party has acted reasonably (see clarification post) or in good faith in relying upon the certificate, then the fact that it is suspended does not prejudice that reliance.

'time': This definition is presumes that the validity of the public key certificate is limited to a specified period of time, which suspension cuts short. Public key certificates whose validity is limited to a particular transaction or by other criteria could perhaps be invalidated after issuance, but this document would not term such invalidation 'suspension'.

16. Technologically reliable

Having the qualities of:

(a)   being reasonably secure from intrusion and misuse;
(b)   providing a reasonable level of availability, reliability, and correct operation.

Clarification

'reasonably . . . reasonable': The reasonableness standard of this definition reflects the fact that security exists in varying degrees, and should ordinarily be evaluated in light of the circumstances. A greater or lesser degree of security is possible in nearly all situations, much like public streets can always be made safer or airports more secure. In a case, therefore, the question should be, not whether the defendant could have done more, but rather whether the defendant exercised an appropriate degree of care in the design, maintenance, and operation of the system in question, taking into account the feasibility and cost of additional measures and the benefits they would have provided under the relevant circumstances. It should be noted that the use of the concept of 'reasonable' can be problematic in Civil Law jurisdictions, although de facto the standards of a bonus pater familias or an orderly businessman can be used to adhere more closely to the concept.

'correct operation': What sort of operation is 'correct' for a system depends on design specifications of the system. The expectations of a user of the system should be considered in light of what can reasonably be expected from the system, given the limits in its design and production, to the extent that those limits are made known to the user.

Commentary

(1) The objectives of a technological reliability are, in essence:

Confidentiality: Securing information so that it is not disclosed or revealed to unauthorised persons.

Integrity: Securing the consistency of data; in particular, preventing unauthorised creation, alteration, or destruction of data.

Availability: Securing access to information and resources so that legitimate users are not unduly denied it.

Legitimate use: Securing resources so that they are used only by authorised persons in authorised ways.

17. Trustworthy

Conducting business in a manner that warrants the trust of a reasonable person active in commerce, and having capabilities, competence, and other resources which are sufficient to enable performance of one's legal duties, and assure unbiased action.

Clarification

'sufficient': The sufficiency of a person's capabilities, competence, and resources and the sufficiency of one's disinterest should both be tested according to standards of reasonableness. In any case, greater effort and investment will have been possible, but the question is whether a reasonable person under the circumstances would have expended the additional effort and investment to obtain greater capabilities, competence, or absence of bias.

Commentary

(1) Trustworthiness is a central concept to all business relationships, and is not a concept that can be closely defined. The commercial assessment

of the risk involved in a certain transaction will always have a central role to play. Of course, there exist professions, such as that of a Notary, which remove much of the element of risk in establishing the legal bona fides of a signature by issuing a certification which takes the responsibility for the accuracy of the facts contained therein out of the hands of the receiving party. Indeed, a notary will remain liable for any statements made in a certificate notwithstanding the fact that there is no contractual relationship between him and the party relying on the statements made.

(2) It will be a matter of commercial risk assessment whether or not a person will rely upon a certification where the ensurer, subscriber and even certifier all lie within the same group. Paper-based examples such as the credit card industry have historically provided examples of unbiased performance of legal duties, despite acting in several roles in a transaction.

18. Valid certificate

A certificate which its certifier has issued or disclosed to another person in circumstances where that person's reliance on the certificate is foreseeable, unless the certifier gives timely notice that the certificate is unreliable, or unless the certificate is a public key certificate which has been revoked or is, at the time in question, suspended.

Clarification

'gives notice': The notice must reach all persons who are in a position to rely on the certificate.

Commentary

(1) A certifier may seek to restrict liability for the contents of a certificate issued either through the contractual relationship with the subscriber, or by means of a general disclaimer in the practice statement, or even in the certificate itself. Care should be taken, however, of restrictions on such disclaimers which some jurisdictions regard as unfair or invalid contract terms. This is especially the case in transactions which are deemed to be 'consumer'.

19. *Verify a digital signature*

In relation to ensuring a given message (digital signature, message, and public key,) to determine accurately that:

(a) the digital signature was created by the private key corresponding to the public key; and

(b) the message has not been altered since its digital signature was created.

Clarification

'Verify': If a recipient person does not verify the said information, then reliance cannot be made upon the infrastructure mechanisms which have been created for just that purpose, and for securing the security of the message.

Commentary

This is, of course, the central element in relying upon an ensured message with a digital signature.

BEST PRACTICES

VII. *Ensuring a message*

1. *Ensuring a message as a Factual Matter*

A message is ensured, as a factual matter, if acceptable evidence indicates:

(a) the identity of the ensurer, and

(b) that the message has not been altered since ensured.

Clarification

'as a factual matter': Distinct from legal significance or meaning, the factual question of ensuring a message is addressed simply to identifying the ensurer and the ensured message from the available and admissible evidence. Such a question seeks to discover simply the facts of who ensured what.

Commentary

(1) Ensuring a message for evidential purposes in proceedings before tribunals is generally to ensure a message as a factual matter. The focus of the inquiry is the genuineness of the proffered evidence and its factual linkage to the persons involved in the controversy. (For example, see the US Federal Rules of Evidence 901 , providing that the evidential requirement is satisfied by 'evidence sufficient to support a finding that the matter in question is what the proponent claims', and listing several examples.)

(2) Ensuring a message can also serve as an indicator of origin, often in an evidential context, where the question is usually the fact of origin rather than any legal consequences of a signature.

2. Attribution and Legal Significance of Ensuring a message

A person must attribute an ensured message to the person who actually ensured the message.

Clarification

'must': Whether any consequence flows from a failure to attribute an ensured message depends on the import of the message. If the message may painlessly be ignored, then a failure to attribute it is of no consequence.

'attribute': The person having the ensured message must consider it to be associated with the ensurer in some significant way, which is often apparent from an accompanying expression of the ensurer's intent, the facts and circumstances of the transaction, course of dealing, or usage of trade.

'ensured message': In light of the definition of 'ensure' (see ante), 'ensured message' here means a message which is(1) intact and unaltered since ensured, and (2) identified with its ensurer.

'actually ensured': In a case of forgery, the forger, rather than the ostensible signer, is the actual ensurer.

In this context, see also the UNCITRAL Model Law art. 11 (attribution of data messages) (1995).

Commentary

(1) The duty to attribute an ensured message to its ensurer presumes that the person having the ensured message acts in good faith, exercises reasonable care in evaluating the ensured message, and lacks timely knowledge or notice that the ensured message is false or significantly questionable.

(2) In ascertaining who actually ensured a message, a person is entitled to receive reasonable further assurances that the ensurer has properly ensured a message. In determining what is reasonable in a case, a tribunal should consider indications of the reliability or lack of reliability of the ensured message, the availability of those indications to the person having the message, as well as the resources required to make further information available.

(3) If a person properly attributes a forged or improperly altered message erroneously and thereby incurs a loss, and if the forgery or improper alteration resulted from a failure by the purported ensurer to safeguard an authenticating device or other fault by the purported ensurer, then the purported ensurer must indemnify or compensate the attributing person for the loss.

(4) The effect of attribution to a ensurer depends on the content of the ensured message, the other facts and circumstances of the transaction, applicable law, the course of dealing between the parties, and/or usage of trade. For example, ensuring the written expression of a contract is customarily taken to indicate assent to the contract, and may satisfy formal requirements for ensuring a message sufficient to give effect or enforceability to the contract. Ensuring a letter ordinarily indicates authorship. Ensuring a negotiable instrument in the manner of an endorsement has the effect of an endorsement.

(5) Attribution or legal enforceability of an otherwise attributable message may be limited by formal ensuring and certification requirements.

3. Ensuring a message by an Agent

If an agent ensures a message and represents himself to do so by authority of a principal, the ensured message is valid as that of the principal if, under applicable law, the agent had sufficient authority to ensure the message.

Clarification

'sufficient authority to ensure': Legal systems differ in the processes commonly utilised for the granting of authority, and particularly in the degree to which implicit or apparent authorisation is recognised and accorded legal effect (see comment (2) below). If, under applicable law, the existence of sufficiency of the would-be agent's authority is reasonably in doubt, the recipient of an ensured message may well have reason to seek further assurances.

Commentary

(1) A person generally acts at his peril in relying on an agent's representation of authority. Rather than taking a purported agent's word for the effectiveness and scope of the agency, a person having an ensured message should require a certificate or other, more reliable proof of agency.

(2) Legal systems differ in the extent to which one may rely on representations of agency by the purported principal which fall short of a valid power of attorney, in cases where the principal later disputes the agency. At common law, 'apparent authority' can arise from almost any manifestation of agency by a principal to third persons. Civil law legal systems have traditionally eschewed recognition of apparent authority, although jurisprudence in some has developed comparable doctrines in cases where the principal failed to dispel the appearance that the agent had authority or failed to stop the agent from acting in the principal's name.

4. Appropriate Practices for Ensuring a Message

An ensurer must ensure a message by a means appropriate under the circumstances.

Clarification

'must': The consequence of a failure to ensure a message properly is that the message may be disregarded. In general commercial practice and unless otherwise agreed, a message may be ignored if the manner of ensuring it either contravenes an agreement by the parties, is not suited to impart the legal efficacy intended by the parties for the message, or if reliance on the message as ensured would not be reasonable under the circumstances.

'appropriate under the circumstances': As the commentary below explains, the means should carry out the intent of the parties, or at least reasonably fit the transactional context. At least, signature requirements had the perhaps salutary effect of requiring a person to use minimal ensuring methods. However, imposing sanctions for failure to comply with form requirements has proved to be problematic. In the common law, case law has tended to weaken formal requirements, perhaps because of difficulty in finding a fitting sanction for non-compliance. In the civil law, there are more rigid forms to be adhered to, especially in the areas where the state might take an interest, such as real property law, inheritance, or commercial registration of companies. Such matters require the intervention of a Notary, as a certifier.

The UNCITRAL Model Law (art 6) would sweep aside formal requirements, and leave the recipient of the message to prove attribution. While this approach is sensible, one sticking point remains: the recipient bears the burden of proof on the attribution issue, but only the sender can ensure the sender's message. The recipient may act at her peril in rejecting a message which, under various current definitions of 'signature', could be treated as authentic. This article seeks to address that problem by establishing in the recipient a right to demand reasonable assurance of an ensured messages authenticity.

Commentary

(1) The recipient of an ensured message may request further assurances of its validity, such as a valid certificate attesting to a critical fact, or replacement or augmentation of the ensured a message using a more technologically reliable method, if ensuring the message either was not accomplished as agreed by the parties, or is not suited to impart the legal efficacy intended by the parties for the message. In the absence of an express agreement, the parties are assumed to have intended a reasonable outcome, and therefore to have intended to use only ensuring practices that are reasonable under the circumstances.

(2) In determining what is reasonable under the circumstances, the recipient should consider facts that the recipient knows or of which the recipient has notice, including all facts listed in the certificate, the value or importance of the ensured message, within the transaction in question, the course of performance between the relying person and subscriber and the available indices of reliability or unreliability corroborating the ensured message, in prior transactions, the course of dealing between the relying person and subscriber and the available

indices of reliability or unreliability corroborating the ensured message, usage of trade conducted by technologically reliable information systems.

The factors are listed approximately in order of importance.

5. Scope of an Ensured message

The creator of an ensured message must clearly indicate what is being ensured.

Clarification

'clearly indicate': The ensurer should both delimit precisely what the message is in order to distinguish it from other matter, and should create a clear link between the act of ensuring the message and the ensured message itself.

Commentary

(1) Since ensuring a message does not apply to alterations of the message, a person receiving the ensured message must determine whether the message arrives intact. Such a determination is only possible if the message has been clearly delimited and linked to when it was ensured. On paper, the delimitation is accomplished by the spatial limits of paper, formatting conventions, and the custom of signing at the end of the message. The linkage between signature and message is often accomplished by including them both within the same paper message, with the signature generally following the message.

(2) Defining the message is complicated by the fact that different systems may present the message in varying human-readable forms. For example, a printer or fax machine may utilise a different size of paper than another. Variance in representations of the signed matter may or may not be significant. With electronic messages, variations are common, even when all relevant information systems are technologically reliable, simply because the capabilities and preferences of information systems vary. A ensurer should express the ensured message in a manner that enables a receiving information system to represent it properly, either in the manner required by law, agreed upon by the ensurer and receiver, or in accordance with usage of trade, applicable technical standards, and/or common practices for messages of the kind. The parties should agree, in specifying the form for their messages,

which variations are to be considered significant. In the absence of such an agreement, the ensurer may specify the variations to be considered significant alterations of the message. Ordinarily, minor variations in the media size, font, spacing, margins, and similar features are inconsequential; however, a change significantly affecting meaning, including a change to the logical structure of the message, should generally be treated as a significant alteration.

6. Safeguarding an Ensuring Device

If a person ensures a message by means of a device, the person must exercise, at a minimum, reasonable care to prevent unauthorised use of the device.

Clarification

'device': If the device consists of a system of interrelated components, the entire system need not be safeguarded. Rather, it suffices to safeguard one or more critical components of the system sufficient to prevent a falsely ensured message.

'reasonable care': 'Reasonable care' is the degree of caution and prudence that a reasonable person would exercise under the circumstances. (for comments on 'reasonable', see ante)

Commentary

(1) The ensuring device should be physically kept in a location where access is limited and carefully controlled. Access should be accorded only to trustworthy persons and ordinarily based on their need to utilise ensuring services. Persons to whom access is granted should be identified by presentation of a password or pass phrase, by biometric information, or other secure means.

(2) Where remedial action is possible following a loss of control over an ensuring device, the remedial action should be taken without delay. In a case in which a private key has been lost, the public key certificate should be revoked, or suspended immediately until it can be revoked.

7. Representations to a Certifier

A subscriber must accurately represent to a certifier all facts material to the certificate.

Clarification

'represent' This can take many forms. It may simply be the statements of the subscriber, or the certifier may have taken extraneous evidence of the matters contained in the certificate. As the certifier will be responsible for the statements made in the certificate, it would be advisable for the certificate to be clear as to how the statement of facts has been arrived at.

Commentary

(1) see generally the definitions in 'Certification', post.

VIII. Certification

1. Effect of a Valid Certificate

A person may rely on a valid certificate as accurately representing the fact or facts set forth in it, if the person has no notice that the certifier has failed to satisfy a material requirement of ensured message practice.

Clarification

'rely': The extent to which one may properly rely is limited to what is reasonable under the circumstances. In other words, one is not entitled to rely when a businessman of ordinary prudence would not do so from substantially the same informational and circumstantial vantage point. This implicit limitation on reliance finds expression in substantive law in limiting relief for deception to plaintiffs who are not excessively gullible or tainted; see, e.g., US Restatement Second Of Torts ss 548A (1977) ('A fraudulent misrepresentation is a legal cause of a pecuniary loss resulting from action or inaction in reliance upon it if, but only if, the loss might reasonably be expected to result from the reliance').

'notice': The UNIDROIT Principles of International Commercial Contracts point out that 'notice' 'includes a declaration, demand, request or any other communication of intention'. (International Institution For The Unification Of Private Law (UNIDROIT), Principles Of International Commercial Contracts, art. 1.9 (1994).)

Commentary

(1) Fundamentally, a certificate is simply evidence of the fact or facts it represents. As such, it is only as good as the certifier is worthy of belief. For commerce to function properly, a society must provide a trustworthy means of establishing critical facts, such as the identity of a ensurer. Certifiers provide such a means, but only if the certifiers are trustworthy.

(2) Where trustworthy certification practices are generally known to be followed, certificates are customarily treated as establishing the facts represented in them. For each transaction, the parties may ordinarily determine whether a particular certificate or type of certificate is acceptable. In certain circumstances, and particularly in the absence of an agreement among the parties, applicable substantive law can often supply a rule determining validity, together with any supporting certification. Such substantive rules may relate to the legal system's supervision of certifiers.

(3) Although a certificate is fundamentally evidence, whether or not a certificate is admissible in a judicial or arbitration proceeding is determined according to the rules of the forum.

(4) All the foregoing presumes that the parties are acting in good faith and without deception or negligence in conducting their business.

2. Accuracy of Representations in Certificate

A certifier must confirm the accuracy of all facts set forth in a valid certificate, unless it is evident from the certificate itself that some of the information has not been verified.

Clarification

'set forth': This applies both to facts explicitly stated in the certificate and to facts on which conclusions in the certificate are based.

'some of the information has not been verified': This has been termed 'Non-Verified Subscriber Information'. See commentary, post.

Commentary

(1) One school of thought holds that all of the information set out in a certificate must have been verified by the Certifier. This would prove to be unnecessarily restricting in commercial practice, as circumstances may exist where it is required to ensure a message, but the ensurer is unable to provide satisfactory evidence, say, of his corporate authority to act.

It should therefore be possible for the certificate to contain a statement to the fact that the ensurer is purporting to act on behalf of a particular corporation, but that this has not been proved. The receiving party is then able to make a commercial risk assessment as to whether to accept the ensured message as it stands, or to demand further proof.

3. Trustworthiness of a Certifier

A certifier must:

(a)   use only technologically reliable information systems and proc-
      esses, and trustworthy personnel in issuing a certificate and in
      suspending or revoking a public key certificate and in safeguard-
      ing its private key, if any;

(b)   have no conflict of interest which would make the certifier
      untrustworthy in issuing, suspending, and revoking a certificate;

(c)   refrain from contributing to a breach of a duty by the subscriber;

(d)   refrain from acts or omissions which significantly impair reason-
      able and foreseeable reliance on a valid certificate;

(e)   act in a trustworthy manner towards a subscriber and persons
      who rely on a valid certificate.

Clarification

'trustworthy personnel': A certifier must make reasonable efforts to screen, train, manage, and assure the loyalty of all employees perform-ing functions significantly affecting the certification process. 'conflict of interest': To be trusted by the parties to a transaction and serve as a trustworthy verifier of facts should a dispute arise, a certifier must not have a stake in the transaction that would compromise the certifier's trustworthiness. 'subscriber': A certifier owes a duty to a subscriber for whom the certifier issues a certificate, and to successors to the subscriber's rights which are dependent on the certification.

Commentary

(1) The trustworthiness of a Certifier is central to the whole concept of certification. This trust in turn is generally founded upon the liability that the Certifier is willing to accept for its statements. The Certifier may seek to limit its liability to a certain level through its 'certification practice statement' (see ante), but in doing so should exercise care that this limitation of liability is permissible within its jurisdiction. The very nature of electronic commerce as an international medium then further complicates this matter, as the Certifier may find that its certification is relied upon beyond its own borders. By the same token, a person relying upon a certificate should ascertain the level of reliance the certifier is expecting him to place on the same.

4. Notice of Practices and Problems

A certifier must make reasonable efforts to notify a foreseeably affected person of:

(a)   any material certification practice statement, and
(b)   any fact material to either the reliability of a certificate which it has issued or its ability to perform its services.

Clarification

'foreseeably affected person': To assure that a certifier foresees an effect, a person who believes himself to be affected may notify the certifier of the person's position and interest, and request a certification practice statement or further information.

Commentary

(1) Foreseeability is a difficult concept, especially when a certificate may be freely circulated, though of course it is an inherent element in assessing a commercial risk.

5. Financial Resources

A certifier must have financial resources sufficient to conduct its business and bear the reasonable risks resulting from the certificates it issues.

Clarification

'sufficient': As between a certifier and its client, the subscriber, the sufficiency of the certifier's financial basis is apparent from their willingness to do business with each other in a setting where the subscriber could have retained the services of another. In relation to third parties, however, the sufficiency of a certifier's financial basis should be evaluated according to a reasonableness standard.

'reasonable risks': The reasonableness of a risk should be evaluated in light of what is foreseeable from the certifier's informational vantage point, and what is likely.

Commentary

(1) It is under this heading that we must consider the impact of insurance, either by bonding or through indemnity insurance. Existing professional certifiers, such as Notaries, are required to carry sufficient professional indemnity insurance to cover such losses as are likely to be occasioned as a result of others relying upon their certifications. Such insurance can be considered as adding to the available financial resources of a certifier, though evidently he will not have access to such resources unless and until a claim is made against him.

6. Records

A certifier must keep records of all facts material to a certificate which it has issued for a reasonable period of time.

Clarification

'facts material to a certificate': The required records include evidence to support all representations made in a certificate.

'reasonable period of time': The duration of the record retention period is difficult to pinpoint, and requires weighing the need for reference to the records against the burden of keeping them. The records could be needed at least as long as a transaction relying on a valid certificate can be questioned. For most transactions, statutes of limitation will eventually place a transaction beyond dispute. However, for some transactions such as real property conveyances, legal repose may not be realised until after a lengthy time elapses, if ever.

Commentary

(1) Most professions already have established rules for the keeping of records, depending upon their nature. There is no reason that these rules should be any different in an electronic world, though added care must be taken to assure the retrievability of the information stored, especially in view of the rapid advances in technology.

7. Termination of a Certifier's Business

In terminating its business, a certifier must:

(a)   act in a manner that causes minimal disruption to subscribers and persons relying on issued valid, operational certificates; and
(b)   turn over its records to a qualified successor.

Clarification

'qualified successor': Another certifier is generally qualified to succeed a withdrawing certifier. A responsible, high-quality archiving service, a professional association, or regulatory agency may also be suitable. The successor need not issue new certificates, but must at least maintain suspension, revocation and retrieval services.

Commentary

(1) If no successor is willing to take over a certifier's business, it may be necessary to revoke all valid certificates outstanding, since the certifier will not be available to support them in the future.

8. Suspension of Public Key Certificate by Request

The certifier which issued a certificate must suspend it promptly upon request by a person identifying himself as the subscriber named in the public key certificate, or as a person in a position likely to know of a compromise of the security of a subscriber's private key, such as an agent, employee, business associate, or member of the immediate family of the subscriber.

Clarification

'certifier which issued': Although the certifier need not confirm the identity or agency of the person making the request, the certifier which issued the certificate should ordinarily be the person to suspend it, because the issuing certifier is in the best position to screen out and ignore requests that are obviously not in the subscriber's interest, such as requests intended as pranks, for harassment, or for improper interference.

'suspend': Since, by definition, a suspension cuts short an otherwise applicable time period, it relates only to certificates whose validity is determined according to time. If validity is measured by some other criterion, such as the scope of an identified transaction, this paragraph may well not apply.

'upon request': The certifier must act in good faith in responding to the request, but need not conclusively confirm the identity or agency of the person requesting suspension. The certifier may rely on the representations of the person requesting the suspension, though there will be an element of verification of identity made by the certifier.

Commentary

(1) Since suspension temporarily invalidates a public key certificate, it, in effect, temporarily severs the association of the subscriber to the public key listed in the certificate. Without such an association, digital signatures verifiable by that public key are not attributable to the subscriber. The subscriber has thus effectively put its digital signature capability on hold.

(2) Although the certifier is not required to identify the authority of the person making the request, it should have some form of procedure in place for the immediate confirmation of such a request. Failing this, the certifier may find itself in breach of its obligations to the subscriber, and liable for any loss arising out of the subscribers inability to use its digital signature.

(3) The ability to temporarily preclude attribution of digital signatures through suspension of the critical public key certificate is one of the principal means for the subscriber to manage the risk of holding a private key.

(4) A contract between a certifier and subscriber may limit or preclude suspension, so long as a person in a position to rely on the certification has notice of the limitation or preclusion. Such a limitation or preclusion could be included in a certification practice statement.

9. Revocation of Public Key Certificate by Request

The certifier which issued a public key certificate must revoke it promptly after:

(a)   receiving a request for revocation by the subscriber named in the certificate or that subscriber's authorised agent, and
(b)   confirming that the person requesting revocation is that subscriber, or is an agent of that subscriber with authority to request the revocation.

Clarification

'certifier which issued': The certifier which issued the certificate should be the person to suspend it, because the issuing certifier is in the best position to confirm the identity and agency of the person requesting the revocation.

'revoke': Since, by definition, a revocation cuts short an otherwise applicable time period, it relates only to certificates whose validity is determined according to time. If validity is measured by some other criterion, such as the scope of an identified transaction, this paragraph may well not apply.

Commentary

(1) The same comments as apply to the 'Suspension of a Public Key Certificate by request' will apply to a revocation, though evidently, a revocation is permanent, and can be regarded as an ultimate step.

10. Suspension or Revocation of Public Key Certificate Without

Consent

The certifier which issued a public key certificate must revoke it, if:

(a)   The certifier confirms that a material fact represented in the certificate is false;
(b)   The certifier confirms that the trustworthiness of certifier's information system was compromised in a manner materially affecting the certificate's reliability.

The certifier may suspend a reasonably questionable certificate for the time necessary to perform an investigation sufficient to confirm grounds for revocation pursuant to this article.

Clarification

'must revoke' If the Certifier does not revoke the certificate, or at least suspend it pending investigation, and can be proved to have notice of any of the grounds listed above, then it follows that the Certifier may be held liable for any consequential loss. Such failure to act may even bring into question the 'Trustworthiness' of the Certifier vis-á-vis third parties.

'compromised' That the information which must be secret in order to safeguard the operation of the ensured message, has been revealed to parties who do not have the right to access such information.

Commentary

(1) It is anticipated that the exact parameters whereby a Certifier would be entitled to suspend or revoke a certificate without consent would be established through the contract between the certifier and the subscriber.

In the absence of such provisions, any court proceedings brought as a result of a loss occasioned would have to establish if the certifier was entitled to act in this way.

11. Notice of Revocation or Suspension of a Public Key Certificate

Immediately upon suspension or revocation of a public key certificate by a certifier, the certifier must give appropriate notice of the revocation or suspension.

Clarification

'give appropriate notice': In determining what is appropriate, the certifier should evaluate the circumstances and make reasonable efforts to deliver notice to persons likely to be significantly affected by the suspension or revocation. Ordinarily for a certificate published in a digital certificate repository, the certifier should likewise publish notice of the suspension in the same repository, in the manner specified by a standard adopted by the repository or a statement of procedures which it has published. For an unpublished certificate, the notice should reach persons whose reliance on the certificate is foreseeable from the vantage point of the certifier and the person requesting the suspension or revocation.

Commentary

If the certifier fails to give notice, then it may find itself at least in breach of its contract with the subscriber, or at worst liable for any loss arising out of the subscribers subsequent use in good faith of an invalidated key.

Conclusion

It is intended that the GUIDEC serve as a foundation document in the application of digitally ensured Electronic Commerce, but it is freely acknowledged that we cannot hope to have addressed all of the issues at once. The whole field of Electronic Commerce is evolving at a rapid rate, and it is necessary that the concepts and definitions inherent thereto also evolve at an equivalent pace. The Electronic Commerce Project of the ICC will therefore seek to apply the definitions and principles as set out in the GUIDEC through further studies into the subject as it is enumerated here, and address itself to additional problems in the field as they continue to be identified. As technology develops, and the commercial world attempts to embrace such techno-logical developments, further revisions and enhancements of this document will be made available, in order that the inevitably complex concepts can be readily understood by the business community, and put to the best use.

ICC GUIDEC

Published in its official English version by the International Chamber of Commerce.

Copyright © 1997 – International Chamber of Commerce (ICC) Paris.

Available from: ICC Publishing SA, 38 Cours Albert 1er, 75008 Paris, France

Appendix 9

AMERICAN BAR ASSOCIATION STANDING COMMITTEE ON ETHICS AND PROFESSIONAL RESPONSIBILITY

PROTECTING CONFIDENTIALITY OF UNENCRYPTED EMAIL

10.3.99 FORM OPINION ON 99.413

http://www.abanet/org/cpr/fo99-413.html

Formal Opinion 99-413

Center for Professional Responsibility

AMERICAN BAR ASSOCIATION

STANDING COMMITTEE ON ETHICS AND PROFESSIONAL RESPONSIBILITY

Formal Opinion No. 99-413

March 10, 1999

Protecting the Confidentiality of Unencrypted E-Mail

A lawyer may transmit information relating to the representation of a client by unencrypted e-mail sent over the Internet without violating the Model Rules of Professional Conduct (1998) because the mode of transmission affords a reasonable expectation of privacy from a technological and legal standpoint. The same privacy accorded U.S. and commercial mail, land-line telephonic transmissions, and facsimiles applies to Internet e-mail. A lawyer should consult with the client and follow her instructions, however, as to the mode of transmitting highly sensitive information relating to the client's representation.

The Committee addresses in this opinion the obligations of lawyers under the Model Rules of Professional Conduct (1998) when using unencrypted electronic mail to communicate with clients or others about client matters. The Committee (1) analyzes the general standards that lawyers must follow under the Model Rules in protecting 'confidential client information'1 from inadvertent disclosure; (2) compares the risk of interception of unencrypted e-mail with the risk of interception of other forms of communication; and (3) reviews the various forms of e-mail transmission, the associated risks of unauthorized disclosure, and the laws affecting unauthorized interception and disclosure of electronic communications.

The Committee believes that e-mail communications, including those sent unencrypted over the Internet, pose no greater risk of interception or disclosure than other modes of communication commonly relied upon as having a reasonable expectation of privacy. The level of legal protection accorded e-mail transmissions, like that accorded other modes of electronic communication, also supports the reasonableness of an expectation of privacy for unencrypted e-mail transmissions. The risk of unauthorized interception and disclosure exists in every medium of communication, including e-mail. It is not, however, reasonable to require that a mode of communicating information must be avoided simply because interception is technologically possible, especially when unauthorized interception or dissemination of the information is a violation of law.2

The Committee concludes, based upon current technology and law as we are informed of it, that a lawyer sending confidential client information by unencrypted e-mail does not violate Model Rule 1.6(a) in choosing that mode to communicate. This is principally because there is a reasonable expectation of privacy in its use.

The conclusions reached in this opinion do not, however, diminish a lawyer's obligation to consider with her client the sensitivity of the communication, the costs of its disclosure, and the relative security of the contemplated medium of communication. Particularly strong protective measures are warranted to guard against the disclosure of highly sensitive matters. Those measures might include the avoidance of e-mail,3 just as they would warrant the avoidance of the telephone, fax, and mail. See Model Rule 1.1 and 1.4(b). The lawyer must, of course, abide by the client's wishes regarding the means of transmitting client information. See Model Rule 1.2(a).

A. Lawyers' Duties Under Model Rule 1.6

The prohibition in Model Rule 1.6(a) against revealing confidential client information absent client consent after consultation imposes a duty on a lawyer to take reasonable steps in the circumstances to protect such information against unauthorized use or disclosure.4 Reasonable steps include choosing a means of communication in which the lawyer has a reasonable expectation of privacy.5 In order to comply with the duty of confidentiality under Model Rule 1.6, a lawyer's expectation of privacy in a communication medium need not be absolute; it must merely be reasonable.

It uniformly is accepted that a lawyer's reliance on land-line telephone, fax machine, and mail to communicate with clients does not violate the duty of confidentiality because in the use of each medium, the lawyer is presumed to have a reasonable expectation of privacy.6 The Committee now considers whether a lawyer's expectation of privacy is any less reasonable when she communicates by e-mail.

B. Communications Alternatives To E-Mail

In order to understand what level of risk may exist without destroying the reasonable expectation of privacy, this Section evaluates the risks inherent in the use of alternative means of communication in which lawyers nonetheless are presumed to have such an expectation. These include ordinary U.S. mail; land-line, cordless, and cellular telephones; and facsimile transmissions.

1. U.S. and Commercial Mail

It uniformly is agreed that lawyers have a reasonable expectation of privacy in communications made by mail (both U.S. Postal Service and commercial). This is despite risks that letters may be lost, stolen or misplaced at several points between sender and recipient. Further, like telephone companies, Internet service providers (ISPs), and on-line service providers (OSPs), mail services often reserve the right to inspect the contents of any letters or packages handled by the service. Like e-mail, U.S. and commercial mail can be intercepted and disseminated illegally. But, unlike unencrypted e-mail, letters are sealed and therefore arguably more secure than e-mail.7

2. Land-Line Telephones

It is undisputed that a lawyer has a reasonable expectation of privacy in the use of a telephone.8

For this reason, the protection against unreasonable search and seizure guaranteed by the Fourth Amendment applies to telephone conversations.9

It also is recognized widely that the attorney-client privilege applies to conversations over the telephone as long as the other elements of the privilege are present.10 However, this expectation of privacy in communications by telephone must be considered in light of the substantial risk of interception and disclosure inherent in its use. Tapping a telephone line does not require great technical sophistication or equipment, nor is the know-how difficult to obtain.11

Multiple extensions provide opportunities for eavesdropping without the knowledge of the speakers. Technical errors by the phone company may result in third parties listening to private conversations. Lastly, phone companies are permitted by law to monitor phone calls under limited conditions.

Despite this lack of absolute security in the medium, using a telephone is considered to be consistent with the duty to take reasonable precautions to maintain confidentiality.12

3. Cordless and Cellular Phones

Authority is divided as to whether users have a reasonable expectation of privacy in conversations made over cordless and cellular phones.13 Some court decisions reached the conclusion that there is no reasonable expectation of privacy in cordless phones in part because of the absence, at the time, of federal law equivalent to that which protects traditional telephone communications.14 After the 1994 amendment to the Wiretap Statute, which extended the same legal protections afforded regular telephone communications to cordless phone conversations,15 at least one ethics opinion addressed the advisability of using cordless phones to communicate with clients and concluded that their use does not violate the duty of confidentiality.16

The nature of cordless and cellular phone technology exposes it to certain risks that are absent from e-mail communication. E-mail messages are not 'broadcast' over public airwaves.17 Cordless phones, by contrast, rely on FM and AM radio waves to broadcast signals to the phone's base unit, which feeds the signals into land-based phone lines. Therefore, in addition to the risks inherent in the use of a regular telephone, cordless phones also are subject to risks of interception due to their broadcast on radio signals that may be picked up by mass-marketed devices such as radios, baby monitors, and other cordless phones within range.18 Further, the intercepted signals of cordless and analog cellular telephones are in an instantly comprehensible form (oral speech), unlike the digital format of e-mail communications.

Similarly, cellular phones transmit radio signals to a local base station that feeds the signals into land-based phone lines. The broadcast area from the phone to the station is larger than that of a cordless phone, and receivers and scanners within range may intercept and overhear the conversation. Although the Committee does not here express an opinion regarding the use of cellular or cordless telephone, it notes that the concerns about the expectation of privacy in the use of cordless and cellular telephones do not apply to e-mail transmitted over land-based phone lines.19

4. Facsimile

Authority specifically stating that the use of fax machines is consistent with the duty of confidentiality is absent, perhaps because, according to some commentators, courts assume the conclusion to be self-evident.20

Nonetheless, there are significant risks of interception and disclosure in the use of fax machines. Misdirection may result merely by entering one of ten digits incorrectly. Further, unlike e-mail, faxes often are in the hands of one or more intermediaries before reaching their intended recipient, including, for example, secretaries, runners, and mailroom employees. In light of these risks, prudent lawyers faxing highly sensitive information should take heightened measures to preserve the communication's confidentiality.

C. Characteristics Of E-Mail Systems

The reasonableness of a lawyer's use of any medium to communicate with or about clients depends both on the objective level of security it affords and the existence of laws intended to protect the privacy of the information communicated. We here examine the four most common types of e-mail and compare the risks inherent in their use with those of alternative means of communication, including the telephone (regular, cordless and cellular), fax, and mail.

Like many earlier technologies, 'e-mail' has become a generic term that presently encompasses a variety of systems allowing communication among computer users. Because the security of these e-mail systems is not uniform, the Committee here evaluates separately the degree of privacy afforded by each. As set forth below, we conclude that a lawyer has a reasonable expectation of privacy in such use.

1. 'Direct' E-Mail21

Lawyers may e-mail their clients directly (and vice versa) by programming their computer's modem to dial their client's. The modem simply converts the content of the e-mail into digital information that is carried on land-based phone lines to the recipient's modem, where it is reassembled back into the message. This is virtually indistinguishable from the process of sending a fax: a fax machine dials the number of the recipient fax machine and digitally transmits information to it through land-based phone lines. Because the information travels in digital form, tapping a telephone line to intercept an e-mail message would require more effort and technical sophistication than would eavesdropping on a telephone conversation by telephone tap.

Based on the difficulty of intercepting direct e-mail, several state bar ethics opinions and many commentators recognize a reasonable expectation of privacy in this form of e-mail.22 Further, in two recent federal court decisions, the attorney–client and work-product privileges were considered applicable to e-mail communications.23 The Committee agrees that there is a reasonable expectation of privacy in this mode of communication.

2. 'Private System' E-Mail

A 'private system' includes typical internal corporate e-mail systems and so-called 'extranet' networks in which one internal system directly dials another private system. The only relevant distinction between 'private system' and 'direct' e-mail is the greater risk of misdirected e-mails in a private system. Messages mistakenly may be sent throughout a law firm or to unintended recipients within the client's organization. However, all members of a firm owe a duty of confidentiality to each of the firm's clients.24 Further, unintended disclosures to individuals within a client's private e-mail network are unlikely to be harmful to the client.

The reliance of 'private system' e-mail on land-based phone lines and its non-use of any publicly accessible network renders this system as secure as direct e-mail, regular phone calls, and faxes. As a result, there is a widespread consensus that confidentiality is not threatened by its use,25 and the Committee concurs.

3. On-line Service Providers

E-mail also may be provided by third-party on-line service providers or 'OSPs.'26 Users typically are provided a password-protected mailbox from which they may send and retrieve e-mail.

There are two features of this system that distinguish it from direct and private-system e-mail. First, user mailboxes, although private, exist in a public forum consisting of other fee-paying users. The added risk caused by the existence of other public users on the same network is that misdirected e-mails may be sent to unknown users. Unlike users of private system e-mail networks who, as agents of their employers, owe a duty of confidentiality to them and, in the case of a law firm, to all firm clients, the inadvertent user owes no similar duties.27 The risk of misdirection is, however, no different from that which exists when sending a fax. Further, the misdirection of an e-mail to another OSP can be avoided with reasonable care.28

The second distinctive feature of e-mail administered by an OSP is that the relative security and confidentiality of user e-mail largely depends on the adequacy of the particular OSP's security measures meant to limit external access and its formal policy regarding the confidentiality of user e-mail. Together, they will determine whether a user has a reasonable expectation of privacy in this type of e-mail.

The denial of external access ordinarily is ensured by the use of password-protected mailboxes or encryption29. The threat to confidentiality caused by the potential inspection of users' e-mail by OSP system administrators who must access the e-mail for administrative and compliance purposes is overcome by the adoption of a formal policy that narrowly restricts the bases on which system administrators30 and OSP agents31 32 are permitted to examine user e-mail.

Moreover, federal law imposes limits on the ability of OSP administrators to inspect user e-mail, irrespective of the OSP's formal policy.

Inspection is limited by the ECPA to purposes 'necessary to the rendition of services' or to the protection of 'rights or property.'33 Further, even if an OSP administrator lawfully inspects user e-mail within the narrow limits defined by the ECPA, the disclosure of those communications for purposes other than those provided by the statute is prohibited.34

Accordingly, the Committee concludes that lawyers have a reasonable expectation of privacy when communicating by e-mail maintained by an OSP, a conclusion that also has been reached by at least one case as well as state bar ethics committees and commentators.35

4. Internet E-Mail

E-mail may be sent over the Internet between service users without interposition of OSPs. Internet e-mail typically uses land-based phone lines and a number of intermediate computers randomly selected to travel from sender to recipient. The intermediate computers consist of various Internet service providers or 'routers' that maintain software designed to help the message reach its final destination.

Because Internet e-mail typically travels through land-based phone lines, the only points of unique vulnerability consist of the third party-owned Internet services providers or 'ISPs,' each capable of copying messages passing through its network. Confidentiality may be compromised by (1) the ISP's legal, though qualified, right to monitor e-mail passing through or temporarily stored in its network, and (2) the illegal interception of e-mail by ISPs or 'hackers.'36

The ISPs' qualified inspection rights are identical to those of OSPs.37 The same limits described above therefore apply to ISPs. In addition, the provider of an electronic communications service may by law conduct random monitoring only for mechanical or service quality control checks.38

The second threat to confidentiality is the illegal interception of e-mail, either by ISPs exceeding their qualified monitoring rights or making unauthorized disclosures, or by third party hackers who use ISPs as a means of intercepting e-mail. Although it is difficult to quantify precisely the frequency of either practice, the interception or disclosure of e-mail in transit or in storage (whether passing through an ISP or in any other medium) is a crime and also may result in civil liability.39

In addition to criminalization, practical constraints on the ability of third parties and ISPs to capture and read Internet e-mail lead to the conclusion that the user of Internet e-mail has a reasonable expectation of privacy. An enormous volume of data travelling at an extremely high rate passes through ISPs every hour. Further, during the passage of Internet e-mail between sender and recipient, the message ordinarily is split into fragments or 'packets' of information. Therefore, only parts of individual messages customarily pass through ISPs, limiting the extent of any potential disclosure. Because the specific route taken by each e-mail message through the labyrinth of phone lines and ISPs is random, it would be very difficult consistently to intercept more than a segment of a message by the same author.

Together, these characteristics of Internet e-mail further support the Committee's conclusion that an expectation of privacy in this medium of communication is reasonable. The fact that ISP administrators or hackers are capable of intercepting Internet e-mail – albeit with great difficulty and in violation of federal law – should not render the expectation of privacy in this medium any the less reasonable, just as the risk of illegal telephone taps does not erode the reasonable expectation of privacy in a telephone call.40

CONCLUSION

Lawyers have a reasonable expectation of privacy in communications made by all forms of e-mail, including unencrypted e-mail sent on the Internet, despite some risk of interception and disclosure. It therefore follows that its use is consistent with the duty under Rule 1.6 to use reasonable means to maintain the confidentiality of information relating to a client's representation.

Although earlier state bar ethics opinions on the use of Internet e-mail tended to find a violation of the state analogues of Rule 1.6 because of the susceptibility to interception by unauthorized persons and, therefore, required express client consent to the use of e-mail, more recent opinions reflecting lawyers' greater understanding of the technology involved approve the use of unencrypted Internet e-mail without express client consent.

Even so, when the lawyer reasonably believes that confidential client information being transmitted is so highly sensitive that extraordinary measures to protect the transmission are warranted, the lawyer should consult the client as to whether another mode of transmission, such as special messenger delivery, is warranted. The lawyer then must follow the client's instructions as to the mode of transmission. See Model Rule 1.2(a).

ENDNOTES

1 As used in this opinion, 'confidential client information' denotes 'information relating to the representation of a client' under Model Rule 1.6(a), which states: (a) a lawyer shall not reveal information relating to representation of a client unless a client consents after consultation, except for disclosures that are impliedly authorized in order to carry out the representation.

2 The Electronic Communications Privacy Act of 1986, Pub. L. No. 99-508, 100 Stat. 1848 (1986), amended the Federal Wiretap Statute of 1968 by extending its scope to include 'electronic communications.' 18 U.S.C.A. (2510, et seq. (1998) (the 'ECPA'). The ECPA now commonly refers to the amended statute in its entirety. The ECPA provides criminal and civil penalties for the unauthorized interception or disclosure of any wire, oral, or electronic communication. 18 U.S.C.A. (2511.

3 Options other than abandoning e-mail include using encryption or seeking client consent after apprising the client of the risks and consequences of disclosure.

4 See also RESTATEMENT (THIRD) OF THE LAW GOVERNING LAWYERS (112 cmt. d (Proposed Official Draft 1998), which provides that confidential client information must be 'acquired, stored, retrieved, and transmitted under systems and controls that are reasonably designed and managed to maintain confidentiality.'

5 Whether a lawyer or a client has a reasonable expectation of privacy also governs whether a communication is 'in confidence' for purposes of the attorney-client privilege. As a result, analysis under the attorney-client privilege is often relevant to this opinion's discussion of e-mail and the duty of confidentiality. The relevance of privilege is not exhaustive, however, because of its more restrictive application in prohibiting the introduction of privileged communications between a lawyer and client in any official proceeding. In contrast to the requirement imposed by the duty of confidentiality to avoid disclosing any information 'relating to the representation' of the client, see Model Rule 1.6(a), supra n.1, the attorney-client privilege applies only to actual 'communications' made 'in confidence' by the client to the lawyer. See JOHN H. WIGMORE, 8 EVIDENCE § 2295 (McNaughton rev. 1961).

6 See infra Section B. It should be noted that a lawyer's negligent use of any medium – including the telephone, mail and fax – may breach the duty of confidentiality. The relevant issue here, however, is whether, despite otherwise reasonable efforts to ensure confidentiality, breach occurs solely by virtue of the lawyer's use of e-mail.

7 A.C.L.U. v. Reno, 929 F. Supp. 824, 834 (E.D. Pa. 1996), aff'd 521 U.S. 844 (1997) ('Unlike postal mail, simple e-mail is not 'sealed' or secure, and can be accessed or viewed on intermediate computers between the sender and recipient (unless the message is encrypted.').

8 Frequently, what we understand to be regular or land-line telephone conversations are transmitted in part by microwave. For example, many corporate telephone networks are hard-wired within a building and transmitted by microwave among buildings within a corporate campus to a central switch connected by land-line or microwave to a local or interstate carrier.

9 It should be noted that the ECPA preserves the privileged character of any unlawfully intercepted 'wire, oral, or electronic communication.' 18 U.S.C.A. (2517(4). The inclusion of e-mail in this provision is important for two reasons. First, implicit in this provision is the assumption that electronic communications are capable of transmitting privileged material.

To argue that the use of e-mail never is 'in confidence' or constitutes an automatic waiver of otherwise privileged communications therefore appears to be inconsistent with an assumption of this provision of federal law. Second, the identical federal treatment of e-mail with other means of communication long assumed consistent with the maintenance of privilege likewise is inconsistent with the assertion that the use of e-mail poses unique threats to privileged communications.

10 See Peter R. Jarvis & Bradley F. Tellam, High-Tech Ethics and Malpractice Issues 7 (1996) (paper delivered at the 22nd National Conference on Professional Responsibility, May 30, 1996, in Chicago, Illinois) (on file with its author), reported in 1996 SYMPOSIUM ISSUE OF THE PROFESSIONAL LAWYER, 51, 55 (1996) (hereafter 'Jarvis & Bradley'); David Hricik, E-mail and Client Confidentiality: Lawyers Worry Too Much about Transmitting Client Confidences by Internet E-mail, 11 GEO. J. LEGAL ETHICS 459, 479 (1999) (hereafter 'Hricik').

11 See Jarvis & Tellam supra n.10, at 57; Hricik supra n.10, at 480.

12 See Hricik supra n.10, at 481.

13 See, e.g., Jarvis & Tellam supra n.10, at 59-61; Hricik supra n.10, at 481-85. Compare Mass. Ethics Opinion 94-5 (1994) (if risk of disclosure to third party is 'nontrivial,' lawyer should not use cellular phone); N.C. Ethics Op. 215 (1995) (advising lawyers to use the mode of communication that best will maintain confidential information); State Bar of Arizona Advisory Op. 95-11 (1995) (lawyers should exercise caution before using cellular phones to communicate client confidences) with United States v. Smith, 978 F.2d 171, 180 (5th Cir. 1992) (finding that there may be reasonable expectation of privacy in cordless phone communications for Fourth Amendment purposes).

14 McKarney v. Roach, 55 F.3d 1236, 1238-9 (6th Cir. 1995), cert. denied, 576 U.S. 944 (1995); Askin v. United States, 47 F.3d 100, 103-04 (4th Cir. 1995).

15 By 1986, the protection under federal law for cellular phone communications was equal to traditional land-line telephone communications. The Communications Assistance for Law Enforcement Act, Pub. L. No. 103-414, 202(a), 108 Stat. 4279 (1994), deleted previous exceptions under the Federal Wiretap Act that limited the legal protections afforded cordless phone communications under 18 U.S.C.A. ((2510(1), 2510(12) (A). Existing law criminalizes the intentional and unauthorized interception of both cordless and cellular phone communications, 18 U.S.C.A. (2511; the privileged status of the communication preserves in the event of intentional interception,

18 U.S.C.A. (2517(4); and bars the introduction of the unlawful interception as evidence at trial even if it is not privileged, 18 U.S.C.A. (2515.

16 State Bar of Arizona Advisory Op. 95-11 (1995). Some commentators have argued that in light of the 1994 amendment and the recent improvements in the security of both media (including the introduction of digital cellular phones), the expectation of privacy in communications by cordless and cellular telephones should not be considered unreasonable. Jarvis & Tellam supra n.10, at 60-61. See also Hricik supra n.10, at 483, 485 (arguing that despite the fact that their privileged status would not be lost if cellular and cordless phone conversations were intercepted, lawyers should consider whether the cost of potential disclosure is outweighed by the benefit derived from the use of cordless or cell phones). Further, 18 U.S.C.A. (2512 prohibits the manufacture and possession of scanners capable of receiving cellular frequencies, and cordless and cellular phone communications have been afforded greater legal protection under several recent state court decisions. See, e.g., State v. Faford, 128 Wash.2d 476, 485-86, 910 P.2d 447, 451-52 (1996) (reversing trial court's admission of defendants' cordless phone conversations violated state privacy act because defendants had reasonable expectation of privacy in such communication); State v. McVeigh, 224 Conn. 593, 622, 620 A.2d 133, 147 (1995) (reversing trial court's admission of defendants' cordless telephone conversations because such communications were within scope of state law forbidding the intentional interception of wire communications).

17 Hricik supra n.10, at 497.

18 See United States v. Maxwell 42 M.J. 568, 576, 43 Fed. R. Evid. Serv. (Callaghan) 24 (A. F. Ct. Crim. App. 1995) (holding that user of e-mail maintained by OSP was protected against warrantless search of e-mails because user had reasonable expectation of privacy in such communications, unlike cordless phone communication) aff'd in part and rev'd in part, 45 M.J. 406 (U.S. Armed Forces 1996) (expectation of privacy exists in e-mail transmissions made through OSP).

19 The risks of interception and disclosure may be lessened by the recent introduction of digital cellular phones, whose transmissions are considered more difficult to intercept than their analog counterparts. New communications technology, however, does not always advance privacy concerns. The use of airplane telephones, for example, exposes users to the interception risks of cellular telephones as well as a

heightened risk of disclosure due to eavesdropping on the airplane itself. Most recently, a world-wide, satellite-based cellular telephone system called Iridium has been introduced by Motorola. The principles articulated in this opinion should be considered by a lawyer when using such systems.

20 See, e.g., Practice Guide, Electronic Communications, in ABA/ BNA LAWYERS' MANUAL ON PROFESSIONAL CONDUCT 55:403 (1996) ('[C]ourts seem to have taken it for granted that fax machines may be used [to transmit confidential information],' citing State ex rel. U.S. Fidelity and Guar. Co. v. Canady, 144 W.Va. 431, 443-44, 460 S.E.2d 677, 689-90 (1995) (holding that faxed communication was protected by the attorney-client privilege)). See also Jarvis & Tellam supra n.10, at 61 ('[T]here seems to be no question that faxes are subject to the attorney-client privilege . . . no one asserts that the use of a fax machine or the possibility of misdirection destroys any hope of a claim of privilege,' citing ABA Comm. on Ethics and Professional Responsibility, Formal Ops. 94-382 and 92-368).

21 The names for the varieties of e-mail described in this section of the opinion are based on those used by Hricik, supra n.10, at 485-92.

22 See, e.g., Alaska Bar Ass'n Op. 98-2 (1998); Ill. State Bar Ass'n Advisory Op. on Professional Conduct No. 96-10 (1997); S.C. Bar Ethics Advisory Comm. Op. No. 97-08 (1997); Vermont Advisory Ethics Op. No. 97-5 (1997). See also, Jarvis & Tellam, supra n.10, at 61; Hricik supra n.10, at 502-06.

23 In re Grand Jury Proceedings, 43 F.3d 966, 968 (5th Cir. 1994) (court considered e-mail messages along with other documents in work-product privilege analysis); United States v. Keystone Sanitation Co. Inc., 903 F. Supp. 803, 808 (M.D. Pa. 1995) (defendants waived privileged nature of e-mail messages due to inadvertent production).

24 Hricik supra n. 10, at 487.

25 See e.g., Alaska Bar Ass'n Op. 98-2 (1998); Ill. State Bar Ass'n Advisory Op. on Professional Conduct No. 96-10 (1997); S.C. Bar Ethics Advisory Comm. Op. No. 97-08 (1997); Vermont Advisory Ethics Op. 97-5 (1997). See also, Hricik supra n.10, at 486-87.

26 Examples include America Online ('AOL'), CompuServe, and MCI Mail.

27 Hricik supra n.10, at 487–88.

28 If the inadvertent recipient is a lawyer, then the lawyer must refrain from examining the information any more than necessary to ascertain that it was not intended for her and must notify the sender, ABA Comm. on Ethics and Professional Responsibility, Formal Op. 92–368 (1992), an obligation that extends to information received by e-mail or fax, ABA Comm. on Ethics and Professional Responsibility, Formal Op. 94-382 (1994).

29 For a basic explanation of encryption technology, including the use of digital signatures, see Kenneth E. Johnson, Dealing with Security, Encryption, and Ethics Concerns, in THE LAWYER'S QUICK GUIDE TO E-MAIL 93-105 (ABA Law Practice Management Section 1998) ('Johnson').

30 For a discussion of some additional matters such formal policies might address (deletion and retention of e-mail messages, remote checking of messages while out of office, etc.), see Johnson, supra n. 29, at 104-05.

31 For example, the terms of AOL's policy forbid access to e-mail except (1) to comply with the law, (2) to protect its own rights, or (3) to act in the belief that someone's safety is at risk. Hricik supra n. 10, at 489.

32 18 U.S.C.A. (2511(2) (a) (i) (It is 'not unlawful under this chapter for an operator of a switchboard, or an officer, employee, or agent of a provider of wire or electronic communication service, whose facilities are used in the transmission of a wire or electronic communication, to intercept, disclose, or use that communication in the normal course of his employment while engaged in any activity which is a necessary incident to the rendition of his service or to the protection of the rights or property of the provider of that service, except that a provider of wire communication service to the public shall not utilize service observing or random monitoring except for mechanical or service quality control checks'). The qualified right of interception of OSPs cannot be argued to create unique risks to the confidentiality of e-mail communications because phone companies (and other providers of wire or electronic communication services) are given identical rights under 18 U.S.C.A. (2511(2) (a) (i)). Moreover, many commercial mail services reserve the right to inspect all packages and letters handled, yet no one suggests this diminishes the user's expectation of privacy. See Hricik supra n.10, at 492. It also is noteworthy that in 1998, the New York Legislature amended the state's rules of evidence to provide that

no otherwise privileged communication 'shall lose its privileged character for the sole reason that it is communicated by electronic means or because persons necessary for the delivery or facilitation of such electronic communication may have access to the content of the communication.' N.Y. Civ. Prac. L. & R. § 4547 (1998).

33 18 U.S.C.A. (2511(3) (a).

34 See e.g., supra n.18. See also Alaska Bar Ass'n Op. 98-2 (1998); D.C. Bar Op. 281 (1998); Ill. State Bar Ass'n Advisory Op. on Professional Conduct No. 96-10 (1997) (users of e-mail maintained by OSP have reasonable expectation of privacy despite greater risks than private network e-mail); S.C. Bar Ethics Advisory Comm. Op. No. 97-08 (1997); Vermont Advisory Ethics Op. 97-5 (1997); Jarvis & Tellam supra n.10, at 61; Hricik supra n.10, at 492.

35 Confidentiality also may be compromised by computer viruses, some of which have the capability of causing the user's document to be propagated to unintended recipients. However, a virus scanning program containing up-to-date definition files will detect and clean such viruses. See generally Carnegie Mellon Software Engineering Institute's CERT(r) Coordination Center Website, http://www.cert.org/index.html, for descriptions of these and other computer viruses.

36 See supra notes 30 & 31 and accompanying text.

37 18 U.S.C.A. (2511(2) (a) (i).

38 See 18 U.S.C.A. ((2511, 2701, 2702.

39 See Katz v. U.S., 389 U.S. 347, 352 (1967) (Fourth Amendment protection extended to conversation overheard by listening device attached to outside of public telephone booth).

40 See, e.g., Alaska Bar Ass'n Op. 98-2 (1998) (lawyers may communicate with clients via unencrypted e-mail; client consent is unnecessary because the expectation of privacy in e-mail is no less reasonable than that in the telephone or fax); D.C. Bar Op. 281 (1998) (lawyers' use of unencrypted e-mail is not a violation of duty to protect client confidences under District of Columbia Rule of Professional Conduct 1.6); Ky. Bar Ass'n Ethics Comm. Advisory Op. E-403 (1998) (absent 'unusual circumstances' lawyers may use e-mail, including unencrypted Internet e-mail, to communicate with clients); New York State Bar Ass'n Comm. on Professional Ethics Op. 709 (1998) (lawyers may use unencrypted

Internet e-mail to transmit confidential information without breaching the duty of confidentiality under state analogue to ABA Model Rule 1.6); Ill. State Bar Ass'n Advisory Op. on Professional Conduct No. 96-10 (1997) (lawyers may use unencrypted e-mail, including e-mail sent over the Internet, to communicate with clients without violating Rule 1.6 of the Illinois Rules of Professional Conduct; client consent is not required absent 'extraordinarily sensitive' matter; expectation of privacy in e-mail is no less reasonable than that in ordinary telephone calls); N.D. St. B. Ass'n Ethics Comm. Op. 97-09 (1997) (attorneys may communicate with clients using unencrypted e-mail unless unusual circumstances warrant heightened security measures); S.C. Bar Ethics Advisory Comm. Op. No. 97-08 (1997) (finding reasonable expectation of privacy when sending confidential information by e-mail, including that sent through a private network, commercial service, and the Internet; use of e-mail to communicate client confidences does not violate South Carolina Rule of Professional Conduct 1.6); Vermont Advisory Ethics Op. 97-5 (1997) (lawyers may use unencrypted Internet e-mail to transmit confidential information without breaching the duty of confidentiality under state analogue to ABA Model Rule 1.6). Two opinions similarly endorsed e-mail as a means of communicating client confidences, but advised lawyers to seek client consent or consider the use of encryption prior to its use, unlike the present opinion: Pa. Bar Ass'n Comm. on Legal Ethics Op. 97-130 (1997) (lawyers should not use unencrypted e-mail to communicate with or about a client absent client consent); State Bar of Arizona Advisory Op. 97-04 (1996) (lawyers should caution client or consider the use of encryption before transmitting sensitive information by e-mail). Two other opinions advised lawyers to avoid the use of e-mail to communicate with or about clients: Iowa Bar Ass'n Op. 1997-1 (1997) (sensitive material should not be transmitted by e-mail – whether through the Internet, a non-secure intranet, or other types of proprietary networks – without client consent, encryption, or equivalent security system); N.C. State Bar Opinion 215 (1995) (advising lawyers to use the mode of communication that will best maintain confidential information, and cautioning attorneys against the use of e-mail). Commentary supportive of the conclusions reached in this opinion, in addition to Hricik supra n.10 and Jarvis & Tellam supra n.10, include William Freivogel, Communicating With or About Clients on the Internet: Legal, Ethical, and Liability Concerns, ALAS LOSS PREVENTION JOURNAL 17 (1996) (concluding that it is not ethically or legally necessary to encrypt Internet e-mail but cautioning them in light of the absence of controlling legal authority). For a list of Web pages containing articles on e-mail and confidentiality, see Johnson, supra n. 29, at 103.

American Bar Association 750 N. Lake Shore Dr., Chicago, IL 60611 312/988-5000

info@abanet.org

Copies of ABA Ethics Opinions are available from the Service Center, American Bar Association, 750 North Lake Shore Drive, Chicago, IL USA, Tel: 1-312-988-5522.

Table of Cases

Table of Statutes

513

Table of Statutory Instruments

Table of European Legislation

Treaty of Rome
Arts 28–30	2.24, 3.47
Art 81	2.25, 2.59, 6.13, 11.9
Art 82	3.4, 3.25, 5.14, 6.12

NOTE: the following are currently in draft form

Draft **Electronic Commerce Directive**   4.1, 4.37, 4.60, 6.6,
6.9, 9.23, 10.50, 11.4
Art 7   10.48

Draft **Electronic Signatures Directive**   4.1, 4.38, 4.60, 6.6,
8.12
Art 3   8.10
Art 5   8.10

Draft **ISDN Telecommunications Directive**   10.23

Index